MEDICINAL RULE

Methodology and History in Anthropology

Series Editors:
David Parkin, *Fellow of All Souls College, University of Oxford*
David Gellner, *Fellow of All Souls College, University of Oxford*

Volume 1
Marcel Mauss: A Centenary Tribute
Edited by Wendy James and N.J. Allen

Volume 2
Franz Baerman Steiner: Selected Writings
Volume I: Taboo, Truth and Religion. Franz B. Steiner
Edited by Jeremy Adler and Richard Fardon

Volume 3
Franz Baerman Steiner. Selected Writings
Volume II: Orientpolitik, Value, and Civilisation.
Franz B. Steiner
Edited by Jeremy Adler and Richard Fardon

Volume 4
The Problem of Context
Edited by Roy Dilley

Volume 5
Religion in English Everyday Life
By Timothy Jenkins

Volume 6
Hunting the Gatherers: Ethnographic Collectors, Agents and Agency in Melanesia, 1870s–1930s
Edited by Michael O'Hanlon and Robert L. Welsh

Volume 7
Anthropologists in a Wider World: Essays on Field Research
Edited by Paul Dresch, Wendy James, and David Parkin

Volume 8
Categories and Classifications: Maussian Reflections on the Social
By N.J. Allen

Volume 9
Louis Dumont and Hierarchical Opposition
By Robert Parkin

Volume 10
Categories of Self: Louis Dumont's Theory of the Individual
By André Celtel

Volume 11
Existential Anthropology: Events, Exigencies and Effects
By Michael Jackson

Volume 12
An Introduction to Two Theories of Social Anthropology: Descent Groups and Marriage Alliance
By Louis Dumont

Volume 13
Navigating Terrains of War: Youth and Soldiering in Guinea-Bissau
By Henrik E. Vigh

Volume 14
The Politics of Egalitarianism: Theory and Practice
Edited by Jacqueline Solway

Volume 15
A History of Oxford Anthropology
Edited by Peter Rivière

Volume 16
Holistic Anthropology: Emergence and Convergence
Edited by David Parkin and Stanley Ulijaszek

Volume 17
Learning Religion: Anthropological Approaches
Edited by David Berliner and Ramon Sarró

Volume 18
Ways of Knowing: New Approaches in the Anthropology of Knowledge and Learning
Edited by Mark Harris

Volume 19
Difficult Folk? A Political History of Social Anthropology
By David Mills

Volume 20
Human Nature as Capacity: Transcending Discourse and Classification
Edited by Nigel Rapport

Volume 21
The Life of Property: House, Family and Inheritance in Béarn, South-West France
By Timothy Jenkins

Volume 22
Out of the Study and Into the Field: Ethnographic Theory and Practice in French Anthropology
Edited by Robert Parkin and Anne de Sales

Volume 23
The Scope of Anthropology: Maurice Godelier's Work in Context
Edited by Laurent Dousset and Serge Tcherkézoff

Volume 24
Anyone: The Cosmopolitan Subject of Anthropology
By Nigel Rapport

Volume 25
Up Close and Personal: On Peripheral Perspectives and the Production of Anthropological Knowledge
Edited by Cris Shore and Susanna Trnka

Volume 26
Understanding Cultural Transmission in Anthropology: A Critical Synthesis
Edited by Roy Ellen, Stephen J. Lycett, and Sarah E. Johns

Volume 27
Durkheim in Dialogue: A Centenary Celebration of The Elementary Forms of Religious Life
Edited by Sondra L. Hausner

Volume 28
Extraordinary Encounters: Authenticity and the Interview
Edited by Katherine Smith, James Staples, and Nigel Rapport

Volume 29
Regimes of Ignorance: Anthropological Perspectives on the Production and Reproduction of Non-Knowledge
Edited by Roy Dilley and Thomas G. Kirsch

Volume 30
Human Origins: Contributions from Social Anthropology
Edited by Camilla Power, Morna Finnegan and Hilary Callan

Volume 31
The Ethics of Knowledge Creation: Transactions, Relations and Persons
Edited by Lisette Josephides and Anne Sigfrid Grønseth

Volume 32
Returning Life: Language, Life Force and History in Kilimanjaro
By Knut Christian Myhre

Volume 33
Expeditionary Anthropology: Teamwork, Travel and the 'Science of Man'
Edited by Martin Thomas and Amanda Harris

Volume 34
Who Are 'We'? Reimagining Alterity and Affinity in Anthropology
Edited by Liana Chua and Nayanika Mathur

Volume 35
Medicinal Rule: A Historical Anthropology of Kingship in East and Central Africa
Koen Stroeken

MEDICINAL RULE

A Historical Anthropology of Kingship in East and Central Africa

Koen Stroeken

berghahn
NEW YORK · OXFORD
www.berghahnbooks.com

First published in 2018 by

Berghahn Books

www.berghahnbooks.com

© 2018, 2021 Koen Stroeken
First paperback edition published in 2021

All rights reserved. Except for the quotation of short passages for the purpose of criticism and review, no part of this book may be reproduced in any form or by any means, electronic or mechanical, including photocopying, recording, or any information storage and retrieval system now known or to be invented, without written permission of the publisher.

Library of Congress Cataloging-in-Publication Data

Names: Stroeken, Koen, author.
Title: Medicinal rule : a historical anthropology of kingship in east and central Africa / Koen Stroeken.
Description: New York : Berghahn Books, 2018. | Series: Methodology and history in anthropology ; v. 35 | Includes bibliographical references and index.
Identifiers: LCCN 2018008442 (print) | LCCN 2018023456 (ebook) | ISBN 9781785339851 (ebook) | ISBN 9781785339844 (hardback : alk. paper)
Subjects: LCSH: Chiefdoms—Africa, Central. | Traditional medicine—Africa, Central. | Africa, Central—Politics and government. | Africa, Central—Kings and rulers.
Classification: LCC GN492.55 (ebook) | LCC GN492.55 .S77 2018 (print) | DDC 306.2/0967—dc23
LC record available at https://lccn.loc.gov/2018008442

British Library Cataloguing in Publication Data

A catalogue record for this book is available from the British Library

ISBN 978-1-78533-984-4 hardback
ISBN 978-1-80073-214-8 paperback
ISBN 978-1-78533-985-1 ebook

CONTENTS

List of Figures and Tables	vii
Acknowledgements	viii
Note on Language	x
List of Abbreviations of Referenced Works	xi
Introduction. Endogenous Kingship	1

Part I. Divinatory Societies

Chapter 1. The Forest Within	43
Chapter 2. Beyond Turner's Watershed Division	64

Part II. Medicinal Rule

Chapter 3. A Sukuma Chief on Medicine	81
Chapter 4. Endogenizing Vansina's Equatorial Tradition	109
Chapter 5. From Cult to Dynasty: Nilotic and Niger–Congo Extensions	131
Chapter 6. Magic and the Sole Mode of Production	173
Chapter 7. Tio Shrines of the Forest Master	191

Part III. The Ceremonial State

Chapter 8. Kuba, Kongo and Buganda 'Miracles': Reversions in Transition	221
Chapter 9. From Divinatory to Ceremonial State: Narrative Proof from Rwanda	252

Conclusion. Reversible Transitions 287

References 298

Index 306

Photographs follow page 166

FIGURES AND TABLES

Figures

0.1	Social versus cultural tendencies in anthropological theorizing	12
0.2	Two dimensions of anthropology	15
0.3	Endogenous transitions of rule in eastern and central Africa	36
1.1	The fertility fractal in initiation	59
3.1	Genealogy of Bulima chiefdom	82
4.1	The social and cultural structure of rule in a historical whole	117
5.1	The Zande cultural complex, based on Evans-Pritchard (1958)	156
5.2	Analytical map of Zande cultural influences	159
9.1	Methods on two anthropological dimensions of culture	264
9.2	Gakaniisha's 20 tales in terms of chronology, variables and reigns	268
9.3	Decimals (x) and positive/negative/neutral scores of variables in Gakaniisha's tales	282

Tables

5.1	Origins of Zande cultural items (according to Evans-Pritchard's informants)	164
9.1	Three levels of coherence between the symbolic relations of Ryangombe's myth	267
9.2	Gakaniisha's 20 tales in terms of their values on all eleven variables	270

ACKNOWLEDGEMENTS

Deep gratitude and a sense of honour dominate when I think about the African men and women who have crossed my path since my first fieldwork more than twenty years ago. They taught me their language. And after deciding I was open enough and would not judge them, they reshaped my mind. The original idea for this book goes back that far. It is the product of a promise I made at the time to a fellow student of anthropology named Stefan Bekaert, as we stood in the library, staring at the filled shelves of unopened monographs waiting to be read. I dedicate this book to his memory. In the same breath I thank Renaat Devisch, who as our supervisor motivated the search, and has continued to do so.

Write-up and additional fieldwork have been made possible by a sabbatical grant, for which I thank the FWO as well as my faculty of Arts and Philosophy at Ghent University. The book was written during the time I coordinated the Belspo-BRAIN project CongoConnect regarding the Hutereau expedition and collection. The present publication is my token of gratitude for Belspo's generous sponsoring of this collaboration with the Royal Museum of Central Africa in Tervuren. Some of my ideas found fruitful friction in discussions with the project researchers Jean-Michel Kibushi, Vicky Van Bockhaven and Hannelore Vandenbergen. I pay homage to them and to the inspiring project leaders Maarten Couttenier from the museum and Chokri Chikha from KASK. For the feedback received, I also thank the Belspo project's advisors Koen Bostoen, Els Cornelissen, Els De Palmenaer and Bert Ingelaere. The late Jan Vansina, whom I unfortunately never met, formed our shared frame of reference. This book is a reminder to carry on his work.

The manuscript has benefited from conversations in the field with people in northern and southern Tanzania, western and eastern Congo, Kenya, South Africa, Benin, and western Uganda. I warmly acknowledge Per Brandström for being my guide over the years on Sukuma life. Some Sukuma friends never ceased coaching me as the work took shape: Ngwana Hande, Sele and Doto Lukundula, Ngwana

Mawe and Paolo Magufuli. Chief Kaphipa has been my sounding board since 1995. Chiefs Kishina and Makwaia I thank for sharing their sense of urgency with me about recording their knowledge. In his eight-hour-long narration on the history of his chiefdom in January 2018, the Busiha court historian Daudi Ngonyeji put me back on track when I had begun to doubt the obvious: 'The basis of chiefship is medicine'. All these people and many more than I could mention have enabled this book.

A great source of motivation and inspiration in this endeavour are my students at Ghent University for sharing their experiences in the field with me, such as Karin van Bemmel, Eva Bleyenberg, Karen Delooze, Dieter Devos, Emelien Devos, Mohamed Ghasia, Mrisho Malipula, Adrien Munyoka, Ivo Ngade, Nick Rahier, Lurdes Rodrigues, Kristien Spooren, Troy Thomas, Wim Van Daele, Anja Veirman and many others, whose names will come back to me. Felix Kaputu deserves special mention for a long-standing intellectual exchange and for guiding me in eastern Congo. Jean-Baptiste Nkulikiyinka has been an invaluable source on Rwandan kingship. Koen Peeters and the friends of Die Keure continue to enrich my thinking about culture. For creating a genuine hearth for thought on affect and materiality I thank Hugo DeBlock, Rozita Dimova, Chris Parker, Marlene Schäfers and the other members of CARAM.

Colleagues who have prompted me, sometimes inadvertently, to explore unexpected paths in this project include Berber Bevernage, Wim van Binsbergen, Inge Brinkman, Miriam de Bruijn, Fr Wauthier de Mahieu, Rijk van Dijk, Sverker Finnström, Ornulf Gulbrandsen, Nathalie Holvoet, Nancy Hunt, Fr Bon Kamuli, Bruce Kapferer, Johan Lagae, Andrew Lattas, Michael Meeuwis, Knut Myhre, Francis Nyamnjoh, David Parkin, Miranda Poeze, Katrien Pype, Knut Rio, Stef Slembrouck, Olaf Smedal, Chris Taylor, Steven Vanden Broecke, Fr Leon Verbeeck, Annelies Verdoolaege, Annick Verheylezoon, Judith Verweijen, and the late Neil Whitehead. Since 2013, several conference panels and seminars have been the stage for bits and pieces of this manuscript. Carine Plancke organized the last try-out in a brown bag seminar at the end of November 2017, coordinated by CRCG at UGent, for which I thank her and the highly motivated participants.

Finally, always last but not least, I express immense gratitude to my family, Vera and Ruben, and Annika. Thank you for your patience, and for tolerating my bouts of mental absence during the summer months. 'I think the problem is solved now'.

NOTE ON LANGUAGE

Bantu words can be spelled with or without indication of tone. This book has opted to follow the spelling adopted by the works cited, which may mean inconsistency. But save for the few times an author marked high tone with acute accent, tone has been disregarded. Double vowels express a long sound. Exceptionally accents are placed on or before a vowel to place emphasis on that syllable. Other inevitable consistencies include pairs of consonants to reproduce sounds such as 'Ch' for Chwezi, which French authors prefer to write as Cwezi (see Chapter 9).

Sometimes variation in spelling is necessary as in the case of the pronunciation of the same word differing between language groups. For instance, my Sukuma informants write *ng'oma* with an accent to express a strong velar nasal, while researchers in Rwanda and Congo do not, hence the inconsistency of encountering also *ngoma* for 'drum' in the same book. Inclusion of the alternative spellings in the index should remedy this.

It is conventional to omit the Bantu prefixes denoting populations, namely mu- (singular) and ba- (plural), and to maintain the prefixes for non-Bantu ethnic names (e.g. Azande for Zande).

ABBREVIATIONS OF REFERENCED WORKS

Nine works have been the object of such detailed referencing that we opted to use the title's initials instead of the standard form of citing year or 'ibid.' We will announce the procedure between brackets in the text after citing the work's title. In order of appearance, with author and year of publication referring to the Bibliography section, the works are the following:

LK *The Lele of the Kasai* by Douglas (1963)

QC *Qui a Obstrué la Cascade* by de Mahieu (1985)

DA *The Drums of Affliction* by Turner (1968)

PR *Paths in the Rainforests* by Vansina (1990)

AR *The Historical Study of African Religion* by Ranger and Kimambo (1972)

AS *Alur Society* by Southall (1956)

TK *The Tio Kingdom of the Middle Congo* by Vansina (1973)

CW *The Children of Woot* by Vansina (1978)

GL *The Great Lakes of Africa* by Chrétien (2003)

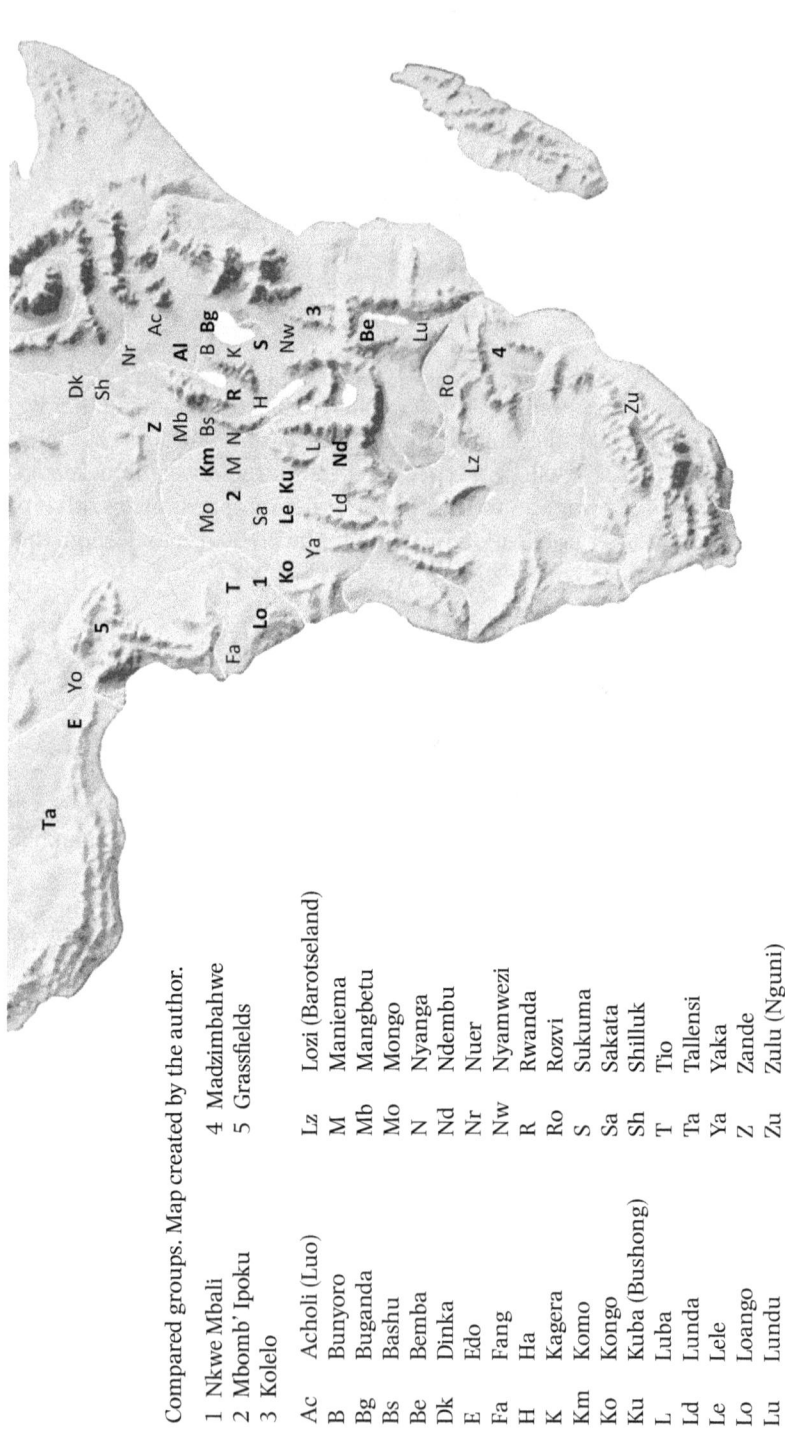

Compared groups. Map created by the author.

1 Nkwe Mbali
2 Mbomb' Ipoku
3 Kolelo
4 Madzimbahwe
5 Grassfields

Ac	Acholi (Luo)	Lz	Lozi (Barotseland)
B	Bunyoro	M	Maniema
Bg	Buganda	Mb	Mangbetu
Bs	Bashu	Mo	Mongo
Be	Bemba	N	Nyanga
Dk	Dinka	Nd	Ndembu
E	Edo	Nr	Nuer
Fa	Fang	Nw	Nyamwezi
H	Ha	R	Rwanda
K	Kagera	Ro	Rozvi
Km	Komo	S	Sukuma
Ko	Kongo	Sa	Sakata
Ku	Kuba (Bushong)	Sh	Shilluk
L	Luba	T	Tio
Ld	Lunda	Ta	Tallensi
Le	Lele	Ya	Yaka
Lo	Loango	Z	Zande
Lu	Lundu	Zu	Zulu (Nguni)

INTRODUCTION
ENDOGENOUS KINGSHIP

Why a book with the words 'Africa' and 'kingship' in the same title? An enormous amount of literature exists on African kingship, so much so that our opening question may have become a truism. Thirty years ago, Gillian Feeley-Harnik (1985: 275, n1) already gasped out that she had to limit her literature review to a representative portion of 'issues in divine kingship', a rubric on the intersection of politics and religion. Most anthropologists today prefer to act as if the subject is closed. Their misgivings remain unspoken: nothing conclusive has come out of the comparison of precolonial political systems in sub-Saharan Africa; the mass of literature on these societies without writing drew on oral traditions that had mostly mythical instead of historical purposes; the precolonial systems have lost all their relevance anyway; and so on.

The reality is that precolonial Africa never ceased to fuel exciting research collaborations. The debate on the history of kingship involves historians, archaeologists, linguists, political scientists and geographers. What has prevented a breakthrough, I submit, is the contribution that anthropology could make. Ethnographically based local models of rule shed light on endogenous processes and lived meanings, away from the safe classifications dictated by European history, such as king and priest, state and religion, government and ideology, rules and beliefs. These classifications encountered in the political sciences tend to lock up interdisciplinary collaborations in the default perspective that may be coined 'the polity prism'. Sounding like a scholar's prison, the polity prism takes the Greek *politeia*, citizenship, for granted, wherein society and political organization are the same. It inscribes itself in the tradition of the classics, basing power on government. Other perspectives on power should be explored. Comparative ethnography can equip historians with a palette of cultural perspectives to interpret sequences of events. The collaboration should disclose the recurring local distinctions and relations of wide-ranging regional and long-term historical relevance. In this part of the world, I will argue, these relations concern medicine rather than governance. Medicine is a perspective that might actually set Europe's own systems of rule in a new light.

Culture and the 'Anthropologizing' of Kingship

To use the label of 'king' for an African leader is not ethnocentric in itself – no word is. But the use of the word can be. If a study defines 'kingship' in terms of governance and applies it to a period when the 'king' headed a medicinal tradition, then the use of the term is anachronistic, and the assumption of its universal validity is ethnocentric. The European explorers of the sixteenth century setting foot on the Congolese shore, heading inland and stumbling on what looked like a palace in a city with well-clad personnel medicating objects had no doubt that these were priests and that the main inhabitant was a king. He was to be the spokesperson for 'his people' in the forthcoming exchanges with the throne in Europe, despite the relative anomaly of states in the region, the medicinal origin of his rule, and his limited say beyond the immediate surroundings. Soon his main role de facto changed into one of governance. The European delusion was self-fulfilling. Did Africanist research, which we will subject to exegetic analysis, commit this error?

Our[1] query about misconstrued kingships makes a hidden claim though: that the many societies in eastern and central Africa have some cultural commonality. If the institution of kingship cannot be the same everywhere, and in every epoch, then the same goes for a region of the world, *in casu* central and eastern Africa. The region witnessed the rise and fall of many types of society, some untraceable to us today. Very few were states headed by a king. These varied again in levels of centralization and autocracy, and in orientation on trade or on military conquest. Were these diverse sociostructural traits subtended by a shared cultural structure? One position this book will maintain is that surrounding groups co-determine the meaning of an institution.

To be on the safe side in our talk of kingship, we may want to drop the English term and stick to the word prevalent in a place, 'the local term'. Yet where does the local begin and end? *Ntemi, mfumu, makama* and *mwami* are some of the terms employed in neighbouring communities for the supreme customary authority. None could serve alone to speak for the institution across the region. And none of those exotic syllables contain pristine meaning. Even within a language community, a word will have its ambiguity masking original differences and developing new connotations – like the old word for witchcraft, *bulogi*, in disuse among Sukuma families after its negative association with the murder of innocent women. The solution I will propose for 'kingship' is not to reject the term but to accept a broadly defined version of the institution and embed it in an endogenous logic relating several systems of rule. By 'broadly' I mean a general category to talk of plural meanings, as in anthropological deconstructions of modernity and witchcraft: Africa has many 'modernities' and corresponding forms of witchcraft (Comaroff and Comaroff 1993; Geschiere 1997). The additional requirement of an embedding logic stems from our insistence on historical comparison.

The postcolonial message has been to leave the issue alone of cultural commonality and of concomitant radical difference between societies, and instead to focus on the multitude of particularities. Anthropology took a deep breath after decolonization and went through a historical turn, demanding we delimit the timeframe of our claims, and acknowledge the researcher's coevalness with the life of the respondents (Fabian 1983). Anthropologists have historians to thank for historicizing their discipline and raising reflexivity about cultural descriptions being products of the epoch (Clifford 1988). After the benefit that anthropology received, might the time be ripe for the converse move, for 'anthropologizing' history?

With the work of scholars from the Global South such as Appadurai (1996) came something of a geographic turn. Researchers no longer look at people in a place, but at places where all kinds of people live, and things pass through. Anthropologists reassured fellow disciplines that 'culture' does not matter (anymore); that we had been too traumatized by colonial ethnographies freezing cultures in time and, since the 1990s, by the culture concept associating people with certain ideas, feeding stereotypes in rightist circles (Bruman 1999). An extreme example of static analysis was Placide Tempels's claim about one philosophy shared by all Bantu-speaking peoples, a project that Mudimbe (1988) cogently crushed, subsuming it under Western inventions of 'Africa'. Ethnographers today seem content with networks or assemblages of things and actors becoming the unit of analysis (Latour 1993). The adjective 'cultural' is limited to an aspect: beliefs and institutions.

Recent developments, in particular the so-called ontological turn we will briefly touch on later, show that anthropologists are not willing to pay the whole price, that is to sacrifice the lifeworld, an endogenous reality with an internal cause – or 'logic' in the broad sense – requiring an adapted holistic methodology. Good ethnography captures the whole on which interconnected parts depend (Parkin 2007). True, a place or an epoch can be that whole instead of culture. To the latter's defence, however, the adjective 'cultural' has the advantage of, on the one hand, attributing meaning to a group uniquely producing it, and on the other hand of permitting the study of cultural systems, for example institutions, without identifying these with the people of the group. The members of the group are subjects, capable of acting according to their own variable frames of experience, which are parts from the whole we tentatively call 'cultural structure'. Events and places know a level of interconnectedness and permanence thanks to institutions embedded in cultural structure, which itself evolves through practice. Our aim is to combine this praxeology with a historical-geographic approach in order to attain the middle between the poles of four theoretical dimensions, schematized further on.

Introducing Medicinal Rule: A Regional Commonality

Signs of precolonial continuities do not cease to interrogate us. A few years ago, thousands of Tanzanians, of all layers of society, queued with their bicycles and four-wheel-drive vehicles to drink the cup of medicine from Babu Mwasapile, a Pentecostal preacher in a remote village of Arusha region. What attracted them? What persuaded government ministers to fly in by helicopter to have a panacean sip? A less embarrassing, easy answer than to evoke gullible citizens is that Babu had struck the right chord by the fusion of politics and religion into medicine. The massive popular interest attested to a special type of power that suffused the cup curing everything but nothing specific (although HIV was inevitably one on the propagated list of ills cured). The medicinal fusion brought everyone a century back to the shrine of the proto-king/healer.

On the negative side, nostalgia in the postcolony for such collective type of medicine most probably stems from the void left by the colonizer's and missionary's joint and all-out effort to remove medicine from people's highly intertwined network of symbols, norms, beliefs and daily practices, sometimes with the help of paramount rulers (see Part III). A postcolonial void, affecting self-confidence, morality and creativity, is a sadder truth than the primitive gullibility alleged by Europeans. By being (mis)construed as the classic counterpart of both science and religion, magic so engrossed missionaries and colonizers that they stereotyped much of the African continent with it, alternating between the obsessive collection of these things of archaic power and their public destruction. In response to the colonial obsession, postcolonial studies downplayed its significance with the no less embarrassing result of dissolving the collective empowering practice of medicine into aspects of religion (ritual), politics (divine kingship) and the medical field (plants, therapy).

On the positive side, a certain model of rule should be acknowledged that is regionally important and has a history. Political sciences cannot understand how African systems of patronage, in which young people aspire to please 'recycled old elites' (Chabal and Daloz 1999: 43–44), deflect into exploitation without considering the gradual disintegration of medicine by those systems. Initiation into medicine, often spirit-led and granting adolescents a central role, had important democratizing effects for society, as we will see.

By 'medicinal rule' we mean an institution embedded in a certain lifeworld. Our working definition boils down to an everyday experience: to guide a group of non-kin members is a forest- and spirit-based initiatory power, made permanent and tangible in a charm or shrine, entailing cultic tradition. The medicine by which one rules does not fundamentally differ from any other form of 'domesticated fertility', which achieves a fusion of inside and outside elements – a transformation experienced by the subject as far from evident yet therefore fruitful. Fertility, of people and land, is an accepted term of cross-cultural significance underpinned by virtually inexhaustible literature on non-modern societies and kingship. The literature cannot be ignored, and will intermittently feature in this book, but the contribution we envisage is to start afresh from a regionally salient ethnographic basis. More generally, we ask ourselves what 'power' (commonly defined as influence) means in societies where fertility, or life, is the one and only mode of (re)production.

Those Africanists who did emphasize the regional commonalities, and tried to explain them, focused on either medicine or rule. Vansina (1990) on 'the equatorial African tradition' gave a detailed historical overview of the diverse political systems in central Africa. Chapter 4 will be devoted to explaining why he did not acknowledge their main commonality: that no chief or king ruled without medicine, namely charm or shrine and the initiation into ritual. Janzen's (1992) *ngoma* cast a regionally wider net to effectively show that the basic characteristics of healing performances in western central Africa were applicable as well in southern and eastern Bantu groups. His examples include the Sukuma 'secret societies', which although influential down to the cities on the Indian Ocean, seamlessly concur with Zebola and Nkita cults operating all the way to the Atlantic coast. All groups had developed collective medicinal rituals for therapeutic, spirit-based communication to treat a wide range of both physical and mental afflictions. In Janzen's (1992: 78) exposé, however, the sociopolitical was the 'independent variable' determining the importance of *ngoma*: cults copied emblems of the state; a state in decline allowed for more cults, charms and therapies; a collapsed state handed over social control to ngoma-type orders, as in the *Lemba* cult enabling and controlling trade (Janzen 1982). The Bunzi shrine that 'gave impetus for the emergence' of a centralized polity in coastal Congo seemed an exception to the rule that Ngoma-type cults of affliction 'have either been brought under the tutelage of government and served the purposes of, and the legitimation for, sovereign power, or they have preserved and perpetuated segments of society not directly related to the state' (Janzen 1992: 75–76). We will argue instead that the cult is the regional model of rule in which the state originated. Gradually solidified into traditions, the cultic practices invariably initiate into medicine. They often, but not necessarily, give rise to a stable association, mostly with a hierarchy of initiatory positions. The dynastic clan presents a special case of medicinal cult.

A number of historians working in East Africa have converged on 'public healing' as the category to situate *ngoma* (Schoenbrun 2006: 1419). Cults that resisted the conquest-state, like in the case of Nyabingi spirit mediums in Northern Rwanda, illustrate the political aspect of public healing (Feierman 1995). In Buganda the dynasty was founded on a shrine that vied with rivalling clans for the preservation of public health and environment (Kodesh 2007: 549; 2010). Public healing, however, shifts attention away from medicine and divination and onto the ritual and charismatic aspects of kingship. An office devoid of charisma, with mediums performing the public healing, would then suggest historical change from a priestly political to a purely political function, as Schoenbrun (2013: 635) has reasoned about King Rukidi from sixteenth-century Bunyoro. In practice, we know that kings have always been the medicine itself. They are 'the drum' – the literal meaning of *ngoma*. Hidden from the public eye, they serve together with knowledgeable healers, named in Sukuma chiefdoms the *banangoma*, 'children of the drum'.

Medicine envelops the ruler's reign. Before enthronement, a medicine for which sacrifices have been made transforms the commoner into a king. Afterwards, the success of his reign depends on rain medicine containing a body part of his predecessor, signalling continuity of power (cf. the Shambaa kingdom; Feierman 1972: 236). Because medicine is the air their reign breathes, kings have attempted to monopolize it. In some cases, such as Bunyoro in Uganda, the medicinal cult was integrated in the state. Even then, Emin Pasha in 1877 wrote about Chwezi healers at the court (according to him 'sorceresses') as a section within a larger group (Doyle 2007: 566, 568). Kingship was an instance of a spatially larger and temporally deeper endogenous history. Facing the diversity of political-religious-medicinal complexes that historians have brought to bear in intricate detail, the anthropologist is invited to trace the model that ties the instances together. We will appreciate how Vansina, versed in both disciplines, situated the meaning of institutions in a 'tradition' – that is, the historically as well as geographically widest context.[2]

The everyday relations between medicine, socialization and leadership will provide evidence to frame the historical data. Janzen's research concentrated on urban areas. The *ngoma* rituals were performed without the comprehensive (including political) impact they had in rural communities, where the national government was far away, and the representatives it sent to the villages (e.g. village executive officers in Tanzania) were ignorant of medicinally based social status. Other regional comparisons, such as Ranger and Kimambo (1972) for eastern Africa and MacGaffey (1986) for Kongo, held the stage for a while, yet each time connecting the religious to the political as two domains. Our attempt is to rethink kingship from the encompassing perspective of medicine.

Part of why bringing medicine and rule together has never seemed necessary is the work of arguably the most influential Africanist anthropologist. Victor Turner's (1968: 198) 'watershed division' between healing rituals and rites of passage in Ndembu villages was responsible for distinguishing between a religious-medical function of treatment and a sociopolitical function of status attribution. Chapter 2 will demonstrate how it artificially shifted attention away from the actual power, the 'cooling' that all these rituals do according to the participants. Cooling with the aim of balancing fertility is the meaning of *poja* in southern and eastern equatorial Africa (and of *lemba* in mostly western equatorial Africa). The meaning expressed in various metaphors prevails in the whole of Bantu-speaking Africa.

Socializing Medicinal Rule:
The Ethnographic Experience

This book tells the story of a transition. It is not a historical account about a people at a certain epoch. We cannot accurately delimit the area or the people to which the transition pertains. Transition is a process with potential for wider relevance. In our case the process concerns the emergence of an institution, kingship, in a certain region. Emergence and origin are vague concepts. Only if confining ourselves to a specific institution of kingship, with a name and place attached, can we date its rise and fall. Even then, the same practice may have changed names over time. And the same label may cover different practices in the history of a society. In the end the task, fit for an anthropologist, is to figure out the meaning of the institution, and see whether and how that has changed. Ultimately, the matter will arise of the region of application. A wide number of groups speaking different languages may be practising and thus participating in the construction of the meaning of the institution.

Who decides on the meaning of a practice? I can think of no better answer than 'the people'. Unfortunately, that mass of voices from past and present, and often transcending borders we initially drew, will never reach us. Yet, ethnography permits a marvellous inlet to hearing culture speak about itself. Practices of socialization (re)produce collective meaning. Therefore, my analysis starts from fieldwork on an initiation in a Bantu-speaking community. The rituals reproduce the local model of rule to speed up adolescents' coming of age. The ethnographic experience offers the researcher a 'where' and a 'when', suitable for the literary methods in the humanities. In the following pages, I will briefly present the initiation, which has elsewhere been the subject of more extensive attention than required for our purpose (Stroeken 2010). The social sciences hand the methodology to analyse the experience. Explicated in a scheme, a two-dimensional anthropology relating matter to idea, and actor to structure, will discern the initiated (and transmitted) cultural structure, entitled 'forest within', and link it up with a sociostructural reality, the polycentric complex. The third step we envisage for an anthropology mediating between disciplines is a return to the humanities, testing the explicated ethnographic experience in various societies in the region.

What is the implication of kings being initiated by other healers? Those that transmit culture have power. They determine what the world is like. The Sukuma chief of Bukumbi evocatively described to me his enthronement in the 1950s – how he was abducted at night at an impressible young age, momentarily buried, and taught medicinal secrets that would keep him alive in his career. The dependence on the medicinal initiator appears also where one would not expect it. In the Luba empire, seemingly the epitome of monarchic rule, the chiefs had to be initiated into Mbudye, the medicinal society of men and women. The condition applied to the supreme ruler as well, before his investiture and reception of the title of the Mbudye's highest rank (Reefe 1981). The incumbent was taught to use the memory board 'longhand of the sacred pool' (*lukasa lwa kitenta*) made of mnemonic beads of various colours that explicitly socialized kings into their duties. The other two *lukasa* boards taught members of the bottom rank of the cult about the early settlers and the organization of Mbudye. Where then did the power lie – in the dynastic clan or in the cult? And why do we assume these two to represent different domains?

In late 1996 I was lucky enough to be invited by my Sukuma host, the elderly healer Lukundula, to participate in an initiation (*ihane*), together with other young men of my age. The invitation was a relief for me because until then the Sukuma healers I wanted to interview had told me that they could not share anything substantial about their medicine unless I had been initiated. I had not understood well that they did not mean by this the completion of training into their medicinal society, which I thought was impossible anyway, but simply the *ihane*, the general training all adults begin with. I had thought (and read) that the institution was long extinct, but in this area relatively close to the city of Mwanza – possibly left alone for that reason by missionaries and inquisitive civil servants – it was vibrant. After brewing four drums of beer, I and five sons of farmers as well as the local schoolteacher could enter into the senior age-grade association of our village before a crowd of one hundred. During the rituals of *bunamhala*, translatable as 'elderhood' by which adulthood is meant, a cultural logic was conveyed with ahistorical overtones. In a region of cultivated steppe, small hillocks with boulders were designated as 'forest', *bu*. An ordeal in the forest staged the death of each novice's former self, the ultimate sacrifice and acceptance of indebtedness to the cult. Provided they paid the fee of a goat, and the ancestral spirits had accepted through an oracle of a rooster, the novices underwent three days of medicinal training in the forest and passed the public exam among the elders in which to prove their knowledge of the forty collected substances and their secret proper names. Medicinal knowledge epitomizes 'forest-mastery'. It is the only formal collective socialization they will undergo.

Our thesis on medicine being the model of rule is illustrated in the ritual consecration of the *ihane* novices after obtaining a medicinal bundle named *bu ya mu kaya*, literally 'forest of within the home' – in short, 'forest-within'. It prepares them to head families and, in principle, larger entities. The village headman was in the first place a *namhala*, an elder initiated into the medicinal association and of highest rank. *Bugota* is 'medicine': among Sukuma it could not get more 'political' than that. Making gifts of beer is rewarded with more secret knowledge, and with a higher title to match. For this reason, too, the elders' association deserves to be called medicinal. The extinct precursory initiation of young men, *busumba*, allegedly followed a similar structure with a riskier corporeal ordeal and fewer medicines than the elder's society. The pendant for elderly women, *bugikulu*, participated during the public scenes of the *ihane*, challenging with ladles the young men carrying spears. I remember how the spear had felt in my hands twenty years ago, when I entered *ihane*, and how hard the women's ladles could hit. A song followed on how we had wed 'male' and 'female' things of life.

The twin set of connected gourds from which the initiated drank beer was likened to experiences of fertility by one of the masters surrounding us: 'A game of African chess goes on as long as there is more than one pebble in the pit'. The forest-within medicine, concocted from the forty ingredients, was used afterwards by the masters to protect their fields against drought and disease. The meaning did not need to be explicitly conveyed to the participants. For me the 'animism' was somewhat unexpected. The perspective on the world that admitted only one mode of production, life, contrasted with my separation between political, economic, religious and other modes of production, which not only marks modernity (Luhmann 1995) but constitutes the scholarly take on society.

I should hasten to add that by a perspective on the world or a 'logic', *in casu* the mastering of the forest in order to no longer fear but harness the unfamiliar wild outside, I do not mean a certain thought or belief. It would be untenable to imagine people possessed by an idea and for this cognitive reality to ground their culture, while anyone of them at any given moment could easily invert it into the opposite idea. The rituals rather initiate the members into affects of the group – inarticulate energies underlying motives, convictions and desires. The preconscious grasp of parts connecting into a whole permits the ethnographer later to intuit which cultural relations in the past might be 'logical' possibilities. The ethnographic experience of context is holistic, best served by the literary style of the humanities. However, in order to function as a baseline for interpreting other studies of leadership, our task is to submit it to analysis and make the whole comparable across cultures.

The association of men and women that organizes the socialization has authority and impact on the members, more than any kind of power a king could summon. What did the association of *bunamhala* tell us about the world? At a general level, the major elements interrelated in the *ihane* were: divination and ritual communication with spirits, obtaining medicine of life and fertility from the forest, initiation of that knowledge after sacrifice, gift giving for personal status, and a cultic-associational model of sociality. The coming nine chapters will unite the elements into a logic of 'forest-mastery', and test its value as an endogenous model to reinterpret anthropological and historical analyses of chief- and kingship in the region.

The implication of the initiated cultural structure is that leaders have no ultimate powers. They depend on spirits or charms. Their dependence is sociostructurally reinforced within a polycentric society safeguarding the autonomy of initiated adults and their extended families. I experienced this situation in Sukuma villages of the 1990s. Each extended compound (*kaya*) was a centre regulating its social concerns, which comprised all aspects ranging from health to decision making to education (school for many boys being an interruption to cattle herding) to rituals and economy. Everybody was expected to master medicine from the forest, possess charms at home or at an ancestral shrine in the compound, and to transmit and have access to fertility. The autonomy of adults primarily manifests itself as the sociostructural outcome of polycentrism.

Half a year after my *ihane* I entered the Chwezi spirit cult (Stroeken 2006). The basis of the ritual was, like *ihane*, a ritual passage in the forest (seen in cults of affliction in western equatorial Africa as 'the passage through the white', cf. Janzen 1992). The emphasis was on healing and multisensory interventions, as patients suffering from depressive and dissociative symptoms participated (Stroeken 2008). The ritual period lasted much longer than *ihane*, and the transgression during the moment of ordeal went further, involving ritual incest. The head-making was more explicit: each received a Chwezi diadem at the end as a sign of new status. Whether this has been copied from the enthronement of kings and chiefs, or vice versa, is a historical question. What strikes the anthropologist is the common cultural structure. The novice picks up the diadem from the pool, purified with charms. This pool of charms is central in cults across Bantu-speaking Africa, from Kolelo in the south-east, Luba in the south, and Mongo in the centre, to Tio in the west and Chwezi in the east and the Great Lakes. Another addition to the forest-within of *ihane* is the role of animal hides, from which the blindfold for the master of ceremonies is made. In brief, the spirit cult's symbolism explores the most feral qualities. This may be why cults look like they deviate from the everyday idiom of magic (cf. Evans-Pritchard's claim in Chapter 6), while in fact, they push magic to its limits.

To sum up, this book seeks to reconcile social sciences and humanities in a feasible methodology for (re)interpreting historical and cultural data. To systematize our comparison, the next section will analytically link the two socioscientific dimensions with the 'historical whole' that the ethnographer experiences. At the same time, the theoretical detour imparts to the non-expert reader some of the main tensions of the discipline.

A Century of Africanist Anthropology in One Oscillation

Africanist anthropology has, since the 1920s, been a token of the wider discipline by oscillating between cultural and social poles of analysis to explain patterns and change. In retrospect, much of what propelled the debates was the will to grant societies an endogenous dynamic.

Radcliffe-Brown's structural-functionalism concentrated on the social organism that is society, in an attempt to snap out of the cultural teleology of social evolutionism by Morgan, Maine, Tylor and Frazer. Their supposed stages of civilization, reflected in the greater rationality of practices, from magic to religion to science, lost all purport in light of the question Radcliffe-Brown asked about the functionality of practices. Magic did as good a job, for what it was meant to do in the studied societies, as science did in the West. Evans-Pritchard, who was most influential between 1930 and 1950, rejected social evolu-

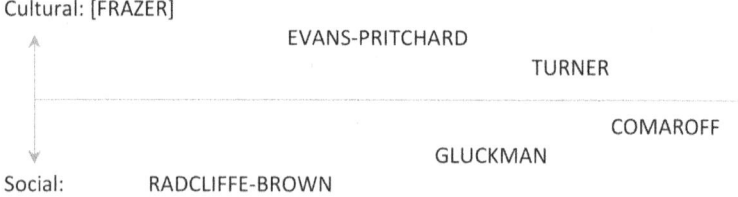

Figure 0.1 Social versus cultural tendencies in anthropological theorizing. Figure by the author.

tionism as well; however, unlike Radcliffe-Brown, he engaged with the lifeworld of the community in which he did his fieldwork. Zande beliefs in witchcraft were no less rational. Only their cultural premises were different. The anthropologist's hope of a natural science of the social was in vain. Humans are historical beings, caught in webs of signification, to be studied by the humanities. Radcliffe-Brown's view of society had been static, downplaying social change. But had Evans-Pritchard been any better at capturing the social processes at play? Zande and Nuer cultures were described as if isolated from the impact of colonization. From reading his work, the civil war after he left Sudan could only come as a surprise.

Max Gluckman tackled the pressing social matter profoundly with his extended case method, hinging the study of macro-processes such as colonization onto the ethnography of micro-situations. Under his tutelage in the 1950s, the British anthropology of Africa flourished. The shift was again to social structures, yet much enriched by the fieldworker's insight in lifeworld (see rapprochement to horizontal line in Figure 0.1). Urban and industrial environments in southern Africa had been neglected earlier. The critical, neo-Marxist stance in the extended case method brought the anthropologist in tune with the postcolonial era, the events of independence, and a new élan wherein Africa was no longer intellectually separate from the rest of the globe.

It would not take long though before the oscillation resurged. Research on industrial zones and town life may have been fashionable, and data collection through survey or from behind the table of a bar may have been practical, but all of it rather dimmed the alterity of non-Western cosmologies. Had alterity – the colonial spectre, the heart of darkness in Joseph Conrad's novel – been a figment of the ethnographer's imagination? Once the independence of African states was achieved in the 1960s, the issue of cultural particularity could be given a second chance. Symbolic anthropologists Mary Douglas and Victor Turner had a keen eye for the cosmologies of central Africa. At the same time, both made sure the cultural particularities they collected served to illustrate an encompassing theory – for example, the role of ritual in society. The distance between the social and cultural poles of analysis shrunk in the syntheses offered by their symbolic anthropology. Published during the Flower Power era, Turner's research on liminality and communitas in collective ritual had relevance beyond Ndembu society.

After the enthusiasm of the early 1970s about African states nationalizing and claiming authenticity irrespective of their inner cultural or 'ethnic' diversity, the critical voice of what became postcolonial studies, and later subaltern studies, sounded ever louder. Mudimbe's *The Invention of Africa* and Clifford's *Writing Culture* built on the theoretical thrust produced by Saïd's critique of orientalism in the humanities. Anthropologists had already gone through the motions of critique on (neo)colonialism, if mainly from the social angle. Now they understood, with the help of historians, the cultural fact that any research is historically situated. From the late 1980s onwards, Jean and John Comaroff, James Ferguson, and many others, carried Gluckman's project through by culturally particularizing colonization and its cousins, the macro-social processes of modernity, globalization and neoliberalism. For Africanists there was no longer modernity except in the plural: African 'modernities'. Magic and witchcraft could perfectly well be modern. We had to give up the Eurocentric concept of modernity, which defined itself in opposition to traditional belief. Witchcraft had lost nothing of its relevance in Africa because it reinvented itself, always and everywhere, to match new circumstances of social inequality and injustice.

As the theoretical currents succeeded one another during the past century, the poles of culture and society intertwined more and more. Their one-dimensional axis now has validity mainly as a methodological pointer: if social structure characterizes a society in the way it differentiates groups, classes, relations, offices and positions, the researcher has to take into account the cultural structure as well, because beliefs, values, norms and ideas form a whole (structure) that determines priorities in life.

What is lacking in this schematization of theories on a one-dimensional axis is the issue of agency. Methodologically it is useful for ethnographers to zoom out to the fantastic construct of a lifeworld whose secrets can be unravelled. Its value has to be proven in instances of behaviour that become explicable only through that construct. Anthropologists observe and communicate with their subjects to verify whether the hypothetical cultural structure actually informs the way the actor experiences the world and makes decisions. Each chapter in our book confronts ethnographic studies by recalling this methodological challenge: what is the cultural structure underlying the author's interpretations, and could it have been really 'lived' by the cultural actors – that is, employed as a frame of experience? The next section introduces this second dimension highlighting agency.

The necessity to dimensionally specify our schematization also appears from its incapacity to situate the recent theories advocating an 'ontological turn'. Basically, the ontologist theorizes that each 'culture' corresponds to an actual world (a more fashionable cognate) rather than to a different perspective on the same world that all humans share, and of which the empirical sciences would have expert knowledge. If we stick to the two poles of society and culture, the turn seems like radical culturalism and a leap away from social anthropology. But since the theory replaces culture by ontology, it as much deserts cultural anthropology. The double leap away from the evolution towards synthesis to a kind of infinity underlines the limits of our distinction between the social and the cultural. However insightful it may be as a division of explanatory factors, the axis fails to situate current theory, at least in the wider discipline.

Interpreting Culture: Anthropological Dimensions

To overcome the limits of our one-dimensional social-cultural axis, we must replace it by two anthropological dimensions that reproduce in a more refined manner the oscillation schematized above. Going by the chain of debates in our wider discipline on the explanation of cultural practices, the most liable candidates are, as a first dimension, the poles of materialism and idealism, and as a second dimension, the poles of structure and agency. Their combination results in four quadrants on which anthropological positions can be situated, in principle with coordinates determining different tendencies towards each of the four extremes (Figure 0.2). How do we proceed from one to two dimensions?[3] To take the example of the increased interest in schooling

Figure 0.2 Two dimensions of anthropology. Figure by the author.

in rural Sukuma villages since the 2000s, an adequate explanation should combine the material factor of the improved quality of schools with another factor, the ideational change: medicinal knowledge and cattle-holding lost their value as criteria for social status. The polycentric system is dissolving as the centre of gravity has shifted towards public spheres, with some, such as education and agriculture, controlled by the national government, which was not the case under traditional central authorities securing the fertility of land and people.

Have we explained practices exhaustively with the ideational versus material dimension? To believe so is to reduce reality to structures or statistical trends.[4] The exceptions on a pattern result from the actors having agency. For example, some adolescents leave school early to start a healing trade, which means that the ideational basis for this practice, reinforced by material reasons such as poverty, should be differentiated by a second dimension opposing structure and agency.

Explanatory frameworks that do not tilt practices towards one of the poles manage to approximate the middle of the dimensions. They avoid the stamp of an 'ism'. Much of anthropological debate has been about probing the opponent's paradigm for one's favourite pole, with the aim of decrying its neglect. The inconsistency of an author inadvertently shifting his or her approach during the same study towards the opposite pole will be maligned too. It is a game of antagonisms that this book is willing to play. The reader will forgive me the somewhat inelegant conjunctions spawned by the two dimensions. Between brackets I put the convenient historical tags to typecast each approach: actor-materialism (the early nineteenth-century Liberal), structure-materialism (the late nineteenth-century Marxist), structure-idealism (the twentieth-century functionalist), and actor-idealism (the postmodern phenomenologist).[5]

A century of debates in the discipline has resulted over time in a positive spiral towards the middle of both dimensions, like the gradual rapprochement in the social-cultural synthesis schematized above. Bourdieu, Latour and Ingold are located closer to the centre than their predecessors Evans-Pritchard and Max Gluckman. The centre means equal distance from the four extremes. Frederik Barth's game theory and Marvin Harris's cultural materialism are outliers, both privileging the role of material necessities in the (re)production of practices. The second dimension is necessary to specify that Barth starts from the actor's choices (*actor-materialism*) while Harris, like Marx's historical materialism, gives primacy to the (material) structures driving history (*structure-materialism*). The functionalism of Radcliffe-Brown, unlike Malinowski's reference to the biology of motivational primary needs, insists on the ideational system shared by members of a society. His *structure-idealism*, like the structuralism of Levi-Strauss, passes over the situation in which an actor has to make decisions between cultural options, and the actor goes against the grain of society. To avoid such cultural essentialism, Geertz concentrated on ethnography of the lifeworld and the subject's acts of interpretation (*actor-idealism*). He did not do so to the extent that Ortner (2006) would, shedding light on subjectivities in various contexts. All these authors, or at least their seminal studies, can be compared to each other using the relative positions determined by the two axes.

Applied to the theme of kingship, the four approaches differ consistently (I do the exercise for the theme of witchcraft between brackets). An actor-materialist explains cultural systems from the material benefits for the actor: the king is an individual seeking power (the one accused of witchcraft is disempowered). A structure-idealist spurns such microsocial explanations and reaches for macroscopic heights of analysis to see the functionality of institutions: kingship (and witchcraft) maintains social harmony in ways that a single actor could not fathom. In response, a structure-materialist will be critical about those institutions by pointing to the economic and political structures that keep certain social classes united under the protection of the king (or regarding witchcraft: that push the underclass into a whirlpool of mutual accusations). Actor-idealists will emphasize, against all three quadrants, the subject's situated ideas and the agency ignored in both material and ideational structures. Kingship is an institution whose meaning depends on people's experiences of it, which may not all be conscious (witchcraft beliefs are not pre-given but take shape in certain situations). This fourth approach, 'actor-idealism', is our book's theoretical point of departure. We try to balance it with the other poles of interest. The experiential frames that an actor employs in concrete situations are significant for our analysis to the extent that therein persists cultural structure.

In the two-dimensional scheme the ontological turn belongs to the quadrant of actor-idealism. However, its nearness to the centre indicates that the two dimensions still do not suffice to register all nuance of the theoretical advance aimed at. Ontologists pursue the interpretive interest of Geertz, yet adamantly avoid, like Bruno Latour (1993), the dualism of nature and culture, of truth and belief, or Dilthey's dichotomy of explanation versus interpretation that kept Geertz on a leash called culture, held separate as it were from the natural world. Viveiros de Castro (2004), Holbraad (2007) and an increasing number of phenomenologists and ontologists carve out their position on a third dimension, which is non-dualist, hence holistic and opposed to atomistic takes on culture.[6]

Their interest, though, is not in how a world, the whole of parts, changes. Their weak spot thus seems to be a fourth, temporal dimension, requiring historical research. The fourth dimension distinguishes diachronic from synchronic studies, for which Chapter 9 will propose an adapted methodology.

The praxeology of Pierre Bourdieu (1980) also belongs in the centre of the two-dimensional scheme. But non-dualist it is not. Praxeology was hailed in the 1990s as the culmination of anthropological and sociological attempts to reconcile phenomenology with historical materialism (the first dimension), while granting people's structured dispositions (habitus) a considerable dose of agency (the second dimension). Practices result from the dialectical relation between the habitus and the field, influenced by the forces of social class. Habitus, which was how Bourdieu operationalized culture, is produced, not fixed – and this in a field, not in a vacuum. However, internalized dispositions (habitus) and the environment (field or context) restore the old duality of a perspective and the world out there, which ontology seeks to bridge. The habitus and the field are respectively micro- and macroscopic entities. How could they 'interact'? Their mysterious dialectics of structure and agency, matter and idea, lack the holistic, visceral meaning of the humanities, of a 'where' and a 'when'.

Both ontology and praxeology are of little help to our study because of the same omission: the historically salient reality of a region. Institutions, such as kingship, cannot be understood without considering different epochs and adjacent places. An endogenous logic, through which a society finds within itself the reason for change, implies a historical whole with geographic scope. It cannot be a set of loose ideas, colliding like atoms, because subjects, including the ethnographer, experience this endogenous logic, for instance the forest-within, during initiation. To discern endogeneity, we propose a 'meso-anthropology'. Its focus on regional history is spatio-temporally intermediate, lying between society and a concrete community, as well as between universal meanings and meaning at the current moment. It seeks to reconcile the two-dimensional scheme, couched in socioscientific terms, with two criteria of analysis requested by the humanities: to bring out the history of an institution while retaining its holistic meaning.

Given our objective, our main frame of reference for a baseline will be the work *Paths in the Rainforests*, an unparalleled exercise of comparison conducted by Jan Vansina, who, until his death in February

2017, remained actively involved in discussing his book's numerous repercussions. Vansina (1990: xii) managed to derive from oral histories and linguistic reconstructions 'a powerful endogenous process, a cultural tradition that had its roots some 4,000–5,000 years ago, and that had maintained itself by perennial rejuvenation, until it withered as a result of the colonial conquest'. It is in honour of his pioneering synthesis that I present the following comparative exercise. Honour in an academic context is always hard won and ambivalent, I admit. The reader may expect relentless efforts on my side to find the imperfections in Vansina's synthesis. Chapter 4 concentrates on the question of whether he had actually distilled the endogenous factors of the tradition and its changes. Chapters 7 and 8 reinterpret the analyses of his two major monographs.

The main impetus of my critical effort stems from teachings of another senior, René Devisch (1993), who made it his vocation in the book *Weaving the Threads of Life* on Yaka ritual and society to develop a genuinely endogenous anthropology. The affect of life-giving was his angle to understand the forces of healing and witchcraft in the lived cosmology of Yaka hunters. My emphasis will be on the cultural structure emanating from the wider region.

Endogenous Process and Transition

An intimate link exists between culture, structure and endogeneity. If it were not for some cultural structure transmitted from one generation to the next and expressed in a variety of institutions, how could we claim that societies have endogenous processes? Structure does not mean fixity, no less than the abstract sequence of DNA should be confounded with its concrete expression after transmission. Exogenous factors meet with a group's inner receptivity for habits to change.

Sahlins (1968) captured the anthropological urge by demonstrating to a wider audience that although aridity was an exogenous push factor for the Neolithic transition from hunting to agriculture, whose beginnings in central Africa are dated to 2500 BP, it in itself was not sufficient cause for a change of lifestyle. Khoi-San hunters and gatherers knew how to sow plants and in the right seasons did so, to eat their favourite berries and wild grains, but to make agriculture their lifestyle was not endogenously logical, for they had developed a nomadic way of life adapted to desertification. By 'anthropologizing' histories we mean this exercise of 'endogenizing' the analysis, shifting attention from causality and directly observable (atomistic) factors to the history of something as hard to delimit as a whole and its systemic modifications.

The endogenous factor in history has not yet been given a fair chance. That is why Jerardino et al. (2014) recently thought, going by their exclamation, that they would startle their colleagues. They observed that cultural influence rather than demic diffusion drove the Neolithic transition in southern Africa. The implied knotty processes of cultural exchange and acculturation countermanded the conventional wisdom that the spread of agriculture was a group trait advancing along with the migration of Bantu-speaking groups from west-central to central, east and southern Africa.

Endogenizing, however, means that we should go one step further and consider multilinear and non-linear explanations. The thesis advanced by Broushaki et al. (2016) attributes the spread of the earliest farming in Asia to independent inventions. A pause is in order to underline the last two words. They muddle up the neat diachronic descriptions of diffusions from the distant past. The charted distribution of the institution's earlier and later occurrences in the region, which initially seemed to reflect a direction of influence, appears to result from intervals between separate influences, even separate inventions of farming.

How could independent inventions happen so close together in time and space? The answer may quite simply be that the groups shared a cultural logic. Think of parallel inventions in music, art or theory in the globalized West: individuals with the same interest independently enact dormant possibilities of innovation. Among Sakata farmers of the central African rainforest, for instance, fertility is reproduced through the insertion of seeds in the garden, as well as through the male insertion of ore and air from the bellows into a female furnace (Bekaert 1998). Farming and iron smelting reproduced for the Sakata the same logic in embryonic form. This is what we mean by cultural structure.

Not surprisingly, the atomistic method cherished by positivists does not welcome the possibility of endogenous logic from which symbolically similar practices would spring. The atomistic unit of analysis is an actor adapting received or socialized practices in response to material needs. To give a taster of the sort of tensions lying in wait, Vansina (1990: 60) deems it very unlikely that the complex technology of iron smelting spread to equatorial Africa as an independent invention from northern Gabon, on top of its diffusion from the Great Lakes, even though that is what the archaeological data suggest. Why could it not happen in Gabon, I ask, if the technology was independently invented in other parts of the world? According to the one-dimensional axis, Vansina's positivist methodology seems well balanced, taking into account both society and culture. The two-dimensional scheme reveals his bias towards actor-materialism, as illustrated later on.

Obstacles to the study of endogenous processes abound. Firstly, our academic specialization of research themes in Africa reflects the functional differentiation of modern society: Vansina focused on the political, Ranger on religion, Turner on ritual, and Janzen on healing. Yet, those classics dealt with the same phenomenon, which is as much political as religious as therapeutic. It is, in one word, medicinal – an adjective seeking to capture the holism of cultural practice. A second obstacle is the scientific emphasis on social structure in the study of processes. Complexification of networks, and economic or ecological factors are easier to conceptualize and analyse than changes in cultural 'logic' that require an insider's experience and ethnography. A third hindrance to comprehending medicine is the aforementioned mix of fascination and a fear of the fetish.

The well-trodden path, following an approach summed up in the conjunction 'actor-materialism', is to imagine kingship as an invented idea whose influence gradually spread, and to explain the diversity of kingships from the integration and adaptation of the invention in different places and contexts. In contrast, this book explores the harder way that brings together data hitherto kept separate. We trace a cultural structure originally shared by a wide number of people now scattered. We disentangle the process through which this structure evolved into various institutions, including kingship. The major advantage of discerning a transition is that it permits one to trace an endogenous logic amidst complex historical interactions. Our comparative data will distinguish three endogenous possibilities: divinatory societies, medicinal rule, and the ceremonial state, all interrelated in the last section of this introduction in terms of earlier forms and offshoots.

History and Anthropology

Jan Vansina merits a special place in our theoretical discussion, for his celebrated use of oral traditions to reconstruct Africa's past poignantly raises the question of whether the historian can do without the anthropological contribution. Where on the scheme would we situate Vansina's historical interpretations? It suffices at this stage to give some examples of his analyses of Rwandan kingship. What is striking is that they do not take cultural structures into account. Vansina (2004: 40) writes that Rwandan people considered the king's leadership as legitimate 'because his lineage had been the first to clear the land of his whole country'. We do not contest that the traditions mentioned bush clearing, but the Belgian historian does not ask himself whether landownership is a concept compatible with agro-pastoralists in the region used to usufruct. Moreover, oral tradition recounts that not the first king or his lineage elders but divination determined the place to clear bush. Is it not the goodwill of spirits, bound to autochthonous peoples, to the forest or to clan ancestors, that keeps the king and his rainmakers in charge?

We notice a certain actor-materialism in Vansina's (2004: 48, 66) claim that the early kingdoms emerged from the demand for military protection in return for the farmer's food. Cattle-herding comrades growing into chiefs figured out that recognizing one ruler was a solution, and so they did. Might their coalition not have had cultic or medicinal origins? The chiefs' success in forcefully seizing all the lands is explained from the materialist tropes of land deficit and cohabitation of farmers and herders on the hills, which '*required* a single managing authority for all. This figure emerged in the form of the strongest of the herder lords who could call on a permanent military force' (ibid.: 42, my italics). Political centralization is presented as an event, a materially based decision. This approach pays no heed to the cultural process that explains gradually changed minds in society.

When culture does appear in Vansina's history, it is not a preconscious structure informing people's actions, but an ideology employed. For many colleagues, his addition of an actor's perspective made history less objectivist. It meant an advance from cultural materialism, which for instance explained the Neolithic transition from ecological change alone. Combining materialism and an orientation on the actor, his supposition was that cultural change results from humans acting according to their self-interest – a view maintained in classical economics, rational choice and game theory, among others. In this view, individuals are invariably strategic rationalists. Vansina (2004: 55) asserts that Ndori was the first 'king' of Rwanda, an immigrant of Hima descent who, rather than taking over the throne, imported kingship. He reasons:

> For the population to accept Ndori as king, a more solid legitimacy than that which flowed from his victories was needed. Since he came from a land in which the institution of ritualists was as well known as in central Rwanda, he eagerly sought to acquire the legitimacy it could bestow and to have himself proclaimed king.

Strategy implies that Ndori would not have believed in the rituals himself. The actor-materialist historian identifies with an individual actor conscious of all material circumstances and rationally responding like the author himself would. His theoretical position leaves little room for cultural process, and thus for the reader to really appreciate the radical break with past beliefs that Ndori may indeed have made. There are no structures with explanatory value, save the one rationality of *homo economicus* oriented on material needs and applying presumably universal logic. As a result, paradoxically, it is this one cultural structure of pragmatism that buttressed Vansina's reconstruction of African history. The antidote is to 'anthropologize', which is to situate oneself on the scheme of axial poles.

As a student of Vansina, David Newbury (2007: 221) is well placed to draw a nuanced picture of Vansina's position in the field. He portrays a courageous academic plagued in his early career by fellow historians discrediting the reliance on oral tradition and therefore deriding him as 'an ethnologist' (an offence according to him), while criticized on the other side of the fence by anthropologists for his literalist approach to oral traditions. Newbury (ibid.: 224) lucidly remarks that both currents in the 1970s, literalists and structuralists, were still after a single 'Ur-text' in the collected narratives, whether it was events for the one, or values for the other. Soon more 'liberal' historians would take over the humanities with the empirically stronger insistence that 'historical narration was still passed on through time, rather than reinvented around core clichés'. The above scheme aides in situating this postmodern stance embraced by Newbury: actor-idealism. The advantage of the scheme is to nuance, in turn, the claim of theoretical superiority. Actor-idealism is just another quadrant with its own potential weakness such as insensitivity to the facts of nature and economy, and to the structure subtending events – to the ongoing past with its degree of cliché and core.

The humanities underwent a postcolonial transformation conducive for historians and archaeologists to collaborate with anthropologists. An 'anthropologizing' moment in the discipline of history was the ideational structures, or epochal mentalities, studied by the Annales school (Burke 2015). Towards the 1990s, this wider focus on the *longue durée* was called history's cultural turn (Kalb and Tak 2005). Historians and archaeologists realized the importance of contextualizing behaviour in the past, and therefore sought to reconstruct the ideational systems of those actors in that epoch. Archaeologists such as Hodder and Hutson (2003: 14–19) understood that grand 'processual' approaches implied a materialism that basically ignored the mediation by culture. Their postcolonial stance was to move from matter, as directly reflective of society, to materiality, as a rapport practised and constitutive of the identity of both the thing and the user. The fourth current described as actor-idealism permits such radical materiality. Subjects experience the world in a way that is not fixed (as in cultural essentialism) but situated. In an actor employing experiential frames, culture is an event mediating between cause (e.g. ecological disaster) and effect (e.g. a changed lifestyle). Because of its preconscious reproduction, a cultural structure may have relevance to understanding similar practices and objects from several centuries back. As I intend to show next, historical studies ignore cultural structures at their peril.

To elicit the difficult wedding of foci, with sacrifices made at both ends of the table, of semantic dearth by the anthropologist and of missing material evidence by the archaeologist, let us look into a constructive attempt by archaeologist Robertshaw to interpret Urewe culture, 'the mother' of the Eastern Bantu expansion and of the first ironworking sites in East Africa. Urewe pottery in rock-shelters in Bunyoro-Kitara is the lead for Robertshaw (2012: 104) to string parts together 'of a religious complex involving caves, wells, and pythons'. He cites Tantala's work on 'priests' of pre-Chwezi provenance, whose cult would have evolved out of the ritual role of elders in the worship of python gods of rainmaking, fertility and spirit possession. The two series of archaeological associations suffice to feed the next paragraphs of anthropological interrogations.

Despite peering together at a period more than a thousand years ago, the ethnographer of lifeworlds in the same area to the west and south-west of Lake Victoria will shiver at the amalgamation of cultural structures. What would s/he bring to the table then? A series of critical remarks, each however inferred from cultural structures possibly helpful for the archaeologist to work with in the domain of interpretation. Each anthropological critique follows from an ethnographically based distinction, opposition or equation.

First of all, the adjective 'religious' evokes a semantic field that is European and unduly overshadows the importance of the medicinal in these parts of the world. Secondly, in the idiom of all spirit cults in the area, beginning with the Chwezi cult, there is no necessity for possession to evolve from elderliness. On the contrary, the spirit-induced call has a penchant for the adolescent heart. The spirit cult is intergenerational. The power structure that ranks cult members, with elders topping the hierarchy, is quite separable from the bodily experience of possession, led by initiated drummers. We have no reason to assume that this was once different. Thirdly, the word 'priest' has a clerical connotation that leaves out the mediumistic experience in contemporary Chwezi cults. Again, the burden of proof should be on the archaeologist for employing liturgical terminology without explaining why the mediumistic experience could not have had relevance in that epoch as it has today in the region. 'Priest', fourthly, excludes alternative or subversive activities at play in the caves. Just as the rock art of hunters in the Kalahari Desert was done outside the regular living quarters, the activities in the caves of the savanna may have deviated from those at the shrines in familial dwellings. Fifthly, we should make the point that unless an imposing form of chieftaincy existed, or people were very isolated, which the demographics and spread of the sites seem to belie, there could have been multiple cults in parallel. This has been the case since time immemorial among Sukuma living near Lake Victoria. Sixthly, from the latter group's medicinal cults under the name of Zwilili, Yeye and Nunguli that honour snakes, we know that the snake-charmer cults have a different concept of spirit from the Chwezi cult. The python is an ancestral spirit communicating with the living through bodily pain. The snake charmers also have a distinct concept of fertility, expressed in the rainmaking symbolism of the thirty cave drawings taught to the novices. To aggregate the medicinal idioms of spirit cult and python cult is to deny the local distinctions and quite plainly universalize the Western idea of an amalgamated occult realm.

Two simple sentences by the archaeologist have just prompted a long series of remarks by the anthropologist. Should the collaboration be deemed impossible? We have no other choice, I am afraid, than to reconcile history and anthropology. Whether the same cultural structure drove medicine and initiation centuries ago the ethnographer can never tell for sure. Historical sources have to come in. But what ethnographers can commit themselves to is that an endogenous logic did exist. Even on anthropology it dawned slowly. The following pages browse, inevitably shallowly, through some of the seminal comparative studies of African kingship to illustrate the European preoccupation with centralization, sovereignty, conquest and the neat division of sacred and secular, and surmise the blind spot: the medicinal and cultic basis of rule. Chapter 8 will revisit the mantra of divine kingship.

The Polity Prism

Centralization has long preoccupied political science in Africa, as much as conflict does these days. In their standard volume *African Po-*

litical Systems, Fortes and Evans-Pritchard (1940) introduced a number of sociocultural factors to contrast two groups of African societies, the first with central government, the second without. The second, 'stateless' societies (Logoli, Tallensi, Nuer) fascinated for transcending the bilateral, transient kin group with lineages that created corporate groups with political functions. Instead of growing into hegemonies, the lineage segments struck power balances, settling disputes in shifting alliances (ibid.: 14). The first group of 'primitive states' (Zulu, Ngwato, Bemba, Banyankole, Kede) had not kinship but territory as their defining principle (ibid.: 11). Their centrality of government correlated with cultural and socio-economic heterogeneity. A case in point was the Kuba kingdom, composed of patrilineal as well as matrilineal groups, moreover speaking different languages. Drawing on the Zulu and Banyankole kingdoms, the authors speculated that the cultural heterogeneity had resulted from conquests before the formation of the state (ibid.: 9). The authors critically remarked that the kingdoms were less affected by the advent of colonial administration than the segmentary lineage systems with their precarious dynamic (ibid.: 16).

The types of livelihood, such as fixed cultivation versus shifting cultivation, varied independently within each type. About the lineages of stateless societies, the authors emphasized their segmentary logic (Fortes and Evans-Pritchard 1940: 21). The leopard-skin chief among the Nuer was merely a mediating figure negotiating between the lineages. His safeguarding of the earth's fertility was a form of mediation too, with the spirit world. The inverse reasoning would apply for states. There rule without mediation is possible. A single head embodies people's norms and beliefs.

It can be disputed whether the kings sought to embody the unified beliefs, especially since the community of a conquest state was always culturally heterogeneous, but the theory of an ideational superstructure getting the many minds aligned appealed to Fortes and Evans-Pritchard (1940: 17, 21), escaping the bland functionalism of their teacher Radcliffe-Brown. They claimed that mystical aura reinforces secular sanctions to maintain the axiomatic character of moral and legal norms. The problem, though, with their religious focus, was to presume a section of reality that can be isolated as non-political.

The separation of church and state is ethnocentric in the description of stateless societies. So is the governmental-administrative model of rule, which assumes every society, and every social unit whether family or festival, to be politically organized. Political aspects can be studied in any group, because decisions will be made and interests defended. This perspective refracts incorrectly, though, once we treat those aspects as forming a system that can be equated with society and be called interchangeably the polity. The polity prism assumes that power, defined narrowly as individual influence and epitomized in the ruler's office, characterizes social structure. Many alternatives are possible to such power: desire or affect or the cosmology of healing could encompass that power. The polity prism tends to obscure the fact that a system looking like a kingdom could grow from an entirely different model than the European one.

Fortes and Evans-Pritchard (1940: 16) did sense the limitations of their governmental focus, although they invented a separation that presumed the African king to be the sum of secular and sacral domains:[7]

> An African ruler is not to his people merely a person who can enforce his will on them. He is the axis of their political relations, the symbol of their unity and exclusiveness, and the embodiment of their essential values. He is more than a secular ruler; in *that* capacity the European government can to a great extent replace him. His credentials are mystical and are derived from antiquity. . . . Into these sacred precincts the European rulers can never enter. They have no mythical or ritual warranty for their authority. (ibid.)

The authors find in the king's ceremonial role under European administration a conservation of the ritual function, as if the colonizer in all his anthropological wisdom had managed a clean cut of a lived reality rather than caused a new reality to arise. 'It is an interesting fact that under European rule African kings retain their "ritual functions" long after most of the secular authority which these are said to sanction is lost' (Fortes and Evans-Pritchard 1940: 21). The precolonial king's charm imposed its rules in the form of spirit obligations and thus decentred the ruler. By separating secular and sacral power, the medicine was now an object without actual power. The matter of the charm became a travesty, a fetish ready for collection and museum display. And the king became a ruler escaping dependency on the object. He could disregard the spirit's will, which paved the way for legitimate autocracy. Part III will describe such transition towards the ceremonial state. For instance, the medicinal rule of chiefs transformed radically after Shaka expelled all rainmakers from his kingdom (Gluckman 1940: 31). The medicine was not coincidentally the focus of Shaka's intervention to become an autocratic ruler – in other words, a king without medicine.

In this book we interchangeably speak of 'kings', 'paramounts' and 'chiefs', if the latter operate in a system without paramount, for all these terms refer to the traditional office of a supreme authority. By this we do not necessarily assume the customary holder to have actual authority. None of our data will warrant to describe chieftaincy as a secular office nor kingship as sacred. Both draw on reciprocal relations with the spirit, through medicinal initiation, sacrifice and divination. If divine rule is the sole system that deserves the label of kingship, we should not use the word in equatorial Africa. We follow Claessen (2011: 6) in subsuming the king under the cross-cultural category of 'chief'. For Claessen, though, the king would differ from a (paramount) chief in the legitimacy to enforce personal decisions. One could then argue that precolonial central Africa had no kings. Autocratic heads of state existed but it was not institutional for their rule and interventions to deviate at will from tradition and common opinion like the despotic kings of Europe. Claessen (ibid.: 5) summarizes the ethnographic literature on chiefs and chiefdoms to list the following elements as defining: an ascribed top position with the capacity to redistribute profits; a sacred effect on living beings; and collective public endeavours including warfare. The medicinal aspect, linked to the chief's supreme responsibility, is lacking in his account.

The comparative study of African political systems by Fortes and Evans-Pritchard set the scene for decades of fruitful interdisciplinary exchange with historians. A series of debates ensued, which began with discarding the racist Hamitic hypothesis on kingship as an institution diffused by the pastoralists of current Ethiopia and Somalia. Torday and Wrigley, among others, objected that a nomadic people limits its cultural and administrative luggage (Ogot 1964). This in turn raised the enigma of Nilotic kingdoms in East Africa. The Shilluk and Bunyoro so-called 'divine kings' were exceptions in the Nilotic spectrum, where stateless societies formed the bulk. An intermediate case was the Alur 'segmentary state'. Murdock remained intrigued in 1959 by the presence of Cushitic Iraqw in central Tanzania: might they be the remnants and evidence of an immigration some two thousand years ago, when the Bantu had not yet moved that far east?

The oral traditions of the Interlacustrine kingdoms, however, are unambiguous in that, before the Nilotic Bito invasion, a Bantu group had formed the Kitara kingdom and a Bantu linguistic mixture had developed, from which sprang Hima-Tutsi dynasties (Ogot 1964: 286). The Chwezi were the dynastic clan ruling Kitara. After the invasion, the Bito founded the Bunyoro-Kitara empire. The neighbouring kingdoms of Ankole and Rwanda were reactions of revolt (ibid.: 292). The historian Bethlem Ogot proposes one explanation for the rise of both the Shilluk kingship and the Bito empire:

A dominant minority imposed its rule over several disorganized local groups, in the same way that the Franks had done in Gaul or the Normans in England. This minority rule gradually acquired solidarity and permanence, perhaps due to the people's sedentary life, coupled with external pressures, probably the attacks of the Fung and the Dinka. Lienhardt has suggested that the Shilluk kingship might have 'strengthened as a focus of opposition to foreigners'. (ibid.: 294)

In the dialogue with anthropology a classification of types of state formation developed. Ogot's quote suggests a process of subjugation (or colonization) and replication, 'planting out sub-dynasties from a central source' (Ogot 1964: 296), which was recognized too by Southall (1956) in the expansion of Lwo clans. An inverse process with the equivalent outcome of political centralization was collateral growth, or what Kopytoff (1999: 91) coined 'levitation', whereby a lineage grows and the founder or his successor heads the expanding hierarchy. Between subjugation and levitation, the coalescence of villages into an encompassing unit is possible, with conservation of the village headmanships creating a two-tier polity.

This processual typification of state formation ignores two characteristics central to our thesis. First of all, it does not consider cultural forces of assimilation or symbiosis entailing centralization and migration. A minority, such as the cattle-holding clans that ruled in the Great Lakes, is presumed to have imposed its hierarchy, if not through war then through ruse at a time of political chaos. Secondly, in the classification of processes, the pivot of theory is the Western concept of 'state'. Could comparative historical research make a difference?

The fourth International African Seminar, which took place in Dakar in 1961 under the auspices of the International African Institute, was an occasion for much excitement heralding a decade of fruitful interdisciplinary exchange (Vansina, Mauny and Thomas 1964). With Mauny and Thomas as chairmen, Vansina as general rapporteur, and anthropologist Daryll Forde as an ever-avid supporter, every bit of data was scrutinized in order to reconstruct Africa's past, all in an atmosphere comparable to the epiphany of disciplinary convergence that anthropology had undergone in the 1950s (epitomized in Max Gluckman's famous series of talks on BBC radio). The historians noted with enthusiasm the contributions by other disciplines such as archaeology and linguistics. They did not mind conceding that '[o]nce more the topics discussed show that the historian cannot be concerned solely with gathering raw data. His task is to discover their *meaning*. This can *only* be done through the knowledge of categories and criteria derived from the social sciences after their immediate significance has been outlined by ethnographic research' (ibid.: 90; my italics). Bradbury (1964: 149) noted along similar lines the need of sociocultural models so that historians contextualize their information from oral traditions and do not mistake history for 'the rationalization of myth'. General progress was to be made through a two-way exchange whereby the historian projects the anthropologist's 'plane of the ethnographic present' onto a timescale. By the latter, Bradbury meant that ethnographers systematically wrote in the present tense to record the beliefs and practices of African societies.

A few years later the tone hardened. Jan Vansina (1966: 247) concluded his overview *Kingdoms of the Savanna* on the history of Central Africa, with an unmistakable instruction: 'The regularities outlined are evident and the link with structural features of the political system are obvious. It is the task of anthropologists to work them out in greater detail'. The possibility of other structures rooted in the subject's motivations and appearing from the anthropologist's ethnography was not entertained. The division of tasks had changed. What happened in the meanwhile? In the background may have simmered the usual interdisciplinary skirmish over funds whereby Vansina could exert pressure as a towering authority after his directorship of the Institute for Scientific Research in Central Africa (IRSAC) in Rwanda. More to the front was the budding consensus during decolonization that many anthropologists had fed colonial ideology by representing African societies as static worlds without history. Despite the historian's warning, many ethnographers until the 1980s imperturbably retained the present tense. It was as if, integrated in the community and speaking the language, they possessed a deeper truth – something that was bound to irritate other scientists working in the same area.

In this respect, Chapter 7 will consider the deeply engrained Western cosmology of linear time that sharply opposes past to present, with concomitant grammar. Is use of the past tense not suggesting more historical accuracy than ethnographic data permit? And is historical accuracy not secondary for the anthropologist searching for cultural structure, something of a less factual nature? Since such structure envelops both past and present, can we use both tenses? Bantu verbs have a habitual marker for a third tense regarding cyclical or repetitive occurrences. Might that suit ethnography better? The habitual tense does tally with the reversible transitions this book will evince. A view on history as 'trend' instead of 'linear flow' requires an adapted language (cf. Braudel's distinction in Chapter 4). The Rwandan concept of oral tradition situates history in trends rather than in sequences of events (see Chapter 9). To endogenize, must African studies not heed the local views? The past and the present constitute a bone of contention that historians and anthropologists still grapple with today.

Taking a closer look at Vansina's (1966: 245) three 'leitmotivs which occur over and over again', we find that the 'structure' he observed in central African history is a material, macroscopic reality. On it, contingent events operate such as the slave trade, whose impact on dynastic rise and fall is emphasized by Vansina. The leitmotivs bear no relation to a lifeworld, cosmology or other ideational structure that local actors may share and reproduce in their practices. The first structural feature of the savanna kingdoms would be the primacy of the figure of the king, causing personalities to very much shape local history. The second feature is the relatively informal system of succession, stimulating civil strife. The third feature, applicable to the major kingdoms, is the system of peripheral territories operating as tributaries with internal autonomy, headed by local or vassal chiefs. Their structural 'indirect rule' has, as a material consequence, the possibility of secession by the outer provinces, especially if undergoing exploitation by the centre, like in the Kuba and Lunda kingdoms. The three leitmotivs are, however, secondary outcomes. They obtain salience only if embedded in practices and the experiences of actors. The relative autonomy of Sukuma agro-pastoral farmers and their extended compound, whereby authority is grounded in unwritten traditions and in an invisible world nobody can monopolize, interacts with the polycentric social structure. The side effect are Vansina's leitmotivs: (1) a rather centrifugal type of power (2) by an influential personality (3) whose succession is not much formalized.

State Formation: Conquest or Alliance?

Conquest attracts as an explanatory concept for it seems universal, needing no cultural translation. Conquest was in most precolonial African states the number one cause for the rise of centralized government – the statement of Vansina, Mauny and Thomas (1964: 88) will not shock. We may see before us a group of warriors, young men sent away or leaving the community after their initiation in the forest, expanding their territory with every victory, their descendants needing government to control the growing population. That scenario is not what the authors had in mind. As far as the data tell, the conquest consisted in an invading group immigrating and making their domination accepted by the autochthones:

> A typical example is the rise of the kingdom of Kongo. The foreign conquerors married in the local groups. But they were accepted and the kingdom was really founded only when the religious head of the autochthonous groups recognized the king. He cured him from a mysterious illness, gave him his daughter in marriage and accomplished the ritual of enthronement. Through these acts the conquest became legalized and accepted by the conquered. (ibid.: 88)

The choice of focus is revealing. Why emphasize conquest over popular acceptance of the newcomer's rule? Exchange established an alliance. That was the decisive factor in centralization. The quote mentions marriage, curing and ritual, each a practice whereby an insider embraces the outsider's knowledge in order to foster life – not oppression. Furthermore, how could the locals have organized a ritual of enthronement, if they had just been introduced to kingship? The groups must have shared a cultural model so that they jointly created a ritual or reworked one from the transcultural cults. Acculturation by a gentrifying group, whose language and culture seem more refined, is a common process worldwide in the growth of societies, and could very well sum up the long-range history of the Bantu languages' success.

The historians discussed two other cases of state formation.[8] Both are logical alternatives to conquest: a process from within or an external power wished for. In the internal development towards a state, one corporate group such as a clan manages to impose itself on the others. This could happen through social reorganization. The Zulu example expounded by Gluckman ([1956] 1970) is that of age sets transformed by Shaka into military units. The other possibility featured in a monograph by Southall (1956: 98). The Alur invited princes to immigrate and organize their community into a state. The commoners were willing to pay tribute, although they got no army for it. What did they get in return? The historians do not mention the medicinal knowledge of the Alur, which made their kingship desirable. The historians' three cases rely on a view of power as in its essence conflictual, pitting in-groups against out-groups, whereas the opposite, endogenous process seems more plausible to explain the successful expansion of Bantu-speaking peoples.

Acculturation is a more likely driver of change in central Africa than conquest or mere mobility. First of all, the numbers of actual immigrants, even in the wars for which the conquest state of the Lunda was famous, were very small. Vansina himself noted that the mobility was limited to localized sections of clans, not much larger than the bands of hunters, which led him to argue:

> [the] grandiose tribal migrations elaborated by authors such as Gouldsbury and Sheane, Lane-Poole or Grévisse, are unlikely. Population movement would occur at the level of clan section migration. Clan sections would be very mobile, but they would move in all sorts of directions. Over the large area, then, the whole population could be seen as a static mass. This view is supported by the cultural evidence, which shows that from one point to any other in the area there is no sharp break in culture but only a gradual change. (Vansina 1966: 88)

Were the agricultural immigrants culturally attractive to their hosts, the bands of hunters and smiths? Initiation (re)produces a cosmology, especially if easily transmittable thanks to 'contagiously' fractal patterns of meaning, which Bantu languages with their noun classes and monemes facilitate. Sociostructurally, the diversity in the region is enormous, but culturally any anthropologist confining the subject to a language group will be embarrassed to admit that as the comparison of cultural systems progresses in the four directions of the compass no sharp break can be observed between any of the Bantu-speaking peoples, and quite far beyond.

The king's rule typically fading from the centre to the periphery (cf. Vansina 1966: 155) is an indication that in the few cases when the savanna groups happened to centralize to organize government and become 'states', their origin and sense of purpose was not the centralized state as encountered in Europe. Territorial rule was divided among chiefs, amounting often to a decentralization like that of the Tio kingdom of which Vansina (ibid.: 108) admitted that it was 'pushed so far that one can legitimately ask if this was indeed a state or not'. The least one can say is that Vansina's kingdom is an umbrella term with relative validity for all types of polity in the region. It may work for scholars who are content with an outsider's account of kingship worldwide, but as our concern is cultural meaning, more purchase should be gained with an indigenous concept of rule. It would be an advance in comparison to non-anthropological histories such as Vansina's description of the rise of the Lunda kingdom as a natural kind of process without cultural reference: 'Also, the people began to believe in the chiefs' influence on the general fertility of the land and gradually to believe in the whole concept of divine kingship' (ibid.: 86). One would nearly forget that those people had a history of traditions and spiritual experiences on which they drew to innovate.

In brief, what has been lacking in precolonial political analyses is a sensitivity for the cultural 'logics' in history. African kingship will always look divine to the European observer splitting medicine into politics and religion (cf. Chapter 8). An antidote is needed – and that we offer in the study of endogenous process. Making sense of disparate data in a region spanning the continent from the Indian Ocean to the Atlantic, it explains in large part how the chieftaincy of medicinal rule could evolve into the kingship of a centralized state. Until now, disregard for endogeneity and commonality has been the safe bet: 'Surely, equatorial Africa is too culturally diverse'. But the data demand a courageous claim.

The Endogenous Logic of Medicinal Rule

As outlined in Figure 0.3 in the next section, and elaborated in the coming chapters as well as recapitulated in the conclusions, we argue that historically the regional model of rule rests on four interdependent elements forming an endogenous logic of innovation: after (1) divinatory communication with the ancestral or nature spirit an individual is (2) initiated and allowed after sacrifice (ordeal, transgression, blood offering) to (3) initiate others ritually into medicinal knowledge coming from the forest, which (4) bestows social status in return for gifts (fee, feast) to an association. The *ihane* village initiation we described enacts that logic. The medicinal knowledge combined with ritual cooling, purifying the novices of all 'heat', including witchcraft affect, gives the novices the status to 'rule', in the culture-specific sense of heading a social unit such as the band of peers, a family, compound or house. A social cephalization takes place. The 'village headman', 'chief' and 'king' are applications of this basic model, epitomized by the cult founder of great renown with many followers. Divination and medicine will emerge as the elements preceding and subtending initiation and gifts for association.

Medicinal rule has been an endogenous force in the social changes of centralized states. Its four elements played a key role in the tensions pivotal to the historical changes in the area, as portrayed in the three parts of this book, of which we give examples here between brackets: (a) the royal struggle against diviners (Rwanda), the attack on divination by autocratic associations (Lele), and the royal discomfort with spirit mediumship (Buganda); (b) the royal aversion to initiation (Tio); (c) the delegation of medicine by the royal founder's distant successors (Kuba, Sukuma, Bemba), and the abolishment of rain medicine (Zulu); and (d) the tension between chiefs and initiatory associations, and the creation of ethnic castes instead of a transcultural cult (Rwanda). A king's invention of an institution to escape initiation or to thwart diviners could typically be undone a few generations later, so the pivots have returned in recorded history. Their origins perhaps date back millennia. The four elements have been pivots between which histories in the region have tended to alternate, their rootedness in endogenous logic causing reversions, besides aversions. Discussed in this book, seeking in the sequence of events an 'ongoing past', are reversions of (and aversions to) divinatory, initiatory, medicinal and cultic tenor. The fact that social changes typically arose in the form of an attack on one of these elements of medicinal rule bears testimony to the model's salience.

The cultural aspects of the colonial intervention itself tend to bear out the hypothesis about medicinal primacy, because at the heart of it, as Chapter 3 will highlight, stood the uncontrollable mobilizing force of local medicine (cf. Rose-Hunt 1999). Several anti-colonial rebellions in eastern Africa drew on claims of magical prowess, in part because of the shared tradition of medicinal rule but possibly also because the rebellions identified medicine as the weak spot in the European occupation (which the colonizer inadvertently confirmed by employing 'witchdoctors' against Mau Mau rebels; Luongo 2006). The colonizer intended to remove the medicinal side of chieftaincy through deontological norms, the schooling of chiefs and a careful selection of the incumbents. My interviews with a Sukuma chief and oral literature will reconstruct a century of succession struggles in the chiefdom of Bulima, seen from the perspective of the main contender. The life history of the late chief illustrates the political role of medicine in conflicts with the colonial administration. The externally designated incumbent of the throne does not know how to make rain. Bulima's fate is contrasted with the clean 'cultural break' in another Sukuma chiefdom, that of Ndagalu, on the occasion of the royal shaving ceremony. In the first case, traditional and colonial expectations clash over medicine, having reverberations many years later in the last appointed incumbent's refusal to climb the throne and his preference to work as a car mechanic in Dar es Salaam. The Ndagalu case stages a chief coming to greet his people, only to bury chieftainship for good, as he conspicuously evades the practice of medicine.

From Divinatory Society to Kingship: Soil, Root, Stem and Shoot of the Transition

The trouble with process is the suggestion of linearity. The metaphor of the tree and its bifurcations has been useful in studies of evolution to evince multilinearity in chronology. I push the analogy with germination a little further by differentiating the sequence of transition in terms of its soil, roots, stem and shoots. Soil evokes conditions necessary for the transition. It contains elements of a cultural structure, such as ideas, implanted like seeds. Roots point to the growth of these seeds into one or several institutions. The stem is the main body of the transition whereby the new institution emerges from the roots. Shoots and branches are bifurcations into institutions derived from the same cultural structure. As a disclaimer, we should keep in mind that 'transition' is a certain perspective on history chosen by the scholar. There is no intrinsic reason why the institution under study should be called the stem. The stem may for other institutions be the root or a bifurcation from earlier practices.

The *soil* of the transition to chiefship and kingship in equatorial Africa is the cosmology of hunting bands and the new ecological circumstances of climate change, deforestation and desertification. An embryonic form of centralized rule germinated during the initiation of hunters that entered divinatory societies, such as those described by Mary Douglas (1963) among the Lele, and by Victor Turner (1967) among the Ndembu. The initiation boils down to the experience of possession by a spirit in the forest sharing medicinal knowledge about the forest and imposing a new identity upon the incumbent with moral obligations. Its basic structure can be encountered today across central, eastern and southern Africa, in medicinal associations, drums of affliction, *ngoma* societies, collective initiatory rituals, and in the personal accounts of traditional healer-diviners on the origin of their medicinal knowledge. It is succinctly portrayed as well in the

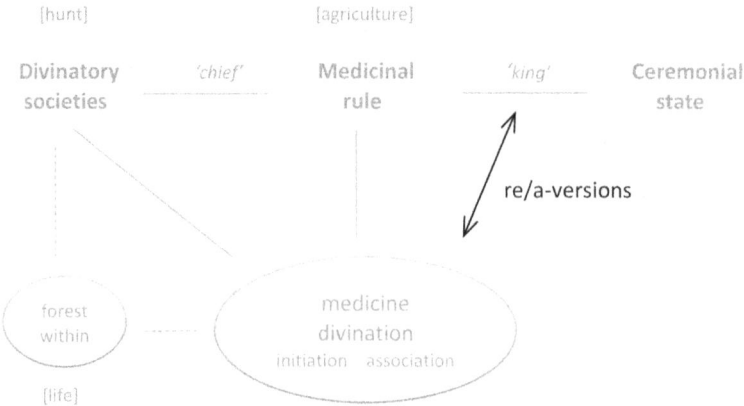

Figure 0.3 Endogenous transitions of rule in east and central Africa. Figure by the author.

first Congo travelogues of the seventeenth century. The divinatory societies, or spirit-based associations, that interconnect bands of hunters represent an institution at the *roots* of the transition leading to the new institution. The two chapters of Part I, 'Divinatory Societies', compare ethnographic and historical cases.

The hunters' societies initiated members of other villagers in return for fees that were redistributed in the community. I propose a rationale on how the new institution of chiefship originated from there. The transition reaches its *stem* as the new institution takes mature form. We choose not to name it 'kingship'. Headman or chief embody 'medicinal rule', the title of this book and of Part II, because they have what is expected of the leader, namely a mastery over and communication with the outside, the forest, spirits, witchcraft and foreign groups. Ethnographers have translated that mastery as healing because across Bantu-speaking Africa the diviner-healer (e.g. *nganga, sangoma*) has become the expert of these activities. All the initiations, whether rite of passage or rite of healing, are called practices of *kupoja,* or 'cooling'. The Bantu verb signifies the regulating of life, which is more than healing. It comprises both the remedying of 'heat' and the acquisition of social status and fame. To be powerful is to have – literally to 'be with' (*kuwa na*) – the medicine. Treatment of an affliction, with the medical purpose of cure, is an offshoot of medicinal initiation, tapping from the powers that the ritual exudes. Ritual rebirth of a group during initiation releases medicine from which individual patients can benefit at the periphery of the occasion.

Part II exhibits in five chapters the wide variety of medicinal rule in central Africa, the Great Lakes, and eastern and southern Africa. Although always materially expressed in medicine, the institutionalized power of headman and chief in the rainforests of the west mostly concentrates on a shrine and rituals for protection against witchcraft and for guardianship over women's fertility, whereas in the savannas towards the north-west, the south and especially the east it more often relies on collective agricultural ceremony, protective charm and rain medicine. The chiefs or 'forest-masters' among Tio in the north-west of Congo exemplify with their shrine representing the chiefdom the primacy of the ruler's medicinal qualities over his personal ones. Autocratic tendencies, clear-cut geographical boundaries and administrative policy are uncommon in the 'stem' of the institution. The chiefs are initiated in a moment of great transgression as incumbents of the highest rank of spirit possession. They collect fees in return for protective rituals that 'cool' the world. In some cases, historical links can be traced with actual cults turned dynastic clan. The forest-masters are as much proto-healers as proto-kings. Carrying a title with stem *kum* (in many linguistic variants) they literally have 'come out' and are 'famed'. Their medicinal rule constitutes the local model for kingship, quite unlike the European concept of rule.

The challenge for us as scholars is to think through the proto-meaning of the institution. What was *kum* like before bifurcating into 'healer' in some eastern Bantu languages and 'chief' in some western Bantu languages? In search of an answer we examine cases of medicinal rule, including roots and offshoots, at the borders of the cultural and linguistic 'whole', which for Vansina exemplified the equatorial tradition. The exploration of the fringes will bring us among others to Tio and Loango west from the inner Congo basin, to Azande and Alur north-east from it, to Bushong and Komo somewhat east, to Lele and Ndembu in the south-east, to Bemba, the Lundu and Rozvi states further in that direction, and to Rwanda, Buganda and Sukuma-Nyamwezi on the eastern side (see Map 0.1 at the beginning of this Introduction). Most of these groups have been the subject of a seminal monograph that deserves to be exegetically examined. Systematic reinterpretation will permit a check of the plausibility of our thesis across the region. Some cases are representative of Vansina's baseline research of the Congo basin (Chapter 4). Others extend the research far beyond the basin. The renowned quality of the ethnography is a criterion of selection for our sample of groups. Taken together, the monographs admittedly still cover just a fraction of the available literature and archival data. In my exegesis, I will add page references between brackets in the text as frequently as possible, sometimes quite frankly to anticipate the likely disbelief of colleagues, because the data in the monographs do not always correspond to the interpretation that has become conventional in the discipline. The endogenous quality of the interpretation is our main concern.

Strictly speaking, the term 'king' is best reserved for the paramount of a ceremonial state. We think of the Kuba, Kongo, Rwanda, Bunyoro and Buganda kingdoms depicted in Part III. As an *offshoot* of medicinal rule, the king interestingly undermines the root affect. He and his palace control ritual in order to overrule divinatory communication with the spirits. With the help of a subjugated caste of priests, the king rids himself of reciprocity with the spirits and governs as an autocrat, possibly to enrich himself. He has unequivocal procedures at his disposal, in ceremony and succession, conserved and recited by court historians, to avoid dependence on people councils, on the capricious wishes of the spirit world or on the fertility from the wild outside, which he in his non-human, constant transgression may rather want to embody.

Confirming the hypothetical interconnections, the offshoot labelled kingship was already noticeable in the very roots of the transition. In the recent past, Lele communities of hunters in the rainforest had been replacing about every ten years the fortune magic of their divinatory societies by the rule of the witch-finding cult that supersedes people's reciprocity with the spirits, and transcends village communities. Such shortened sequences are of special interest in our study for revealing the pivotal elements of the cultural model. They could be coined the 'radicles' of kingship. Similar examples are the recurring tensions between which social changes pulsate and to which temporary revolutions revert, as if they are too fundamental to disappear: the divinations prohibited by autocrats; the ritual initiations the incumbents try to evade and abolish; and the spirit mediumship the dynastic families disparage. An extended, long-term version of a pivotal tension, leading to the bifurcation of divination and kingship, is revealed in Rwanda's oral traditions from four centuries of dynastic history. All these cases illustrate the historically grown cultural structure that endows chief- and kingship in eastern and central Africa with another meaning than the European institution.

Notes

1. I will employ the first-person plural as the verb form to refer to you and me reading this book. The singular form is reserved for the author's personal position or experience.
2. An example of a multidisciplinary reconstruction of history is the online website by Rhonda Gonzales, 'Societies, Religion, and History: Central East Tanzanians and the World They Created, c. 200 BCE to 1800 CE', http://www.gutenberg-e.org/gonzales/index.html. The absence, however, of wider context, such as Vansina's equatorial tradition, limits the validity of hypotheses about that narrowly delimited 'world' and its cosmology.
3. A standard illustration for undergraduates of medical anthropology is the mortality statistic of the Titanic disaster. Proportionally more victims fell among the lower than higher classes. To explain the outcome, we must consider the proximity of the lifeboats to the expensive cabins above deck. The 'social effect' corresponds to material advantages (e.g. the nearby lifeboat) for the higher social classes. This social effect must be juxtaposed with the cultural expectation to save 'women and children first', which accounts for the statistical fact that more men died than

women and children. The 'cultural' effect results from an inculcated idea. An explanation allowing for both effects in equal measure will be situated on our scheme in the middle between the extremes of materialism and idealism.
4. In our example of the Titanic, the many 'deviant' cases are visible too in the statistics of survivors and casualties, such as those passengers below deck alert enough to save themselves and those on deck too inebriated to wake up for a walk to their lifeboat.
5. The fourfold typology has relevance beyond anthropology; see Andrew Feenberg's (1998) four approaches to technology, respectively instrumentalism, determinism, substantivism (dystopia) and constructivism (critical theory), whereby the latter two came up thanks to insight in a second dimension, namely the cultural values within technology.
6. In Africanist anthropology, we should note, the ontological turn has not taken off, despite its promise of truly capturing the local endogenous dynamics. The theory tends to unnerve Africanists whose postcolonial turn was the historically logical culmination of the schematized oscillation and centripetal spiral. The acknowledgment of a shared postcolonial condition globally is crucial for the Africanist's critical project. The decolonizing project controverts the existence of separate worlds, each with their own morality and priorities. The quest for radical difference in local terms, like Marilyn Strathern's (1988) for Melanesia, and Viveiros de Castro's for Amerindians, could not preoccupy those working in the multidisciplinary field of African studies, which has in its ranks political and economic researchers doing pretty well without ethnographic fieldwork and without the perspectival shift and openness to alterity.
7. The irony is that the founding father of functionalism, Radcliffe-Brown (1940: xxi), who in his preface to the volume was eager to reprimand the two editors and rising stars at the academic firmament, figured that out in his own way: the political and the ritual are one office, hence the state should not be the Africanist reference. His ensuing solution to conceive of all polities, centralized or not, as regulators of sanctions was a simplification to obtain common ground, complying with Evans-Pritchard's take on the Nuer lineages as feud-settling alliances, while conveniently forgetting that Nuer leadership was an earth- and fertility-bound role, despite the pastoralist mode of livelihood.
8. Lemarchand (1977: 304) distinguished four types of kingship: theocratic kingship (Ethiopia), stratified kingship (Rwanda, Burundi), ethnic kingship (Swazi, Lesotho), and incorporated kingship (Buganda, Ankole, Yoruba). His focus, however, is on the recent past, as can be derived from the last two types. The typology differentiates insufficiently for our region of study, central and eastern Africa. More informative anyway is a typology of kingdoms anchored in processes of origination, like that attempted by Vansina, Mauny and Thomas.

PART I

Divinatory Societies

Chapter 1

THE FOREST WITHIN

The aim of this book is to highlight the cultural continuity of an institution. How to go about it? We have older ethnographies by colonials and missionaries at our disposal, as well as diaries of explorers going back to the early seventeenth century. Although the descriptions suffer from ethnocentrism of the day, they can be scrutinized for elements that are known to still have relevance, such as local terms and recognizable practices. The cultural logic that holds the elements together cannot be derived from those documents. For that integrative dimension of cultural cohesion, prevailing partly at a preconscious level, we have ethnographic fieldwork. To attain the intercultural experience that is required for cultural comparison, the most effective way is gradual initiation and ritual participation as one of the novices. By visiting other ceremonies afterwards and learning from novices of nearby peoples entering the same cult, the researcher develops a more composite sense of cultural structure or logic, defined as a set of adaptable frames to experience the world.

Our first piece of historical evidence is Dapper's description of Loango society around the early seventeenth century. At that time the institution of kingship was well established, yet traces of its cultic origin were still visible. The king owned the paramount medicinal shrine. He sat behind a large cloth demarcated by other statues operated by nobles for his protection. The kings of nearby smaller groups behaved like cult heads whose authority depended on initiation. Inheritance of a title through descent, matrilineal or patrilineal, was an obvious solution to ensure continuity in the management of a cult, but due to the principle of classificatory kinship the succession was rarely unequivocal. The ancestral spirits were thought to communicate their preference of a successor in dreams and oracles. The fact that kings normally have to be initiated, and some are known to have tried to escape that obligation, is an important trace of the original link with the healing cult. Chiefs under the paramount had territorial responsibilities for settling fees, not unlike 'chiefs' of cults welcoming new members. In seventeenth-century Loango, each chief or *mani* – whose stem *man* etymologically alludes to 'the knower' – specialized in a medicine. Each *mani* had a shrine for it, which functioned as a reminder of the personal obligation he received in a dream or in the forest.

Before examining the historical evidence, we turn to the anthropology of divinatory cults among Lele hunters to obtain a glimpse of the earliest model of centralized rule. The analysis continues with an introduction of the fertility symbolism in initiations. Authority is normally limited to heading the kin group and, in a consultative rather than hegemonic way, to heading the residential unit. A chief or king transcends kinship and residence. Their source to draw on is the medicinal and divinatory power obtained in the forest through spirit-led initiation. The personal transformation generates fertility. To illustrate the required transformation, we end with an interpretation of the Mwindo epic about the origin of chiefship.

This chapter displays three of the sources at our disposal for reconstructing Africa's precolonial past: the historical evidence of a travelogue, the oral traditions, and the ethnography of social change. Social change may be cyclical and thus of long-term historical relevance, as in the Lele case of expanding divinatory societies and the cyclical emergence of witch-finding cults (Douglas 1963). A second case is the gradual standardization of parallel ritual initiations in Komo society (de Mahieu 1985).

Lele Divinatory Societies

To 'endogenize' African history we should restore the role of divination in (un)settling power structures. Divination is commonly defined as prediction of the future, through communication with a supernatural or invisible world. Yet what do foretelling and the future mean in a society with other concepts of time and knowledge? 'Pre-dicting' is ritually saying how the future will be. To know, with the stem *man*, is to prefigure and redirect fate.

East of the Busho(o)ng speakers who founded the impressive Kuba kingdom, which features in Part III, live groups of Lele hunters in villages. Their precarious livelihood and lack of authority structure were the object of study by anthropologist Mary Douglas (1963: 270) in her classic monograph *The Lele of the Kasai*, shortened in the following references as 'LK'. What should interest us are the many divinatory societies lingering in the background of her study, downplayed by scholarship at the time. Lele society is a counterpoint to the neighbouring Kuba kingdom, and a reference point in the region for discovering what the cultural structure may have been, out of which the kingdom grew.

The Lele clans, matrilineal and devoid of ritual heritage, did not command their members. The villages were headed by the oldest male member of the clan that founded the village (LK 68). Despite his double seniority, a primacy in age and in autochthony, his role was only mediatory. No special qualities or ritual investiture were required of the head, the *kum* (*a bola*, 'of the village'). He did not keep the village treasures, which consisted of raffia cloths obtained from cult fees and marriage fees (LK 181). Those were guarded by the spokesperson, a young adult making his announcements every evening around the village compounds. How is power differentiated in a more or less egalitarian (if gendered) society? Seniority is important: *baotale*, 'big ones', is the category comprising both elders and ancestors (LK 204, 223; its stem is proto-Bantu *tal*). Yet seniority is an attribute that everybody possesses sooner or later. The capacity of divination appears to be a more salient discriminator among individuals.

Possibly influenced by Vansina whom she cites in reverence, Douglas treats divination separately in her monograph as a religious activity, despite linking medicine with religion and realizing its wide social significance (LK 205). Looking closer at the statistics in her village (LK 214), we discover that no less than half of the non-Christian males are *bangang*, diviner-healers; divination and healing (*-kang*) are the same. They are initiated into at least one of the oracular societies, or cults (*bu-kang*). They accumulate this divinatory vocation on top of their voluntary membership in the society of 'Begetters' – villagers who have fathered a child. Those who have begotten twins must, for their own sake to remain blessed in life, go through the rites to enter the divinatory society of twin-parents. The villagers who fulfilled the condition for entering the Pangolin cult had done so. The condition was to have a male and a female child from the same wife, and to be fathered by a member of the autochthonous clan.

Divination seems foremost a quality of individuals, who have learned to master their fate by predicting it. Only a few members turn the quality into a profession. Every village has an official diviner (*ilumbi*) joined by a younger successor. They communicate with nature spirits (*mingehe*) to ensure a successful hunt and sniff out witches to protect the village. A special case is the diviner of 'god' (*njambi*) living ascetically in isolation, although regularly meeting with colleagues from other villages to discuss matters of common concern (LK 213). This makes divination the basis for any decision making beyond the village level.

All these cults were organized by the village. The associations interconnected the Lele villages into a country. Fees were collected for transfer of medicinal knowledge and for the climbing of cultic ranks. Thus the village made hay of people's divinatory vocations. Far from a marginal activity, these divinatory and medicinal associations lay at the heart of village affairs. A source of kingship, as in neighbouring Bushong, could be the union of all those village cults in a territorially encompassing association. The source of kingship is less likely the diviner reading the augurs for individual clients than the official diviner catering for the collective and addressing the spirits on the group's behalf. The good hunt and fertility he promised will be to his credit. The things that did not materialize will be on his account as well. We must bear in mind that this is an egalitarian society, without ascribed status or hierarchy. So, if divination is the prime source of authority, the latter will be ambiguous. The knowledge of sorcery the diviner is supposed to possess makes him the number one suspect of sorcery among Lele. The conundrum is, as Douglas emphasizes, that identification of a sorcerer requires the diviner's skill. Villagers were pragmatic about it, distrusting their own fount of knowledge.

The felt ambiguity about the local oracles paved the way for accepting the claims of the anti-sorcery movement, a phenomenon at the roots of the transition we want to study. This local witch-finding cult typically emerged fast to oppose the village diviners and actually forbid all the aforementioned cults (LK 213). The intense impact on Lele society could be compared to the banning of the poison ordeal by the Belgian colonizer, after which villages remained in limbo because suspected diviners could no longer take the oath and prove their innocence. A lot has been published about the witch-finding cults emerging in the first half of the twentieth century (LK 256). Their contemporaneity with colonization seemed no coincidence, hence historians saw in them political revolt. The idea attracted academically for hinting at an adaptive tradition. But equally coeval with colonization is written history. There were no precolonial archives to contradict that the witch-finding cult was new and resulted from colonial violence. A drastic revision followed at the end of Douglas's work. Her data support our thesis on an (anti-)divinatory reversion rooted in endogenous logic. The witch-finding cult would not be an anticolonial reaction but the antipode in a recurring cycle of divinatory societies gaining and losing control, depending on the success or otherwise of hunts in the forest.

> At first I had been inclined to regard anti-sorcery cults as a modern response to the abolition of the poison ordeal. But inquiry soon showed that the cults and the ordeal had existed side by side long before the law of 1924 prohibiting ordeals and therefore much longer before that law was effective in Lele country. Professor Vansina cites evidence that Miko Mi Yool among the Kuba was one of a series of cults extending back into the past. (LK 257–58)

The symbolical anthropologist Douglas breaks with the historicist account of cults, and earns the master historian as ally. In the 1950s, Lele informants identified five successive anti-sorcery movements at ten-year intervals (LK 244). The cases offer a marvellous opportunity to verify the endogenous process in which a cultural structure, quite unfamiliar to us, interacts with sociostructural elements to create an amazing regularity and long-term alternation characteristic of the region.

A pattern recurred. News was heard about a cult that ends all sorcery, which in local terms amounts to millennial belief. Repeated failures in hunting turned around initial scepticism. The failures discredited the official diviners. At the same time, the neighbouring villages had succumbed to the millennial lure. As soon as the village could collect one hundred raffia cloths and four camwood bars they bought the power to install the witch-finding cult. At that point, so everybody knew, all ritual offices and divination were suspended.

The diviners accepted the cult's rule. True to the autonomy principle, they became members too or else laid low, knowing unlike colonial administrators and missionaries the temporariness from previous such cycles. In a few years, during Douglas's fieldwork, the anti-sorcery movement peaked. The key to its success was a belief that would in the end be its downfall as well, for it was hard to maintain. After instalment of the cult, the village was cleared of all medicine. A sort of supernatural law was thought to materialize: every act of sorcery would rebound and automatically cause the sorcerer's death (LK 247). The dead were from then onwards the only guilty ones, and, because of their sorcery, were denied a proper funeral.

The news about denials of funeral rippled through the region. Strong protest invariably ensued, by kinsmen from other villages. Their demand of a funeral upset the cult's rules. The upset in turn threatened the lives of the initiates of the new cult, whose characteristic strictness of rule they had learned to fear. The new converts thus engaged in an all-out effort to initiate the other villages as well (LK

249). The cosmological transformation was no small thing since the contingency of hunt to which divination was attuned had to be ignored. A procedural take on ritual had to be imposed, whereby people would be remarkably persuaded that the bought medicine to initiate the village would eradicate sorcery entirely. Besides cleansing the village, the anti-sorcery rite introduced an alternative cultural structure, namely the belief in a kind of divine law. Once the procedure was correctly applied, there could no longer be any witch alive in the village, and there could be no death, save that of witches.

The old anthropological distinction between witch and sorcerer, based on Evans-Pritchard's 1937 reading of Zande cosmology, comes in handy to explain the cosmological shift, with social and psychological implications. The witch-finding cult conflates the two figures. It morally reframes the villager's everyday use of medicine as an unconscious act of evil that is witchcraft. All sorcery, except the magic of the cult, has become immoral behaviour of witches. A strong identity and sense of exclusion is attached to the cult, for not only are the initiated absolved of evil, the cult prohibits interaction with those who are impure because of being uninitiated (which was an additional motive for conversion, LK 249). Divination has lost all legitimacy through its association with forbidden magic.

In this cyclical movement of the divinatory system ebbing and flowing from one generation to the next we discern the pivot around which the cultural structure of medicinal rule evolves. Most practices and symbols are modifiable as classificatory extensions of root meanings. However, as soon as a shift takes place from spirit reciprocity to divine procedure, the potential is there for a radical change towards state formation. Institutions arise enacting a new frame of experience. It is no coincidence that divination and medicine or magic, both elementary in the endogenous logic, are aimed at in the cyclical rise and revolt of the witch-finding cult. Sustain such cultic revolution and the ruling associations like in Congo's eastern uplands may evolve into a state. What in a social change gets replaced, or people revert to, reveals to the observer what was central to the previous system. With this rule of thumb, we underline the significance of *buganga*, medicine-divination, for precolonial rule in equatorial Africa. As a converse confirmation, the banning of the practice for years at a time could not prevent its continuous resurgence. Connoted by cosmology, desires and beliefs, *buganga* was thus closely entwined with daily life.

In this first comparative exercise, three sources of validity have cropped up for confirming our thesis of medicinal rule. The first is the ethnographic exercise imbuing the researcher with another lifeworld.

The fieldwork generates insight that defies preordained interpretations. The second source of validity is situated in the stories transmitted across generations. Oral tradition conveys the tenor of what matters to a community, from which cultural structure can be derived. The third source of validity concerns historical process. Which changes disturb the sequence of events, and get unmade in case of a return to the old system? Each source of validity avoids the ethnocentric common sense of the methodological individualist, the actor-materialist.

The *ilumbi* Diviner as Proto-king

Given the 'corrosive' belief in the irrational motive of the witch, Mary Douglas wondered how Lele social order is possible (LK 222). Educated in the functionalist school, she emphasized that diviners pinned responsibility for deaths on outsiders or on marginal figures whose downfall could not split the village (LK 235, 226). The *mimbera* curse (cf. widespread Bantu stem *bil*) rectified injustice suffered by a deceased (LK 228). Nobody could get bewitched without prior consent by a clansman, since only kin hold 'rights' over life (LK 221). Although Douglas overestimated entrenched belief, a corollary of structure-idealism, her symbolic anthropology also had the capacity to peer beyond idiosyncratic histories and to acknowledge the cyclic collective process of a witch-finding movement, whose radical change towards a kind of millenarian fundamentalism, perfectly represents what the cultural structure of divinatory societies is not. Because of recurrence of the reversions, the process should be relevant for the historian.

The figure wherein all threads converge is the *ilumbi*, the village's official diviner. He supposedly is the 'arch-sorcerer', able to dance with the witches (LK 231). Reminding of royal taboos that we will discuss, any illegitimate sexual relations with him are life-endangering. He is an intimate of the forest, the place of pure and undomesticated fertility, so observing taboos regarding his company is a way of keeping his life-giving powers safely in check. Transcending the sorcery of personal conflicts, he defends the village as a whole against foreign attacks of magic (LK 229). He complements the village head and the *ndwi*, the village warrior. His rituals serving the peace (*polo*, LK 251; proto-Bantu stem *pol*) of the village and collective well-being evoke activities of the proto-king. At the beginning of the dry season he convokes the village to administer potions against illness (LK 230). Like the leopard chief in the Nuer acephalous segmentary system, the *ilumbi* brews the cup of peace to establish a permanent truce with the rival village. Equally intriguing is the association between diviners and their supposed control over leopards sent to chase away game (LK 255), reminiscent of royal symbolism. An *ilumbi* of high repute at hunting and healing will be invited to practise in other villages. '[E]scorted home with drums and much wealth in camwood and raffia', he spices the village treasury with his earned fees and receives a portion for himself (LK 232). Sustained success of his cultic activities meant alliance with, and effective influence over, villages in the district. A nascent chiefdom under his ritual guidance could be the next step.

In case of a failing *ilumbi* who cannot be exiled or condemned with the poison ordeal, the Lele village resolves the impasse by recourse to the witch-finding cult. Medicinal knowledge remains the reference for law and justice. Douglas notices in the whole region the general pattern applicable 'to the anti-witchcraft movements which have swept through Central Africa, including Mcape and Bwanali-mpulumutsi, which also have some of the characteristics of an ordeal substituting its final verdict for that of the poison ordeal' (LK 256). The anti-sorcery cult plays in the same league as the *ilumbi*, because it takes full responsibility for health in the village (LK 247). Both occupy the sphere of collective healing, which Feierman (1995), Schoenbrun (2006) and Kodesh (2010) associate with kingship. The medicinal model of rule will surface in our observation that kings practise collective ritual where diviner and witch-finding cult no longer have primacy. In brief, the source of kingship seems not to be the leadership of a village head, who is content with representing the group and tackling its concerns. In the Lele case, the seeds of political expansion are divinatory-medicinal. The next two sections explain the relation between the divinatory-medicinal and the forest in an ancient chiefdom on the coast and in the village initiation of a decentralized community in the rainforest.

Loango *nkisi*

In the Dutch book *Naukeurige beschrijvinge der Afrikaensche gewesten*, published in 1668, the author Olifert Dapper synthesizes descriptions of the economic and political system, religious practices and everyday life as observed by European explorers and traders in the villages and kingdoms of coastal Africa. Dapper did not travel himself. The evaluation he makes of the documented customs is mired in the sensitivities of the epoch, such as his observation that the god of the locals is merely nominal and that they mock the idea of an afterlife but strangely believe in the influence of ancestral spirits (Dapper 1668: 544–48). Much of his account fascinates for depicting precolonial institutions that bear a striking resemblance to current ritual practices. Many of the local terms for specific traditions, such as *nkisi* (amulet) and *mani* (chiefship), can be verified today. Most revealing is the way some of these practices and beliefs were connected in that period through symbolic relations that latently exist today but whose semantic origins have faded over the centuries as the uses of the various concepts within and across societies diverged. Some directly concern our comparative exercise to determine the cultural origins of the local institutions of kingship: the relation between spirit, *nkisi* and taboo, between forest and initiation, between leopard and king.

This section examines the depiction of the Loango kingdom, named Lovango by Dapper and according to him also known as the land of the Brama. Dapper (1668: 4) bases himself on the travelogues of Samuel Blomert, combined with those of Filips Pigaset and Samuel Brun (whom he calls Sam. Bruno). The description of life in Loango in the 1600s offers insight into the earlier origins of kingship, since Loango is one of the three kingdoms, with Kongo and Tio, that according to Vansina could together have formed one model of rule. That model would be a political competition between alpha men, so-called 'big man'. According to the contrasting model we propose, the source of power is cultic, befitting the tendency of Bantu-speaking settlers to acculturate locals through alliance and social exchange rather than through warfare. Cosmologically, the migrants found a way of matching agricultural fertility with the hunter's success. Their ideas, and the language connected with these, were sufficiently attractive to spread in equatorial Africa at a pace that did not depend on the migration of the settlers alone.

Following Dapper's (1668: 546–47) account of Loango, the key idea around which practices of power and ritual seemed to cluster is that of obligation, a formal promise (*oplegging* in old Dutch). The promise is made to a spirit, represented by the *nkisi* statue (plural: *mikisi*). A bracelet worn on the left or right arm has the same function of mnemonic about the duty to fulfil or the prohibition to obey.[1] Next to the general obligations for men and women, such as dress code and food taboos, and the clan-specific prohibitions, each Loango citizen grows up with a personal obligation. It ranges from the sort of fruits, spices, meat or fish one is prohibited to eat, or is obliged to eat in private with any food remainders to be buried deep (so no dog could dig these up), to behavioral prescriptions, such as hairstyle (e.g. shave or not), and whether or how one should cross water (with a canoe or not). The specifics are conveyed in an oracle after the diviner has been entrusted with the personal obligations of each parent and each grandparent. As long as the obligations are respected, the individual should feel protected. Negligence can cause death. In seventeenth-century Loango the strictest obligations were the king's, but these presented no cosmological breach with those of the citizens. Everyone lived with the divinatory-medicinal condition of knowing a personal spirit's taboo and having protective charms.

Unwilling as Loango presumably are to accept natural causes of death (Dapper 1668: 546), the burial after three days of mourning is concluded with an oracle conducted by a diviner, 'Ganga' (proto-Bantu *kang*), in the backyard of his house: 'So and so has died, we have buried him. Has he been killed by magic, or did his *Moquisien* kill him?' (ibid.: 531; author's italics, our translation). The fetishes, *moquisien* or *mikisi*, can turn against the owner who has not met their obligations. The alternative is killing by magic, referring to someone else's *nkisi* activated for evil purposes. That person is a witch, 'Dokki' (*ndoki*, proto-Bantu *log*), who has a personal obligation permitting acts of witchcraft. Through the *nkisi* the witch can send a curse, 'Takka' (cf. *ndagu* in Kisukuma), to inflict madness (cf. the *ndagu* curse today of *mayabu* patients), to make cripple or blind (ibid.: 526). After the answer obtained through mediumistic possession, the next question of the oracle concerns the possible involvement of kin. The family elders consult various diviners and travel for months between neighbouring villages to investigate every *nkisi* until the truth comes out. If no confirmation is obtained but there are suspects, the family can request from the king to have his experts, 'Konda', organize a poison oracle (*bonde*). The poison ordeal takes place on a hillock outside the village. Those able to urinate after ingestion are considered innocent and will be given the antidote. Falling on the ground and screaming is a sign of guilt, after which the audience may drag the suspect to the road nearby and cut him up in parts with a machete (ibid.: 528).

Some of those who have fallen after the test, and thus should be witches, may be spared. They live on in Chilongo, the province ruled by 'Manibeloor', a lord or chief (*mani*) ranked under the 'Manilovango' chief, but with relative autonomy and the ability to cure people from the consequences of Bonde poison (ibid.: 533). What distinguishes this chief from other people is a special ability in the field of medicine. All chiefs appear to have their specialties with medicinal duties connected to it. Dapper makes a disputable choice of translation for 'Manilovango' (*mani loango*). Eager to identify the monarch in a hierarchy of titles, he speaks of the 'king' of Loango. However, the man's local name is simply *mani*, chief, in his case of Loango. That chief or lord is specialized in detecting witches through the poison oracle. What distinguishes him foremost from his peers heading the other chiefdoms is the quality of his medicine. He possesses the *nkisi* charm with the highest status, *ma-lemba*, which protects him against all illness and witchcraft (ibid.: 551). Hereby established is the link of rule with medicine, more exactly with the cooling medicine of the Lemba cult we discussed in the introduction.

The elders of the clan chose the lord. To him they assign an elderly woman, 'Makonda', the primus inter pares among *konda* experts. Characterized as a queen mother by Dapper, she rather reminds of the legendary cult founder Nkwe Mbali, a mother excelling in medicinal knowledge (see Chapter 7 on Tio). She advises the *mani loango* but also has the power to kill him (ibid.: 535). The importance of this type of knowledge shows in the cloth laid out before the king's seat surrounded by *mikisi* and the operators of these objects working in his service. The *mani loango* is himself a *nkisi*, the people say. In the 1600s all the chiefs had a territory they represented and 'ruled' in that they exerted influence over it. But significant for our thesis on the historical origins of their rule is that their title refers to a certain knowledge. The *mani mata*, 'lord of the bow', specializes in weaponry (*over 't geweer gestelt*). The *mani boma*, lord of the fort (near the sea), controls the sea. *Mani iniami* rules the hill, which everyone is obliged to cross by foot instead of by carriage. 'Manibas' and 'Manikinga' take care of the knowledge of trade. 'Manidonga' knows how to guard the king's women. Are these specializations of government, or of medicine? The data above point to a proto-meaning from which both types of knowledge have diverged.

The political translation of *mani* into lord, chief or king is assumed to be neutral, yet does not capture the *mani*'s double acquisition, of a title and a charm. He is initiated into both at once, charm and title. Also etymologically we have evidence for the medicinal model to inspire rule. A probable derivation is from the verb *ku-mana*, 'to know', referring to divination and initiatory knowledge. Deeper inland in Congo certain medicinal associations are called *mani*, indeed the same term as the one designating the chief in the coastal areas.

Lemba, the Loango king's fetish or charm, is one of the most renowned initiatory systems of the region (cf. Janzen 1982). The Lemba cult as a 'drum of affliction' focuses on healing. Might the king's fetish have been an inspiration for a cult conveniently tapping from the symbolism of royal power? Knowing the creativity and opportunism of healers today, such a direction of influence from a political tool towards medicinal purposes may have taken place at several moments in history (as suggested by Doutreloux, in MacGaffey 1986: 139). But logically such influences came after kingship was established, which means something else preceded that. In many places healing cults existed without or before the institution of kingship. The least we can infer is a cultural affinity between the two institutions. The question of a coherent initial model brings us to the earliest written records on the situation in the 1600s, when a frame of experience was shared and practised among cult members that was less rehashed by the inflation of ranks and political offices than it is in ancient cults today. The initiation into *nkisi* forms a coherent frame of experience, with several features on which the institution of kingship could have been modelled. To be the incumbent of a title or throne was to be the incumbent of a charm. Dapper's text offers an engrossing account of how fetishes were made in Loango. The origin of the *malemba* fetish and of every other *nkisi* was spirit possession. The possession unfolds as a ritual initiation. The resulting *nkisi* subsequently became a protector (*voorbehoeder*; Dapper 1668: 545). Some people, obviously with the means for it, acquired several *mikisi* to cancel out the jealousy between their protective charms. How did one become the incumbent (*aensteller* in old Dutch) of a *nkisi*?

> To make these statues of demons, they have special teachers, in their language named *Enganga Mokisie*, whose main instrument is a drum, and who make these when having reached the right age and being preoccupied by troubles, affected by illness or affliction. (ibid.: 545, our translation)[2]

On the teacher's advice, the incumbent or patient begins by organizing a meeting to announce his initiation to all members of his clan (*geslaght* in old Dutch) and the neighbourhood. The following fifteen days he will spend in seclusion in a small hut made of palm leaves, obeying the prohibition on sexual intercourse. He will not talk for nine days, as signalled by the two parrot feathers at the corners of his mouth. We will encounter those nine days as well in the initiation of kings. He will not clap his hands in reply to a greeting, but for that purpose holds in his hand a little wooden cylinder with a cavity in the middle and a small hole above, connected with a shaft to the sculpted little head, which he should hit with a stick in reply to any questions. A similar cylinder with cavity and stick is used for divination in the region, among others in Yaka villages. The cylinders come in three sizes and will be hit by the teacher once the patient becomes possessed. Usually this happens after the subsequent coming-out ceremony in which the spirit is propitiated during three days of dancing. Patients and family encircle the drum, standing in a clearing in the forest. At possession the dancing stops. The teacher paints red and white dots on his and the patient's temples, eyelids, chest and limbs. Possession can be violent with screaming, grabbing and biting in fire. The possessed may run away deep into the forest, covering himself with plants and living there like an animal for several days. The search party will look for him while sounding the drum that should control his possession and bring him back. Led back into the circle, he should be ready to announce his personal obligation. The spirit speaks through him, after which he may die of his illness, or possession recedes and he gets well. A bracelet is tied to his arm as a reminder of the obligation he should observe in life.[3]

Dapper's description from the seventeenth century sums up the universal theme of healing across Bantu-speaking Africa, discussed in the introduction. An ancestral spirit has a wish in the form of an obligation concerning a commoner, typically a descendant. As long as this obligation is unknown the wish remains unmet. This situation manifests itself in the body as an illness, madness or recurring misfortune. Only divination can unveil the obligation. Divination is part of the medicine. Knowing the obligation and thus establishing a relation of reciprocity with the spirit ends the crisis. The *nkisi* charm is a material consequence of the treatment, perhaps the most dramatic and visible one to the outsider. The incumbent should never forget the medicinal cult (the 'drum') that initiates and supervises acquisition of the *nkisi*.

Loango knew a wide variety of types of ritual initiation, each named after the obtained *nkisi* (ibid.: 548–52). Each initiation is both divinatory, in communicating with the invisible world, and medicinal, in finding a cure for one's malady. *Mani* is a ritual that achieves initiation into adulthood, but patients attending can also heal from it. We will see chiefs invested after completing a similar ritual. To comprehend the ritual from the perspective of the participants, we should not look at it as the application of a custom but as an investiture. It is social cephalization, enabling the novice to do the extraordinary thing of heading a group of people. The ritual is not reserved for a certain cast. The divinatory-medicinal practice benefits patients, professional healers and chiefs alike.

The Komo Fractal of Life: The Medicinal Origin of Status

The similarities between ritual patterns in all societies from coastal Congo to the Great Lakes and beyond are important in our search for a cultural structure with which to interpret history in equatorial Africa. How can we confirm that these similarities are not coincidental? *Gandja* circumcision ceremonies among the Komo, described and analysed by Wauthier de Mahieu in his classic monograph *Qui a obstrué la cascade?* (abbreviated as QC) from 1985, enlighten us further. The Komo live in eastern Congo, about halfway between the coastal Congo and the Nyamwezi-Sukuma groups whom we will discuss in Part II. The geographical distance does not show in divergence of beliefs. Raising the question of common cultural origin, the Komo initiation connects life, power and personal calling into a cultural structure permeating Loango and Sukuma initiations as well. The symbolic connections are replicated on different scales of social structure as if they form a fractal.

Gandja, which literally means semen and evokes fertility, is also the name for madness. One incurs madness as a punishment when not obeying the prescriptions or prohibitions of the institution one is initiated into (QC 27; so too for Loango, the madness of the possessed is the sign of needing initiation). The *nkisi* fabricated in Loango reminded the holder of the personal obligation towards a spirit. In the Sukuma village initiation, the snitch divulging the secret of plants, prohibitions or ordeal dies of madness. Punishment sounds like a response incidental to the institution, serving the collective socialization according to Van Gennep's rites of passage (cf. next chapter). The reader is invited to let go of that angle and consider the healing power affecting participants as the primary cause of the ritual. The following data indicate that this medicinal dimension, with its socially uncontrollable power, is pivotal to the institution. Tellingly, concrete interventions of polishing the ritual have sought to control the medicine and facilitate an impersonal, chieftainship-oriented view on ritual that suited the encompassing geopolitical evolutions in the region. Medicinal practices turn into rites of passage if the personal obligation imposed by a spirit becomes a socially sanctioned duty with corresponding initiatory rank.

De Mahieu portrays an intriguing historical change in Komo society. Before the standardized hierarchy of subgroups in the *kentende* initiation, several types of initiation prevailed in the region that paralleled and resembled each other (QC 32). The anterior *dokpo* initiation was itself a polished version of the old *mondaa*, feared for its violent ordeal. Reminiscent of the chief in centralized states, the novice held a leopard's tail in his hand. Circumcision resulted from the novice's prolonged leopard dance during which masters chaotically inflicted cuts on his foreskin, thus enacting the ritual murder of the leopard. *Kentende* initiation associates the novice with (edible) game such as the antelope. The institution took over the area, surfing on the wave of Arabic globalization in eastern Congo controlled by Tippu Tip. *Kentende* remained long enough to become standardized.

Over time the initiators smoothened the ceremony and a hierarchical organization arose. Nevertheless, the initiatory symbolism always drew on the therapeutic ritual (QC 30). More exactly, it revolves around the domestication of fertility, represented in the Komo case by the removal of the foreskin. Divination is essential too, like in the Sukuma *ihane* some thousand miles to the east, where an oracle revealing in public a swelling (*nhebe*) on the rooster's spleen is the sign for participants to drink beer from two interconnected gourds. Among Komo the augural sign of initiation is a successful hunt, followed by the sharing of two plates of meat, one for the novice's parents, the other for the ceremony officials (QC 49).

Almost seamlessly do the various ritual initiations of Bantu-speaking peoples tie in with each other, their common origin being medicine. The Komo fixed formula '*belame*' at the end of *gandja* verses is translated as 'May we be healed' (QC 62). The root of the verb is *lam*, an archaic greeting to honour Sukuma chiefs that they may 'live long'. The regional Bantu penchant of the term is towards life rather than cure. A major part of the Komo circumcision ritual is the investiture of the master of initiation, whose new role is accredited with the words 'Should he not be healed?', and the public's response 'That he be healed' (QC 225). The fixed formulae in a rite of passage celebrating the attained status of adulthood underline the medicinal model of investiture (QC 45).

In Komo symbolism, red ingredients represent the lightning sent by ancestors for the sky to open and life to regenerate (QC 279). At the end of the ritual cycle, when the novices return from the forest, the master of ceremonies has symbolically died. He is compared to a leopard waiting in the forest to devour the uncircumcised (QC 290). Exactly like in the main phase of the Chwezi ceremony known as the 'big forest', purification of the participants happens at termite hills, which house the ancestors from the forest. The Komo novices and patients inhale ancestral vapour, as in the *umba* ritual therapy, de Mahieu observes. So too do the Chwezi novices at that stage. The *gandja* ordeal of fustigation resembles the smearing of shivering-cold medicinal mud (*lutaka*) during a nocturnal dance in current Chwezi rites (QC 301–2). Komo novices are smeared with red oil as a sign of recovery of health. On the elder's request to the ancestors they shall give birth to many children (QC 362), which can also mean many future initiations (*kubyala*). The new master of initiation will have his head shaven save for a tuft of hair in the middle, symbolizing his higher rank and new role (QC 302), just as the Chwezi masters tie a bored bead or rounded shell in a tuft of hair at the top of their head to attest to *bumanga*, their capacity for spirit mediumship. Their novices wear the *shishingo* diadem. Those who did not complete the ritual cycle have as a reminder (*ibelile*) a bundle of straw tied in their grass roof. Grass of the roof is a classificatory extension of hair on the head. A successful hunt after the red smearing by each initiated marks the end of the Komo ritual (QC 362). The classificatory extension of an oracle is the hunt, or possibly the other way around, as hunting is the ancient livelihood.

The experiential fields of hunt and fertility are united in recurring metaphors (QC 161). Just as a large *mbau* pole penetrating a hole in the ground covered with leaves articulates the Komo symbol of fertility, the Sukuma sons of farmers who have come back from the forest with a bundle of plants plant their spears in the 'female' threshold of the house, where their wives await them (cf. QC 284). On the next day elders will want to fertilize their land with their plants' concoction. The symbolism of prepuce removal in Komo initiation enacts the cutting of the umbilical tie and the subsequent opening of the male sexual organ for intercourse (QC 237).

Experts of comparative anthropology may be slightly dazed at this stage to see the old theme of fertility symbolism in non-modern societies rehearsed. Yet, the symbolism itself is not what interests us. What it does, matters; how it gets reinvigorated within obviously porous geographical and linguistic borders between communities. The symbolism works like a fractal, each time reinvigorated because replicated at another scale: from the leopard's ferocity, to prepuce removal, to the adolescent's termination of his childhood, to the healing of the whole community. More generally, the affect of letting the 'other' in is basically how men and women start a family. 'Let the other in' is also what the participants of an initiation do when venturing into the unknown terrain of the forest, at night and guided by spirits they cannot control. What they do is to replicate at a socially higher scale the life-giving act between two people (represented in Figure 1.1 as triangle and circle, man and woman). The pattern becomes a fractal as schematized, based on Ron Eglash's (1999) work on 'African fractals'. A third scale of fractal replication is to welcome an outsider for

Figure 1.1 The fertility fractal in initiation. Figure created by the author.

his medicine to lead the group, or a migrant population welcoming the autochthonous people to appease the spirits of the land and accredit their stay (as succinctly articulated in the pygmy enthroning the king). The hunt, the oracle and shamanic possession form another serial replication encountered cross-culturally, this time pivoting on the experience of contingency, on the affect of feeling blessed after gratification in a situation of dependence.

What the fertility symbolism actually does is to establish divinatory communication. The linchpin of the Komo ritual is for each novice to receive his ancestral obligation, causing illness in case of disobedience or defective application of the ritual (QC 165). The knowledge characterizes the investiture of adulthood. In the background, outsiders momentarily join for an aspersion (QC 275). They appear to be patients of infertility, which underlines the medicinal life-giving discharged by the ritual. The ritual formula concerns them too ('that he be healed'; QC 166). The healing and investiture originate in the forest. The acquisition of both resembles a hunt and a union with the spirits (QC 134, 143).

The Mwindo Epic: On Medicine Civilizing

Although less informative than ethnography and oral traditions on specific historical events, myths are most significant in providing the local view on origins and cultural models. The Mwindo epic narrated in Nyanga communities describes in about hundred pages of text (translated and edited by Biebuyck and Mateene, 1969) the journey of a pygmy-like, physically challenged boy who will succeed his father as chief but does so by installing a new kind of rule – non-violent, respectful of life and conscious of magic and ritual. The Mwindo epic offers a unique glimpse of the way in which Bantu artists recount the origins of chiefship. Medicinal rule is the gist.

The story commences with chief Shemwindo of Tubondo forbidding his wives to give birth to a son. When his preferred wife cannot hide the sounds of the baby boy called Mwindo and dubbed Little-one-just-born-he-walked, his father orders the live burial of the child under a pile of leaves. When the atrocity fails, the child is locked up in a drum submerged at the bottom of the river. Heavy rains ensue, causing famine in Tubondo. Again the boy escapes. Upstream he goes through ablution ceremonies. He sets out on a dangerous journey to cross the dense forest and visit his paternal aunt, who was married out to the water serpent Mukiti. During a subterranean peregrination, he performs magic. His miraculous feats play into the symbolism of medicinal rule. He conjures up water where it is gone (Biebuyck and Mateene 1969: 78). He heals the yaws of the female spirit Kahombo (ibid.: 95, n172). He observes taboos on terrestrial food. His medicine cures the chief Muisa. He makes iron tools cultivate for him (ibid.: 98). His enemies are defeated not through violence but by his use of words and an object, the Conga sceptre.

To understand the murder attempts, Mwindo conjectures that his father preferred daughters because of the profits of bridewealth (ibid.: 92, n165). The father confesses he actually feared the son for wanting to replace him as chief (ibid.: 123). For his malice, the chief insists to the council that he be deposed. However, Mwindo who lives on the 'father mountain' (*ntata*) grants his father governance over the 'child mountain' (*mutundu*), the less valued lower half of the land. His father confers on him all the paraphernalia of chiefship. The epic ends with the hero hunting down and killing the dragon, after which the dead are resuscitated to live on the mountain (ibid.: 134). Climbing up with the assistance of the spirit of lightning to the realm of Sun, Moon, Star and Rain, the new chief receives his personal prohibition. He should never kill, human or animal, lest the fire of the sky be extinguished and he be taken away without saying farewell to his people (ibid.: 139, 143).

The myth sheds an emic light on the relation between magic and chiefship. At the outset, chiefship appears as merely leadership by a village headman, so use of the term 'chief' is questionable. The father's preoccupation with material gain and his lack of magical knowledge contrast with the innate capacity of the unwanted son. Can medicine spawn real chiefship? Equipped with the Conga flyswatter sceptre, whose antelope tail is used in the *kiowa* possession dances by the Nyanga (ibid.: 56, n67; and in the *shishingo* diadem of the Cwezi spirit possession cult in Interlacustrine Africa), the successor completes a journey into the unknown that is reminiscent of the ordeal in cultic initiation. The commoner headman of old transforms in his generation into a chief with ritual capacity. Mwindo is brought back to the village by Nkuba, the divinity of lightning, who is rewarded with the prescribed white fowl and with female novices wearing a copper ring. From then onwards a cult is devoted to Nkuba (ibid.: 143). The final song hints at the cultural revolution established by Mwindo. He embodies the paramount (*muhanga*; ibid.: 141, n276) who reigns over more people than the chief (*mwami*). He displays genuine concern for the common people.

Rainmaker (*muntanga mbura*) and diviner (*mukumu*) make their appearance in the contemporary world, sung about in the last verses (ibid.: 199). In the mythical period, divination was hinted at indirectly. At the arrival of Mwindo's paternal aunt Iyangura and her family in a guesthouse where a room had been prepared for them by the groom, the verses go: 'They seized a rooster to clean the teeth. In this guesthouse they had Iyangura sit down on an *utebe*-stool' (ibid.: 50, n41). The authors note the anomaly of the visiting party seizing instead of giving a chicken to the groom, and they remark that the bride should not be sitting on a sacred stool reserved for women whose head is shaved at the end of mourning. In Sukuma divination, however, the *(n)tebe* is a metaphor for the mark on the rooster's spleen indicating presence of the spirit and the validity of the oracle (note also Mwindo sits on the *utebe* to sing his song; ibid.: 115). Oracles, forbidden by colonial administration and the Catholic church, are disguised throughout the epic, as is the prevention of witchcraft, which could motivate consultation of an oracle. Culturally speaking, divination would be the sensible thing to do before concluding an alliance through marriage with a foreign clan and, in the subsequent verses, before letting the daughter have sexual intercourse with the groom Mukiti. The kinship position of paternal aunt, moreover, has a medicinal connotation. In Nyanga stories about people getting lost in the forest, the paternal aunt turns out to be the ideal guide for showing the way out with her whistle from a reed-flute (*mpingu*) (ibid.: 100, n186). The paternal aunt combines the features of insider (as family member) and outsider (emigrated to live in her husband's clan) that render her structurally suspect of witchcraft. Her kinship position can be associated with the ostracized and with the one anticipating on the ban by fleeing into the forest to come back renewed. As the typical refugee, she has had a deeper experience of the forest than hunters themselves. She can help those lost. The paternal aunt knows the place where the king comes from and belongs.

In our interpretation, the story recounts Mwindo's initiation into chiefship as his founding a cult dedicated to rain and life, the fertility of land and people. Next to the convergence of ritual chiefship and the founding of, and initiation into, a divinity cult, we note the shift from profane to magical rule. From a Western perspective it is a counterintuitive evolution. Yet, magic is the path towards non-violent rule. The evolution from physical power to medicinal rule permits adults to behave and interact adequately, that is without verbosity or excessive emotion (cf. ibid.: 110, n207). Magic in that sense civilizes.

In the Rwandan ceremonial state, oral tradition displays an opposite sequence of events, from a leader dependent on magic and oracle to a contemporary king relying on solemn ceremony and correct procedure (see Part III). The direction of the shift matters less in our search for cultural structure than the two poles pulsated between: medicine/magic on one side and procedure/ceremony on the other. Chronology, which is essential in chronicles, is not normally what myths are about. Lévi-Strauss therefore famously limited himself to synchronic analysis, relating the recurring themes or 'mythèmes'. As his power grows, Mwindo's society reverts to a less complex state of affairs. Previously the animal tails, the ritual parts of shot game, went to the chief's elder brother (ibid.: 140, n269). Now Mwindo asserts the right as paramount, on top of his privileges as chief. Formerly differentiated functions get conflated. The counterintuitive evolution might frustrate those seeking to squeeze history out of oral tradition, unless they are content like we are with obtaining salient pivots of local cultural perspectives.

Synchronic analysis reducing the myth to a number of symbolic relations permits comparison with the Sukuma cosmogony of Shi'ngwe'ngwe, narrated south of Lake Victoria some 500 km to the east of Kivu where the Nyanga live. Both Nyanga and Sukuma groups trace their descent back to Interlacustrine Africa. In the Sukuma myth a young man, Tricks-to-be-taught, who seems fatherless and acquires magic during an initiation-like stay in the forest, leaves his mother and all certainties behind to fight Shi'ngwe'ngwe, a paternal figure represented by a monster in the forest. After the father's death, all humans and animals he had swallowed return to Earth, and the boy becomes their king. In both myths the monster is divided up in many parts like a sacrifice (ibid.: 134). Both the Mwindo and Shi'ngwe'ngwe tales mention cattle as swallowed, while unlike the Sukuma the Nyanga have none.

Biebuyck and Mateene (1969: 119–20, n226) cogently posit that the myth containing cattle symbolism predates the Nyanga migration from their pastoralist cradle in the East African grasslands (whose main centre was possibly called *Bisherya*, ibid.: 136, n263). The Sukuma probably share that cradle. Like the patrilineal Nyanga, the Sukuma group designates healer-diviners as *kum* and uses another term for ruler, which in the case of the Nyanga is *mwami* like in Rwanda. Nyanga are culturally closer to Rwanda, Bunyoro and Toro, from where they migrated.

Nyanga came to live in cultural and political symbiosis with the much smaller local population of pygmy hunters. Those hunters fulfil a ritual function in the enthronement of the Nyanga chief. They also supply one of his wives, whose firstborn will be the 'chief pygmy' (ibid.: 1–2). It seems that their implication as autochthonous representatives in the succession ceremonies of the chiefdom, which just consists of villages and their headmen, is necessary for the royal office to persist. Part II will link these semantic fields of chiefship, autochthony, forest and life into one cultural structure. First, we must break with the scholarly divisions that keep the fields apart, starting with the one between affliction and life-crisis, maintained by Turner in his study of rituals.

Notes

1. We use the present tense to reproduce Dapper's account. The past tense would have suggested more historical factuality than is justified, or needed.
2. 'Zy hebben, om deze gestalten der duivelen te maken, byzondere meesters, geheten op hunne tale Enganga Mokijïe, wier voornaemste werktuig een trommel is, en maken dezelve, wanneer ze tot een bequamen ouderdom gekomen zijn, en hen dan eenige zwarigheden over 't hooft hangen of geladen hebben, en met ziekten of aenvechtinge bevangen zijn.'
3. The original phrase reads: 'als dan wort den zelven een ring aen den arm gedaen, waer by hy altijts kan gedenken, wat zijne oplegginge zy' (ibid.: 546).

Chapter 2

BEYOND TURNER'S WATERSHED DIVISION

Cultural similarities can be expected between distant groups whose languages have enough shared features to suggest a common origin. Migrants speaking languages of the Bantu cluster reshaped almost half a continent in symbiosis with autochthonous groups. Ethnographic particularism, the refusal to zoom out geographically and sacrifice the sharp resolution of the field experience, has prevented anthropologists from exploring the regional recurrence of the power symbolism reiterated in the previous chapter. Etic speculations about regional cultural patterns published under supervision of armchair scholars may leave ethnographers aghast at the loss of local meaning. But is there no way of bridging the gaping space between the particularism of the field and the universality of *anthropos*, the human?

Victor Turner's ethnography was of exceptional depth, richly weaving case studies and personal accounts of Ndembu collaborators into the smooth fabric of his analysis. His symbolic anthropology has been rightfully acclaimed for excelling in the two scales of research. It systematically ignored the gap in between. Can we develop a meso-anthropology, with an appropriate ethnographic methodology, comparative and geographically historicized? As cultural inventions are transmitted, their meaning may change, yet never without some lasting ties to their origin such as a preceding or initial idea. It is this historically built-up logic of rituals that a meso-anthropology envisages. At the price of loss of resolution in relation to the field experience, the cultural structure manages to link up a single community with its region.

Turner's work on rituals among the Ndembu of Zambia in the 1960s cannot be vaunted enough for thoroughly engaging the reader with the field. His classic *The Drums of Affliction* from 1968 (abbreviated here as DA), referring to the local healing cults, laid the foundations for a performance-oriented anthropology as well as for the later interdisciplinary collaborations on therapy management groups. His work has been most instrumental in paving the way for an ethnography that respects the local views and brings cultural particulars to the fore in order to learn more about humanity as a whole. The unmet challenge was to describe what happens in between the culturally particular and transculturally universal.

Insight in the regional pattern of rituals could have come from conducting a survey of the wider area. Edmund Leach (1960) had done so for the Kachin and the Shan in north-east Burma. As a result, he treated these peoples as forming one region because they employed the same set of ritual symbols; he addressed historians explicitly about the issue. The striking resemblances between rituals over wide territory in Africa remain implicit in Turner's analysis. His comparisons of Ndembu with neighbouring groups in Zambia and RD Congo drew attention mainly to the differences, such as puberty rituals conducted before instead of after the first onset of the menses among Luvale (Turner 1968: 99). Theoretically influenced by Lévi-Strauss's structuralism, Turner primarily noticed the synchronic meaning of ritual symbol; how it relates to other symbols, although he did study how the symbol was used as well as talked about (DA 17).

Nobody easily shed the shackles of British functionalism. Turner explained the cultural practice of witchcraft accusations from the contradiction between matrilineal descent and virilocal residence. Ritual symbols were efficacious because of their bi-polarity, endowing the norms, instilled in the pupils, with the libidinal qualities symbolized (DA19). He referred to Radcliffe-Brown's types of religion and confirmed that, of all these, the veneration of ancestors is most intimately connected with social structure (DA 52). Ndembu villages held together a fairly labile, socially controlled society thanks to people's membership in at least one of the decentralized, non-territorial associations venerating the spirits.

Although anthropologists will propose terms that approximate the local experience, like Turner writing 'shades' for spirits, they inevitably play with units of analysis provided by the discipline: cult, association, polity, ritual, symbol, social structure, and religion. In practice, informants rarely if ever use these terms. They talk of concrete remedies. The next chapter will point out the scholarly neglect of the proper name. The proper names equate the medicine with the spirit. We must avoid writing about medicine without spirit, or about spirits as such, for instance as separate forces. The meaning of remedies is fused with the effects or forces operative in them.

'Ritual' is another term concealing what the participants experience, which can be ancestral empowerment or particular remedying acts. The first ritual episode in the *nkula* drum of affliction is named *ku-lembeka*, the linguistic derivation from the stem *-lemba* suggesting a shared endogenous logic or even historical links with the Lemba cult on the Atlantic coast. *Kulembeka* is the main sequence of the ritual and yet remarkably deals only with medicines – collecting, preparing and applying them (DA 55). Ritual in the liturgical sense fails to capture the medicine at work.

The Watershed Division of Rituals

In the following pages, I argue that all data collected by Turner on the many Ndembu rituals concern the cultural history of one and the same medicinal complex. In his mind though, he observed 'the major watershed division between rituals of affliction and life-crisis rituals' (Turner 1968: 198). The simplest counterargument is that traditionally in Bantu-speaking societies all healing equals initiation, and vice versa. It is just Turner who decides to translate the same words *chimbuki* (also *Chi-mbanda*, DA 56; cf. *Ku-banda*, the Rwandese name for the Chwezi cult) and *muyeji* respectively as 'doctor' and 'patient' in the case of affliction rites, and as 'adept' and 'candidate' in the case of life-crisis rituals (DA 57; cf. Sukuma tradition of naming patients *bahemba*, 'fee-paying initiands', so the role of patient seems secondary). His observation of a division of rituals was slanted by the aforementioned structural-functionalism of his day, imposing preconceived Western categories: the anti-structure of religion versus the structure of politics; the medical sphere of affliction versus the educational sphere of life-stage. In his theory on the bipolarity of symbols, he struggled with Europe's psychoanalytic tradition on the tension between norm and desire. The poles of respectively analytic and synthetic thought would correspond to divination and ritual. Hence he claimed that, in contrast to drums of affliction, life-crisis rituals were never preceded by divination (DA 27). The theoretical division does not hold for Sukuma rites of passage: a swelling on the spleen in the chicken oracle must demonstrate the ancestor's acceptance of the initiation rites.

What Turner's analysis and his watershed division ignored is telling: fertility not only occupies a central role in healing but also in initiation. Its presence depends on the spirits' wishes, communicated through oracle. His analysis leapt from the local metaphor to a psychological explanation, instead of capturing the regional complex in between that could truly evoke cultural difference. The drum of affliction 'represents aggressive drives of human nature', with patients feeling 'guilty', engaged in 'self-punishment' (DA 182) as well as homosexual conflict, masochistic parturition, and the sociological scapegoat mechanism (DA 192). The author jots down guilt without asking what it could mean in this society.

Turner's watershed division conceals what unites the rituals. Whether ceremonies of wedding, enthronement, healing, and so on, rituals should be understood from the perspective of the participant counting on their power. Why would the power they enact amidst contextual noise not be one and the same? Turner cites White at length about the Luvale rites of circumcision, stating that these are 'typical *rites de passage* in which the novices are reborn as men after a symbolic death' (DA 152). Procedurally this is true. The *mukanda* rite of circumcision for Ndembu boys contains the three phases like the girls' *nkang'a* puberty rite: causing to enter (*kwing'ija*), seclusion (*kung'ula*) and coming out (*kwidisha*, DA 185–86). But the rite of passage is not the local semantic model. The Ndembu informant Muchona emphasizes healing instead. He literally says that the purpose is 'to cure [a novice] that he may be strong, that he may catch power' (DA 153) – the last word translated as *ng'ovu*, denoting bodily strength and health.

The novice was not ill in the narrow physical sense. Uncircumcised though, an adult man would be permanently polluting his environment (DA 154). That is a condition to be treated with a healing rite, which includes circumcision. Initiating a generation of boys in Mukanda brings treatment at village level for a condition that would otherwise put the entire community at risk. The leading role, in return for his sponsorship, is reserved for the village headman (DA 159). He acts like the highest ranked officiant of a cult. The last verse of the *kwing'ija* song, 'the son of a chief is like a slave' (DA 190), perhaps evinces that the novices are treated impartially, as they are equally impure. The implication is also that after initiation none could be a slave. The rites are 'cephalizing', head/man-making. They free a person from the bonded state of affliction or pollution. A structural-functionalist approach emphasizes the change of social status, and applies it to any ritual (as in the theories of Van Gennep and Henri Junod, cf. Turner 1967: 94). Yet, the indigenous model to comprehend headmanship, we have argued, is the forest-within, a hunt that cools and makes whole.

Turner stated that rites of passage in life-crisis (e.g. puberty) are dogmatic and ahistorical, occur at regulated phases and replenish the principles of the Ndembu social order, whereas rites of affliction are ad hoc, more dependent on context and patient, and challenging the social order as they respond to disturbance (DA 87). Are these not logical differences between healing and attributing status that could have been deduced without fieldwork? In practice, both types of ritual tap into the symbolic universe of fertility, hunt, spirit and forest to initiate people in need of a new status. There is no local terminology dividing the rituals in two categories. Turner's proposal of such cultural structure has to be rejected unless the actor's actual frame of experience supports it. To wit, Ndembu villagers tackling a disturbance would never think they are challenging the social order. It is rather eccentric for an individual to believe in an inner truth that defies the view of the collective. In the oracle, the client becomes one with the collective. Far from a cold analysis, divination provides a soothing synthesis like any other ritual. Turner's logical inference that oracles and rituals would differ in that only the second are redressive (DA 26) collides with the ethnographic fact that clients obtain relief from an oracle. Hearing the otherwise unattainable ancestor identifying the cause of evil is a liberating experience, emboldening the client enough to subsequently resort to magic against the witch (Stroeken 2010).

Initiation, Medicine and the Cultic Basis of Kingship

A piece of key evidence, almost lost in the textual flow on the sequences in the *nkula* drum of affliction, is the name of the fee paid for treatment: 'the tribute of Mwantiyanvwa' (*mulambu wa Mwantiyanvwa*, DA 77). Mwantiyanvwa is the name for the king of the northern Lunda empire. The preposition 'of' should probably be translated as 'for' (rather than 'from') because the received fees are subsequently distributed by the senior practitioner among his adepts. In cults across the region, fees refer to the highest initiated, who as representative of the cult's founder in principle receives all collected tribute that shall be divided among his regional deputies, themselves responsible for sharing the proceeds among their clients.

Two centuries ago, the Mwantiyanvwa sent an expedition to subdue the autochthonous Mbwela, the amalgam of which resulted in Ndembu society (DA 9, 94). The *nkula* cult is said to come from Mwantiyanvwa (DA 55), more exactly from the 'woman chief' who founded the dynasty (DA 58) and whose blood is called *mukula* (DA

86). The *nkula* cult, from *ku-kula*, 'to grow up' and 'to become great' (proto-Bantu *kul*), connects social cephalization to fertility. It has the medicine to form healers and to cure women suffering from menstrual disorders or infertility. The various elements point in the same direction, suggesting historical grounds for the claim of our book. The Mwantiyanvwa descended from a female healer, whose cult preceded the Lunda kingdom, itself established long before the Ndembu expedition. The tribute he obtained as king was originally a fee paid to him for initiation into the cult. In the expanding cult the intermediate lower ranks of the hierarchy were 'great' ones, the later headmen or chiefs, who had been trained into the ritual knowledge and were disseminating it in their localities in return for fees. I see no other reason why the diviner would first address ancient chiefs to activate the *Kayong'u* spirit of divination (DA 33). Any scholar presupposing that chiefs and divinatory-medicinal associations were counterparts, condemned to be either rivals or allies in the image of kings and priests, state and church, should think twice. They are probably accomplishing the anachronistic feat of explaining the past from the present. Before being categorized by the colonial administrator as a surrogate governor, the chief was primarily an initiatory authority in the medicinal field. The divide between political and religious domains, and its corollary of priestly worship legitimating royal authority, looks like a decoy in this part of the world.

At his instalment, the Ndembu chief, or titled senior headman, becomes initiated into a medicine by a ritual officiant, *chivwikankanu* (DA 134). The medicine deviates from the common protections, for it enables the chief to create a sorcerous familiar, manifest as a snake with human face (*ilomba*), an elephant, hippopotamus or giant crab, which harbours the chief's external soul and can only be killed by a weapon of the night. Out there in the forest at night, the chief's shamanic warfare and peacemaking takes place, invisible to those possessing no *nsompu* medicine to wash their eyes with. Some have acquired the knowledge, but the chief's familiar, or 'medicine-body' as Turner's informant says, surpasses them all. The name for this creature is *chiswamu chawanyanta*, 'a place to hide in of chiefs' (DA 135), which indicates that the medicine and its cult belong to the chief. It is not a medicine from a cult (the religious domain) given to the chief (the political domain). In that which enthrals everybody, the chief simply ranks highest.

We provisionally conclude that the chieftain model among the Ndembu underwent an evolution, of which the earliest phases were a shamanic complex and divinatory association, as in the Lele case.

The symbolic remainders suggest that the hunter's lifeworld informs the agricultural community ruled by kings. Medicinal rule is the pivot between hunters' divinatory associations and the centralized ceremonial state of the largest kingdoms. Within medicinal rule, distinct evolutions appear yet again, such as between the initiated who become travelling professional healers, mobile like 'flying squirrels', and those becoming increasingly attached to a territory and shrine, making hay of autochthony in function of their kinship group (cf. DA 116–17). The latter are about to head a chiefdom. Membership in cults is typically non-territorial, transcending hamlet or village, but at the level of the wider area, 'the district', the cult attributes territories to ranks. If the cult leadership adopts the rule of clan-based succession, a chiefdom arises. Remainders of the original situation, the cultic basis, are traceable in kingdoms like Kuba, where the successor is supposed to have a spirit-induced vocation and must be ritually initiated in a cult, which logically preceded kingship. Enthronement systematically is an initiation in seclusion. A cultic origin of kingship tallies with cultural assimilation in the region rather than with conquest.

Why did Turner not consider the implications of the fee's name referring to tribute for the first king? The attribution of anything cultural, including medicine, to a king is taken as self-evident, however contradictory this may sound according to his division between politics and religion. Before the bifurcation into non-territorial initiatory cults and territorial dynastic cults, which we name kingdoms, there existed positions with the proto-meaning of healer-king. Concretely, the fee of a cult is named after the first king if the latter led the cult. In those early days, he was not a 'king' in the Western sense of a non-medicinal sovereign. The alternative interpretation seems unfeasible, that he as such king introduced a cult that naturally competed with his authority.

Comprehending the region's traditional principles of authority in their own terms could shake established political theories of the state to their foundations, especially those that presume the universality of patronage and gradual centralization. The traditional principles reappear in an interesting case of the early 1960s recounted by Turner, about the discussions of an ex-chief with the colonial administration on reinstating him (DA 94). Feuds arose between chiefs adopting the colonial emphasis on territory and borders. They had abandoned the traditional concept of a chief's diffuse and centrifugal scale of control (DA 98–99). But in the heat of the dispute, contemporary criteria meant nothing. In the two cases discussed by Turner, the paid tribute was the argument put forward by a chief (*kanongesha*) to give proof of his status. He did not invoke rights on land or property, nor his political or popular support. What persisted from the earliest model of cultic kingship was, besides his line of descent, the right to collect tribute for Mwantiyanwa (DA 94). The hierarchy of ranks in cults dictated his reasoning. The collector of tribute from other headmen and for the king is not a king's servant but by definition of higher standing than the givers, hence a chief. Until well into the period of transition towards national independence, the paramount chief sought to conserve his influence mainly by according chieftain crowns in return for a fee (DA 95–96). To give the certificate of chiefship in return for great favours remains a powerful privilege in many corners of the Niger–Congo area. Far from a strategy of despair or an act of patronage, we encounter king- and chiefship reduced to their bare essence: the exchange of precious possessions demanded by the spirit (a sacrifice) in return for a title and charm. The essence of medicinal rule does not include power games or charisma, which no title can guarantee.

Ritual Power: From Symbol to Medicine

Given Turner's awareness of a symbol's polysemy and thus volatility, he might never have meant his reference to a watershed division of rituals. He must have noticed that the *chishing'a* in the Ihamba cult, a white forked branch bare of bark representing luck, features in rituals on both sides of the division (DA 183–85, n1). In the *musolu* rainmaking ceremony, the wood of the *mudyi* tree is used for making the miniature bow of 'female procreativeness' (*lusemu*); in the girl's puberty rites the *mudyi* tree symbolizes lactation for its milky sap (DA 207). A semantic division of rituals denies symbolic acts to be medicinal interventions activated in various contexts. The list of symbols employed for their medicinal power, irrespective of the type of ritual or practice, is endless: nakedness during the seclusion phase in healing, in female puberty rite and in boys' circumcision rite (*mukanda*); the lighting of the new fire in honour of the spirits, the kindling of the fire and the obligatory silence in its vicinity in hunting cults, initiation, and affliction rite (DA 211); wearing the hides of game to mimic ferocity; the bow inserted in the apex of the seclusion hut (DA 214); the Kasenzi white beads to represent the purification one has undergone for fertility in initiation, in affliction and spirit possession rites, in hunting cult, rainmaking, and marriage ceremony, where the beads are shaken out of the bride's hair after the first nuptial night (DA 214); the *kuleng'a* dance and the throwing of leaves in *nkula* and *nkang'a* (DA 220); the hut poles in the shape of 'legs of parturition' in *nkang'a* and affliction rite; the *kasasenji* tree for bodily strength in *ihamba* and in circumcision rite (DA 188–89); the termitary representing the hunter's grave (DA 191); the walking backwards in puberty and affliction rites to keep the medicinal power intact (DA 64); the anointing of objects with *mpemba* white clay or kaolin (DA 69), bargaining play between men and women during the public parts of ceremony (DA 223), rebirth after ritual death, and so on.

Turner does not deny the 'common fund of symbols' in the region (DA 115), although limiting it to 'west-central Bantu tribes': Chokwe, Luvale, Lunda, Luchazi (the linguistically adequate yet anthropologically incomplete 'west-central Bantu culture area', cf. also his monograph *The Forest of Symbols*, Turner 1967: 151). But the limit is the product of his choice to not extend the comparative effort. The similarities go further than generic features such as dance, songs and drums in healing. To proceed with the previous list, virtually all rites in central and eastern Africa emplace a shrine for ancestral protection, after which the group leaves to the forest with a winnowing basket (*lwalu*) to collect medicine for the ritual (Turner 1968: 159). The medicines are cooked in a broken calabash (DA 73, 163). Turner mentions in passing the licence songs during the *nkang'a* puberty ritual (DA 219). However, they are the hallmark of spirit cults across central Africa. A novice's friend having to steal food like a 'hyena' resembles the condition of the novices in the Chwezi cult just after spirit possession, who are treated like animals and get their food thrown at them. Puberty rite and healing ritual ignore the watershed division because medicinal power is their preoccupation. As a result, the symbols have historically deep roots of regionally wide significance, which a culturally limited account without comparison simply overlooks.

During the first phase of the *nkang'a* puberty rites, the girl enters seclusion (DA 233). During the second phase she performs a coming-out ceremony, *kwidisha* (DA 249). The core act is the evocation of rebirth after death, which explains the use of medicinal symbolism reminiscent of the Lemba cult and the Loango archetypal case. The second phase of the rite of passage reintegrates the novice into society, the universal trope from Van Gennep's study of rites of passage that so captivated Turner. Twenty-five years after my undergraduate years I am perplexed to reread his Ndembu study through the prism of medicinal rule. Ndembu reintegrate the girl by basically organizing a marriage ceremony during her coming out. The ritual is centred around the arrival of the bridegroom, with beer in one hand, an arrow in the other, and accompanied by his relatives, all ready to meet his future wife's party (DA 249–50). The taunting scene between both parties challenging the men's virility is a classic too in the Sukuma wedding ceremony (*bukombe*). 'Can the groom handle our women?' Will he be able to unite his male 'bow' (also in Ndembu: *mwanawuta*, 'son of the bow', DA 94) with the female 'back', so that healthy socially recognized children – 'of bow and back' – are born? The challenge probes for man's domestication of fertility. For all the convergence of data, the continuity between puberty and marriage ritual does not strike Turner (DA 264). With the parties' noteworthy skirmishes in mind, he instead maintains that almost every episode in *nkang'a* betrays the contradiction between matrilineal descent and virilocal marriage (DA 279), which does not apply to the patrilineal Sukuma in any case.

If the *nkang'a* puberty ceremony transfigures into a marriage ceremony, it should be noted that both ceremonies eventually refer to healing. At dusk after the bridegroom has given an arrow to the girl's mother as a pledge to pay bridewealth as soon as the girl leaves her seclusion hut (DA 201), the village headman appears on stage to invoke the ancestral spirits. His opening words betray the root of the puberty rite: 'that she may remain well, not be ill' (DA 202). The rite of affliction resurfaces. The songs chanted by the audience about puberty cannot conceal that the operative core of *nkang'a* is the rebirth that is medicinally organized. Stronger still, the novice of the puberty rite is said to suffer from *chihung'u*, an affliction. She will stay in that state of crisis until she undergoes her healing rite in 'the place of dying' (DA 213). Again rituals overlap: because they tap from the same source of power.

The bride's coming out is the occasion for payment of bridewealth (DA 250). Formerly the payment was done during the night of the rite. May we actually be observing a gradual evolution towards ritual specialization and separation of puberty and marriage ceremonies? A medicinal amulet will help the bride to step out in public. About the washing and shaving at the girls' *nkang'a* and the boys' *mukanda* (circumcision), as well as at *Ihamba*, Turner laconically ruminates that it is 'an integral part of the culminating rites of all cults of affliction' (DA 254). In brief, he had all the data to debunk the watershed division between healing and life-crisis, medicine and education. Would it have changed the history of our discipline, or paved the way for systematic studies on the remarkable ubiquity of the forest-within fractal?

Contrary to monotheistic liturgy, participation in the chronology of ceremonial steps is far from strict in the Ndembu ritual. Some people join the *ku-tumbuka* sequence of rites, the second half of a *nkula*, without having first passed through the *ku-tembeka* episode, because they want to become healers and will therefore do the *ku-tembeka* later (DA 68). The power in the medicine of the ritual is what matters, and apparently does not depend on context. The concept of medicine sheds a brighter light on our data than that of symbol. 'Ritual' inaptly connotes procedural steps. Ritual rule is not the model we observe.

The equation to comprehend juxtaposes medicine, life and the wishes of the spirit. On the one hand, medicine serves to remember the *mukishi* spirit (DA 62), which more than an imaginary act is to materialize the spirit and bring it to life. On the other hand, Turner's informant Muchona literally states that life means medicine (DA 66) and that those forgetting the spirit fall ill (DA 68). Therefore, getting healed is to be dedicated to the afflicting ancestor and inherit his or her name. In *nkula* the afflicted moves her neck round and round, shaking because she is caught by the spirit. The trembling is as much a classificatory extension of spirit possession as is speaking in tongues. (The head of the Chwezi cult, Ngwana Hande, told me that for him personally dancing is a manifestation of spirit.) The red *ilembi* bead stands for the *nkula* spirit and is worn on the head (DA 64), analogically to the aforementioned bead or shell the Sukuma medium (*manga*) weaves on top of her head. A series of semantic and linguistic associations can be derived that establish a common historical origin for *ilembi*, the *ihamba* affliction, the medicinal phase of *ku-lembeka* during *nkula* treatment and initiation (DA 65), spirit possession and the Lemba cult on the Congolese coast. The *nkula* cult, as suggested by its derivation from -*kula*, 'to mature' and become 'great' (-*kul*), enables victims to become healers themselves. Then it is not far-fetched that the ritual of affliction could turn into a celebration of maturity in puberty rites. The cultural structure is not the watershed division but rites applying classificatory extensions of power and cephelization.

Our comprehension of practices in a particular group is improved by comparing data on related groups. The meaning of a practice should not solely depend on what members of a linguistic group assert about it. As an endogenous logic, meanings from a distant past get rekindled and modified. Regional comparison in an area transcending one linguistic group can unravel those latent layers of meaning. For instance, Turner learns from the Ndembu to translate *(kwa-)hola*, the absence of witchcraft, as 'coldness' (DA 65). He would have benefited from comparing cosmologies of nearby Bantu-speaking groups, which converge on a common metaphor to denote peace (and absence of witchcraft). The metaphor is not exactly coldness but 'coolness', derived from the proto-Bantu stem -*pol*. It is the root word and meaning in Bantu languages to describe what Westerners think of as health or well-being, and the absence of heat. Its opposite is indeed 'heat', like in Kisukuma, *n-sebu*, which refers to breach of taboo, the violation of the Loango 'obligation', and in everyday terms to fever. Witches too are 'hot'.

In the late 1990s Sukuma elders were worried about the disappearance of *ihane* initiation. The concern they voiced was not about the rite of passage, the youngsters' incorporation into the group fulfilling a Durkheimian social function. Refraining from village initiation would postpone the rains, they said, hence cause drought and famine. It meant a breach of the collective cycle of life and fertility. I witnessed the relief of hundreds in the audience after a *ihane* was completed and clouds of rain packed together. The medicine of initiation had always been inserted in the fields to ensure a fertile year. To organize the initiation of youth, turning them into worthy successors, pleased the ancestors. Perhaps the educational function lingered in the background. I never saw it. Hunger, an affliction of the community, was prevented by a communal rite. The forest-within replays the Neolithic transition by blending hunter semantics with agricultural goals. Like a fractal, it has modelled symbolic structures across the region. The fractal shared by neighbouring Bantu speakers lubricates the insertion of symbols from other cults, because either these symbols are returning to where they were at home once or they stem from similar cultural structure.

Classificatory Extensions

Now that we elicited the cultural structure of domesticated fertility, 'forest within the home', around which the various rituals revolve, we can concentrate on the classificatory extensions by which the structure acculturated. The clearest Ndembu expression of (probably early) classificatory extensions comes not surprisingly from the putatively oldest association, the *Wubinda* hunting cult, to which several initiatory rituals belong (DA 157).

Every hunter sooner or later in his life has to cope with the curse of bad hunts embodied by the Mukala (or Kaluwi) spirit. The treatment 'can be regarded as a phase in the complete cycle of hunter's ritual' (DA 121). Already before the Neolithic transition to agriculture, the natural contingency experienced by the hunter in the forest may have inspired the belief in spirit, and in remedy coming from the forest. Success and failure in hunt still inform the cosmology of agriculture (also the subsistence cultivation of cassava is associated by Ndembu with hunting, DA 9). Nightmares of Mukala are curbed by placing at junctions and on top of termitaries the peeled forked branches *ayishin'ga* (sing. *chishin'ga*) of the hunters' cult. The hunter's cult creates mystical bonds between non-kin that are almost as strong as matrilineal ties. 'The blood of huntmanship' and 'the blood of motherhood or procreation' are experienced as two types of ties that should not mix (DA 179). Just as the hunter spills his luck through an act of procreation the night before a hunt, parturition requires that all hunting gear in the vicinity is removed. Turner noticed a radical opposition between taking life by the hunter and giving life by the mother. It may also be that their strong affinity makes the one type of fertility jeopardize the other. Too close an affinity, by classificatory extension, is often the reason for taboo. The two types of human ties are classificatory extensions of 'life': luck for the hunter, fertility for the parent and farmer. Their commonality, rather than opposition, is corroborated by the Ntambu cult (or 'drum') administering the red gum of the *mukula* tree to provide the hunter with luck (Turner 1967: 132). The ancient hunting cult calls this medicinal use of the red gum '*mukula*'s blood'. An alternative, which may have preceded it, is the sounding of the *nkula* drum of reproductive affliction, named after the *mukula* tree. We shall later link the cultural structure and its extensions to a unique linguistic property of the Bantu cluster.

Descent in the Hunting Cult

In our search of cultural structure accounting for the development of cult into kingship, several elements converged to reveal the close affinity between medicine, life and power. These elements characterize the hunter's lifeworld at a time before the rise of chieftaincy. They constitute the roots of the transition. The remaining condition for the transition from cult to chief- and kingship to happen is the succession of powerful medicine along lines of descent. Again we turn to concrete historical cases. A precursor to this institutional invention entailing kingship seems to be the *ihamba* gun-hunters' ritual.

Turner (1968: 176) situates the origins of *ihamba* in the mid nineteenth century, when the cult *Wuyang'a* celebrating the introduction of firearms was spread by Luvale and Ovimbundu slavetraders. *Ihamba* is the central upper incisor of a deceased hunter. The relative who has dreamt of him can be accredited by the cult members to possess the tooth as a lucky charm (DA 178). The left incisor is inherited along the maternal line, the right incisor along the paternal line (in analogy with the region-wide custom of left- and right-arm bracelets referring to maternal and paternal ancestors). Each member of *ihamba* receives a secret name during a ritual, metaphorically described as 'causing to cook'. Each hunter is someone else's successor, his incisor charm representing a hereditary title – compare chieftaincy. The successor receives the medicine following a mediumistic type of vocation combined with initiatory knowledge bestowed by elders. Inserted in a mush of corn and blood of slaughtered game, and covered with two cowrie shells representing the 'eyes' to see game, the tooth is safely kept in a white pouch (*mukata*) hung at the ancestral shrine and carried during hunting. The shrine (*katunda ka wuyang'a*, DA 178) stands in front of the hunter's hut. Its architecture of a classificatory house – essentially, woven branches converging at the top, sometimes thatched and on stilts – resembles the ancestral altars found in several parts of equatorial Africa, including the Nyamwezi-Sukuma area.

Central themes of kingship discussed later are prefigured in the hunter's cult. Luck in the forest comes with possession of a charm, in fact one of the smallest shrines imaginable. Like the king's shrine, the tooth is a remainder of the predecessor (a Sukuma word for charm is *shitongelejo*, literally 'predecessor'). The bodily remainder is a vehicle of the deceased's blessing. The spirit is ancestral and not a mere entity of the forest. After every successful kill in the forest, the shrine should be propitiated with a blood sacrifice to domesticate this source of life and avert its potential working against society (DA 180). *Ihamba* also refers to the ritual of removing an escaped tooth that entered the body of a patient through the evil mediation of a witch in the village. The intrusion affects the victim in the form of an illness, such as leprosy. An *ihamba* 'falls on' the victim (DA 181). Of a spirit possessing, the same is said. *Ihamba* is indeed nothing less than the *mukishi* or spirit of the hunter (DA 182). Among the Luvale and Luchazi, the *lihamba* is a manifestation of a spirit inducing affliction. Ndembu use the word *ihamba* as the general category to which specific spirits belong such as *Kayong'u*, which is an *ihamba* giving a person the permission for divination.

The healer resembles the hunter in that their knowledge concerns the forest and that they learn about it through dreams. Upon entering the forest, the healer addresses the *ishikenu*, 'the tree of greeting'. That tree is the 'elder' (*mukulumpi*) among the medicinal ingredients he seeks to collect. *Musola* is the *ishikenu* for the *Ihamba* ritual, hence the 'dominant symbol of the medicinal complex', Turner concludes (DA 159). More than dominance, the tree of greeting hints at seniority. In Bantu traditions, elders are respectfully greeted every morning by having their line of descent acknowledged, through which they represent senior authority in the area. This principle of cultural structure is replicated in the user's relation with plants and ancestral spirits. In Sukuma-speaking areas and further down south, each cult has its own set of secret plants headed by a tree or shrub called the 'chief'. Turner admits about Ndembu rituals that 'some of these dominant symbols are at times actually *identified* with certain manifestations of ancestor spirits, and not merely regarded as representing them' (DA 20, his italics). The author shifts from representation, whereby matter is shaped after meaning, to identification: things carry meaning within, in the shape of effects, which actors want to discover. The mind is not another mode of production than matter. This basic paradigm shift paves the way in Part II for a holistic understanding of materiality.

Part I has introduced the initiation symbolism of small communities where hunting and forest have not disappeared and the influence of the practice on the model of rule is visible. This chapter has ended with Ndembu cultural structure. What to the outsider looks like a variety of rituals classifiable according to symptom and remedy, are for the participants entities discovered in the forest producing a bundle of effects, as can be derived from their naming of remedies. *Kayong'u* helps to find things hidden, heals afflictions of the chest, but is also the spirit who entitles a person, in return for payment, to become initiated into divination (DA 175). A deep asthmatic wheezing noise gives away that spirit's voice (Turner 1967: 144). The spirit and the medicine are entities with their own qualities, like the plants the initiated learn about.

Part II will retrace the endogenous logic of the forest-within that led to sociostructural changes and the medicinal rule of chiefs. We set off by discerning a chief's understanding of medicine, which Europeans would more narrowly label as magic.

PART II

Medicinal Rule

Chapter 3

A SUKUMA CHIEF ON MEDICINE

Ethnographies and lexicons permit one to compile lists of cultural elements prevalent in neighbouring groups. Could they provide the baseline for the comparison of institutions, as they did in several studies discussed in the Introduction? In a holistic understanding of culture, wherein all parts are interconnected, a list of decontextualized elements has no meaning. It will at best reflect the author's cultural background. A proper start therefore is a lifeworld one has experienced as an ethnographer. My reference is a Sukuma-speaking community as it evolved since the mid-1990s in the chiefdom of Bulima. It had stayed relatively aloof from the radical Christianization in some other parts of Tanzania and on a national scale in neighbouring Congo, Uganda, Burundi and Rwanda.

The chapter starts with a Sukuma chief's account of the fairly recent past, and proceeds with oral literature and archaeological reports on the region. Together the data confirm that the endogenous model of rule revolves around medicine rather than governance. It is what adults are initiated into and what the community's enemies are feared for. At stake in the unarmed battles between the Sukuma chief and the colonizer's figurehead was the knowledge of rain medicine. Because the Tanzanian post-independence government mainly adopted the Western standard of rule, chiefdoms could organize enthronements well into the 1990s. Their medicinal and ritual power did not collide with the governance imposed top-down in the capital. The district officer was not bothered by the fame a chief enjoyed among villagers, who treated him as a special type of healer concerned with the collective and with the contingencies of nature a farmer faces. As far as the farmers knew, the chiefs had always been doing their duties in secret. The rainmaking was part of the larger field of medicine. The field was less populated now by cults than by professional diviner-healers, who had become accustomed to individualizing the etiology and the treatment (Stroeken 2017). In 2015, for instance, I worked in the Morogoro region with a diviner-healer initiated into the old Kolelo cult who, following the dissipation of Kaguru chieftaincy, was invited by community council members to make rain. They had to ask him informally so the district head would not hear about it. Chieftaincy returned to its bare essence before it vanished in Tanzania.

Figure 3.1 Genealogy of Bulima chiefdom. Figure by the author.

Part II, forming the core of our book, extends the argument in the next five chapters to the central Congo basin and then to the edges of our region of study. Equipped with an adapted theory of medicine in terms of magic and materiality, developed in Chapter 6, the next and final chapter of Part II then examines the Tio kingdom in north-west Congo. It illustrates how the initiation into medicinal charms could lead to ranks in a hierarchy of power, more or less geographically defined. We observe an endogenous process of centralization, including tendencies of transition towards a ceremonial state.

An Emic History of Bulima Chiefdom

In November 1996, my collaborator Paulo Magufuli and I did two interviews with a Sukuma chief (*ntemi*) at his home in Nange. Stanislaus Kishina, chief of Bulima, also gave his unpublished biography to copy. I last revisited the compound in September 2015 for interviews with his descendants. Chief Kishina was born in 1922. His father, Kisabo, had succeeded Nkondo, whose predecessor was Lunyalula. After the First World War, German Tanganyika had become British. The principle of indirect rule meant the local chiefs had to be integrated in the colonial administration. A palace was built in 1920 for court hearings and the storage of files. Oral traditions on the dynastic genealogy were collected in 1923. In these traditions, it is said that eighteen successions before Kishina, Shimawa founded the dynasty (Kishina n.d.: 48). Assuming roughly fifteen years on average for each reign, like the last four, this should have been around 1700.

Shimawa, or Semawa, was a hunter whose father Isamasongo emigrated from Kagunga village in Buha, at Lake Tanganyika. Isamasongo stayed as a guest in Buyombe chiefdom in what is now Geita, near Lake Victoria. He was the oldest son of chief Kabeza of Buha. Whether he was the victim of succession disputes, or sent to rule elsewhere, is not clear. Together with his younger brother Kilugabuha he made quite an impression helping the Bayombe to fight their local wars. He became their chief, to be later replaced by Kilugabuha, who was bad news for his brother's sons. The oldest, Kanami, moved to find a chiefdom to rule in Mwanza. The traditions explicitly state not knowing what made him rule there. They go on to recite why in Bulima, some fifty kilometres to the east of Buyombe, Shimawa could overshadow Kalugulwa, son of Mlyambisi (cf. strikethrough font in Figure 3.1). The people in Bulima requested Shimawa to be their chief after he let them discover salt and fire to cook food. His success resulted not from conquest, but knowledge. Ever since, it is said, the successors of Shimawa pay at their installation two heads of cattle to the clan in Buyombe. Officially, they thereby honour their kinship on the father's side, denoted as 'of the bow' (*ya ku buta*). It is not clear why they would have to pay allegiance to a chiefdom that Shimawa had to flee, unless part of the knowledge was the medicine a chief would need. He must have acquired this from his clan in Buyombe. Application of the rain medicine indeed commences with respectfully attributing its origin to the dynastic clan founded by Shimawa.

After three hours of interview we had become accustomed to each other. Kishina's genealogy gained salience as he framed it in terms of his personal experience during application of the rain medicine. Three names of ancestral spirits (*masamva*) then always come to mind, he said. First, he greets Shimawa, his 'director' (*ng'hulugenji*). His invocation 'descends' down the family tree to Lunyalula and Nkondo. Through the classificatory extension (in a vertical line) he has involved all the ancestors of the clan. Classificatory extension is important in Sukuma kinship. The royal dynasty is no different from any other Sukuma clan in that the brothers participate together in the duties of fatherhood. In this horizontal extension, any paternal uncle is a father. A younger paternal uncle may be called a 'little father' (*baba ndo*). Sons gain from treating the senior paternal uncle as their father, especially the uncle who has inherited the herd in the extended family and been given the responsibility for procuring bridewealth for all men of the sons' generation. Seniority is important in authority, but proven skill can overrule primogeniture in the decision on an office. The chief's clan adopts this principle in the choice of the successor. The latter will consider the predecessor as his father.

Kishina's father Kisabo ruled the chiefdom from 1938 until 1950 when he quit because, in the version of Kishina to which we limit ourselves here, the chief was fed up being humiliated (*kunyanyaswa*, Sw.) by the English. In 1938 he and the administrators got off on the wrong foot. After his enthronement, a group of eight armed soldiers led by the district's English administrative officer (*Bwana Shauri*) had travelled by boat to the southern tip of Lake Victoria and moored on the shores of Bulima. The party threatened to arrest Kisabo after accusations received in the city of Mwanza that he had usurped the throne. Two 'enemies' belonging to Bulima's seceded chiefdom had conspired with the influential clerk for native-authority affairs; however, the large crowd present at the lake shore to support their new chief in Bulima convinced the administrator. During the last two successions, the chief's councillors (*banang'oma*) had chosen the descendant whom the chief had appointed earlier as his caretaker. So too had the old Nkondo signalled to believe in the vocation of Kisabo. The twenty-five *banang'oma* had followed suit. They consisted of clan members, inhabitants of the court, and vassals of the court (*basese ba ng'wikulu*) living elsewhere. Nkondo Gwamhuli was a popular chief and successful rainmaker; he could not read or write, but had taught himself English to deal with the foreign authorities. He wanted someone to safeguard traditions.

However, pressure on Kisabo increased. The humiliations included systematic negative feedback by the district commissioner of Mwanza, fed by the 'government sociologist' Hans Cory, known locally as Ng'waninyami and described by Kishina as no less than wicked (Kishina n.d.: 14). Kisabo saw himself as a Sukuma chief continuing the tradition. The governor of Tanganyika had summoned him in Dar es Salaam to remind him that a chief was expected to serve the colonial government. To the governor's request to step down, Kisabo retorted that being a chief under the colonial administration 'he was glad to stop his service under the English, such service being bad for African countries' (*anayo furaha kuachana na utumishi wa waingereza ulio mbaya kwa nchi za kiafrica,* Sw.; Kishina n.d.: 15).

The unimaginable had happened in Bulima history. A king would be succeeded without a burial preceding. No ceremony would take place whereby the deceased king's head would be embalmed, placed in a shrine, and replaced in his grave by his predecessor's embalmed head. As a further token of the uninterrupted transmission of life in the chiefdom, the incumbent was supposed to enter the palace as the corpse of his predecessor was being carried out at the back. Nothing of the kind could happen now. The new king would have to be prepared in the hut of installation without standing on the predecessor's grave or smelling the freshly dug earth. The medicinal side of the political tragedy was bound to be spurned in the governor's office. The local engagement of officers was limited to integrating the local 'polity' into colonial administration, debating about such things as the correct name for the head of a chiefdom since the Sukuma have no paramount. The administrative organization was tangential to the one concern of those directly involved – the fertility of the land and its people.

In February 1951 at the age of 29, Stanislaus Kishina Kisabo won the vote in a public election that was organized by the administrator, accompanied by Hans Cory and two native governors, Segese Makungu and Shindano Kilumba. Kishina was the native candidate proposed by influential *banang'oma*. He won the election against the only contender Francisco Gama Ngalula. In his address to the crowd he reiterated his father's controversial emphasis on tradition by comparing the chiefdom to an old tree that should not be cut lest birds lose their shelter to breed. He accepted to travel to the area of Ntuzu, in Maswa district, for his training by another chief in English service, Ndaturu Ilanga Masanja. Teachings concerned two matters central to the colonial employment of native authority: the hearing of court cases and the collecting of taxes.

His high spirits could temporarily muffle the prediction of his grandfather Nkondo back in the year of 1937, when famine struck the nation and colonial presence grew, that the last member of the royal clan of Bulima had been born (Kishina n.d.: 21). In December 1951 after four months of training he was invited to a hearing in Mwanza attended by five chiefs, Cory and the district commissioner. After two minutes of pregnant silence, the English commissioner spoke. He accused Kishina of sexual assault on a granddaughter of his host chief Ndaturu. Kishina denied, and pleaded to ask the chief himself and to be confronted with the young woman. Cory responded that he might have to be imprisoned. Kishina wondered aloud why he had not been heard by the commissioner of Ndaturu's district, where the assault supposedly happened. In the next meeting the province commissioner of Mwanza deposed Kishina, after telling him the English government threatened to blemish the entire royal clan of Bulima. Culturally well informed, by Cory probably, the commissioner demanded Kishina hand back his *ndeji* bracelet, which was then given to Francisco Gama Ngalula, the administration's candidate from the start. Ngalula had been educated at the prestigious government school of Tabora.

Attempts by the retired chief Kisabo to restore confidence in his son were in vain. As soon as violent protests emerged in the area's commercial hub Misungwi, the next accusation came against Kishina, this time of him having stolen money from the chief's treasury. Kishina demanded an official complaint so a judicial case could be opened for him to defend himself. Receiving the remand a few days later frightened him, but he knew that his opponent Ngalula had made an unlikely claim that was bound to raise the judge's suspicions. He said that Kishina had borrowed the keys of the treasury from him. In his trial on 24 January 1952, Kishina was acquitted (Kishina n.d.: 34).

Besides disregarding the royal court councillors and overruling the popular vote in favour of the better educated candidate, the colonial administration appointed with Ngalula the son of the predecessor's sister. Gama was the wife of Mamba, who in the Sukuma exogamous patrilineal system did not belong to the royal clan (see Figure 3.1). Hereby the colonizer had de facto commenced a matrilineal line of succession. Archival research, lying outside the scope of this book, might determine whether this was an intervention deliberately pursuing the stereotypical African ideal cherished by colonial administrators for preventing wealth accumulation by royal families in patrilineal societies.

In the next fragment Kishina speaks of chief Ngalula as 'this cousin of mine', denoting him as someone whose membership of the clan passed 'through a woman', which implies that the dynastic bond between father and son is severed. He added that the shrine containing the head of the predecessor, embalmed in lion fat, would wait in vain for its successor. Hereby ended the unbroken line of royal descent associated with the fertility of the land and safeguarded by the taboos of Bantu-speaking chiefs (e.g. prohibition on spilling blood, on leaving the court and walking on soil during planting season, and on a chief's death being paraphrased other than as 'a drum broken'). The successor, Kishina's father, died in solitude outside the palace. The new family in charge did not have a patrilateral tie with grandfather Nkondo and the line of nineteen chiefs to be named at enthronement. The colonizer had 'fixed' everything for the cousin, who would work for them. They did not want chieftaincy to depend on what the oracle shows.

[Ndikuwila giki ndugu wane ungwenuyo wali ng'wana wa nkima. Yalitaboneshija giki aitawala isi. Na mambo gakwe aganayo ahogalibeejiwa, ubise abakwipanda lya kumigongo yakwe tutalifiwa giki Ngalula wachaga ahenaho.	I am telling you that this cousin of mine was a woman's child. It did not show that he should rule the land. With this matter fixed for him, we on the side of his mother's line of descent (kumigongo, 'on the back') were not notified that Ngalula had died there.

Sukuma descent is patrilineal, so that many years later when his rival Ngalula died he was not informed. Ngalula's family did not have to invite matrilateral cousins to the funeral. Kishina had been alienated from the affairs of the court. He decided to write down for future generations the history, the dynastic genealogy and the secret recipe of rain medicine. In our discussion with him, he appeared to notice a pattern in history, leaving him embittered about European interferences. Long ago, Ngumila, a predecessor who had lost a succession battle, had convinced the Germans to split off the most fertile part of Bulima at the shore (nkilo) of Lake Victoria to create a new chiefdom, which installed a matrilineal line of succession (see Figure 3.1). After the

First World War, Nkondo from the remaining Bulima (*ya ndinga*) managed to persuade the English administration to restore the situation, but Ngumila got the last word from the English after fighting back in an alliance with the neighbouring chiefdom of Bukumbi. Kishina could not conceal from us his irritation over the current situation that reminded him of the chiefdom's fission in the past.

Francisco Ngalula remained chief of Bulima until his death in 1992. It was interesting to see what would happen next without colonial interference. In haste the palace appointed a grandson, Jackson Mabula Ngalula. Tragically, he died a few months later, obviously kindling suspicions of witchcraft. A police officer knocked at Kishina's door one early morning in September 1992 to tell him about the king's death and the boy's enthronement. Was he on a mission to verify secret accusations? Kishina could only reply that the deaths were news for him.

Because chiefs were not officially recognized in post-independence Tanzania, chiefdoms either disappeared or, as in the case of Bulima, the chiefs could play an adapted role in fairly unhampered fashion. The law is one thing, and in these villages far away from the capital a very remote thing at that, but the perspective of the local population is something else. All respondents from Bulima told me that Ngalula had gained much sympathy since the 1960s by being accessible to commoners. The rains had always been good and he had mediated well in some conflicts between famous elders, which always involved magic. Popular opinion was that he and his *banangoma* – elder men living below the palace whose unwillingness to speak to me and whose sense of secrecy always reminded me of the atmosphere in compounds of famous healers – probably did their job well, which involved practices nobody ever knew anything about. In my interviews with the chiefs of Bulima, Ndagalu and Bukumbi, none of whom are active now, it was striking how they and the elders in the villages nearby spoke of their rule in the present tense, and never cheekily. The make-belief in those few districts with abiding chieftaincy in a country without official chiefdoms was possible thanks to the importance of medicine, an invisible practice.

How did the palace react after the new incumbent's sudden death? The information we obtained in 1996 from the daughter of Ngalula was that she had become the queen mother because the palace – in fact, the few *banang'oma* living in – had appointed her son. Madaha Sicora lived in Dar es Salaam and worked as a car mechanic, but would soon return to Igokelo to claim the throne of Bulima. He never did. The queen mother was very reluctant to give details. Probably her son Madaha saw no point in accepting an unremunerated job, moreover bound to entice sorcerous retaliations from the royal patriclan of Kishina, deposed forty years previously and hoping for a second chance. His mother lived at the palace as household head and was not planning to move out.

Rain Medicine and Sukuma Chieftaincy

Kishina (n.d.: 38) had never accepted his substitute's rule, dubbing it in Swahili *utawala wa bandia*, a 'puppet government'. He could not endorse any successor. It is striking that, reaching this turning point in history, Kishina's document suddenly changes into a recipe book for medicine. The Bulima chief's main medicine for rainmaking consists of the pounded roots of twenty-six trees mixed with twenty meaningful additives (see Illustration 8). Instructions are added on how to dig them up and to apply with the correct formula of words. All this medicinal knowledge must be kept secret. The obligation is no different from any other initiatory group punishing betrayal with heavy fines.

In the next section of his manuscript he lists the dynastic genealogy, before continuing with an explanation of how he became reinstated as chief. To an outsider, the list of medicinal ingredients and procedural steps of application look like a mismatch in a historical account. These are ahistorical data belonging in an annex. Yet, from their central place, we may deduce that they represent the climax of his account. In it he proves his medicinal knowledge against the claims of the competing dynasty. In an introductory paragraph, he reminds his intended readers, mainly his grandchildren, of the essence of kingship. The royal capacity of healing could get lost in a chronicle focusing on the chain of events. The kind of anthropological or 'endogenized' history we advocate falls in with the chief's spontaneous write-up, and takes the chronicler to task for omitting the cultural meaning of medicine.

The document subsequently displays the genealogical list of chiefs, depicting him as nineteenth incumbent. The twentieth, Ngalula, is put between brackets, which conforms to his grandfather's prediction of the royal clan's extinction. The genealogy is followed by a third list, enumerating the years of famine in the chiefdom, about thirty-eight between 1800 and 1994. Each has a metaphorical designation, such as the 'famine of the hide', *nzala ya ndili*, in the year 1815, referring to cases of people chewing on cowhide to suppress hunger. The years are used as temporal references in oral traditions and have sufficient natural basis to estimate historical periods. The list of famines (*nzala*) caused by droughts also underlines the direct link between the chief and his responsibility over the land's fertility.

In 1993, a group of *banang'oma* came together in the village of Bugisha and agreed to re-elect Kishina. His chieftaincy never formalized into a stay at the palace. In his eyes, he had been the rightful incumbent since 1951, while living in Nange as a relatively poor man with his family in a small compound ten kilometres south of the palace. He was primarily known in the region as a rainmaker. By lack of court to live in, his rain medicine was the bare essence of kingship to which he was reduced. Igokelo palace had hidden the royal bracelet (*ndeji*). He had quarrelled over its return, but the material sign of kingship did not matter for rainmaking. Kingship had died in Igokelo palace, he said, because he knew that the powerful medicine named *shilala*, which Francisco Ngalula had obtained elsewhere, was finished. Nobody was left in Igokelo with knowledge to make rain (*kugimbula*). That was the big secret he was pondering over whether to give it away. As for his *ndeji*, he received a new one when he travelled to his relatives in Buyombe, the medicinal cradle of Bulima's chieftaincy.

The chief has his experts for ritual and protective magic. The medicine (*bugota*) he personally specializes in is for rainmaking, *bugemi wa mbula*, literally 'an attempt at rain'. Kishina was trained by his father Chief Kisabo, who had been taught by his. First, he learned about the plants for rainmaking. Then he received the knowledge of the *shingila*, which activates the medicine. The third step was to recognize weather patterns: the clouds of heavy heat (*nhungwiizi*), the small clouds (*mahilimbi*) blown from the ocean announcing rain, the big clouds (*mahuuli matale*) of torrential rain, and wind blowing forth the good rains from the south or Ukerewe Island. In response to our query, Kishina emphasized that the signs were not a matter of divining or dreaming, and that there is no 'group' (*shikundi*, from Swahili *kikundi*)[1] that guards this expertise – save the dynastic clan itself.

Shali shitiho ishikundi *isha bagemi ba mbula*. Isipokuwa *duhu uyo alibyaalwa* uwa bukoo *wenubo uwa* ntemi *lazima abitile nzila yeniyo*.	There is no group of rain-triers. It is just that the one born in the family of the king should pursue this path.

Interestingly, however, the death of chieftaincy and the reduction to its bare essence meant that he no longer needed to hide the fact that the rain medicine is cultic knowledge. At the time, he had two novices learning the exclusive trade of rainmaker. He called them *bahemba*, like all candidates acquiring medicinal knowledge from a healer or cult for a fee. They paid five head of cattle and ten goats, five times more than novices of the average medicinal cult. Granted, the collective impact of a chief's medicine makes this a special cult. The teachings concentrate on defensive acts (*lusumbo*) against enemies ruining the weather and on two types of rain typical of the region (*kateelegwa* and *kusombela*), which correspond to medicine applied on rain stones (*ng'homango*) and placed in the courtyard's campfire (*kikome*). We have no reason to assume that, at its incipience, this rain medicine from Buyombe was any different before giving rise to Bulima chiefdom. The thing called *shilala* was the last survivor of the dynasty, as it had been the source.

Chieftaincy as Medicinal Cult

Contrary to how I as a European was taught to think about chieftainship, namely as a political office and, if endowed with ritual capacity like in Africa, bound to be 'divine' on top of it, Kishina treated the tradition as a type of cult and knowledge, only special in its intention of a dynastic clan protecting the fertility of land and people. It is illuminating how Kishina systematically juxtaposed chieftaincy and initiatory association, or cult, as two counterparts adopting the same cultural logic and therefore in principle excluding each other. A chief may acquire the medicinal knowledge of 'other' initiatory associations, but is not allowed to climb ranks in these, as he presides over the dynastic cult.[2] In the following fragment about the medicinal society of the BaGalu, founded in the late nineteenth century by Gumha and most famous across Sukuma communities as a dance society, Kishina compares the hierarchy of his dynastic clan ('we') with the Galu cult's ranks, occupied initially by Gumha's descendants (*bang'wa Gumha*) but later on by non-kin as well.

Bakabyagi na masumbi giti hagenaga duhu ga butemi. Batadugije duhu munhu ungi ukupanda icheo tuhaye giti bang'wa Gumha. Benabo bali na mbika jabo, ubise nise. Mfano nulu giki niingile ko uku BaGalu natiko ukwihusisha sana na mambo genago, isipokuwa uku BaGalu kwenuko nane nalikachoolako mabugota fulani.

They have their own ranks, like those of chieftaincy. Someone else cannot climb the ranks that concern the kin of Gumha. They have their cause, we have ours. Even if I enter there at the Galu I would not concern myself much with their affairs, unless it is to go to the Galu to procure some specific medicine.

Chieftaincy and cult are not only equipoised. They are actually of the same order. Does his statement, surprisingly countermanding the claim of political office and sovereignty of chiefs, reflect the opinion of a frustrated incumbent? Or is it expressing a common belief about medicine's centrality in life, which has been more readily voiced (in the local language) ever since there became nothing more to be gained from the centuries-old confusion of Europeans eager to find a true equivalent for their sovereign at home (whether it was for signing deals in the economic scramble over Africa's resources or, still valid today, for persuading a donor to invest in a country)? The second option means we would have to revisit our concept of rule, chieftaincy and kingship in this part of the world. Summed up in the concept of medicinal rule, the above data support it. But there is more.

Kishina's discourse was replete with parallels between chieftaincy and medicinal cult, which went beyond their drawing on the same cosmology. Nobody will deny the particularity of chiefs having to retreat into their palace to spend the ten months of the cultivation season, engrossed as they were with people's expectations of the land. At the onset of this period around November, *ng'weji gwa igabanha*, the first month of the old Sukuma calendar, the *busunzula* ceremony takes place. The hair of the chief is shaven, made ready to grow like the crops on his fertile land. For this occasion, however, the chief must offer like every head of a medicinal society a treat of traditional beer to the members, which in his case are the *banang'oma*, clan members acting both as benefactors and recipients of the organization over which he presides. The head shaving is done in privacy in the round seclusion hut, *itemelo*, where the chief was installed and his predecessor buried (see Illustration 2). As soon as his head is shaven and he has dipped his finger in the beer, he steps out of the seclusion hut to be hailed by the public: '*Untemi ufuma*', 'the chief has come out'. The same verb expresses initiation after spirit possession and the healing of a patient. He wears a *ndeji* bracelet made with fibres of the *ng'hoja* tree and a shell (*shilungu*) like that of healers. The royal bracelet of Bulima is enwrapped in the hide of a monitor lizard (*mbulu*). The slight deviation from forest animals towards creatures common at Lake Tanganyika honours the dynastic cult's particular origin. Other variants exist, such as the five *ndeji* worn by the chief of Nera, and the *ndeji* worn on the forehead by chief Fundikila from Bunyanyembe, in resemblance to the diadem worn by Chwezi spirit mediums. Although emblems of chieftaincy are popular in cult symbolism, there is no reason to assume that chieftaincy preceded ritual initiation. All Sukuma chiefs have their caretaker: *ntemi ng'hoja*, 'the cooling chief', named after the secret tree.

At ceremonies, he sips the beer and asperges the ancestral altars with it. The expert leading the royal ceremony is called *kanumba*, literally 'small house', which is also the title for the master of ceremonies in the Chwezi spirit cult. The ritual expert medicates the seeds so the chief can offer these on banana leaves to every 'headman of nine homes' (*ng'wanangwa wa kaya kenda*). The leaves may be indicative as to the origin of the ritual. Banana trees are much more common in Buhaya and in the west of the Great Lakes region, from where the Chwezi cult spread, than in Bulima or five hundred kilometres down south in Buha.

In February 1996, nine months before our interview, I had attended a belated *Busunzula* in the chiefdom of Ndagalu, south of Magu. None of the ritual songs explicitly mentioned titles of chief- or kingship. The lyrics seemed to relate to any cultic practice, preceding the era that led to the institution of chieftaincy. In the song of inauguration, the vulture, a carrion-eater, and the heron, a snake-eater, feast on the corpse of the incumbent, symbolized by the leopard, an animal of the night. The lyrics, repeated in variants over twenty times, seem to evoke the liminal phase before the incumbent is enthroned.

Imbeshi nikugombola, hii baba.   The vulture will pick at you, man.
Ing'hona nikulya ifuje.   The heron will eat until satiated.

To be reborn as chief the young man must perform a hunter's kill, not for food but to obtain the ruthless power of the night. To 'give birth', *kubyala*, means to initiate. The new chief will prove to be fearless and then receive gifts together with the headman, who later on will collect tribute for him. Chief and headman engage in reciprocal exchange with the villagers.

Wabyala boba, ng'wana Masanja   He has given birth to fear, child of
Linjachi. Ubugosha wa ki ubuni-   Masanja Linjachi. What kind of man-
wakogoha shilanga? Wabyala na   liness would fear the weapon? He has
ng'hwe Nchimani ng'wanangwa.   given birth to it with Nchimani, the vil-
Bise tulatula kaliki? Ali kaliki   lage headman. What shall we give him
ulashoshe.   as a gift? He will return something.

The song inaugurating the ceremony replays the chief's initiation. The symbolism of the last fragment (in which the name Mabumbuga makes historical connections we cannot bring home) is most revealing.

Katunile wa Mabumbuga.   Let's cry over Mabumbuga. He has
Wasononhile subi, usumba wa   killed the leopard, the young man with
shilanga, wasononhile. Wafungwa   a weapon, he has killed. He has been
kabubi ku miso.   tied a blindfold over his eyes.

The last act makes reference to the blindfold of leopard skin worn by the *kanumba* at the start of Chwezi initiation when he must clear the ritual ground of evil spells by inserting protective medicine along the fence. The symbolic connection between chieftaincy and cult thus attains intriguing historical overtones. The Chwezi cult probably originated from the royal dynasty called Chwezi and ruling Kitara in the hectic era and area of the Great Lakes. After its destruction by a Luo clan in the late sixteenth or early seventeenth century, the survivors of the dynasty, among them the culture hero Ryangombe, moved south in the shape of a cult (de Heusch 1966: 37). Is it a coincidence that not much later the first chiefdoms emerged in the Sukuma-Nyamwezi plains? Rather than wondering which institution came first, cult or chieftaincy, it is the ease by which the one transforms into the other that should draw our attention. Why is the main medicinal plant of initiation called *ntemi*, 'the chief'? Why are the holders of high ranks, responsible for collecting the fees of initiates in the districts, denoted literally as 'chiefs' (*batemi*) under the head of the cult? The two institutions of cult and chieftaincy have a cultural model in common so that the one readily evolves into the other. That is why the primarily political interpretation of chieftaincy falters.

Festival-Based Chieftaincy

In the Busunzula ceremony I witnessed, chief Kapunda Ndalahwa Kishosha II of Ndagalu made a public speech that contrasted inadvertently with his traditional outfit of black garment, diadem and *ndeji* bracelet, as well as with the aforementioned inauguration song evoking images of blood sacrifice and royal rebirth. What was key in Kishina's account seemed beside the point in Kapunda's address. His aim was to play into the postcolonial concerns of the Tanzanian officials present. He thus buried the issue of customary authority.

Huna lulu, badugu bane. Ishida iyo tulitumamila ahenaha iti giki tulichoba butemi wa madaraka gitumo wali buli. Tuliita historia ya kulekela bichiswi. Mhayo untale historia. Buli munhu lazima amanile ifumo yakwe. Ubebe ufumile he. Abang'wing'we ikala bitaga kinahe. Igete twalitutemilwa na bazungu duhu nulu kinahe?	So, my brothers and sisters. The thing we are working on here is not that we seek kingship as it used to be. We are making history as it was bequeathed by our people. The main word is history. Each person should know his origin. Where you came from. What did our people do in the past? Is it true that our only government was that by Europeans?

Kwa hiyo ulu giki mapicha genaga gakayubonekana, basi abanhu bose. Abana byalwa nulu giti bado bakwandya kumana gikigashina ikale twali na bakiongozi bali giko. Bise ishughuli yise yeniyi kuimarisha ubutamaduni wenubo. Kwa hiyo huna lulu badugu bane, hi shabaha nhale.	Therefore, once the pictures of this event will be visible, all people of all generations and small children too will learn to their pleasant surprise how our leaders in the past were acting. Our activities are about strengthening this culture. So, brothers and sisters, that is the big objective.

What was the contrast between Kapunda's discourse and Kishina's? One word – medicine, *Bugota* – the phrase repeated like a chorus in the account of the Bulima chief. The Ndagalu chief did not mention it once in his hour-long speech. Instead he pleaded to his audience of several hundred for a cultural role squarely locked in history. In such culture reduced to history, someone's origin (*ifumo*) is a memory fading with the linear progress of time, lost in the 'ethnographic past'. Such culture is not a source of life, regenerated in innovations of the present. Etymologically, though, this second, regenerative meaning of the concept of *ifumo*, origin, is suggested by its stem *-fum* (equal to *-kum*), which is shared with the stem of 'healer', *mfumu*: literally the originator, and professionally a restorer of life. That kind of rule Kapunda shunned, because precolonial government had to resemble the European prototype.

The pictures he spoke of showed the *ntemi ng'hoja* backing his king as it should (see Illustration 1). Several members of the initiatory associations invited for the occasion to perform told me that they were reassured by this man's presence and about medicine being used. But in public, curiously, no ritual acts had been performed nor shrines addressed. Nor had there been an open competition between the dance groups of the medicinal societies, as I was used to watching in the plains between villages, with thousands swarming between the two rivalling groups directing magical attacks on each other. Instead, Chief Kapunda had much good advice about care for the environment, solidarity and the problem of witchcraft beliefs. The waning enthusiasm of the crowd during his speech illustrated what was lacking. His insistence on celebrating culture as history meant to dispel fears that intervention in society, hence political change, would actually be envisaged. Besides me, a European student, the audience counted in its midst some government officers dressed as civilians. They were not on official duty. By day, the chief was a civil servant too. Did he fear his colleagues might scrutinize his customary-chief speech for subversive demands? Important for our angle is the unconscious reduction of life by the postcolonial chief. His separation of culture and society, the first regarded as traditional (and gone), the second as political (and actual), prevented traditional medicine from mattering. It is the anachronistic take on African kingship that we want to avoid.

Long-Range Sukuma History

Oral traditions converge with the archaeological survey of Mwanza region by Soper and Golden (1969) foregrounding the early seventeenth century as the period of the first Sukuma chiefs. In the previous century the intrusion of Lwoo-speaking peoples in Bunyoro and Buganda had caused southern migration of Hima, Hinda, Tusi and Chwezi. Historians Holmes and Austen (1972: 380–81), in a little gem of an article, convincingly reject the thesis that these people, designated in European literature and some oral traditions with the racist superior label of 'Hamitic' (which the Tutsi too were granted), had to be the founders of chieftaincy. The first chiefs' ascendants had most probably been Nilotes and Cushites a few generations earlier. They had already undergone 'the ubiquitous Bantu assimilation process'. Going by the oral history on their origins, several Sukuma chiefs were descendants of Bantu groups around Lake Victoria that had mixed with those migrants from the warring Interlacustrine kingdoms and had already been culturally influenced by them. The new idea transmitted according to Holmes and Austen was centralized authority.

It is hard to believe though that autochthonous groups would welcome the idea of losing their power to an individual from outside. The change is only feasible if something followed that all could benefit from, and if the outsiders were not a rivalling group and they had privileged access to that thing. Before Rwanda's ceremonial state emerged on the instigation of King Ndori, it had known medicinal rule, whose ritual and medicine the medium Ryangombe putatively carried along in his migration south after the Lwoo invasion (see Chapter 9). Sukuma oral tradition explains chieftaincy from the 'efficacious magic' offered by the newcomer. Holmes and Austen hurry to mention problem-solving skills and technological expertise instead of magic (ibid.: 381). Due to a predilection for administrative discourse, and unfamiliarity with local medicine, they omitted oral histories detailing the newcomer's spirit-based knowledge to control the fertility of the land. People must have recognized the rain medicine as a novel form of something they had, magic. Holmes and Austen repeatedly state that Sukuma groups were particularly apt at absorbing strangers into their community.

That cultural openness did not mean that the farmers would welcome change. There was something about the proposed chieftaincy that already made sense culturally. And it was not the king's privileges, palace or court that it would later give way to. If we accept that it was medicine at the collective level, desired by former bands evolved into village communities, then we have an explanation for the 'mutual accommodation and acceptability rather than conquest' (ibid.: 382) surfacing in each of the foundation histories of Sukuma chiefdoms. The authors ponder whether the institution of chieftaincy was not a revolution for Sukuma after all. We contend that it was not, since chieftaincy lay in line with healership.

Cultural structure is never easy to discern, but unless we go for the easy way out, which is to presume the universality of the *homo economicus* and reduce all motives to fleeing war and making profit, we must find endogenous reasons for clusters of villages independently from each other agreeing with the rule of newcomers. The deal must have been culturally inviting. Medicinal rule was an arrangement whereby extended families could maintain autonomy and live dispersed. Of course, what the first deal looked like and how it evolved are two different things. But even in the later evolution, the initial premises should persist, if only negatively in the form of resistance or turmoil when the premises were altered. An example is how settlement patterns were affected by the trade routes in eastern Africa, blooming in the nineteenth century. Sukuma were in such high numbers that Arabs and Swahili did not contemplate enslaving them; and Sukuma chiefs did not participate in that trade (ibid.: 390). But the few chiefdoms located on trading routes did carve out a profit by imposing a transit and hospitality levy (*hongo*). The toll inadvertently changed the cultural structure by introducing the principle of territoriality. In the densely vegetated terrain of the rainforest in western equatorial Africa, where villages were territorially marked entities, the effect of the new principle would have been minimal, but among Sukuma it fundamentally affected the custom of dispersed dwelling and free travel. Territorial disputes soon arose between adjacent chiefdoms, a turning point in local history, indirectly suggestive of the prior cultural structure. Together with cattle-raiding and brigandage, in the slipstream of transit trade, an atmosphere of threat reigned that caused the southern chiefdoms of Busiha, adjoining the Nyamwezi, in the late nineteenth century to concentrate dwellings. The household's autonomy eroded. Villages were fortified. Land erosion and shrunk harvests ensued.

Bordered in the west by Lake Tanganyika, in the north by Lake Victoria and in between by the Ruwenzori mountain range, the cultivation steppe of western Tanzania had for over a thousand years been the scene of wide-scale migrations by small groups of Bantu hunters and gatherers with variable notions of farming. They had supplanted the first occupants, probably the Hadza of today and traditionally named the Bahi, whose traces are left in caves with rock paintings. Holmes and Austen (1972: 378–79) make an interesting observation about the cultivation steppe after comparing their archaeological data with contemporary ethnography:

> The people seem to have come from practically every direction of the compass. Given these factors it is somewhat surprising that the basic Sukuma-Nyamwezi language and culture structure have sustained their essential homogeneity. But this is testimony to the dynamic powers of assimilation of the fundamental culture.

Larger immigrant groups from the south such as the Minza were later remembered as clans, in whose name elders are still greeted today (*Iminza*). Remembered to this day as hunting bands, the Minza converted to agriculture after the abundant game diminished. Bantu farmers joined them from opposite directions. Balaturu had come from the Nilotic highlands in the north-east, introducing cattle, which among Sukuma would never attain cultic status but did function as the supreme means of exchange and bridewealth. The Balaturu were famous for offering their services as diviners to the chiefs. Divination originated in the east, every Sukuma healer will say. The Nilotic source of oracles sounds like an enigma, although a cultural logic supports the historical claim. Oracular truth remains unspoilt if communicated through an outsider, uninfluenced by local rumour. The Balaturu, whose mother tongue was Nilotic, fit the profile. Up to this day, Sukuma prefer faraway diviners. The east is moreover the direction from which cattle came, the symbol of riches and fortune that oracles ultimately deal with. The chief, *ntemi* (plural: *batemi*), must have been pragmatic about engaging Balaturu, for he was himself familiar with divination techniques and the use of medicine:

> The traditional *batemi* were primarily sacerdotal rulers, high priests in an ancestral cult, who exercised few administrative powers and duties. The *ntemi*'s primary role was as an arbitrator among social and supernatural forces which were considered to dominate the fate of the society. It was expected that he would seek to control destiny and manipulate the factors for success, not through political power but sublime influence established through necromantic spirit mediums known as *bafumu ba ntwe* (ibid.: 383).[3]

The *ntemi* had to exhibit persuasive impact on natural forces, primarily rain and calamities of disease or vermin. Tales abound of chiefs exiled for failing their duty. Deposing them was alleged to be rare at first (which would be from around 1700), but frequent from the mid nineteenth century onwards when the chief's rain medicine became essential in securing agriculture (and secondarily livestock). Farming was the main livelihood after the forest cover had vanished under population pressure and due to trading routes budding between the coast and Buganda (ibid.: 386). The chief was the superior judge and military commander too, but without him elders would have continued performing those tasks. Chieftaincy was, like healership, a matter of affect management. Sukuma had grown up in wide open undulating plains without any particularly fertile bits to fight over (except for the dry season watering places, *malambo*, but those were communal). In the dry season all rivers run dry. In the rainy season precipitations are erratic everywhere. Going to war as a family man was not obvious. Nor was it for a young man in search of an honourable deed, as he might offend the ancestors (ibid.: 384). That uncertainty about invisible interference prompted many of my Sukuma friends' everyday decisions in the late twentieth century. Centuries before, when the colonial construct of Sukuma ethnicity had not come into existence, it was an equally open society that would not discriminate between the ancestors of other clans or even groups speaking another language. The retribution feared of the opponent's supernatural guides if going to war was a democratic moment in itself. As the safety net for mankind's experiments in the Great Lakes and East Africa, the plains of western Tanzania not surprisingly hand the clues to grasping medicinal rule. How to understand 'ntemiship' as a European? Corresponding to the cultural structure we will discuss, the social hierarchy in which the *ntemi* fitted was such that superiority was not in terms of how much constraint one exerted on other mortals but how good one was at communicating with entities that impacted on mortals.

The political-administrative structure was balanced for a sustainable non-hegemonic chieftaincy. In his court the *ntemi* was checked by his family's *banang'oma*, consisting of the main kin members, their descendants and allied dependents that had collaborated with the predecessor in the joint medicinal endeavour. Succession was mostly matrilineal. Along Lake Victoria and closer to the Interlacustrine kingdoms succession was patrilineal, which prompts Holmes and Austen (1972: 385) to speculate whether the rule of succession may have arbitrarily depended on the kinship position the first chief happened to have in relation to the original *ntemi*. By the latter, one should think of a cultic founder handing out rain medicine to family members willing to emigrate and thus expand the network. In families possessing chiefly medicine, the oldest brother inheriting the farm stayed in the fertile areas up north at Lake Victoria, together with the father. Perhaps they set up a chiefdom there thanks to their medicine. A younger brother or cousin, accompanied by a sister he could marry out for bridewealth, had to migrate deeper into the south and prepare her children for succession. Mediumistic vocation is another parameter mitigating the chance of purely hegemonic endeavours.

A second counterbalancing institution was the *igunguli*, a sub-chiefdom or county, which was headed by the *ng'wanangwa*, chieflet. He was often also kin of the chief. Together with the other *banangwa* he focused on decision making, as opposed to rainmaking. Decisions, sanctioned by the chief, mainly concerned land distribution, agricultural cooperation and communal feasts. The counterparts of *banangwa* were, on one side, the village youth associations (*elika*), and on the other side the advisory council of elders (*banamhala*). On top of this multilayered equipoise, there was the inhabitant's eternal right to leave the area. That too could soften the regime of chief and chieflet. Their prestige depended on the signs of fertility: the number of inhabitants, that is adherents to this system of letting a foreign clan rule.

Sooner or later, chiefs discovered the unwritten limit as to how much a chiefdom could expand. Thorough centralization like in the Interlacustrine kingdoms never took place. Too large a territory for a collective guarantee of rain could motivate sons to establish an adjacent small chiefdom (ibid.: 386). In return for a frugal patron–client relationship, the old chief would give the son the necessary regalia (*shitongelejo*) to placate the 'royal' clan ancestors responsible for fertility and rain. Fission due to conflict happened as well, like in the old Kwimba chiefdom that split into Nera and Busumabu. The second half of the nineteenth century was tumultuous for these northwestern Sukuma chiefdoms, especially in the 1880s, as Mutesa, the Kabaka of Buganda, had his eye on them from his vessels on the lake. The southern Sukuma chiefdoms suffered invasions by the notorious Nyamwezi chief Mirambo.

Since warfare did not befit the ritual function of chieftaincy, the southern matrilineal chiefdoms designated chieflets to act as warlords. Remarkably, the northern patrilineal chiefs led the campaign themselves (ibid.: 395). The contrast with the northern, more pragmatic definition of the office, raises the question of degrees or types of medicinal rule. Might the northern chiefdoms approximate the Interlacustrine model of 'ceremonial states' (see Part III)? Or has their medicinal rule from the onset been more of a business enterprise than a mediumistic call? It would be hard to characterize chiefdoms though, and why for instance some of them have been caught in succession struggles or have seen a chieflet toppling his chief. In the northern chiefdom of Busumabu, the chieflet (greater headman, *ng'wanangwa ntale*) by the name of Linjachi became so powerful as to elect the chief, still he would not aspire to the office himself. He may have known that the expectations were too medicinal for him to qualify or even take interest. He was no healer-rainmaker, nor perhaps willing to pay the price of living virtually incarcerated in the palace to keep the chiefdom's fertility integral.

Ntemi chieftaincy has a medicinal bent at the top of the hierarchy. The lower the rung of the ladder, the more direct and less ritualistic the impact is. Still in the 1990s my impression from speaking to chief Kaphipa from Bukumbi chiefdom about his enthronement (a nocturnal abduction and ritual burial) and to the oldest *banang'oma* of Bulima was that in their early days the court had been a family business specialized in organizing the ritual domestication of fertility. The theme is cross-culturally relevant: the rains fall from the sky via the king, situated outside the social order of daily life and bearing in him the signs of the wild, symbolizing the land itself (Tcherkézoff 1983). The whole family was involved. Agricultural ceremonies required the queen (*ngole*) and the head counsellor (*ngabe*) to place themselves over the farmers' piles of seeds and imitate a pregnant woman in the act of birth (Millroth 1965: 171).

Death of the king was economically alarming for the family business at the palace. There was one occasion when I had encountered a similar atmosphere. In the Sukuma ward of Mondo, I witnessed the destitution and sense of denial that persisted among the dozens of assistants and novices after the death of their renowned healer, Kisununha, dubbed *Mungu wa pili* in Swahili, 'the second god'. One close assistant of his could not find the words to tell me that the healer had died when I visited the compound. At the burial of the healer, like the king's, mourning was not allowed. People were supposed to cheer and dance, as I had done myself a few months before at the funeral of my neighbour, a leader of the Buyeye cult of snake charmers with the title of *ntemi*. Kisununha began his career as an itinerant healer, a medicine man with a bag full of charms – I would dare say, like an outsider about to enter a foreign community to gain fame with a special medicine – and created a chief-like reputation for himself (see Illustration 3). He was one of many such figures whom I had visited in different parts of the Sukuma-speaking region. He had his own fenced hamlet the size of a football field containing fenced compounds for patients, assistants and novices, all participating in the daily routines he had invented. The absolute cynosure was his life-size sky-blue-painted pedestrian 'car' made of tin scraps in which he could drive around thanks to an assistant who kneeled under him to play the engine. By the time I met him in the mid-1990s, he had passed his peak. He stepped out of the tin car in a uniform heavy with medals, wearing an eternal glittering smile under a colourful hat. The interview led nowhere. Like a king, or spoilt Liberace, he had his spokesperson leading the talk and keeping it short. His dignitaries were pushy, seemingly concerned to shield him off lest rumour spread about his frail health and senses. The king never dies. Soon he did. His bureaucrats were confronted with the challenge of prolonging the reign of the second god from which they profited. Succession had no basis. The person-oriented cult made it hard to organize succession. Only a new charismatic healer would do, but such nascent stars had never ceased to pop up elsewhere in the region. The awe-inspiring fact of monopolizing a mass of followers could have spawned an institutional structure, had it not been for the Tanzanian state they had to obey. A medicine, a charm or shrine substituting for the person, could have guaranteed survival had it not been for the contestation by Christian churches, school and civil servants regularly visiting Mondo ward. The region counted a dozen initiatory associations, snake charmers, porcupine hunters, drum cults, and so on, all of them medicinal and most of them not importing nearby traditions, but originating from the founding act of a *mfumu*, diviner-healer, who had managed to institute a lasting successional structure. An overarching leadership for all those associations never existed.

The study by Hans Cory (1951) on Sukuma rites of chieftaincy, potentially a major reference, was not exactly an epitome of ethnographic depth. Its value for us lies in showing the limited salience of the author's polity prism. Cory's data, which were faithfully rendered, confirm to us that the chief could not be distinguished from the healer on the basis of their political traits. They were different specialists of medicine, the encompassing model. In this eastern part of Bantu-speaking groups, *mfumu* is the word for healer (not king or chief, like in the west). The *mfumu* is a 'coming-outer', a term according to some of my Sukuma informants invoking his former seclusion in the forest; their association with *-fuma*, 'to come out', may have an etymological basis in proto-Bantu (see Chapter 7). The chief or king is *ntemi*, derived from *kutema*, 'to cut'. I was told the verb refers to the judging of difficult cases. Cory's informants, fifty years earlier and thus perhaps more reliably, explained the verb from the act of cutting down trees, which the first settlers did to build villages. Before the coming of chiefs, the headmen were the 'cutters'. The new immigrants subsequently adopted this existing title after establishing their rule over whole valleys of villages in return for their rainmaking, arbitration, and possibly their new type of livelihood involving cattle. Little or no lore exists on a major upheaval or conquest war in these plains. The shift towards centralization seems to have happened peacefully, possibly precipitated by the newcomers' stories of expansionist groups in the north-west from where they came, and bound to advance, such as Karagwe, Rwanda, Bunyoro and Buganda. Not weaponry but magic seemed the specialty of the new rulers. Bulima's oral traditions staged them as employing rain medicine to attract people into their realm and settle. (Likewise, the annual harvest dances, *mbina*, organize popularity contests between cultic groups in which the performance attracting the largest crowd wins, assisted with *samba* magic.) In keeping with the peace idiom, the autochthonous 'cutters' were not ousted. The function of the former village founders was renamed *ntemi ng'hoja*, literally 'cool cutter'. The reader will remember this 'cooling chief' homonymous with the sacred royal tree, backing his chief. He fulfilled a special function at the enthronement by initiating chief and ritual wife into their duties. A synonym is *ngeba*, a term that the newcomers knew from the north-west for the same function.

In Sukuma courts the *ntemi* and a chosen *mfumu* operated together in a division of tasks whereby the greater knowledge of the latter complemented the former's royal ancestral charms and shrine. Let us take the example of warfare, which should epitomize the king's function in public affairs. After an oracle by a *mfumu* helped to determine the prospects of the war expedition, the war practitioner (*mfumu wa vulugu*) took his turn to prepare magic to be administered to the soldiers together with the *ntemi* (Cory 1951: 64). In the concoction of powdered roots of the *mkonola* tree (Annona chrysophylla) he inserted a *shingila*, symbolic additive, consisting of bits of the tongue, heart, penis and scrotum of a killed enemy leader, as well as the gullet of a lion, some wild bees and big black ants (*sungwa*). *Ntemi* and *mfumu* stood on each side of a wooden tray containing the medicine mixed with the meat of a herd's strongest bull. In some southern chiefdoms the potent additive was the flesh of a boy sacrificed by being treaded upon by the army. Implication in transgressive violence on a young member of the community may have transformed farmers into soldiers? Together chief and healer held a bow through which each of the warriors put their head to take a piece of meat in their mouth and swallow, before lining up.

The public speech was held by the *mfumu*. In it he not only explained to the troops the purpose of the magic, but surprisingly he also detailed the tactics of the attack. Cory (1951: 65) interprets as follows:

> In this way the *nfumu* directed the leader and his soldiers as to how the campaign should be conducted, and as he was the priest whose opinion was derived from the spirits by magical means, his orders were followed implicitly as religious commands. In this way differences of opinion among the leaders as well as among the rank and file were prevented. Then the *ntemi* made the warriors walk round in a circle and called prominent warriors by name; this was called *kuguba* – to excite.

The terms 'priest' and 'religious' direct the reader towards the theme of religion legitimating politics. The terms operate on the presumption of what a king is, a political office-holder in need of popular support. The ethnographic data, however, make it quite plain that he, the *ntemi*, acts as an 'exciter' and mediator of ancestral blessing, like a charm itself. What the actual wishes of the ancestors are, which brings us closer to actual policy as in this case of warfare, is conveyed through the *mfumu*. Is he then the real political power? The question itself is problematic, for it keeps our analysis confined to the Western cultural structure, with the real risk of a biased or at least lowly salient account of ntemiship. To analyse the practices of chief and diviner, the political is not the most relevant distinction, since on that level they resemble each other too much, as expected from their common proto-meaning, which is the medicinal. We must be careful about discerning cultural structure, because it is the prism refracting our ethnographic observations.

The appropriate alternative is a cultural structure adapted to the regional variations of kingship – an arrangement of ideas, norms and orderings of reality that can be hierarchical or lateral. In all the ethnographies discussed in this book, the political dimension, defined as pertaining to government and the public affairs of a country, is incorporated by the medicinal – that is, the healing properties of rule at the collective level. Magical obligations, prohibitions, rites and recipes rather than policy, ideology or the governing of a territory dominate the activities, office and institutions. Moreover, the strong similarities between initiation rites in such seemingly distinct institutions as healing, spirit possession, age sets, and kingship cannot be disregarded. They cross-cut the division between political, economic, educational, familial and religious aspects, which only garble the meaning of the cultural practices.

To finish my list of objections against the polity prism and modern interpretation of African kingship, I want to give another brief example of how the political perspective can muffle striking data. Out of the blue, and without any chance of being picked up by the unsuspecting reader, Cory writes about a trend, which we must situate in the Busiha chiefdoms of Shinyanga, unfortunately without precision of era. An important duty of the king is to organize a ceremony purifying the parents after the birth of twins (*mabasa*), a condition potentially endangering the rains in the realm.

> Years ago the chiefs had sold all rights in the *mabasa* ceremonies, especially in the more remote parts of the country, to their village headmen (*banangwa*), and as this payment was made once and for all, when a *ng'wanangwa* died his successor had only to prepare beer for a ritual cleaning of the drums which had been bestowed upon his predecessor as a sign of the acquired right. The price was thirteen goats (Cory 1951: 55).

The polity prism and modern division, separating political and economic subsystems, cannot compute. How can a political activity be sold? The layman is not supposed to pay attention. Just read on. The fieldworker though will recognize the model of healership. The *ntemi* acts like a *mfumu* who sets up a trade of medicine whose success can be capitalized on by selling the right to it. The most thriving healers are founders of their own medicinal cult. The drum plays a central part in the cult, as it does in the establishment of a kingship. The drum, *ng'oma*, stands for the kingdom. Rwandese myths recount the wars fought to retrieve the royal drum (see Part III). Across the Great Lakes, the death of a king is symbolized by the drum bursting, after which the hide needs replacing. The hereditary courtiers, who chose the king's successor, are called *banang'oma*, literally 'the children of the drum'. Their title suggests apprenticeship into the healing cult.

The twin ceremony is called *ng'oma ya mabasa*, the drum of the twins. We remember Turner translating the healing cults as 'drums' of affliction, which as many forms of *ng'oma* (cf. Janzen 1992) spread across central, east and southern Africa. The ceremonies almost invariably emulate the structure of a ritual initiation. The cursed not only gets cured, but becomes knowledgeable after the final ceremony with the right to initiate and diffuse his or her knowledge in an offshoot of the cult, if the master's oracle permits. Profit, mainly cattle, can be made from ceremonies, after master and initiated agree that the former retains some rights in the form of tribute by the latter. That is when the master, either healer or chief, cuts up his cult territorially. In Cory's example, the king did not sell his right of twin purification to the headmen of the villages nearby his palace (*ikuru*). This healership most practical to tend he did continue. In medicine converge the many economic, political and other aspects of chieftaincy.

The End of Chieftaincy

The village elders never needed the king for their ritual affairs. They had their own ancestral cult. They had an organized medicinal basis of power, in the twentieth century in the form of the *ihane* initiation of the *bu-namhala*, the society for elders. During the *ihane* I participated in, at the end of three days of intense training into the secret medicinal plants and symbols, each novice was told to hold the 'Sukuma feather', *inana lya kisukuma*. In this uncommon moment of ethnic consciousness, the initiated was guaranteed that wherever in 'Sukumaland' (*Busukuma*) he would show the medicinal bundle of *bu-namhala*, he could count on hospitality, food and a home. It is unclear whether the village initiation had a region-wide orientation already before chieftaincy and the chiefs built their ritual structure around this one, or whether the ritual was a later countermeasure of the commoners to unite across chiefdoms against an increasingly imposing chieftain structure. In both cases, chieftaincy is a cultural invention that actors react to. The associations spanning clans compete with it or inspire it.

In the late twentieth century the chiefdoms had lost almost all relevance. Tanzania's founding president Nyerere, himself son of a chief in the north of the country, abolished customary authority after independence in 1961. In practice, the average Sukuma farmer's social networks had already long covered areas much vaster than their chiefdom after effective exogamy, resettling of families, the migration of clan members, and especially the accumulated memberships in various medicinal associations. One important track is that of the latter, initiatory associations filling 'the social and spiritual vacuum' as Holmes and Austen (1972: 401) put it, which was left after chiefs became implicated in colonial government and effected a 'secularization of ntemiship'. The German administration in 1898 intervened in Nera to support the *banangwa*, the pragmatic elders, in their struggle with *basumba batale*, the young spokesmen, who not surprisingly conspired with *bafumu*, healers, probably by lack of the chief's backing, but also because these young leaders were used to cooperating with healers for the village initiation. It was again a healer and dance leader, Ng'wana Malundi, who a generation later led the resistance movement against the colonial imposition of cotton cash crop cultivation, which impinged on the families' agricultural autonomy. He was arrested and imprisoned, leaving the chiefs with the moral dilemma of whether a healer had not done the duty of a real chief embodying the collective. Was Ryangombe's revolution in Rwanda several centuries before of a similar order? In all these examples, medicinal rule is pivotal, slipping from chieftaincy into medicinal association, and back. Thus we comprehend the medicinal aversions of colonial governor and postcolonial chief and the reversion by a deposed chief to rain medicine without centralized government.

The king's dilemma for his rule to remain medicinal does not appear in the historical accounts of Jan Vansina. Was the model absent in the Great Lakes and to the west, as far as the Atlantic coast? Before verifying, we revisit Vansina's comparative study and then boldly extend our model of medicinal rule to the whole Bantu-speaking region and its fringes.

Notes

1. This is the fragment (with the Swahili words in normal font) the next chapter refers to, in order to caution about the lexico-positivism of Vansina's method of 'words and things' in cultures where an institution exists under various specific names but not as a generic concept. Respondent and interviewer had no option but to use in their KiSukuma conversation the Swahili generic term *kikundi*, 'group', for cult. The local absence of a generic concept for the institution prevents historical linguists from inferring the cultural significance of cults. Oral traditions, if available, could mitigate the problem for the historian. Then again, as in the name Mabumbuga figuring in the song further on (perhaps referring to a cult through its founder, as is the practice in oral literature), very often those specifics are no longer remembered either.
2. His substitute, chief Ngalula, was unlucky to have fathered twins (*mabasa*). Customarily these children were removed from the palace lest their excess of fertility jeopardize the chief's capacity for safeguarding

the life of people and land. The Bulima palace did not welcome other twin children either. Ngalula's unprecedented solution was to get himself initiated into the cult of twins. After purification he could, like any commoner, keep his children at home. To Kishina, the initiative of his cousin added insult to injury.
3. The literal translation of *bafumu ba ntwe* is 'healers of the head'.

Chapter 4

ENDOGENIZING VANSINA'S EQUATORIAL TRADITION

To accurately situate the origins of the model of rule in a locality is impossible. It would falsely suggest that cultural processes begin and end like historical events, and that cultural exchanges stop at the border with other groups or languages. We have tackled this limitation by shifting attention from historical sequences to the logic or structure of the endogenous process. We may estimate, however, that the palette of systems schematized in Figure 0.3 would have existed by around AD 1,000 when, we will learn from Vansina, a new cultural stability was reached in central and eastern Africa after immigration by Bantu-speaking peoples.

The Cameroon Grassfields are designated as the cradle of the Bantu migration. Fascinated by the fact that a language structure, notably slow in changing, is shared by adjacent groups in central, eastern and southern Africa speaking 'Bantu' languages, Roland Oliver (1966) speculated about the journey of the first emigrants and their descendants about three thousand years ago. He proposed four stages of the Bantu expansion, which despite having been detailed and amended since, have retained their main contours. The first wave pushed south through the equatorial woodlands, albeit in two separate directions, west and east. From the eastern nucleus in Interlacustrine Africa, known as the Urewe culture and dated around 500 BC, a second migration spread southward and to the eastern coast, which announced the Iron Age. From a nucleus in south-east Congo, the savannas in the north-east and the south were subjugated. Whether the autochthonous peoples, namely hunter-gatherers in the west and Afro-Asiatic pastoralists in the east, were really 'colonized' is a contentious issue. The Bantu languages probably expanded through both migration and acculturation.[1] Because of the two-way exchange implied in the latter of those two interlaced processes we will include current Nilotic and Niger-Congo groups in the analysis. To learn more about the culture of the first migrants in the grassfields, we will also turn our gaze to the forgotten direction, the neighbouring cultures in the west (see Chapter 5).

Acculturation leaves remnants for many generations. Like the evolution of grammar in language, the cultural models underlying institutions change slowly. In the Western linear perspective of modern art, where defiance of the established rules is a principle in itself, it is unthinkable that the same style would be replicated for centuries, as in the case of Egyptian frontalist painting. In a broader time perspective, though, Western styles do exhibit cycles, reverting to deserted positions and rediscovering grandparental forms, and over say three centuries betraying a cultural penchant for, among others, individualistic expression. This book deems cultural structure essential in studying common historical origins. The spectre we combat is extrapolation from sociostructural – may we say 'superficial' – similarities between systems of rule. Processes of the same form are not the same. Their meaning is cultural, which has always grown historically. Meaning contains a particular history.

The puzzle of the Bantu expansion as framed by Oliver formed the background to Jan Vansina's classic *Paths in the Rainforests* from 1990 (abbreviated to PR in our references). In it he described 'the cultural tradition' of equatorial Africa as 'a powerful endogenous process' dating back to the emigration from the grassfields of groups speaking 'proto-Bantu' and abruptly ending with colonization (PR xii). This chapter begins with the observation that Vansina never treated the process leading to the equatorial tradition as endogenous, that is as having an internal cause in which originated historical events and institutions such as kingship. The criticism sounds harsh and must be substantiated. By the time Vansina published his regional comparison, he was aware of the predilection in his explanations of change for exogenous pressures such as ecology and economy as well as the cultural diffusion from invaders (PR 69, 194). We will demonstrate that besides this materialism the opposite lurked in his analyses, namely the idealism of fixed beliefs governing a people like an inescapable structure. The approach we defended in the Introduction, whose roots lie in the interpretive anthropology of Geertz ([1973] 1993), has actors sharing logics that symbolically frame the world, permitting diverse innovations as well as independent inventions of similar practices. In contrast, Vansina's take on culture has an atomistic bent.

I will attribute it to a faulty understanding of culture's relation with language.

Language and Culture: Words as Things

As a pointer, let us start with the lexical associations he established between iron and stone in both western and eastern Bantu languages. How come Vansina (1990: 60) admits no other explanation than 'diffusion from one centre'? Independent inventions from a common ancestral logic elude the atomistic approach to social change, which traces how one event causes another, as opposed to a whole (such as a logic) relating and producing many parts (such as inventions). The focus is on the diffusion of words and ideas, as if they were things. The endogenous logic from which separate groups develop innovations is an unwieldy parameter the student of diffusion prefers not to reckon with.

For instance, how to explain the commonality we will establish between the fertility cults of water spirits in Zambia and Malawi giving rise to kingship (Ranger and Kimambo 1972: 6), and four thousand kilometres to the west on the Teke plateau the spirits of the waterfall of Nkwe Mbali consecrating the royal charms, *biri* (Vansina 1973), and halfway between them at Mbomb' Ipoku, '*the* spirit of the lake and the senior spirit of the whole region', where the first strong chiefdom of the Congo basin was located, undeniably of cultic origin (cf. Vansina 1990: 121)? Their similar origin shimmers through in the whole rather than in the particular cultural elements held together by that whole – in the recipe rather than the ingredients of the medicine. So one may truly wonder whether the diffusion of cultural elements from a centre explains the pattern. Of course, a naturally selected cognitive disposition to a type of belief need not have a cradle from where the belief spread for it to exist in both Africa and Asia. But specific beliefs and practices that are extensively related to each other raise the pressing issue of an endogenous cultural logic pervading communities. It should be the first query to settle before the historian concludes on diffusion from one point.

Historical claims on the diffusion of an institution that are not based on ethnographic observation or on written archives reiterate a purely lexicological or archaeological reality. The equation of the origin of a practice with the origin of a word or with the first find of an artefact can mislead. Relying on the first appearance of a generic word for relic, Vansina dates for the Mongo area the incorporation of relics in charms in the seventeenth century (PR 118) – a practice universal to homo sapiens and probably homo erectus almost a million years ago. On the rare occasion when Vansina mentions the variety of terminology and makes abstraction of the words to derive the institution they refer to, he presupposes the diffusion of the institution (PR 149). Independent inventions from a common cultural logic seem out of the question. His emphasis is on the spread of word roots, not of meanings. Thus it remains a mystery why terms for 'chief', with different linguistic stems yet similar etymology, can be encountered in Kongo and thousands of kilometres away in the east as well: respectively *ntinu*, 'the cutter' (PR 156) and *ntemi*, 'the cutter'. Are these not separate inventions following a common cultural logic?

At the basis of the interpretive lacuna lies the 'pointillist' methodology Vansina promotes to reconstruct history from archival data, 'painstakingly fitting together small slivers of evidence exactly as tesserae finally yield a mosaic' (PR 31). Can his lists of local words and their regional distribution (PR 9) capture the holistic quality of meanings? The method of historical linguistics he swore by, to venture into depths of the past unreachable by oral history, lets the cultural distribution of an institution depend on the linguistic distribution of the word that stands for it. A methodological problem arises in cultures where an institution exists under various specific names but not as a generic concept. Galu, Gika, Cheyeki, Yeye, Chwezi and Nunguli are all different proper names for initiatory associations in Sukuma communities, each with their own medicine and their members paying fees to climb ranks in a solidarity network. Like many similar ones before them, the name of the medicine and group will vanish after its popularity wanes.[2] The previous chapter cited a fragment of an interview in KiSukuma wherein respondent and interviewer feel compelled to borrow the Swahili generic term *kikundi*, 'group', to talk about cults. The omnipresence and indubitable significance of initiatory societies could not be inferred without input from observation, since the language has no concept for the institution. The word is what the so-called 'method of words and things' relies on. The method, we object, is atomistic. It verges on treating words as things. The danger could be averted on the condition that the historian has oral traditions of the period to consult, which make up for the linguistic shortage of information. Even then, proper nouns very often feature in those traditions that nobody can bring home anymore, like the name Mabumbuga in the royal hymn (see Chapter 3), possibly relating to a cult founder, which 'cultural heroes' in legends often are. Artists cherish the indexicality of specific names for its capacity of innuendo. The unease with indexicality and disregard for it, which amounts to 'lexicological positivism' if allowed to determine our view of history, can be shown to systematically (mis)direct Vansina's gaze, not coincidentally away from medicine.

The origin of a word, in this book too, is a clear-cut starting point to reconstruct the historical development of the institution it refers to. The method we would not advocate, of words-and-things, does help to imagine the regional pattern of institutions, reflected in proto-Bantu vocabulary, and to trace local modifications, registered with lexicostatistics and glotto-chronology for the modern Bantu languages. Our criticism on the method is the positivism of omitting to say what one cannot see, namely the many ephemeral specific names for institutions without a local generic term. Another criticism concerns the exact opposite tendency: the method shows more than there is. Why would a change of word, even a divergence in its literal meaning, necessarily indicate a change of the institution? *Nogi* and *ngwiboneeji* are synonyms for 'witch', the second an innovation replacing the first, however without changing the meaning. The same goes for *isamva* and *ng'hulugenji*, both meaning ancestor. Those two recent synonyms *ngwiboneeji* and *ng'hulugenji* have a Swahili root (respectively *onea*, to treat badly, and *mkurugenzi*, director) which facilitates the Sukuma healer in reaching non-Sukuma clientele. In both cases the reason for replacement is to evade a recent trend of negative connotation, a local phenomenon that the historian centuries later could never guess.

Finally, in the Sukuma field of medicine, where novelty is stimulated, it is common practice to introduce neologisms (which Bantu monemes stimulate) or loan words (e.g. from an influential neighbouring group). The names take over purely for aesthetical or marketing reasons. Bemba chieftaincy, which very much resembles the Sukuma institution of the *ntemi*, has the word *mfumu* (from *kum*) for the institution – exactly the term the Sukuma reserve for the diviner-healer. Although at a general level confirming the once common semantic root of 'chief' and 'healer', the switch or modified use of the word in the region seems arbitrary. No new institution emerged. It might be that Sukuma imitated prestigious Great Lakes terminology. Healers aspire to fame (*kum*) by signalling fame, in which words and names are tools. Linguistic borrowings and modifications over time appear to develop independently from cultural meaning, against the methodological premise of the linguistic dynamic exposing the cultural dynamic. In any case, cultural diversity does not correspond with linguistic diversity (and neither with political structure), as Vansina (1978: 4) had found out himself much earlier in his study of the internally diverse Kuba society combining matrilineal groups with patrilineal ones and overlapping chiefdoms.

The historical linguist David Schoenbrun (2012: 298) tackled the problem by relying on contexts of use to trace the history of words close to their local meaning. Overlapping fields of connotation direct the linguistic search for common grounds of meaning. Insight in connotations increases with the quality of the corpus. Does meaning, however, derive from semantic chains, which the linguist appends and intertwines? The lexical atoms still lay the groundwork. Our counterpoints in this book draw on the cultural whole, or perspective, we derived from the holistic quest known as ethnography.

The Limits of Social Structure: Revisiting the Ancestral Tradition

Can a perspective be combatted? It can be replaced by another one. Vansina's concept of kingship leans towards the exogenous, Western idiom of the state that foregrounds politics, administration and government. The polity prism shines through in his conviction that the Bantu tradition's 'greatest contribution . . . to the general experience of humanity' is in 'the sociopolitical realm', which he moreover considers the essential first domain of study for getting to know a community (PR xiii, 101). He shows the rich tapestry of political systems in the rainforest, which roused fellow historians from their slumber, many of them until then denying equatorial Africa anything other than one and the same static 'neo-lithic polity'. However, his price for specializing into the political is to obscure endogenous logic. We should acclaim, on an ethical basis if nothing else, his dismissal of popular stereotypes about the primitive rainforests; that 'society here was congruent with kinship, not kingship' (PR 5). The latter institution, however, seems for him the sublime outcome of human history and is his implicit point of reference, which raises the risk of an imperfection he always warned about – anachronism.

How apt are sociostructural approaches for capturing endogenous process? Vansina's ancestral tradition of equatorial Africa is couched in terms of social structure, with the addition of a psychological motive. To sum up: the house (a residential unit of bilateral kin), the village and the district are three socio-spatial units that interlock to form a polity, respectively ruled by a big man, a headman and, in case of centralization, a chief or king. The relative influence of the three units has shifted in history, milestones being situated in the years 1000,

1500, 1700 and 1880. Spatially, the protagonists are the western, central and eastern parts of the Congo basin rainforest. Within this shifting field of power stands supreme the competition between big men intent on keeping their autonomy.

A counterargument immediately crops up. Is this tradition characteristic for the region? The socio-spatial units and autonomy can be found in eastern Africa as well, and far beyond. Without a non-arbitrary rationale such as a group's endogenous logic, the tradition has no spatial or temporal confines, as attested by Vansina's own minimizing of the ancestral tradition suddenly at the end of his overview (PR 127): 'Are the changes not of such a magnitude as to eclipse the common origin and render it of no moment? House, village, district, and big men as leaders never really went away, but how much does this matter in the face of the very different houses, villages, districts and leaders found by the mid nineteenth century in different parts of the inner basin?' The answer will not come from more social structure. Cultural structure explains why the equatorial tradition did not abruptly lose its endogeneity or momentum, despite the colonizer's interventions in the social structure of groups and power elites in the district (PR 245). In the next section a cultural value, namely autonomy, will cast doubt on the 'sacredness' of headmanship, which Vansina is compelled to deduce from data denied their basic medicinal quality.

A baseline is necessary to compare societies at different moments and infer change. We chose as baseline an ethnographic experience because of its cultural, endogenous logic. The holism of the latter has more validity for our comparison than the historical accuracy of a set of disparate cultural traits. Vansina systematically opted for the set of cultural-linguistic atoms. His wish however has always been to capture the cultural tradition. Therefore, already about his earlier research on the Kuba, Vansina (1978: 88) had expressed his 'nagging dissatisfaction' with what was principally a court history. His book *The Children of Woot*, which will be discussed in Chapter 8, 'reopened the case'. He reworked the data on the Kuba kingdom that had been collected twenty years earlier and published in Dutch. The theoretical question of an insider's (emic) approach to culture, which we will see lacking in his Tio monograph, received attention in a chapter on 'the Kuba sense of their history' (PR 15). Vansina lucidly applied Braudel's distinction between history as a flow of events and as a trend to emphasize that the first is a much rarer catch in precolonial African history than the second (PR 10). In defence of the second, our Chapter 9 on Rwandan kingship will show oral traditions revealing a local view on change and the initial cultural structure, indirectly detectable and sometimes explicitly couched in time-honoured reflections on historical trends. Vansina instead stressed the historical accuracy of events. In the Kuba study the first rays of his words-and-things approach glistened. Thanks to the linguistic data, the first cracks appeared in his historical materialism, although in the form of rather inconsequential observations: 'Religious practice was more uniform in the kingdom than was social organization' (PR 319, n10; he realizes the overrepresentation on political history, PR 11). If not relegated to a footnote, the insight could have led to studying the role of cosmology, for instance divination, in decision making, and might have changed our idea of the motor of centralization.

Making no secret of the 'ethnographic present' (PR 90, n1) he must surrender to by stretching the temporal validity of collected data, he courageously delved into the scanty ethnographic record on Mongo-speaking peoples in the past century to deduce what the forebears of the Kuba were like around 1500. His baseline to reconstruct the history of the Kuba resulted from comparing linguistic and ethnographic data about southern Mongo and Kuba, and deriving their commonalities. How could one otherwise for oral societies without archival records before 1892? The obtained set of disparate cultural elements raises a methodological problem though. The Kuba of the earliest recorded period determine both the baseline (of cultural commonalities) and the end result (of previous historical change). By lack of archaeological data, errors must be averted through linguistic evidence and through dynastic periodization of oral traditions and concepts therein. The dupe of the method, however, is insight in the endogenous process we have proposed, from divinatory society to ceremonial state. To take the important example of the spirits of ancestors, surprisingly they are not venerated by the Kuba. Might they not have been at some time in the past, until their divinatory unpredictability cost them support from the autocrats who built the Kuba state? Diviners could capitalize on popular belief in ancestral spirits to play a vital part in countervailing the possible hegemony of a king. Logically, the reversion away from belief in ancestral spirits during a distant and unknown past will lower the salience of this institution in the baseline of recorded data. If the institution of ancestral sacrifice is not included in the baseline, and no oral tradition (carefully sanctioned by the court) currently mentions it, we cannot know its role in earlier systems of rule, nor estimate whether the kings abolished it.

The ethnographic holism of a cultural logic, admittedly without accurate timeframe, should mitigate the risk of projecting fractured bits from a partially shrouded past. Figure 4.1 situates our histor-

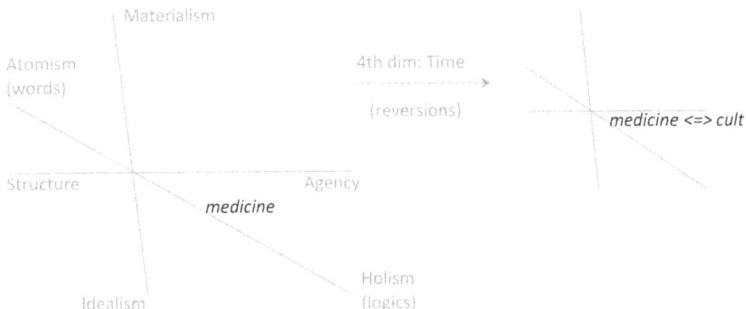

Figure 4.1 The social and cultural structure of rule in a historical whole. Figure by the author.

ical anthropology, as envisaged in the Introduction, somewhere in the middle between holism and atomism, the third dimension in our anthropological approach. The fourth dimension was time, which the figure expresses in a warped copy of the three-dimensional axes. The 4D approach should shed light on the reversible evolutions, among others between divinatory and ceremonial society, and between medicine and cult, which feature further on.

Inner Congo: The Mongo Centralization towards Sacred Kingship

To all intents and purposes, anthropology without history is as pointless as the inverse. Positivist, etic (outsider's) accounts fail as soon as a cultural perspective partakes of the reality studied, which is mostly the case in the humanities. Much escapes the outsider's gaze that fieldwork would have brought into view. For example, archaeologists unearthing many metal objects in the Mongo area, despite the rarity of ore, are entitled to presume trade in that area (PR 104). Such etic reasoning cannot be applied with the same assurance, though, to infer cultural elements such as values, which are articulated in intentions.

Linguistic indications of a Crow system of kinship in Mongo society around AD 1000 convince Vansina that wealth and patrimony became central values and that the accumulating family ('house') overshadowed the village. In Crow kinship, the children of a woman for whom bridewealth was paid are greeted as if of a higher generation than the children of the bridewealth's recipient. From this system, Vansina concludes that '[f]or the Mongo, a woman was not quite of equivalent worth to the valuables given as bridewealth' (PR 103, cf. 152). His interpretation misses the point in societies where this greeting of one's aunt's children as of the parental generation anticipates the situation of levirate whereby the wife and children of the deceased recipient of bridewealth will be inherited by the aunt's son. The institution indicates a preoccupation with social security for fatherless families, possibly due to times of war or epidemic. Moreover, most Bantu-speaking societies have at some point separated the spheres of exchange, for instance between commodities, prestige goods and people. In these, people should not be compared to things. Bridewealth (or 'brideprice') is not the price for a bride, but an intermediate gift by the bride-taker awaiting the return gift one day of a woman from his clan to the bride-givers.[3] Therefore, the institution of bridewealth suggests prolonged relations of debt and credit between residential families (clan sections) who built alliances in a growing network, wherein women's compliance is essential. Confirming the network of alliances are Vansina's own data on villages becoming 'allies' (*noko*) after intermarriage (PR 105).

Another novelty in Mongo society was that the spoils of a leopard hunt, hardly of any purpose save ceremonial, had to go to the headman of the senior village of the district (PR 109). This piece of evidence points to a network of ritual and cultic significance. If, according to Vansina, the patrilineal system was most efficient in defending the community against invaders (PR 111), we append that the matrilineal network supported by such cultic as well as marital alliance need not be less so. Indeed, just north of the Mongo, the Doko villages adopting *noko* alliance and resisting patrilinearity 'swelled to towns'. The authority of the founder-headman grew, which 'was attributed to supernatural support'; he 'gradually acquired most of the attributes of sacred kingship' (PR 113).

How this important evolution could happen, and gradually so, we do not get to hear. Why would belief in the sacredness of the king take several generations to grow? What then was the intermediate phase, between headman and sacred king? Most of all, about that alleged sacredness: is it plausible that egalitarian groups of hunters would begin to worship one of their fellows? Given the emphasis on each house's autonomy that all scholars seem to agree on, it is more likely that hegemony was counterbalanced from the start, in the form of spirit reciprocity. The leopard had to be brought to a man with a rank of ritual value, but that did not mean that he was sacred. The ritual features of the developing kingship had a medicinal basis, we argue, rather than a religious one. Otherwise the big men and their communities would no longer have 'autonomy' (cf. PR 119).

Re-aggregating East and Central Africa, Politics and Religion

The rest of this chapter will scrutinize Vansina's comparison of the three areas sharing the equatorial tradition: the western, central and eastern areas of the Congo basin rainforest. Each would be a variant of political centralization. In this view, big men, a notion from Melanesian anthropology, gradually grew into kings, while religion in the form of magic and ritual was their legitimating practice. Our endogenizing effort will consist in undoing this explanation refracted by the polity prism, and in questioning his assumption that the kingdoms of Kongo, Loango and Tio in the south-west of the Congo basin, on which his thesis is based, exemplify the original model of the region. Because of his focus on these kingdoms, he presented as an exception the eastern uplands of Congo. There no less than a transcultural network of initiatory medicinal cults controlled precolonial society at district level. The situation bears out our conclusions in the previous chapter on the medicinal dimension of the political.

Moreover, about the western area, as the last chapter of Part II will demonstrate, Vansina's (1973) detailed monograph on Tio society allows us to revisit some of the conclusions he drew in 1990. The monograph could hardly conceal that the king and chiefs are masters of the forest, summoned by the spirit and initiated after which they obtain a shrine. It is an important observation for the entire western part of the Congo basin, since he identified the Tio kingdom as coming closest to the original system from which the three kingdoms developed.

What probably tilted the balance for him and his followers, all about to get trapped between cultic and political readings, were the data on the central area of the rainforest. Here the ideology and institution of *nkumu*, the chieftain, dominated. We put his methodology to the test by verifying whether 'the tesserae of evidence' speak for themselves. Do the historian's atoms denuded of cultural structure unequivocally articulate the whole they portray? The next fragment is quoted at length to underline the perspectival decision taken by Vansina, which was slanted away from the most probable, medicinal track of interpretation.

> The traditions do not tell us how the ideology of nkúmú arose. Thanks to a painstaking study by E.W. Müller, we know how the institution spread among the Ekonda, the eastern neighbors of the Bolia. When a rich man wanted recognition by his peers as an exceptional achiever, he took the title nkúmú during a lavish feast to which the great leaders of the vicinity were invited, especially those who had already taken such a

title. At this feast the candidate was given a bit of the sacred emblem of his colleagues and was then entitled to wear or display other emblems, plant special trees around his compound, and assume special etiquette and taboos. He also in turn gave honorific titles, recognized by all, to some of his spouses, junior kin, and followers. Henceforth all would accept the leader's pretensions and honor him as nkúmú. In some villages several nkúmú could coexist and their feasts were less lavish than in other villages, where only one leader could be nkúmú at any given time. (PR 121–22)

This fragment is supposed to ooze (political) leadership and (religious) sacredness, yet none of these, nor governance or worship, are manifest. The co-existence of *nkumu* chiefs in one village in fact belies the very idea of sovereignty. The medicinal exchange in return for gifts is exactly how members of spirit cults today climb the ranks, and occupy positions entitling them in turn to bestow titles such as chief or chieflet on their followers.

The author sums up the origin of kingship in Bantu-speaking groups. *Nkumu*, with cognates *kum, fum* and *pum* as its linguistic root, is the common word for king or chief in the Congo basin (as it is for healer towards the east we argued). Neatly in line with his hypothesis of big men ruling villages and after centralization growing into supreme authorities, Vansina follows the German ethnologist Ernst Wilhelm Müller (and Erika Sulzman referring to the '*dorfhauptling*', village headman) in emphasizing leadership, that is the political rather than religious or medicinal aspects in the local development of kingship. The cited fragment describes the bestowing of a title by men who have already taken the title. Why does the author not acknowledge the initiation that is plain to see? The initiation is medicinal as the newly initiated receives plant knowledge and charms. The portrayal conjures up the Lemba cult as depicted by Janzen (1982: 4), with its initiatory healing, lavish feast and ensuing permission to initiate others.[4] One clan head actually told Janzen that the consecrated medicine (*nkisi*) of Lemba aimed at 'ruling' (*wangyaadila*; ibid.: 5). Similarly, MacGaffey (1986: 17) writes about precolonial Kongo that 'chiefship itself was an expensive form of initiation into one of the many cults'. The investiture of a *mfumu mpu* can only take place after he has fallen ill and been secluded for a year (ibid.: 149–50). That by all means recalls the healer's vocation. Chiefs were 'persons initiated to the cult of a particular spirit on behalf of the groups they represented' (ibid.: 148). As indicated by the word for investiture, *kubyala*, which the KiKongo dictionary translates as 'to rule, or to be consecrated' (ibid.: 150), enthronement is an initiation. In KiSukuma, it means 'to generate, give birth', and in the passive form, *kubyalwa*, 'to be invested' as well as 'to be born', the metaphor is used for becoming initiated to enter an association (as well as for the groom allying with a new family through marriage).

As we dig deeper into authors' interpretive frameworks, familiarity with medicinal practice seems an asset. An informant in one of the Laman archives consulted by MacGaffey wrote that the medicinal charm did not exist in the early version of the rite (ibid.: 149). According to the author, that would render magic a later elaboration of the initiation (ibid.: 151). We thus understand his focus on religion instead of magic or medicine. But can there be a rite without magic? If his religious focus is meant to counter the political interpretation, the dupe is medicine. Spirit possession comes in as a close second for it is only briefly mentioned in MacGaffey's study of 'Kongo religion' (ibid.: 161). How could initiation or therapy after affliction be possible without the discontinuous moment represented by the spirit's calling? Interventions always entail magic in some form, whether an ancestral obligation, a mnemonic bracelet or a protective charm. The source of one's promise to the ancestor is oracular, not written down but materialized in medicine or charm (cf. the common stem of Bantu words 'medicines', *bilongo*, and 'taboos', *min'longo*). The concurrence of magic and spirit possession is also demonstrated in the hunters' divinatory societies discussed in Part I. The *nkumu* aspects, comprising the high rank, the heading, the communication with spirits, the emblems and the secret knowledge, converge in the concept of medicine.

For Vansina, however, medicine and initiation are religious practices that evoke the field of ideology. The mediumistic condition muddles up the polity prism, and so we read: 'The one who did the most miraculous thing, and there was always a purported miracle, was the choice of the nature spirits. . . . [B]elief in the supernatural basis of the nkúmú's authority . . . reinforced the whole institutional complex' (PR 122). The matter and cultural innovations of plants and charms fade into the background. Mediumship serves to legitimate chief- and kingship; medicinally based initiatory status signifies sacredness. That the holder 'became a sacred person' is simply countermanded, I argue, by the proliferation of titles (PR 125). The 'even more exalted status by giving another feast' after which he could drop the taboos very much recalls the consecration ceremony every initiated member of the Chwezi cult has undergone, as I have in 1999, two years after initiation.

Big men with growing houses wanted the *nkumu* title out of vanity or a search for prestige, and as a 'springboard for further expansion' (PR 123), therefore they made 'payments to the higher-titled chiefs'

(PR 125). It is hard to believe that the big men suddenly accepted higher ranks unless these did not weaken their autonomy (in a Western political sense) but continued the cultic network. Surely, each installation as *nkumu* was not 'a great potlatch' but a treat to the already initiated. The more centralizing effect of the title was the unforeseen development. In many cases '[t]he title itself gradually disseminated farther without leading to the formation of chiefdoms' (PR 123). In several groups the *nkumu* emblems proliferated in a 'titled association', the village association of big men in some societies functioning as a 'government by association' at the district level (PR 125). Could we then not turn Vansina's argument on its head: the chiefdoms that were rather exceptionally engaged in the governance of militarily conquered lands were an outgrowth of an originally cultic institution and network?

Linguistic support may be provided for our ethnographic definition of medicinal rule in the Introduction. The proto-Bantu root *kum*, referring to the *nkumu* system, has a 'proto-meaning' suggestive of the endogenous model of rule from which chiefs and kings evolved. We are hinting at a meaning preceding the distinction between the concepts of 'healer' and 'chief'. In Bantu-speaking Africa the ancient term for ruler, with the root *kum* or *fum* (proto-Bantu *pum*), bifurcated over time to primarily mean 'chief' in the south-western parts (see BLR3, 3746 KUMU in Guthrie's Bantu zones L and M),[5] and to primarily mean 'healer' in the eastern parts (see BLR3, 2118 KUMU, for the long list of zones). If a proto-Bantu language was shared by the emigrants from the Cameroon Grassfields, then we should consider proto-meanings of the terms that spread along with them. According to Schoenbrun (1997: 203), Great Lakes Bantu is the protolanguage of the noun with stem *kum(u)* glossed as 'healer, diviner'. He proposes as an etymology: 'Innovation by semantic shift from older meaning of chief, leader, respected person'. The suggestion characteristic of historical linguistics is that the older meaning corresponds to a known concept in the researcher's language, in this case 'chief'. The two supplemental translations, leader and respected person, appropriately broaden the semantic scope. Are they, however, cultural translations? Endogenous logic implies that the arisen innovation is related to and thus tells something about the original meaning. Eastern Bantu has not simply borrowed *kum* from the west. It gave a new meaning.[6] Since the new meaning of the old word is widespread and applied in several forms, nouns, verbs as well as adjectives, we may assume that the new meaning (healer) specializes in an aspect of the older concept (proto-chief/healer). The semantic layer (governing) blanked out by this innovation may be filled in by a new word (chief), the two words together revealing a bifurcation within a family of languages. The next paragraphs explain the endogenous logic whereby the proto-meaning of *kum* becomes in western Bantu a king or chief, and in eastern Bantu a healer-diviner. Dapper in the seventeenth century described Loango possessed leaving the forest with 'their prohibition' imposed by a spirit (see Part I). The personal taboo they obtained lent power to found a new cult. The coming-out ceremony was the foundational event. The semantic (and possibly linguistic) connection with the verb *ku-fuma*, 'to come out', will lead us to translate proto-chief/healer *kum* as 'coming-outer'.

With this cultural logic in mind, the historian can select the connotations and semantic relations that tie terms together in the lists of lexical reconstructions. For example, in Rwanda, *fum* (*umupfumu* in full) is a 'diviner, magician; representative of *imáana* [the supreme being] to protect against calamities caused by *abazimu* (the ancestral spirits)' (Schoenbrun 1997: 204). Some background knowledge is required. Except in highly professionalized settings, the diviner is usually a healer, and vice versa, because communication with spirits and mastery over animals and plants go together. Before professionalization, chief and healer are almost interchangeable functions in terms of responsibility. They should entertain reciprocal relations with a spirit, blessing the collective, and preventing group calamities. The diviner-healer specializes in a capacity that all adults have acquired to some extent since their adolescence.

Fame, *lu-kumo*, is a key concept for Sukuma farmers living south of Lake Victoria to describe their desire to expand the social network through descendants, cattle and the accumulation of cult memberships. We note that the Bantu lexicologies of 'fame' (*kumo*) as well as of 'healer' (*fum/kum*) drawn up by linguists of the BLR3 project fail to mention the Sukuma-Nyamwezi linguistic zone F, located between C and E. Neither does Schoenbrun (1997) mention *mfumu* for the Sukuma language. The influences of medicinal cults via chiefs emigrating from zone J, Rwanda and Burundi, can explain this linguistically unexpected strong cultural tie, especially in the south (*dakama*) of the Sukuma-speaking region, and hence the spread of loan-words regarding medicine. Used in parallel to *nganga*, medicine man, the word *mfumu* stands for an influential healer, who has the potential to innovate tradition and start a cult of his own. The anthropologist can further help the linguist by detailing the semantics: fame and healership fit together, hence the possibly common root. For Sukuma farmers, there could be no genuine fame unless it is medicinally based. Chiefs and kings must be medicinally superior. A person who came out of an ordeal or seclusion is reborn and ready to head a family, to heal and lead in fame. That acquisition of power is what the *ihane* village initiation replicates. Schoenbrun's (1997: 204) example of the Rundi use of *kum* supports our thesis on the medicinal model of power: 'That former Hutu family who "became" titled healers and married Tutsi women'. Through the acquisition of the medicinal title a family achieves a transformation of status. Across the region the institution of kingship adopts the same principle. The successor is called by the spirit to undergo an initiation, often headed by an elder representing the autochthonous population. After the seclusion and coming out, he is the owner of a powerful, medicinal shrine – expressing fertility, mostly in the savannas in the form of rainmaking medicine, and in the more humid climates of central Africa in the shape of water spirit charms at a waterfall or lake.

A final remark on the cited key fragment is necessary. Vansina dates the origin of the *nkumu* system. What is he actually dating? No more than a name it seems. The timeframes he juggles with are so recent, from the end of the fourteenth century to the early seventeenth century (PR 121), that we should ask which system preceded the *nkumu*, and which one came before that, and so on. I argue that we have no reason to conceive of *nkumu* differently before the rise of the system among the Ekonda, and its later development into the Kuba kingdom. The proto-Bantu *kum* harks back to the five thousand years of cultural tradition the author sought to uncover, and not to a few centuries of recent history. It is interesting to note the historiographic difficulty of studying the endogenous process. Endogeneity has no chance of appearing if the unit of analysis is a certain institution at a given point in time. The more we focus on historical origin, on the *chronos* in chronology and on an institution 'arising', the less chance we have of insight into the endogenous source of cultural creativity.

The Associational Model

The hypothesis of initiatory associations, defined as socially structured cults, reproducing an endogenous logic that eventually resulted in chieftaincy and kingship, has never been tested, although the data point in that direction. Many a regional expert has momentarily toyed with the idea, before casting it away. 'In a remote past', Vansina writes with unusual imprecision due to the absence of glottochronological data, and in an area as wide as Congo's whole western area as well as Nigeria and the Cameroon grasslands, 'secret societies' for men and women contributed to the cohesion of villages and the district (PR 130, cf. 136). Hunters, who were used to associational life, conditioned the evolution into an agricultural and trading network.[7] Nevertheless, Vansina deems it logical that the Nge association of men regulating relations between houses and the district in western Congo around AD 1500 was 'a counterinnovation' against the patrilineages of neighbouring Sanaga-Ntem speakers (PR 134). Why would the patrilineage, an agricultural enterprise, not be a reaction against the association with hunters' roots? A corporate lineage group steels the young men's spiritual loyalty to their divinatory society of shamanic initiation. Grown up with the Western ideal of the nuclear family, we tend to think of associations as a cultural achievement overcoming our natural tendencies from which kingship universally evolved. Lévi-Strauss (1949) grounded society itself in the rule prohibiting incest and stipulating social exchange beyond the kin group. The kin group, or 'house', is supposed to be the endogenous social structure of the Nge, while the initiatory association would be an exogenous factor, whose occurrence needs to be explained.[8] If we, however, admit as our perspective the band of hunters (or closer to home, in case of adolescents, the weekend peer group) on whose success each livelihood depends, the nuclear family with strictly established blood relations rather constitutes the supplemental institution needing explanation.

The extent to which Vansina could differentiate local political histories in the Congo basin is impressive: two kinds of segmentary lineage societies, four kinds of associations, five kinds of chiefdoms or kingdoms (PR 191–92). The diversity nuances his process of centralization from big man to king, via chiefdom, principality and dynasty (PR 164). But his model of a nuclear family swelling into a kingdom remains. Given the local tradition of creating cohesion through association, it does not seem obvious to me that the family's patriarch or big man grew into a king. We must figure out what it means for a man to be seen as 'a special type of wizard' possessing a *nkinda* village charm (PR 146).

Centralization is not the only way to socially organize a set of villages, or a district. The first linguistic trace of centralization, which may predate AD 1000, is *nkani* translated as 'judge', someone reconciling between residential groups, possibly through divination. Later followed the chief, termed 'master of the land' (*ngaa n(t)si*; PR 147–49). His function, Chapter 7 will argue, started within the association as a rank specializing in land- and forest-oriented responsibilities corresponding to local nature spirits (*nkira*) managed through charms (*nkisi*), after the example of the 'earth-priest' in the west of the wider area of Niger–Congo speakers. North of the three kingdoms of Kongo, Loango and Tio, before these radically influenced the region, the default structure was a stateless centralization in the form of a village association for boys and a spirit-based society for adult men gathering at the village shrine, *mbanja* (PR 158–59). Some of these groups, such as the Mbede and Alima-Likouala, went a step further and 'invented an association of chiefs' (PR 161). This too is perfectly in line with the associational model.

The Transition from Charm, Initiation and Association to Kingship

The third geographic area studied by *Paths in the Rainforests* offers the most direct expression of our thesis. The eastern uplands of the Congo basin ascending towards the Great Lakes illustrate how politico-medicinal associations gave way to chiefdoms. The Maniema and their neighbours in the south-east of Congo have, for many centuries, maintained associations, whether voluntary or imposed (brotherhoods), determining the power relations beyond the village level. The cases we end with here are pronounced versions of a cultural structure less visible in other groups. The next chapters will pay most attention to those latent cases of medicinal rule, because the plausibility of our thesis is predicated on their successful reinterpretation.

The chiefs of Bashu clans in north Kivu are not sovereigns, we gather from Packard's (1981) study in the vicinity of Beni. Packard pursued the symbolic-anthropological course of Luc de Heusch, the intellectual counterpart of his supervisor Jan Vansina. He framed the clash between Bashu paramount and colonial government as cultural: the chief knew that his people judged him on the basis of the rains and annual harvests, and that he would lose their allegiance if acting as their supreme administrator as the colonizer expected (ibid.: 169). Were these data no blow to the polity prism? Furthermore, the chiefs in this eastern part of Congo, approximating the area of my ethnographic research, do not form a pyramidal hierarchy. Bashu sustain cross-cutting alliances with other clans within the encompassing Nande group: the Bashu chief receives tribute from the Baswanga and in turn pays tribute to the Basongora (Kisangani 2016: 462). One could not expect otherwise from cults and their kind of rule.

The endogenous logic of initiation and association, subtended by divination and medicine (cf. the four aspects of medicinal rule in the Introduction), accounts for the ease by which a certain element can historically evolve into another, and back. An exemplary case is the *mambela* association, originating among the Bali living at the Aruwimi river. The cult began as a collective village initiation. Whether or not as a reaction, like Vansina argues, against the threat of Mabodo in the south organized in patrilineal segmentary lineages ready for war, the initiations got at some point linked one after the other to create a network of allied villages (PR 174). That network became a cult with a war leader, *kam*, the term used north of the Great Lakes for 'king' (PR 175; cf. Makama in Bunyoro). A similar example is *lilwa* circumcision among the Mbole, a rite that transformed into an initiatory association (PR 183). The same rite can be of passage or of healing depending on social context (see Part I). The transition from rite to cult epitomizes the birth of medicinal rule. The alternative transition, equally product of the endogenous logic, is the popularity of a medicine giving way to a cult. In response to Zande invasions, the Mangbetu turned the *nebeli* war charm (cf. *biri* charms in north-western Bantu) into an expansive association (PR 177). In brief, ritual initiation, medicinal charm and cult are cognatic institutions giving way to each other. Together with divination, they constitute the pivots we proposed for medicinal rule.

How come these transitions did not inspire Vansina to posit an endogenous model of rule? As argued, the method of historical linguistics that lent ground to trace historical developments at the same time tied him down to what was retrievable via lexicon and oral literature. Like cloth and wood in archaeology, the proper names of most cults founded by once formidable individuals leave little or no trace after a few generations. Initiatory associations do not require a generic term, just as the proverbial water imperceptible to fish. When people do categorize them, they may use the word for a conspicuous element, such as the dance, *mbina*, or the drum, *ngoma*.

The three groups that migrated to the eastern uplands were the northern Maniema speaking a mix of Buan and Sudanic languages, the southern Maniema with mixed eastern and western Bantu background, and the eastern Bantu from the Great Lakes. Vansina writes: '[T]here is no evidence that any type of association was important in any of these traditions at the time of their immigration, although rituals of circumcision may have been' (PR 178). Next to the fact that absence of linguistic proof is no evidence to the contrary either, as we have argued, he underestimates the cultural interconnectedness and mutual intelligibility between groups whose common origins date back to the early Bantu expansions and whose healers continued to travel (like Sukuma to Beni region to buy aggressive magic). The circumcision rites whose wide occurrence he cannot deny carry the ritual principles within. Their potential for association, within and beyond the village, is dormant and easily activated. The rites are simply unthinkable without medicine and medicinal knowledge transmitted to the boys. Vansina may have momentarily thought so too. In a footnote, some retrospective doubts crop up about his own interpretation of the data. We catch him reasoning aloud, following archaeological evidence by Pierre de Maret (1985) and observations by Biebuyck, that the shell currency dating from AD 800 in the area must have been for social payments, which would date in a distant past the primacy of association before chieftaincy (PR 180, n40 and n43). Would it make his position tumble, about big men embodied in chiefs? More evidence was at his disposal to suggest that cult and kingship are cultural cognates. The terms *bwami* and *mwami* – respectively for the association of the Lega people, which had governing duties, and for the king of nearby Rwanda – have a common linguistic root (PR 183).

Recovering his poise, Vansina grants political primacy only to the voluntary association of the southern Maniema. The reason he gives is that people explicitly refer to this cult's history (e.g. changes of rites and titles) to chronicle their past (PR 181). Only 'associations' would assign political status. 'Brotherhoods' would not be political but teach medicine only. The first would be proper to the southern Maniema, the second to the northern Maniema (PR 180). The distinction between association and brotherhood safeguards his analysis but is artificial, reiterating Turner's watershed division. Because both institutions initiate into medicine, the one readily spills over into the other, as in the case above of *mambela* and *lilwa* village initiations transforming into medicinal societies. Still today, Sukuma 'brotherhoods' could not survive without assigning ranks in return for large treats of beer, which translate into community-wide social status. The medicine and divination acquired in an adolescent's village initiation concords with and prepares for membership in the other medicinal associations when older.[9]

Medicine can be dreamt by an individual, suddenly gain massive renown, spark off a cult as in the Mangbetu example, and undermine older associations to replace them, as witnessed in the past century in Sukuma communities. In contrast, once a dynastic clan monopolizes the medicinal charm, not just anyone can compete to head the dynasty. This fact may explain the relative stability of kingdoms. Wealth and members/commoners are accumulated under the same name and will not stop growing unless the dynasty itself is undermined. Royal dynasties are more liable to endure and thus to be encountered by historians as examples of centralization. Patent examples of medicinal rule without dynastic basis are exceptional, although they exist. In the eastern uplands, *bukishi* was an overarching 'secret' (more exactly medicinal) association that governed Songye groups under guidance of an elected head living at a sacred grove, *eata*. Occupants of higher ranks were removable 'chiefs' (PR 183) as befits the associational model. Northern Maniema looks like the seam between the central African and eastern African practices of medicinal rule, because here *bufumu* associations met *nkumi* associations (PR 183) with the same purpose and linguistic root (*kum*).

Such testimony to the sociocultural interconnectedness of the whole inner basin did not convince Vansina. He was adamant about associations of a decentralized polity not planting the seeds of chieftaincy (PR 191). Despite their dominance in decision making in northern Maniema, he objected to considering the brotherhoods as 'ruling' (PR 190). Only during an actual ritual performance were they supposedly active (PR 189). The polity prism cloaks the informal power inhering initiation, which the ethnographic fieldworker has observed. A polycentric society considers autocratic kingship, and any imposition of hegemony on autonomous families, as a deviation from the tradition. In this part of the world, as soon as a state is in crisis or fails to garner the costly means to rule, the community reverts to a deeper track. Informal networks take over, including medicinal associations. One of many examples was the *ndunga* association regulating trade in Kongo during waning kingship in the nineteenth century (PR 221, cf. 225).

Indeed, just as rites and medicines can grow into cults, and as cults can become territorial and centralize to found a hierarchy with a king, those politico-medicinal systems can lose momentum and disintegrate to be superseded by associational networks. The region's history exhibits an alternation and reversion between cult and kingship, instead of a linear evolution towards kingship.

Notes

1. This was the gist of the counterpoint that Vansina (1995: 194) later put forth based on new linguistic data: any 'vast migration' must have been exceptional. Like the ripples of water left by a pebble thrown into a pond, he analogizes, the spread of language can be mistaken for the movement of people. Many spikes of diffusion took place. Still, in discerning the main directions, Vansina lowered the resolution of the picture, if less so than Oliver did in his sketch of the 'Bantu expansion'.

2. Associations and rituals from elsewhere are a less obvious reality and seem worth remembering lexically if they have a trait deviating from the common model. For instance, the Sukuma concept of *bubeni* refers to the cults of ritual murder of innocent victims, for which the Beni region in eastern Congo, 'to the west' (*ng'weli*), had built a reputation (PR 175, n23).
3. The intermediate gift of bridewealth itself requires a counter-gift of valuables sooner or later, cf. the opening, return and intermediate gifts in Kula circuits in Melanesia (Malinowski 1922).
4. To illustrate the correspondence with *nkumu*, we quote Janzen (1982: 4) in full: 'In typical drum of affliction manner, Lemba doctor-priests took the "sufferer" in hand and administered the initial purification. If he could muster further sponsorship, he would undergo full therapeutic initiation before the priests and priestesses of the locality. A ceremonial Lemba marriage with his leading wife, a lavish feast for Lemba priests and priestesses as well as for the public, and extensive instructions made up part of the initiatory ritual, before the priestly couple were qualified to themselves perform Lemba's therapy'.
5. We rely on 'Bantu Lexical Reconstructions 3' (BLR 3), based among others on Malcolm Guthrie's classification of Comparative Bantu. The BLR 3 database was consulted at the Royal Museum for Central Africa's (RMCA) website http://www.africamuseum.be/collections/ browsecollections/ humansciences/blr.
6. Therefore Vansina's general warning seems not to apply here: 'It is not uncommon for a protowestern Bantu form to be later borrowed by eastern Bantu languages bordering on western Bantu languages and vice versa. The reflexes on the genetic tree then give a false impression and lead the analyst to attribute the ancestral form mistakenly to proto-Bantu' (PR 13).
7. The traps, *-teg*, the hunters set become in their trading network the word used for selling (PR 147, 295).
8. Misapprehension of local affects also shows in the European discomfort about the Bantu custom of intra- and extra-familial adoption of non-orphans.
9. Corroborating the affinity we proposed between rituals for healing and those for social status acquisition, the *bunamhala* induction among Sukuma elders used to be preceded by the *busumba* initiation at a younger age whereby a healing ritual set the scene for the youngsters' rite of passage (cf. *esomba* and *umba* rituals of manhood, PR 188).

Chapter 5

FROM CULT TO DYNASTY
NILOTIC AND NIGER–CONGO EXTENSIONS

Local myths of origin portray the first kings – those who did not import the institution from elsewhere – as spirit mediums.[1] Why should we reject the historical value of that portrayal? We have no reason to imagine gullible commoners indoctrinated by oral traditions of courtiers justifying divine kingship. Oral traditions, linguistic uniformities and archaeological traces of, among others, mining shafts indicate that the Mutapa empire associated with Great Zimbabwe grew in the fourteenth century from the nuclear Karanga empire 'founded by a certain NeMbire from north of the Zambezi' (Abraham 1964: 106). With our hypothesis in mind we may delve into the following bit of oral tradition: 'He adopted the title "NeMbire", which he passed on to his descendants' (ibid.: 107). His people – who might be cult members – would later be named Mbire. They influenced the material culture of the Rozvi and their king, the *mambo* (ibid.: 108). We obtain an important lead as to the transition from cultic to clan-based rule.

What kind of title could be passed on to descendants, before kingship? A healer initiating his children into his craft could pass his title on, and with it a medicine. The professional job of itinerant medicineman would be too disconnected from a village shrine or cult. The healing came from a cult into which this newcomer from the north, who travelled across the Zambezi, had been initiated. A cultic title that resembles it in eastern Congo is *nibeli*, with the same proto-Bantu stem *bil* (which in Bantu languages is phonetically equivalent to 'bir') and wherein the vowels 'e' and 'i' are interchangeable. Later the royal ancestral spirit cult, *mhondoro*, functioned as an association of mediums (*masvikiro*) who maintained the oral traditions of the court (ibid.:

112). 'Zimbabwe' derives from *madzimbahwe*, the burial place for (royal) ancestors (ibid.: 113). Hence, the medicinal cult did not totally vanish at the court, but something blocks the view for it appearing in historical analysis: by the time a leader is worthy to be perceived by us as royal, settled with a dynastic past, the spirit mediums at the court occupy subordinate functions. They look like 'priests', ideological add-ons to serve kingship. But they specialize in the spirit mediumship of the healer-founder, since spirit-based rule is not evident for a successor chosen on the basis of kinship yet expected to have a vocation like in non-dynastic spirit cults.

We shall turn our gaze to another part of Africa, which according to the rationale in the Introduction should tell us more about the original model of rule in the Cameroun Grassfields from where Bantu speakers emigrated. The ethno-historical record of West Africa exhibits many references to medicinal rule, compelling us to broaden our scope. The relevant geographical expanse brings us beyond the Bantu-speaking area to the inclusive family of Niger–Congo languages.

West African Developments: Title Associations and Lineages

Like the city of Ife for the Yoruba empire of Oyo, the old city of Benin was the capital of the neighbouring empire speaking Edo, a language of the Kwa branch of the Niger–Congo family. Rough estimates suggest that about four thousand years ago the Edo language had begun to diverge from its current neighbours in the west and the east, Yoruba and Ibo respectively (Bradbury 1964: 150). The medicinal quality of reign shows in the fact that after the loss of effective political influence around AD 1400, at the rise of Benin, the city of Ife retained its centrality as a ritual metropolis and home of spirit for the kings (ibid.: 152). The Benin and Yoruba had Oranmiyan as a common ancestor and founder of kingship. Each king (*Oba*) had an *orun*, a spirit double in the sky. An autochthonous group of kingmakers installed the king's heir and received a fee for it (ibid.: 154), which is different from having the backing of divine law; it suggests a previous cultic tradition. The palace had graded associations (ibid.: 157). The kingmakers (Oyo Misi and Uzama) had several titles. These titles now correspond to chiefdoms but once designated statuses, which leads Bradbury to speculate in a footnote about whether the kingmakers 'represent a pre-Oranmiyan phase of political development affecting both the Yoruba and the Edo of Benin' (ibid.: 155, n9). In other words, were the chiefdoms not the territorial reflection of a primary factor, namely a grade or title in a cult?

In the Edo case we see what happens when clans or lineages have no effective control over positions of authority, like the Yoruba lineages have. A cult of unrelated members rules. Initiatory associations with rites by leaders 'to make surpass' (ibid.: 157) the novices, socially cephalize them, distribute the important titles among the Edo. These are non-hereditary titles, open to competition or to the fortune of vocation. The villages in the Benin kingdom were governed on the basis of membership in title associations (ibid.: 158). Among the Yoruba, on the other hand (ibid.: 159), a strong lineage structure prevented the monarchical autocracy that developed in the Edo-speaking state of Benin. Unlike the Yoruba groups, Benin had formerly known a centralized power with 'religious cults' (ibid.: 152).

Might these Niger–Congo associations of rule have developed, independently, from the same cultural structure that spread in equatorial Africa? Since migration typically weakens lineages, the Yoruba path of lineages and clans was less likely in the beginning than the Edo path of cults. Benefactors of the lineage-based privileges have no reason to move away and give up their rights of autochthony. The emigrants, typically younger, could fashion a new political system based on the titled association they knew and in agreement with the autochthonous groups they joined. Emigration meant travelling with a partial political system. The severed bit concerned the loss of autochthony, which opened up the space for rapport with future host populations. Emigration thus conditioned the cultural structure of rule carried along and transmitted across generations.

Nilotic and Bantu Interactions of Rule

The cultural connection with West Africa expands our geographical scope. To the east of the Niger–Congo languages there is room for connection as well. To assume otherwise would be as absurd as excluding cultural influences between Germanic and Romanic peoples in European history on the basis of their linguistic difference. The Nilotes form roughly two categories. The nomadic pastoralist Dinka and Nuer have for centuries roamed a semi-arid territory at the borders of Sudan, Ethiopia and Kenya. The second category, of Lwo-speaking groups, emigrated to the south, consisting among others of Acholi and Alur in the centre and Luo further south (Ogot 1964: 287). The nomadic category sustained stateless societies. In the second group, as was theorized above for Benin, the 'plurality' that comes with migration and with loss of autochthonous tradition facilitated the rise of centralized state and kingship (ibid.: 300).

Ogot distinguishes four types of Nilotic rule (ibid.: 299): kingship (Bunyoro, Shilluk), segmentary state (Alur), an acephalous plurality of royal clans (Acholi, Luo) and the stateless segmentary lineage system (Nuer, Dinka). In the fifteenth century, Cushitic immigrants from Sidamo had introduced Ethiopian crops around Lake Victoria (ibid.: 286). Nilotic influences spread as well. As mentioned earlier, in the same century the Lwo-speaking Babito clan had founded Bunyoro-Kitara after chasing the Bantu-speaking Chwezi dynasty from Kitara (ibid.: 292). Previously, if we follow Ogot, who bases himself on Oberg's study from 1940, the Chwezi had imposed themselves on the Bahima pastoralists and their agricultural Bairu neighbours, which led Bahima to get organized in a state (ibid.: 295). Until then the Bahima disputes had been settled through elders applying the segmentary lineage system like that of the Nilotic Nuer. The kingdom of Ankole, like that of Rwanda, grew in response to the Nilotic Lwo pressures in the region. In the same way, the Nilotic migrants arriving in the socially dynamic and conflictual Interlacustrine region had survived by taking on a more centralized government. The cultural-linguistic distinction between Bantu and Nilotic groups was secondary to the sociopolitical decisions made.

Missing in Ogot's account is the endogenous logic, the pull factor that complements the push factors of conquest and war. The sociopolitical decisions had a divinatory and mediumistic quality, which is not specific to Bantu-speakers. In Nilotic societies with kingship, like among the Shilluk, the founder Nyikango (who was a headman, *jago*) empowering his successors was a medium of the deity Juok. Perhaps the kingship, which implied openness to mediumship as well as pyramidical hierarchy, explains why the Shilluk were the first Nilotic groups to accept Christianity. To call the kingship divine, though, is stretching the facts. The health of the king, independent from the god's will, was believed to affect the state of the nation. It recalls the pull of fertility symbolism encountered across central, eastern and southern Africa.

South-East Africa: The King's Territorial Cult

The collection entitled *The Historical Study of African Religion* by Ranger and Kimambo from 1972 (referred henceforth with the initials AR) can be read as a belated answer to the seminal volume of 1940, *African Political Systems*, edited by Fortes and Evans-Pritchard. The latter book had focused on indigenous politics and economy while treating religion and worldview as unchanging. To remedy the lacuna, Ranger and Kimambo (1972: 2) set out to detail the histories of African religions. These explicitly included Islam and Christianity, without abstracting political history from them.

As historiographers they had no trouble in heeding Evans-Pritchard's (1965b: 17) critique of earlier studies of 'primitive religion' that missed out on ethnographic richness and reduced religion to psychological or sociological causes. Nor did they engage in evolutionist speculations, which Evans-Pritchard warned about, on necessary sequences of events. Carefully proceeding from the present to a slightly more distant past, they put the word 'origins' between quotation marks to indicate its asymptotic nature. The authors could also benefit from debate in the 1960s, actually fuelled by Vansina among others, that demonstrated the religious variety in the kingdoms of the central African savanna. The debate had cogently discarded the thesis of a Sudanic system of divine kingship explaining the political-religious similarities across sub-Saharan Africa. The papers in Ranger and Kimambo had the maturity of foregrounding religious institutions in particular regions.

However, juxtaposed in a conference, the presentations inevitably raised the question of remarkable regional resemblance. The similarities converged on cults, in the broad sense of systems of veneration, that were organized by kings or chiefs in eastern and southern Africa. The main insight of the conference was summed up in the book's introduction and was largely based on the chapter by Matthew Schoffeleers on the M'bona cult in the Lower Shire Valley of Malawi. In his and the two editors' interpretation, the similarities in symbolism between the fertility cults of M'bona in the Lundu monarchy, Dzivaguru in the Mwene Mutapa kingdom of north-eastern Zimbabwe, and Mwari in the Rozvi empire of south-western Zimbabwe, as well as other cultic centres in Mozambique and the Transvaal, point to a common origin (AR 5). All were 'territorial' cults in the sense of being attached to a geographical area and devoted to the fertility of the land. By the time they were the subject of research under the colonial administration, their cosmology had an 'active, personal High God', but Ranger (1973: 596) made the conjecture in a comparative study on the Mwari cult that this god was antedated by *jukwa* water spirits. The spirits were responsible for the life-giving of women and the fertility of the crops. Their locus being water, they conjured up the rains.

In the beginning of the twentieth century, towards the north in the Uluguru mountains of Tanzania, the Kolelo cult organized rituals at a shrine for water spirits in response to people's needs of fertility and fortune. The medicinal cult encompassed a society without monarchy. The rituals happened quite significantly at a waterfall (Gwassa 1972: 207), reminding of Nkwe Mbali's waterfall for making charms, all the way down to the north-west of Congo (see Chapter 7) – Mwari and Mbali may very well be cognatic proper names. Ranger and Kimambo observe that the medicinal ritual catered for the farmers' concerns, suggesting co-origination with 'the agricultural opening up of the southern Tanzanian region' before kingship got involved (AR 7).

Are these observations on a fertility cult to which kingship attached itself in south-eastern Africa not in accordance with our inferences on central Africa, thus bearing out the thesis for the wider region? They would if we limited ourselves to the claim that kings traditionally had ritual tasks. Ritual is not yet medicinal rule. Rituals do not necessarily require the endogenous logic of spirit initiation. The possibility remains that these centralized organizations of collective veneration were an invention by the leader in order to govern land and people like a divine king. That ritualist possibility would be a blow to our thesis on the grass-roots development of kingship out of the cultural structure of medicine (or sometimes concretely out of some medicinal association). Contrasted with the polity prism and the commonsensical model of a chief-levitated-from-headman, our purpose is to defend the idea of a chief-descended-from-cult founder. As a reminder, Kishina addressed the spirit of the first ancestral king as a 'director' in matters of healing. I expect a history of medicinal-divinatory associations (as in the Lele case) bifurcating into non-territorial and territorial versions, with this second version forming centralized states that later subjugated the first version whenever encountering it. The first version of medicinal association can last for many generations and be encountered today. The second version implies a brief transitional phase that can take many forms before kingship and is not unequivocally observable as being a transition, which makes our thesis admittedly more difficult to prove. A king inheriting medicine is not conclusive proof for our thesis on the model of rule. Our thesis necessitates that we at least exclude the invention of religion by an already established leader.

What do the data of Ranger and Kimambo's volume tell us? Sure enough, where the mentioned cults function within a monarchy they lend spiritual support to it. They sacrifice to the dead kings. But a number of elements indicate that the cults were endogenous developments of rule before developing into, or being taken over by, kingship. First of all, statecraft did not lie at the heart of the cult's cosmology since the personalities of the spirits addressed were not dynastic. They could change, subject to historical contingencies, like in today's cults where Danish co-operant spirits possess Sukuma women. Permanent, and thus essential, were the symbols addressing concerns of well-being such as the layout of the cultic headquarters and the ritualized relations between rain, forest, land and fertility, which we come across in the whole region (AR 6). The symbols were not associated with any power group, clan or dynasty.

Secondly, the M'bona symbols – to be subsumed under the medicine, which the authors systematically fail to mention – were not Lundu inventions arising with kingship and after chieftaincy, but a 'secondary diffusion' characteristic of conquest states (AR 6–7). Phiri chiefs presided over the cult before the Lundu kings. Consequently, the latter adopted the local cult. Prior to any form of chiefship, the M'bona already existed among the Mang'anja farmers, who had migrated from Congo. In short, the cults had at some point been made to serve kingship. Would kingship have been possible without the subjugation that transformed initiatory institutions into royal cults?

To name the cults 'territorial', like Africanists did in the 1970s, is somewhat of a misnomer, unless referring to a variable. Territorialization is a process that results from successful internal growth or from appropriation by an already grown organization such as an immigrated lineage. The regional cult covers a territory centrifugally without the borders being fixed. The territory may wax and wane, van Binsbergen (1977) noted about the polarity of Barotse regional cults springing from non-regional cults, and then reverting to a decentralized rhizomatic condition. Ranger and Kimambo give an example of patent territorilization though in Upare, Tanzania, where King Nguta during the *cha-njeku* ritual designated a sacred bull to progress along the borders of the territory to demarcate the Wabwambo state (AR 10).

The cult's mythology changed with the subjugation under kingship. In the founding myths of M'bona by the Lundu as well as Dzivaguru by the Mwene Mutapa the healing-cult founder (Schoffeleers speaks of a prophet) is joined by the newcomer, a king who kills that healer and subsequently dedicates a shrine to his spirit. Also, the cult's theology underwent change following the rise of centralized authority. In this respect Schoffeleers speaks of 'High God' cults, because the spirits are headed by a single divinity who is fairly unique in the region by operating in the same plane as humans, namely responding to their sacrifices and intervening in human affairs, for better or worse. This active involvement of a supreme being seems a later invention, coinciding with people's experience of the changes in the institution of kingship.

Before Christian impact, several local cosmologies had gone through an anti-shamanic phase, specifically where states were forming. The transformed concept of supernatural entity attests to the wider social change. Ranger and Kimambo cite Marthinus Daneel on the personification of Mwari into a deity, this due to the influence of the Rozvi empire. The god 'became less remote through His interest in the political cohesion of His people . . . Mwari could eventually be consulted at His shrines. European presence had temporarily turned Him into a militant God, whereafter He assumed, in addition to His rain-making activities, His present role as champion of traditional law and custom' (AR 24, n11). Was kingship a stage in agricultural history driven by material factors of change such as denser population, climate change and military organization? The anti-shamanic phase, territorialisation, cult subjugation and theistic personification are indications of something else, namely an endogenous process whereby a trait of the cultural structure is subjected to radical change. In the non-monarchic cases, we saw that mediumship and medicine were democratic and idiosyncratic in the form of a personal obligation and a dreamt or personally inherited recipe of plants. Yet, that pivot has transformed into a veneration sanctioned by priests collaborating with the court. It culturally prepared people for a person-oriented rule such as kingship replacing their democratic initiation into medicine. Hence, together with sociostructural factors, kingship grew endogenously out of cultic organization. It is the victory of an offshoot over the stem (see Part III). As emphasized in the Introduction, we do not conceive of cultural evolutions as linear or irreversible; such a concept of evolution has become theoretically and empirically inacceptable. The Lele in Part I alternated between cross-cutting divinatory societies and the orthodox witch-finding cult. The court-based cult of priests is an instance of the latter, which among the Lele did revert to spirit possession.

Respect for the actor's autonomy is what sustained a millennia-long tradition of belief in spirits located in the forest and the practice of shamanic possession open to anybody experiencing it. However, Ranger and Kimambo cite their respondents to situate the origin of spirit possession practices in the decades of sociopolitical upheaval at the end of the nineteenth century (AR 12–13). They propose that the phenomenon of 'democratic' spirit possession, by which they mean spontaneous mediumship without cultic ranks, is that recent. The authors revel in the idea of an African discovery of a free concept of spirit, breaking with the elder's social control over it. We can safely assume that their respondents referred to specifically named practices and not to the phenomenon the authors have in mind. The cultural structure of mediumistic possession experienced by an individual, irrespective of cultic institution, is probably as old as humankind. Spirit possession is logically the first form in which mediumship gets to appear and to become a profession. Whether the spirit is an elder, a natural force, a deity or Danish co-operant depends on historical contingencies.

Moreover, no form of spirit possession, democratic or other, could be said to break with the hierarchy of ranks in cults, because these are not essential for a spirit cult. The ranking of initiation is a subsequent specialization in groups of practising mediums that managed to establish a cult. How would the authors account for the medium retreating alone in the forest of spirits in the Loango kingdom of the seventeenth century, two centuries before the supposed onset in Africa of democratic possession? Today, the cultural structure is reproduced in the speaking-in-tongues of Pentecostal services (cf. AR 13). Had the authors allowed for endogenous process with the inclusion of cultural reversions, they would not have made claims about an invention that conflates a historical practice of a hundred years ago, the institution of spirit possession, and its underlying cultural structure which has taken many forms.

Much advance has been made since the 1970s in the study of African religions. We find an elegant example of endogenous transition and reversion in Wim van Binsbergen's (1977: 169–70) distinction between two cults of Lozi living in Barotseland. The non-regional type, territorially unbound due to autonomous factions, is 'a substratum' out of which a regionally organized cult can grow. Most importantly, to this non-regional condition the cult may return. Sociostructural factors drive the process: the Nzila cult in town gets organized, the Bituma cult in the villages does not. Van Binsbergen cites Parkin's (1966) observation about the capacity of voluntary associations to attune their members to the African city's organizational structure. The objective of our interpretive framework is to discern, on top of the sociostructural, the cultural-endogenous factors that drive cultic changes. Disparate people coming together to organize a ritual initiation, without being associated together in one entity, reproduce a cult, broadly defined as a system of veneration or devotion (to an object, spirit or knowledge). Since the ritual is the same for these groups, they either used to form one network in the past or they share a cultural structure. These disparate groups could easily interlace to become –

revert to – one network. The next step, theoretically, would be their forming a chiefdom.

Southern Extensions: Bemba Shrines of Cult and Chiefship

In the 1930s, as British social anthropology flourished under the guidance of Malinowski and Radcliffe-Brown, a massive amount of fieldwork data from various locations came within the purview of their doctoral researchers. Their analyses of societies inevitably acquired a comparative angle. One of those researchers was Audrey Richards (1940) doing fieldwork in north-eastern Zambia. She framed her description of Bemba governance within the larger cultural comparison of African political systems: a community was not the result of prior conquest, but an outgrowth of migrant groups occupying a habitat for three to seven generations before splitting or moving on as a lineage group. The lineage system therefore structured power and decision making. The member of the descent group with most authority headed the community (ibid.: 83, 94).

Her frame of reference was the village headman combining descent and autochthony as two sources of leadership. In practice, though, his duties were ritual and divinatory, oriented on the village shrine. He also oversaw the small tribute to the chief. Autochthony was his bond with the spirits of the deceased first settlers. The chief of the district had mainly this second source to draw on (ibid.: 103). The chief was chosen among a number of potential matrilineal heirs. Generation was not specified so a clash often took place between the primogeniture of the deceased's classificatory brother and the propinquity in kinship of a sister's son (ibid.: 100). The chief spat blessings over the land (*ukufunga mate*), presided court and heard cases of witchcraft, which for greater chiefs included the organization of the poison ordeal (*mwafi*). The chief acted territorially for ceremonially initiating the annual agricultural cycle. He had his messengers, mostly for his family matters or to accompany a child to be educated in another chiefdom to strengthen alliance. Administrative officers worked for his estate, which had a bigger population in precolonial times.

Beyond the level of the village no general meeting took place. This was unlike the system of the southern Bantu chiefdoms out of which grew the Zulu and Swazi kingdoms, with the *pitso* assembly among the Sotho and the *libandla* among the Nguni (ibid.: 107). Their centralization differed from the growth of ceremonial states in central

Africa and the Great Lakes discussed in Part III. Democratic fuelling of governance is not what medicinal rule is about. The affinity of chiefdom gatherings with the Western concept of democratic government enticed Richards to remark in a tone addressing the British administration that Bemba elders of the community had little say in the affairs of the chiefdom (ibid.: 110). She may have overestimated the democratic value of the chief's general meetings, which rather served the colonial state's central government to impose its policy. Bemba society had a bottom-up structure with decentralized decision making. Democracy at the level of the chiefdom would have artificially created governance at that level. Devoid of a general council for politico-administrative issues, the paramount chief did act for the whole population medicinally. He acted as a king in his rites for rain and in the series of sacrifices (*ulupepo lukalamba*) he performed at his home, after which these were carried on at the shrines of all advisers, chiefs and headmen in the land.

To state that someone is elected to 'occupy a chieftainship' (ibid.: 97) gives the wrong impression that these chiefdoms were imposed from above by an overlord. Is chieftaincy the heritage of a sovereign, a big man or an autocratic regime? Supported by oral tradition, our data regarding the Sukuma chiefdoms among others have pointed in the direction of descendants of a once charismatic, ritually inspired leader, whose influence spread along medicinal lines and with growing membership in the next generations. The membership centralized and increasingly mingled with local decision making. In Bemba society too, the chiefs and the paramount's advisers (*bakabilo*) were initiated in the same tradition of medicinal rites. The chiefs lived in the paramount's estate (*umusumba*, from *umb*) while the hereditary advisers lived away, but both categories underwent an initiation at their ascent, and inherited a shrine to match (ibid.: 109). Each adviser played his part in the enthronement, burial, annual ceremonies, and care of the royal drum, which established the tie with the ancestors. Emblematic of the mitigated power of 'Bantu kingship' is the destitute paramount whom Audrey Richards met in 1934 (unfortunately deserving no more than a footnote; ibid.: 110, n1). He lived in a grass hut waiting in suspense because the *bakabilo* were displeased with his behaviour and refused to medicinally bless his new estate.

Bemba villagers were related to the headman or had later joined the community, which makes kinship or alliance instead of conquest the principle of society. Members did share a sense of belonging, expressed in the common name (*Bemba*), language, bodily incision, transmitted oral history and loyalty to the paramount chief (*Citimukulu*). Inhabitants of a chiefdom identified themselves by the name of the chief preceded by the noun *mwine*, translated by Richards as 'subject of' (ibid.: 92). Villagers were subjects of a chiefdom. A few pages later when discussing the chief's title, *umwine chalo*, her translation of *mwine* is the exact opposite: 'owner of' the chiefdom (*mwine* is preceded by a 'u' that does not change the meaning; ibid.: 97). The suggestion sticks that the chief owns the chiefdom – if not the people, then the land. The translation 'owner of' has been widely adopted in texts and by a Bemba indigenous rights platform on the Internet. How to explain her contradiction? In translations of everyday texts, the word *mwine*, like *mwenye* in KiSwahili, means 'the one of', which denotes location, belonging or relationship, implying custodianship at the most.[2] A much more neutral meaning appears than ownership. Without intercultural translation, the analysis sets off in the wrong direction, too much in line with Western parlance on sovereignty. We should here remind of the Bantu word for 'having', *kuwa na*, whose literal translation into the neutral 'being with' gives a better sense of how people perceive their possession of anything, including a charm. The ease of classificatory extension makes for a less individualistic understanding of ownership, as in this case of the chief towards 'his' chiefdom.

The intercultural challenge for Richards in the 1930s resumes as we read on. A four-faceted structure can be discerned in the way she had learned to compare African political systems – the first biosocial, the second territorial, the third socio-hierarchical and the fourth generational. Medicinal rule has no chance of coming to the fore. To start with the biosocial (in the more elegant sense of the British eye for the pedigree), the locally recognized legal unit of society was the lineage group, *in casu* matrilineage, with a certain residence type after marriage, here matrilocality. The lineage determined rights of inheritance and succession of special statuses, which have mostly been banned since colonization. The wider descent group, the clan (*umukoa*), served as a repository for legends and totemic symbolism but also legally for the exogamous choice of a spouse. The smaller descent group was the 'house' (*inganda*) formed by the descendants of an ancestress and headed by a patriarch. They dealt with ritual and marital obligations, and organized the ceremonies for the ancestral spirits (*imipashi*). Closer still to ego yet transcending legally recognized descent was the bilateral group of the kindred (*ulupwa*) one lived with or regularly visited and welcomed at home (ibid.: 88), which Richards identifies as the lived reality and kin-based atom of society.

From the smallest kinship unit sprang a second dimension, which territorially subdivided society, ranging from the unit of the village (*umushi*) consisting of a headman and his relatives to the district (*ichalo*) ruled by a chief. The latter is named *mfumu*, in aforementioned contrast with the Sukuma word meaning healer. The common origin of the fields of rule and medicine also appears in the stem of *bu-sumba*, the Sukuma initiatory association of the young (cf. Varkevisser 1973), of *e-somba*, the Komo initiation, and the word for royal palace in Buganda. With the same stem, the Bemba word for the chief's village is *umusumba* (the shared root of *lu-sumba* initiation in eastern Congo is suggestive for a place where medicinal power was obtained). It housed the village shrine with sacred relics (*babenye*) of the first chiefs, whose spirits guarded land and people (ibid.: 97). Cross-cutting the biosocial and territorial division is the social status attributed to clans and to chiefdoms. Chieftainships nearest to the paramount's capital consider themselves as of higher rank because of the appointed chief's closer kinship with the paramount. The latter's influence – and his shrine's – is concomitantly weak in the peripheral chieftaincies (ibid.: 92).

The lateral, generational classification of society is the fourth structuration. Richards notes its remarkable absence in Bemba society (ibid.: 94). It has no age sets, nor boys' initiation ceremonies or secret societies. She assumes therefore that where the associations exist in the surrounding groups, they have been 'adopted' at some point. Wherefrom? And those in turn wherefrom? Ad infinitum. In our view, endogeneity is the parsimonious hypothesis: the Bemba village shrines have the medicinal power for the land which boys' initiations elsewhere specialize in. In comparison, Sukuma villages have no central shrine (family compounds have several) but their initiation of adults bonds the community members medicinally. The discussion is a matter of cultural structure and which institutions qualify as viable classificatory extensions of that structure. The village shrine draws on a hunter's logic for good fortune, from which cults develop. Hence, the Bemba case rather supports the existence of a common origin in the wider region for domesticating fertility and ritual head(man)-making. The territorialized medicinal cult, the village shrine and the chief's initiation are specializations that in terms of the cultural structure of medicinal rule are interchangeable.

The Nilotic Fringe: Alur Rain Medicine

The main lead to this section is the regret of Aidan Southall about his book *Alur Society* from 1956 (henceforth AS) to not have named the Alur chiefship (*ker*) a kingship, for the chiefs did master the craft of rainmaking.³ Although one could object that the craft should not distinguish chief from king, it is striking that he associated rain medicine with kingship. Remarkably indeed, among the Alur a chief's son was sometimes kidnapped by neighbouring clans in order to found a chiefdom and rule it as a 'chieflet'. It can be surmised that the commoners counted on the rain medicine the princes obtained from their father (cf. AS 191). The importance of medicine is allusive. Other aspects of rule, such as impartial arbitration, were not unique to them, and the Alur chiefs did not possess armies (AS 231). What else than medicine could have made the sons so attractive a presence? The princes to whom my eye was thus drawn from the start emerged as the book's real heroes. Not coincidentally did Southall in the preface liken his role in the field to a prince, abducted to protect and act as mascot of the local community (AS xi).

Southall missed the opportunity of adding an etymological profundity. The mascot, who brings good luck, is the diminutive of the French Provençal word *masco*, witch. Part III will touch on the double-edged sword, an almost universal ambiguity, of a human incarnating the body politic. Among the Alur too, chiefship and witchcraft are intimately connected. It is not just that the king exposes witches (AS 142). The witch belongs with the king. The intriguing closer connection is mislaid among a series of field notes in small font citing an Alur informant about unexpected costs of witch-killing: 'A witch is like a child of the chief, therefore they have to pay to kill him. They had to pay a girl if they had one available, but if they entreated the chief he would let them off with only a bull or even a goat' (AS 143). No analysis ensues. Later we learn that the Alur heads of lineages and clan sections enjoy the highest authority and prefer self-help, considering the chief as the last resort to turn to in case of trouble (AS 144, 237). His knowledge of the invisible realm may exceed that of common diviners, but his interventions can be costly. As the ruler of a 'segmentary state', he offers a service to peripheral zones over which he has limited sovereignty and whose allegiance can shift to other chiefs (AS 248).

Power fades out from the centre in this political system, situated between the segmentary lineages of the Nuer or Dinka and the unitary state of Buganda or Bunyoro. Unitary states signify administration centralized under a sovereign, who has no spirit or medicinal charm to obey, whereas segmentary lineages are not ruled, save by the councils of elders. Southall proposes the intermediary system as the prototypical origin of states worldwide. Since '[r]itual supremacy is often accepted where political control is not' (AS 261), the centralization of governance would be more ritual than political in segmentary states. We subsume ritual under medicinal, as not the liturgical procedure is meant but life-giving power or fertility. That medicinal supremacy, sought in pre-unitary states, would come before stately power. But then one can hardly maintain, like Southall felt obliged to despite his repeated description of rain medicine as the most guarded vivid secret of chieftaincy and the 'essential clue' to the polity (AS 379), that '[t]o the ethnologist, Alur rainmaking is just one of the methods of validating political power' (AS 94).

We can think of a plausible scenario, both historically and culturally, for people who have grown up in segmentary lineages. The idea of a central government encompassing non-kin groups was not obvious to them. They were familiar, though, with certain features of centralizing power. These mainly concerned the medicinal field: initiatory societies, cults, ritual mediation such as the leopard chief, and the annual organization of collective ceremony. That is how states could rise endogenously from the local cultural structure. Medicinal rule could have been the lubricant for state formation. Here too at the north-eastern fringes of equatorial Africa, it seems that first came the medicine, then kingship. The opposite direction has been the unreasoned premise.

The segmentary state survived not through force but by virtue of the social exchange between the chiefly lineage and the subjected lineages constituting the chiefdom. What was guaranteed in return for respect, food and modest forms of occasional tribute (AS 121, 181)? Protection against internal strife, witchcraft, infertility and drought, which required medicinal knowledge. According to Southall, what characterizes the Great Lakes as a single region is the interrelationship between chiefless societies and immigrant aristocracies that were accepted by the former to peacefully dominate them (AS 229, 234). The Belgian colonizers misconstrued at their own peril the interrelation as one of oppression. So, they were surprised to meet resistance by the chiefless groups such as the Lendu and Okebo subjected by the Alur. The Belgian colonizers saw themselves as heroes for a greater cause – namely the African polity of their dreams – by extracting those groups from Alur society and moving them to a separate location with their own chiefs to match (AS 230–31, 222). The colonial cultural structure ranking presumably universal values, which reserved hegemony for the whites (possibly complicated by repressed Flemish desires for regional autonomy after the First World War), could not grasp the local meaning of slavery or serfdom of war captives and vagabonds, which seemed to replicate the mentioned oppression. Serfdom among Alur normally was transient after intermarriage with the next generation (AS 234).

Medicinal rule was a model spread across the region inhabited by a variety of groups. It sublimated warfare into a complementary relationship. What preoccupied the local band or village was the immigrants' rain medicine, something they as outsiders could offer – and why not – which they themselves may have been less confident about at first (cf. fragments of interviews in the appendix of Southall's book). Both the Alur and Hema immigrants who came to rule the Lendu were tellingly called *zhi*, the Lendu word for rain (AS 154). The Lendu bands of hunters were adept at ironwork and according to their oral tradition were tied up in ongoing small-scale warfare with bow and arrow (AS 154). They allegedly welcomed the Alur, who introduced cultivation and cattle-holding as well as arbitration through an embryonic form of chiefship (AS 173, 181).

There can be no doubt that the Alur chiefs were regarded by their subjects as rainmakers. But to claim that they as Nilotic speakers introduced rain medicine to these mostly Bantu-speaking peoples, and with it invented the new type of rule, would be a step too far. An observed anthropological complementarity says nothing about the chronology of historical events. Especially in this culturally highly diverse region, at the crossroads of very different linguistic and economic traditions, the influences must have gone to and fro for centuries. From the data available, it rather seems that medicinal rule existed in the region long before the Alur arrived to fill in the position of rainmaking chief.

Southall waits for an appendix to enlighten us more about the matter. Apparently the rainmaking shrine that is most revered, even by the chief of Ukuru, never was in the hands of the Alur (AS 370). The shrine Jok Riba, located on a small cliff above Lake Albert, originated from the Lendu themselves. Chiefs lose all prerogatives in its vicinity. Transcending and probably predating the institution of chieftaincy, Riba is served by a priest who has sole access to the shrine and makes the annual offerings of first fruits of maize and finger millet. His counterpart is a medium who 'is *like a chief* in his regalia and in his treatment at accession, death and burial. The Lendu origin of the veneration of Riba is further attested by the Lendu flute set which provides the essential music for Riba rituals' (AS 371, my italics). The medium would be imitating a chief, rather than the other way around? The assumed direction of influence betrays the polity prism at work. Southall gives no more details about the rites or whether initiation was involved, but many of the parameters encountered at the shrines of Nkwe Mbali and Kolelo are there so as to recognize a fertility cult, a so-called territorial cult, not unlike that in the rest of equatorial Africa.

Quite different from the Riba, the shrines of chiefs contain pots of earth dedicated to the line of royal predecessors. The earth in the pots comes from the Lwo-speaking homeland. These shrines known as *abila* connect the Alur to their new home. The right-hand shrine, *tipu Lwo* (spirit of the Lwo), represents all agnatic descendants of the chiefs. The left-hand shrine, *tipu jumiru* (spirit of the subjects), refers to the other clans. The walls of the shrine hut consist of stakes of the *kango* tree. To stress the continuity of the agnatic line, a stake of the old shrine is inserted in the new *tipu Lwo* (AS 99; we recognize the symbolization of continuity of life in royal burials). Quite some variation exists among the chiefdoms. In Ukuru, additional shrines are dedicated to all male and female patrilineal ancestors (*Jok Matar*). Mediumistic divination reveals whether a special shrine should be built to appease a maternal ancestor. Chiefdoms that trace their origin to Bunyoro in the west (instead of Lwo) tend to build single *abila* shrines (AS 117). They do not seem to entertain the nostalgic bond with a distant homeland in the north-east that had led the Alur to double their chiefly shrines.

Defining a Society: Language versus Culture

As his comparative analysis of the internally diverse society unfolds, Southall anticipates on an ongoing postcolonial debate. He gets to doubt the very concept of a delimited group of people having a culture. Who actually belongs to the Alur segmentary state? Without clear-cut borders and central administration, the issue is not readily settled. He eventually allows for other dynastic influences to enter into his partition of Alur society (AS 218). He begins by redefining the lowland chiefdoms such as Ragem. Are they not satellite chieflets of Bunyoro rather than Alur? Their geographic proximity as well as historical kinship point in that direction. The groups may in his time not have identified with 'the Bantu culture of Bunyoro from which they had come' and rather have underlined the joint dynastic ties with Bunyoro through historical figures such as king Nyabongo, but Southall begins to discern cultural reasons for describing the Ragem as non-Alur despite their speaking the Alur language (AS 219). Firstly, the Ragem and their lowland neighbours were sticking to single *abila* shrines. Secondly, like the Bunyoro and the Acholi, they absorbed foreign groups by delegating political authority to those groups' clan heads, something quite unthinkable to the Alur chiefdoms which invariably expanded by planting kin members as authorities in adjacent territory. Culturally, the Ragem are not Alur, despite their language and social identity.

A few pages later the dissolution of the identity between culture and language is complete, with the inverse movement. The isolated Mambisa speak Lendu instead of Alur, yet as will be argued, their political system and ritual cosmology lend sufficient footing to rate them as Alur (AS 222). How to decide on criteria in this discussion? In the above it appears that the simple fact of speaking a certain language should not be normative in determining cultural belonging. Although leaving the matter largely implicit, Southall decided by relying on structural correspondences between cultural practices such as the mentioned delegation of power.[4]

Certain clans are designated to initiate the chief's successor. They teach him all rites concerning the land's fertility (AS 87). Other clans of the chiefdom should somehow feel involved as well. The clans of lower status, mostly at the lakeshore, take pride in the control they have over the rain clouds before these reach the prestigious chiefdoms on the high plateau. The location of the ancestral shrines depends on spirit possession. Supernatural forces (*jok*) inhabit them (AS 93). Not unlike chiefs, commoners build shrines. For these too the father's spirit is supposed to decide who will erect the shrine, containing the stakes for future shrines. That person is not necessarily the eldest surviving son. In polygynous families, it is rarely the most senior person whose shrine has the stakes to take from. Lineage elders must keep track of which son is the oldest survivor of those assigned to erect the shrine in honour of the deceased father. Familial oral tradition recounts who had that patriarch's stake inserted to continue the line of materiality (AS 105–6). The inherited stake transmits authority and the medicinal power of *jok*.

The general term for chieftain shrines is significant for our comparative exercise: *Jok R/Lubanga*. Known in Bunyoro as the Chwezi spirit of twins, Rubanga is the first ruler of Northern Kitara (AS 371). The Acholi who presently live there use the name of this supernatural principle, or creator, to refer to the Christian god. It is interesting to observe how the widespread connection between twins and kings, via the value of fertility, is expressed in this part of equatorial Africa. The Alur symbol for *lubanga* is the twin-necked pot (cf. double gourd of *ihane* Sukuma initiation in the Introduction). It contains the umbilici of twins. The pot was carried by the first Ukuru chiefs into this land. The set of data led Southall to conclude that the spiritual (Bantu) concept of Lubanga was adopted from the mysterious Bunyoro-Kitara empire. The adoption must have been prior to the Bito invasion. The Bito took over the concept too, as did Bunyoro's Bantu-speaking neighbours from the kingdoms of Buganda, Toro and Nkole. There are many such parallel derivations, Southall remarks, due to the dynamic exchanges between these ethnic groups, which also include the Lwo, Madi, Lango and Bari (AS 372, n1).

An illuminating case to imagine the incipient interrelation between dominators and subjects in the Great Lakes is that of the Mambisa, a group living in isolation from their fellow Alur. The Mambisa were at the time without paramount chief. Southall situates their changing, 'fluid' political system between the stable small chiefdoms of the Alur lowlands and the expansionist large chiefdoms of the Alur highlands (AS 227). According to Mambisa lore, their arrival in this area, whose first occupants were Mbuti Pygmies, was preceded by that of Nyali, Lendu and Bendi groups. The migrants succeeding Mambisa were Bira who split off from their home community after conquests of Zande in the north-west and Mangbetu in the south-west pushed Momvu-Lese peoples closer to their area (AS 222). The Mambisa cluster of villages, surrounded by Lendu and Okebo groups, is thirty miles from the nearest Alur in the north-east and sixty miles from the main Alur chiefdom of Ukuru in the highlands. The Mambisa lost their Alur speech and spoke Lendu (cf. supra: culture is not language and vice versa; AS 218, 222). Yet, stereotyped as very tall and black, and as outsiders because their daughters could never be married by non-Alur, they could pursue their role as rainmakers and settlers of dispute. They had conserved the rituals from the time they left their Alur ascendants:

> [T]he rain medicine in a cow's horn put in a stream to make rain and taken out to make the sun shine; the spear of chiefship put at the chiefly ancestor shrine and a special plant waved at the rain to drive it away when excessive; the prayers and sacrifice at the ancestor shrine for seasonable weather and for general plenty and fertility (AS 223).

In return, they expected food and services, and they treated as subjects all those joining their communities. Conquest was not their thing. Those who did not play along would suffer 'terrorist tactics': the Okebo smiths made 'leopard claws' of metal for Mambisa to supposedly savage their victims (AS 223). In the region only the Hema were said to also use these leopard claws (which were made famous by a sadly iconic statue at the colonial Africa Museum in Belgium, cf. Van Bockhaven 2013 on the *aniota* murders).

Southall was under the impression that the Mambisa felt destined to rule. Collaborating without a paramount chief surpassing them, their leaders were incipient chiefs, not yet confirmed in a 'coming out of the forest' ritual like the Alur rulers. The situation was conducive to abstruse tactics of intimidation whenever their natural confidence did not suffice to persuade their subjects to conform. The situation may be named a political system, in terms of centralization set somewhere between segmentary lineage systems and the segmentary state, but would it not be fairer to highlight the leaders' attempts at translating medicinal capacity into rule? This kind of intermediacy comes nearer to the local concerns expressed in various discourses on witchcraft, protection, ritual and the management of life and death. The political idiom of conflicting ideologies and implemented policies that suffuses Euro-American scholarly debate simply does not capture the thrust of the chiefships under study.

If rainmaking is so essential a clue to the polity, why not work the other way around and forget about the polity so as to focus on the medicine? Although rain medicine appears to be what each Alur chiefship revolves around, Southall feels at ease in the functionalism of his day: 'I take the view that the political aspect of society is universal, though specifically political institutions are not. A society may lack statehood or government, but then inevitably its political needs are served by more generalised institutions: family, totemic clan, age set, lineage. Every society carries out political functions' (AS 28). And so he is willing to make the effort of detecting the political in each of these spheres. The degree can vary, as in familial authority being less political in modern societies. The cultural structure of Western scholarship is well known. Parallel to the Cartesian division of mind and matter, spirit and nature, the soft and the hard, modern society managed to separate church and state. The feat continued in the division of social subsystems replicated in domains of research: political, economic, religious, educational and familial.[5] The cultural structure spawned much research as any coherent ordering of reality probably does, but whether the 'needs' to be served by society's institutions are as 'inevitable' as suggested may have been the functionalist delusion. A cultural structure other than the modern one of functional differentiation should have been more fruitful to comprehend society south of the Sahara.

Zande Perceptions of Cultural Structure: The Place of Associations

Practices have a cultural identity. They are a reference point for determining the cultural belonging of people in the past whom one cannot ask. The language that people speak, mother tongue or acquired tongue, is not in itself a determinant of societal belonging. Mambisa speak Lendu, yet they identify with Alur; and because of their practices, namely their medicinal institutions, they are regarded by their Lendu neighbours as Alur. The historical fact of their emigration from Alur groups dating from long ago and their constituting a society with Lendu today cannot trump this cultural identification, which is part of their preconscious cultural structuration. How to put one's finger on something preconscious?

South-west of the Alur in Uganda and Congo one finds an equally multi-ethnic state, and mainly non-Bantu as well: Zande society. Its heterogeneity stemmed from consecutive conquests by a group of 'aristocrats', very much unlike the mediation of feuds and rain medicine that propelled Alur expansion. Evans-Pritchard (1960, 1963, 1965a) published three succinct papers in the 1960s on the cultural origins of objects and institutions in Zande society. Packed with historical and linguistic data on more than three hundred items, the papers not only show the extent of cultural exchange in the region, but also that Zande attribute ethnicity to the things they have at home. Evans-Pritchard's informants identified groups inside and outside the Zande state as the originators of certain cultural items. We propose an analysis to demonstrate the logic of classification behind their cultural attributions. The local, subjective attribution is more important for our purpose than the historical factuality of attributed origins (which linguistic analysis of the local terms could retrace). It will permit us to formulate a hypothesis on the forest-within fractal, and extend its cultural logic to the wider region, thus including the Niger–Congo family of languages in the discussion this chapter began. Extension means we accept the reduced resolution of meso-anthropological comparison necessary to zoom out to regional patterns.

I should mention a second reason why derivation of a cultural structure, endogenous and with pre-colonial roots, is of importance for Zande ethnography. Evans-Pritchard (1937: 512) writes: 'Whilst caution is desirable in trying to account for the introduction of closed associations into Zandeland, we may commit ourselves to the statement that they were not only introduced after European conquest of the country, but also are functions of European rule and a sign of breakdown of tradition'.

For Evans-Pritchard our thesis of medicinal rule, implying an associational model, could not be further from the truth: initiatory associations are a novelty without precolonial past, and they break with tradition. His statement applies to the Zande, a non-Bantu group, but I have reason to object anyway. I will argue that his anthropology is in a way 'too' historical, or chronistic, to accept that the new initiatory cults either tap into an age-old cultural structure, or are reversions to formerly deserted practices. A diversity of institutions can express the same cultural structure. Some institutions in Zande society clearly exhibit familiarity with it. They offer an endogenous reason for the rapid popularity of the cults, on top of the instigating factor of (anti-) colonial reaction. The caution Evans-Pritchard observes, moreover, concerns precursors of medicinal cults that may have existed in the conquered groups and were expelled by the aristocratic clan (better put: by the cult that gave rise to the aristocracy, if we apply medicinal rule). The trope of resistance movements in the form of closed associations arising in the turmoil of colonization sounds attractive, but assumes the situation encountered by the first white colonizers to be representative of the precolonial past. It also ignores the internally diverse history of Zande society: could none of the conquered subgroups, including Bantu-speaking, have a cultic history? Finally, it overestimates the invasive impact and, quite plainly, the importance of administration (colonial or other) in this society.

On an implicit level, though, the anthropologist Evans-Pritchard assumes Zande to have cultural structure, otherwise he could not make claims about what is culturally 'abnormal', or normal:

> I have several times emphasized that witchcraft, magic, witch doctors, and oracles form a system of reciprocally dependent ideas and practices. None could be left out of my account without seriously distorting the others. But were I to omit a description of the closed associations it would not be of great consequence. If they had not been penalized the associations might have become stable institutions. As it is, they strike one as foreign and abnormal modes of behaviour. (Evans-Pritchard 1937: 512)

He does not offer ethnographic data to substantiate the division between healing and association, and as I will show, his trilogy of papers published thirty years later indirectly disproves it. Historically the cults may be foreign, but culturally they are not. Their apparent deviation from the normal, in order to bring the dangerous wild into the villagers' purview, is a characteristic of these cults in the whole region. Several photographs in Evans-Pritchard's monograph plainly exhibit the core of initiation, the forest-within, which we initially limited to Bantu-speaking groups (see Illustrations 4 and 5). The Zande shrine in the village, a tree with medicines in honour of spirits and surrounded by plants for medicinal preparation, brings the forest into the centre of the compound (see ibid.: 358).

Our structuralist exercise begins with the two-dimensional symbolism distinguishing domestication from fertility, as well as inside from outside, whose combinations create cosmological categories that are interrelated: inside and fertile, inside and domesticating, outside and fertile, outside and domesticating. These can be verified in the Sukuma village initiation. The novices are men carrying spear and bow in honour of their clan (*ya ku buta*, of the bow) and aim for the house's threshold controlled by the women with their ladles (*ya ku ngongo*, of the back). The fractal of domesticating fertility is reiterated on a more encompassing spatial scale in the confrontation of peer group and forest, generating the medicinal bundle *bu ya mu kaya*, the forest-within. The fractal is articulated in the ethnographies of Bantu-speaking communities, among others in the cited studies by Turner, Devisch, De Mahieu and Janzen. These lived cosmologies systematically symbolize as a source of fertility the undomesticated outside, which according to the logic of classificatory extensions includes the forest, the invisible world, the spirit world, foreign peoples, not-yet-allied exogamous clans, and so on.

'New situations demand new magic' is a famous quote by Evans-Pritchard to capture the colonial situation, deservedly cited by postmodern anthropology (ibid.: 513). For him, it stressed the cults' deviation from the ordinary in Zandeland, their recent origin, their indication of 'social change' (ibid.: 511) and 'breakdown of tradition' (ibid.: 513). I acknowledge the foreign elements in the initiatory cults: the language of the Mani spells, the damming of water (ibid.: 535; like in Komo initiation), the symbolic reference to snakes (ibid.: 533, 536; like Buyeye and much earlier Urewe complex west of Lake Victoria), the *luduta* creeper (ibid.: 535, yet appearing in the Zande 'witchdoctor' initiation anyway) and steam medicine, both common in the Chwezi initiation from the Great Lakes (ibid.: 531). But the medicines, their botanical and metonymic constitution, their location in the forest for purity before domestication (ibid.: 517) and their secrecy (ibid.: 515) follow as much the logic of the Zande witchdoctor's magic he had described (ibid.: 537). Water and river feature centrally too in Zande initiations (ibid.: 527). Most of all, the norm of gender equality in the initiatory associations (the term we prefer over closed or secret associations) cannot be attributed to social change. The defiance of everyday gendered social hierarchy is a property of all initiatory societies in the wide region attributing their medicinal powers to spirit intervention. Violating the norm of male/female separation characterizes the ritual of fertility. To call the cult's gender equality a social change is to overlook the dynamic experiential structure of multiple frames activated in context with concomitant normative shifts.

In sum, both the heterogeneity and the cosmology of Zande forest-fringe society reserve room for a structural outlier. In eastern and central Africa, initiatory associations have – traditionally – been that outlier. Their presence in itself cannot be a sign of breakdown of tradition. The more one knows about the history of a cult and the founder's personal, often traumatizing, experience it is informed by, the greater the temptation to attribute its rise to a unique epoch. In the case of Maria N'koi from Congo, her followers' search for a clean slate by replacing all charms by hers, seemed symptomatic of the colonial 'nervous state' (Rose-Hunt 2016: 65). Anthropologically, the replacement in search of a clean slate is a reversible change. It is reminiscent of the long-lived alternation between divinatory societies and witch-finding cult, as mentioned for Lele society. Evans-Pritchard's removal of cultic initiation from the Zande symbolic system had motivated commentators to classify these institutions as innovations and as 'religious movements' characteristic of the turbulent colonial era in the early twentieth century (De Craemer, Vansina and Fox 1976). We argue that the success of cults among Zande, who are not Bantu-speaking, was moored in precolonial cultural continuities. Throughout this chapter the linguistic criterion to demarcate a region as a unit of analysis has proven fallacious. The openness to alterity as a source of fertility and power is not limited to Bantu speakers. In fact, the alterity of Bantu groups may have made the adoption of their practices attractive to some Zande. In the following I show that Zande associated surrounding ethnic groups with certain practices, and vice versa. Stronger still, they most probably did so according to the aforementioned two-dimensional symbolism of medicine. Unfortunately, our symbolic analysis cannot be checked with Evans-Pritchard's informants. Then again, can the opinions conveyed by informants have the last word on preconscious structure, let alone be dubbed the 'perspective of the people'? To endogenize history, we must explore alternative methods to detect expressions of cultural 'logic'. The following is an example.

The ethnicity Zande attribute to things appears indexical of sociocultural relations between groups. The comparison can be made with Bourdieu's (1979) survey confirming that Europeans (preconsciously) express their economic and cultural capital in their music taste. Among Zande, not social classes but symbolic distinctions are the focus. In medicinal rule the power of symbols counts. The next paragraphs expound the method used to bring the disparate items of Evans-Pritchards' trilogy of papers together according to ethnic attribution, and to subsequently verify which symbolic relations the obtained ethnic classes of items express.

First, we map the various groups that Evans-Pritchard (1958) listed as constituting the Zande cultural complex. The rectangle in Figure 5.1 outlines the area in degrees of longitude (23° to 30° East) and latitude (3° to 6° North) where the Zande language was spoken during the early 1900s when the ethnographer Van den Plas did his linguistic study. Within the rectangle twenty-seven ethnic groups are identified that together compose 'the Azande'. The groups share the cultural traits of the complex to varying degrees, with outliers such as Palembata and Makere much less influenced. The white ovals on the map roughly estimate the size and draw the location of each group as described by Evans-Pritchard in terms of longitude, latitude, and their orientation from one of the streams of the Nile–Congo watershed. Underlined are the ethnic groups that later on featured in Evans-Pritchard's trilogy of articles on the cultural influences that the Azande have undergone. In this region, where the Nile and Congo basins abut and the countries of Congo, Central Africa, South Sudan and Uganda today border each other, a unique cultural admixture grew with Bantuic, Nilotic and Ubangic languages intersecting. The integration of their cultural exchange within one society resulted from the dominance by the Avongara clan (ibid.: 97). Had the exchange been purely spontaneous, then all instead of less than half of the groups would have been underlined, and there might not have been a dominant language.

All Zande cultural items discussed by Evans-Pritchard (1960, 1963, 1965a) in the three articles were arranged in general categories, like cultivation and arts. The articles mention item after item, each time indicating the group of origin that imported it according to the informants. The informants' claims cannot be considered historical evidence, at least not by definition, and that makes them extra interesting. Their ethnic identifications of objects and practices are interpretive. The association of a certain item with an ethnic origin, and sometimes with a preceding disseminator, results from cultural classifications that are only in part historical, and especially dubitable if concerning the distant past. Table 5.1, located at the end of this chapter, should therefore be captioned 'Evans-Pritchard's informants' version of the origins

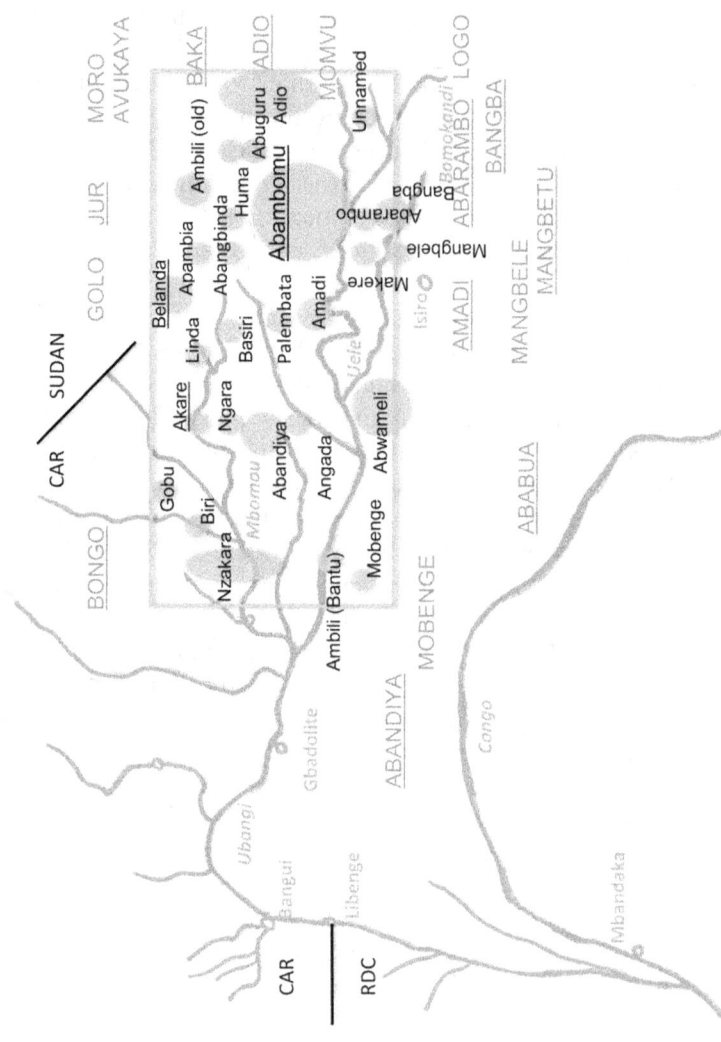

Figure 5.1 The Zande cultural complex, based on Evans-Pritchard (1958). Figure by the author.

of Zande cultural items'. An excel sheet accurately reproduced the list of 300-plus items with their data such as local name, their attributed origin, and ulterior origin if known.[6] No pattern showed, except that the Zande cultural complex was highly diverse.

Once the criterion of classification was switched, patterns did come into sight. After sorting the items under each ethnic group, a clear difference in intensity and type of influence appeared. Each row of Table 5.1 corresponds to a group, each column to a category of items. The correlation between ethnicity and item-category is the main observation the table allows us to make. The four prominent ethnic groups, in bold type in the first column, not only stand out in number of items but also in the type of items on which they had influence. Their impact being specific rather than diffuse raises the question of whether the type of influence reflects actual historical events, or rather the Zande perception of intercultural relations among the four groups. Whatever the answer may be, each of the four groups appears to specialize in a number of items. The bold lines in the table outline four salient categories for which one of the four groups each time scores best.

Examining the table, we notice the linguistic diversity of the Zande area. The two main language families in sub-Saharan Africa, Bantu and Nilotic/Nilo-Saharan, are represented. Predominant is yet a third family, the Ubangian languages of the Central African Republic, which most linguists classify as loosely part of the Niger–Congo family. The font of the groups in the first column indicates language family, as categorized in the Linguasphere database. Italic font stands for Ubangic, normal font for Bantuic, small capitals for Nilo-Saharan Sudanic, and small capitals with engraved font for Nilotic East-Sudanic. Four bold lines in the first column separate the language families.

The data analysis we now introduce is a simplified version of what can be done with spatial-symbolic associations, for our criterion of significance is just quantitative: number of items. From the second column of Table 5.1 onwards the vertical and horizontal bold lines visualize our analysis. In each column the highest number of items is in bold, to reveal an 'influencer' – that is, an ethnic group influencing the Zande for that item. We let the four main influencers determine which columns of item categories should be placed together in a series, in order to visualize their symbolic relations. Marked in the table as boxes in bold, each series shows the item categories on which the four main influencers score a high number of items (number in bold in case of highest score in the column). Thus the box reveals an ethnic group's cultural specialization. Between three boxes of influencers were put intercalary columns of shared top-ranking places. Each intercalary column suggests overlapping significance of these item-categories for the two adjacent influencers.

What is the point of the whole procedure? The significance of our ethnic arrangement of item categories can be verified on the table. The level of significance shows in the frequency of numbers in bold in an influencer's box. The validity increases if the influencer's columns outside the box have fewer or no items. Variance with the other groups' scores on the columns inside the box further confirms our selection. It confirms that the selection of main influencers and their box of salient items is not arbitrary.

What are the results of the analysis? Before looking into the semantics, we notice formal patterns. The first four columns of items are those headed by the Miangba, scoring three maximums out of four, and one second place. The Mbomu are the most impressive influencers as they have seven maximums on seven, of which one is a shared first position. They share first place on the column intercalating with the next series of columns. That box shows the Amadi (better known as Madi, yet we stick to Evans-Pritchard's notation) having three maximums out of five, and two second places. Finally, the Mangbetu score three maximums out of three, and a second place in the intercalary column, on which the Amadi are placed third. Together these four boxes and two intercalary columns cover all the cultural items featuring in Evans-Pritchard's trilogy on Zande cultural exchange. In other words, the mutually exclusive categories turn out to be exhaustive.

The ultimate question is whether the boxes stand for more than a set of high scoring categories. We want to prove that the item-categories relate to each other in a specific symbolic way. Each box of seemingly disparate items has a symbolic meaning, a preconscious reality that – thanks to the method – could surface. The four meanings are interrelated, reproducing the cultural exchange of ethnic groups in the wider Zande society. We will argue that this cultural structure is nothing less than the fractal of domesticating fertility, which corresponds to the model of medicinal rule.

Two groups stand out for counting most items. They occupy the top of the table: the Abambomu, or Mbomu without the plural prefix, and the Bangba, also known as Miangba.[7] Whenever Evans-Pritchard's informants refer to the 'true Azande' they mean the Mbomu, whose language their Avongara rulers speak, so it is only logical that they should occupy the first rank of influencers.[8] The reader should now take a moment to go over the meaning of the categories in the columns and do the exercise of picking items that belong together. The two main boxes of items can be compared in terms of symbolic distinctions that are salient in the region. The Mbomu brought maize, groundnuts, and other subterranean plants into the diet. The Bangba specialize in crops above ground, especially millet or sorghum, which have a male and often honourable quality as opposed to maize, a crop free from bird pests and rapidly processed, hence supposedly preferred by women (sometimes reflected in ritual procedures and in the division of supplies after divorce; cf. Varkevisser 1973, Stroeken 2010). Maize happens to be the only high-growing plant of the Mbomu. Its female quality goes hand in hand with the Mbomu introduction of domestic tools and architectural styles, as well as the female activities of pottery and home-brewing. The Bangba stand out as the originators of oracular techniques, a male activity in Nilotic societies, and through them oracular traditions from the east have penetrated. Oracles are ways to communicate with, and domesticate, the erratic voices from beyond. The Bangba also are the source of a dance. The comparison in terms of male and female may have historical origins in past traditions of marital alliance between Mbomu clans of the bride and Bangba clans of the groom. Our overall comparison next suggests an encompassing symbolism though.

The third and fourth influencers are the Amadi and the Mangbetu. This pair cover a smaller number of items, but still more than the remaining groups. The region designated as 'South' is an aggregation of groups responsible for many items but it does not have an ethnic identity like the four mentioned, and contains about every category of item. Amadi exhibit a certain class of specialities. They invented funerary rites and ways of reshaping the body, as well as medicine, shrine, initiation hut, and cult. They are intermediaries for similar practices brought from elsewhere: bodily incision and dance (see the curve of the arrows in Figure 5.2). The Bantu groups from the west introduced

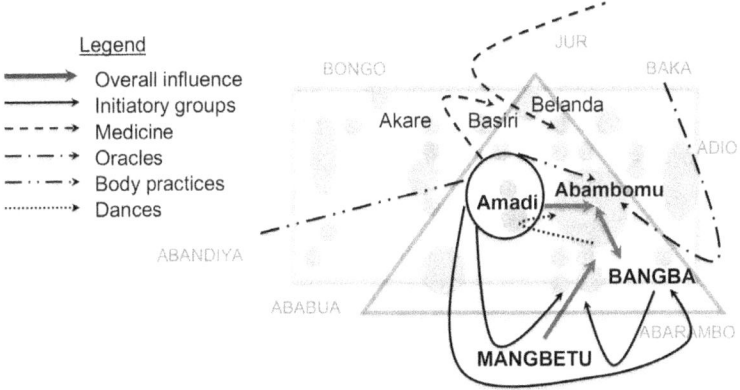

Figure 5.2 Analytical map of Zande cultural influences. Figure by the author.

incisions and body markings. Artisanship (typical of courts), aggressive weapons and high-energy (fast) foods such as fruits are attributed to Mangbetu, a neighbouring conquest state in the south. They are also the source and the group of passage for initiatory cults. The Bantu-speaking south is where many cults originated. Evans-Pritchard's statement about the abnormality of initiatory cults for Zande habits disregarded this internal cultural diversity. He did not envisage the dynamic visualized through a method such as this analytical map.

Amadi and Mangbetu groups lie at the periphery of the Mbomu–Bangba nucleus. In relation to the latter's interiority they contribute exteriority, but they do so in a very different way. The outside can refer to public (versus private) activities, but also to the power or fertility of the wild (versus domestication). Amadi specialize in the latter: rituals for dealing with the dead and with ancestral spirits for initiatory and medicinal purposes. Their fertility is not that of women in the house, like the Mbomu, but that of the dangerous outside. With the Amadi the Mangbetu share exteriority. Yet, Mangbetu are outsiders in their capacity of reputed conquerors specializing in the public activities of war, artisanship and cultic initiation. If the Amadi offer fertility from the outside, the Mangbetu represent external domesticators. Thus, to relate the four main influencers (the nucleus and the two peripheral groups), we must recast the one-dimensional opposition male/female of the Mbomu–Bangba nucleus into two dimensions: domesticator/fertility, inside/outside. Combined they make for four possibilities. The Mbomu are reinterpreted as offering an interior type of fertility that the Bangba domesticators marry into. These two prominent groups, with the highest number of items, specialize in items according to the cultural opposition of domesticator (including items with male traits) and fertility (including items with female traits). Translated from the Sukuma idiom, the outside or forest (*bu*) is opposed to the inside or home (*kaya*), while domestication (*buta*, 'bow') is opposed to fertility (*ngongo*, 'back').

Most significantly, however, the fractal of domesticating fertility is replicated on a larger scale. Through the classification of things, we discover how the Zande think about the outside groups, Amadi and Mangbetu. The Amadi fulfil the mediatory role of included third, between Mbomu and Bangba. The Amadi symbolize the external source of life and death (see arrows in Figure 5.2). The Mangbetu enact forest and domestication, which together evoke the inimical neighbouring kingdom they represent. In brief, the items in the table seem unstructured unless seen through the prism of the fertility fractal – our alternative to the polity prism.

It is in the nature of symbolic interpretations to not be compelling. We could apply the mentioned two dimensions that characterize medicinal rule, or we could start from the fertility of Bangba wedding Mbomu, and on a higher scale recognize the initiatory power of the forest generated by the Amadi entering this nucleus. The entered pair forms a triangle penetrated by a fourth, the Mangbetu, yielding a special type of power (see triangle in Figure 5.2). What else could a 'domesticating outsider' be than a conquering warrior? The Mangbetu had that reputation, historically based, in the region.

The next chapter will evince the principles of a lifeworld wherein all events and things are supposed to be interrelated. The above analysis anticipated the interrelatedness by showing that, because of the alterity of their language and culture, even a neighbouring people can symbolize something – if not discursively, then at the elusive level of the Zande preconscious and affect. The main principles of this symbolization tell us what a certain group deems important, which for the Zande too appears to be the fertility fractal.

The above data and reanalysis permit us to revisit Evans-Pritchard's depiction of initiatory associations as 'foreign and abnormal modes of behaviour'. The associations seemed an unwieldy appendage to Zande cultural structure, which was supposed to be exhaustively covered by the triad of magic, witchcraft and oracle. More than any other method, ethnography emboldens the researcher to compare and declare what culturally belongs and what does not. But the assessment remains subjective, predicated on local opinions about normality (which may differ) and the researcher's openness to internal diversity. Several indicators contradict Evans-Pritchard's judgement. The first contradiction comes from his own data. The papers from the 1960s show that, contrary to his statement thirty years before, the initiatory associations had their origins within Zande society. Although the Mangbetu were seen as introducers of these traditions from the exterior, the Bangba and the Amadi were the actual originators, as schematized in the full arrows on our analytical map.

Furthermore, we cannot ignore how convenient the assessment of associations as culturally foreign must have been for colonial governors tasked with weeding out liabilities without violating the principle of indirect rule. The political reading of 'secret societies' dominated the study of the Zande by Mgr. Lagae in 1926. The editor of the book series Edouard De Jonghe had also reported on this phenomenon as an aberration serious enough to alarm the administration (Janzen 1982: 11). Mgr. Lagae's book was amply cited in Evans-Pritchard's monograph. Nevertheless, his influence may have been underestimated, putting an entire line of ethnographers on the wrong track – that is, away from a medicinal reading that would reveal the cultural correspondence with the socialized local principles of magic and initiation. Lagae's (1926: 117, our translation) chapter on initiatory groups opens with the following paragraph: 'Secret societies were imported in the Zande region by foreigners, or at least founded under foreign influence. Not one dates back further than a generation, and not one may relish to have had, in the beginning, the support of the Avongara chiefs'. Their near absence in the north of the region would 'prove how little they conform to the Zande mentality' (ibid.: 120). Lagae therefore doubts the ethnographic value of studying secret societies. In his days, ethnography literally meant description of a people.

Moreover, the supposition was that chiefs represented their society's traditions and polity. Secret societies had 'nothing customary'; 'stronger still', the chiefs formally opposed them, initially at least (ibid.: 134). The author identifies with the chiefs and regrets to see how some of them join ordinary Zande to enter an association, thereby putatively losing their prestige (ibid.: 130). The monseigneur forgets that for the majority of the population the Avongara chiefs epitomized the outside: historically as conquerors, and symbolically as bringers of ritual powers from the wild. The cults belong to a regionally encompassing endogenous reality, with a long history of cultic peaks and declines. From the subjected populations of Zande society we may expect that top-down destruction of any one of their associations did not terminate the institution itself, or their adoption of new cults. The early studies by Six and Camus, discarded outright by Lagae because of situating the origins of the associations in the Zande region (ibid.: 119), confirm the general fact that cults were not culture-bound but travelled and crossed borders. Far from ethnically unique, the spirit continues to pull the rare individual into the forest to return with a remedy, or to find adepts to resist against oppression. For Lagae, though, the secret societies form 'un Etat dans l'Etat', a state within the state, because they remove their members from the chief's authority (ibid.: 117); he claims that had it not been for the colonizer's presence, they would have been eradicated by the Avongara chiefs, who would not tolerate any competition. The chapter ends with a warning that these societies may soon turn against the European occupiers (ibid.: 134).

We notice the mentioned trope of public healing and resistance (Feierman 1995; Rose-Hunt 2016). Yet, in enumerating the many activities of the associations, Mgr. Lagae strikingly comes up with no actual instance of political resistance. The activities are medicinal, applying the principles of magic. In a next chapter the author does not deny that the study of these ubiquitous practices 'requires a volume of its own' (ibid.: 150; a need probably well understood later by Evans-Pritchard). Moreover, about the *nzula* medicine and the *magaya* whistle acquired through the cult's initiation, he underlines the aggressive goals and the extortion of fees (ibid.: 128). But rebellion is nowhere to be seen. As his descriptions progress, the initiation turns out to treat 'patients'. They are asperged by the whistle dipped in water. Neither is the aggressive magic unequivocally deviant, since it avenges wrongs someone else committed. The seam side of the cult's aggressive magic is therapy: anyone feeling ill – surely a number exceeding that of the actually avenged – may attribute his or her condition to such vengeance, which the association subsequently treats with *nzula* medicine. The association is widely consulted by Zande for the medicine. Does this not make it, objectively, a medicinal cult?

The monograph describes *mani* and *nebeli* associations organizing a seclusion, food taboos, initiation into medicine, blindfolded application of protective magic, therapeutic medicinal fumigation, sacrifice of rooster, and public coitus (ibid.: 122, 126–27). These are all features common to cults of affliction such as the aforementioned Chwezi, Kubandwa, and the ngoma (Stroeken 2006). In the Wanga cult of elephant hunters, presumably of Nilotic provenance, the chiefs own a spirit altar made of branches converging into the shape of a cone (Lagae 1926: 132). So do the ancestral altars of Sukuma and Nyamwezi elders.

Right after having smirkingly remarked that patients are obliged to stay in the ceremonial house (*basa*) in the forest until they pay the fee, the author reluctantly mentions the 'so-called' re-education of the adept, undertaken for no less than four months by the master of ceremonies, *lubasa* (ibid.: 129). Across the region, the practice of healing has always been a business next to a vocation. Primary in the cults is the medicine, not political resistance. A better formulation, given our thesis, merges both qualities. Out of the blue appears proof of the fusion of the medicinal and the political when the bishop sheepishly notes that chiefs let the cult head judge quarrels between 'his people' (ibid.: 129, 133). Many Zande are such people marked as initiated.

The chief respects the authority of the cult head, and vice versa. How to make sense of such mutual non-intervention and legal parallelism? Cult head and chief partake of the same field of medicinal rule, of which a state and an initiatory association are different manifestations. Kishina of Bulima alluded to it in 1996. Court historian Ngonyeji of Busiha reiterated it in his own way in January 2018 when urging me to think of chiefship as medicine.

Table 5.1 Origins of Zande cultural items (according to Evans-Pritchard's informants)

	Miangba	Mbomu	Amadi	Mangbetu	Abandiya	Abarambo	Adio	Basiri	Bongo	North (Wau)
fruits	1	1	**4**							
stool, carving	1	2	**11**			1				
spear, knife			**7**	1		1				
initiatory cult			2	3		1			1	1
burial			**1**					2		1
initiation hut			**1**							
body practices			**5**			4				
medicine	1		**1**	1				3	1	
shrine	1	1	**1**							
dance, drum	1	6	1							1
house, tools	11	**18**	1	5			1			
shields	1	**3**	3							
beer	1	**3**	3	1						
pottery		**10**								
maize		**4**								
groundnuts		**2**								
subterran crop	3	**12**		1					1	1
low crop	**11**	5					1			1
sorghum	**1**	1								
millet	**5**								1	
Oracle	**2**		1							

164 Medicinal Rule

From Cult to Dynasty: Nilotic and Niger–Congo Extensions — 165

Ababua	1		1						
Abuguru	1			1					
Akare		1							
Ambili/Abile			1		5	1			
Bakongo	1	1	1						
South	2		8	1	6	**6**	1	1	
West⁹	3		3						
ABISANGA	1			1			1		
BAKA	3	1							
EAST							1		
BELANDA	2			1			1		
DINKA	1								
European, Arab	3			2	1				**4**

Notes

1. This opening sentence refers to the Mwindo epic at the end of Part I. The alternative of cultural adoption hints at the famous Lunda myth attributing the origin of kingship to Chibinda Ilunga, who imported the title (together with hunting) from his Luba clan.
2. Check for a sample at https://scholarblogs.emory.edu/bemba/speakers-reflections/.
3. Southall's comment came to me by way of personal communication from David Parkin.
4. A postcolonial critique could be that cultural and linguistic belonging is not a merely academic issue. Then again, the issue would be overpoliticized if a survey had to give the local majority the last word on something that had not preoccupied them before.
5. See Luhmann 1995; we may add the medical domain, which refers to the scientific profession and does not contain the medicinal.
6. I thank Karolien Coolen for meticulously listing all the items of the trilogy in an excel sheet with the corresponding specifications from the articles.
7. The plural prefix Mi- here replaces Ba-. We loyally follow Evans-Pritchard's use of prefixes, at the expense of linguistic consistency in our book.
8. Evans-Prichard (1958: 97) writes: 'The Avongara are the ruling aristocracy in by far the greater part of Zandeland. The Ambomu are their original subjects, and it is their language that the Azande speak. When one speaks of Azande one speaks of all those who use Zande as their mother tongue'.
9. West includes King Tembura's area, South includes south-west, North includes Nilotic and Wau. Abarambo includes the Avumaka clan.

Illustration 1 Kapunda Kishosha II, the chief of Ndagalu, reads out his sermon to inaugurate the cultivation year, flanked by his courtiers. The 'cooling chief' (*ntemi ng'hoja*) in the back surveys the crowd (picture taken by Koen Stroeken, 1996).

Illustration 2 Chwezi healers await the arrival of Chief Edward Makwaia at his initiatory hut (*itemelo*) across the courtyard of the palace of Busiha chiefdom in Tanzania (picture taken by Koen Stroeken, 2018).

Illustration 3 The famous healer nicknamed *mungu wa pili*, 'second god', is sitting on his chiefly chair and listening to the plea of an elderly novice, who is addressing him indirectly through the other healer in white coat, acting as a courtier (picture by Koen Stroeken, 1996).

Illustrations 4 and 5 The *shishingo* diadem with strings of beads worn by the Chwezi healers in Illustration 5 resembles the headdress of the Rwandan king Musinga and his queen-mother in Illustration 4 (courtesy of KMMA). The Chwezi in Illustration 5 prepare an inverted altar for the author's initiation (picture by Koen Stroeken, 1997).

Illustrations 6 and 7 Illustration 6, a photo taken by Evans-Pritchard (copyright Pitt Rivers Museum, University of Oxford, 1998.341.13.2, published with permission) shows a medicinal shrine of a Zande family. Equally in the middle of the compound, and to the right of the three ancestral altars, stands the Sukuma shrine called *shigiti* containing medicinal gourds (picture by Koen Stroeken, 2018).

Illustration 8 A great-grandson of chief Nkondo stands before the royal shrine in Mbarika and shows the main charm of rain medicine: ancient hoes of the Balongo ironsmiths (picture by Koen Stroeken, 2018).

Chapter 6

MAGIC AND THE SOLE MODE OF PRODUCTION

At this stage, before the last part of the book, we should be able to situate the medicinal model of rule within a frame of experience. According to the actor-idealist approach, a frame, or structure, of experience shapes the way a subject feels and thinks. The subject shifts between several frames in a culture. An abstraction of this dynamic is a cosmology, in the broad sense of an ordering of the world, society, nature and the invisible world. The cosmologies we encountered subsumed magic under medicine. Are we as Western scholars adequately trained to grasp magic and its materiality?

Magic as Communication

On Zande magic, Evans-Pritchard had some penetrating remarks. His eye for the importance of the natural environment in medicinal thought could rival Viveiros de Castro's (2004) contemplation sixty years later about animism in Amerindian cosmology. Evans-Pritchard's allusion to the obstacle facing the reader separating mind and matter bears on the whole of Western academia and should not evanesce. The fragment below makes a suggestion that could actually have ruined the title of his book: forget about magic, see only medicine. Medicine is in the trees, the herbs, the roots. It brings home nature, but not in the positivist sense.

> [K]nowledge of the medicines means knowledge of the art of a witch-doctor. It is not magic words nor ritual sequences which are stressed in initiation into incorporation of witchdoctors, but trees and herbs. A Zande witchdoctor is essentially a man who knows what plants and

> trees compose the medicines which, if eaten, will give him power to see witchcraft with his own eyes, to know where it resides, and to drive it away from its intended victims. The Zande witchdoctor exercises supernatural powers solely because he knows the right medicines and has eaten them in the right manner. His prophecies are derived from the magic inside him. His inspiration does not spring from the Supreme Being nor from the ghosts of the dead. (Evans-Pritchard 1937: 157)

The fragment sheds light on the cosmological gap the academic has to bridge. What is a society like that situates the mind in the thing one perceives or ingests? From the viewpoint of the Zande, the transformation that colonization caused is not secularization. The ideas of governance that in Europe built on Cartesian dualism and segregated Church and State, did not make people lose God. One lost matter, and with it the means to intervene in the world. A thing was not interrelated any longer with all other things. It could no longer be many things. A thing, such as a charm, lost its reality and interconnection with life. More accurately put, matter as such came into being, decontextualized from the practices it existed in. The colonizers looked at de-spirited things, and after impersonating the African gaze they saw the African's spirited things. They revelled in these things for their enchantment of the other's gaze. The obsessive collection and display in museums attest to our dualist re-enchantment, as Michael Taussig (1993) famously argued. In the meantime, the Pentecostalist speaking-in-tongues that wins over parts of Africa is making up for the material absence of spirit.

In the frame of experience that was first described almost a century ago by Evans-Pritchard (1937: 167) about the Zande, the healer's words spring from the medicine. They are activated by ingestion, or by dancing. The matter of medicine is inseparable from the human life-world. Dancing makes the connection more effectively than keeping the world at a distance in reflection.

> The witchdoctor runs to look into his medicine-pot. He gazes for a while into the medicated water and then springs forward into a dance. He dances because it is in the dance that medicines of the witchdoctors work and cause them to see hidden things. It stirs up and makes active the medicines within them, so that when they are asked a question they will always dance it rather than ponder it to find the answer. He concludes his dance, silences the drums, and walks over to where his interlocutor sits.

As scholars we may fail to reconstruct the medicinal mindset. We observe the object, and subsequently ask what to do with the thing. Two concrete questions proper to our study are particularly challenging for a Cartesian, positivist mindset. First of all, how to do justice to a thing being many things? For this multiplicity to appear in an academic context I propose to shift attention from the thing to the frame in which a thing is used, and, via the detour of the many frames, acknowledge the many things. By a frame of experience, I mean a basic set of standards or criteria for perceiving and judging events. Cultural structure is the more or less ordered totality of such standards in a group. It amounts to an order of moralities, like social structure amounts to an order of social classes. Frame of reference is a synonym for frame of experience, yet somewhat underrating the preconscious, biographically and historically unique as well as subjective status of those standards. Goffman (1974) and Bateson ([1972] 1990) have each proposed a way of analysing frames in communicative settings. Those settings of interacting people limit the research to what is shared intersubjectively. It saves the researcher the trouble of having to enter a person's consciousness at a given moment. Instead, the researcher's insidership sticks to the public reality of a frame and its elements constituting a successful communication.

Secondly, how to do justice to a thing being part of the whole and therefore affecting it? Belief in the existence of one mode of production only is necessary. Life, also fertility, has been the label for the one mode throughout this book. If everything participates in life, whether a word, a theory, a belief, a thing, and so on, then an affect shaped in a charm can interconnect in 'magical' ways. In the medicinal ingredients, magic communicates intentions. Each ingredient conveys a part of the message, like Bantu languages communicating through stem and affix.

My collaborator Paulo Magufuli, son of a Sukuma healer, spontaneously created the word *shikolanijo* for a potent metaphoric object propitious for magical use. It is composed of the stem 'resemblance' (*-ikol-*) and an affix with the moneme for 'simultaneous' (*-anijo*) articulating a reciprocal influence. The constitution of the word suggests that magic is something resembling something else simultaneously. The temporal element denotes the resemblance as a propitious event instead of a symbolic representation. The fertility the patient longs for resembles the red sap of the tree, as much as the sap does the fertility. Communicated at the right time in the right way, the longed for will happen. Patience is required. None of the participants in rituals I attended expected a sudden force to intervene. In that case the belief in medicine would have withered away long ago. Multiple communications of magic that never end resemble our everyday conversation. The sociologist Niklas Luhmann (1995) has built his career on the puzzle of communication. People engage themselves during their whole life in ongoing chains of talk, because a perfect moment of mutual understanding is never achieved. Momentary feelings of success alternate with doubts and despair. So too does magic never end.

The building of words from stems and monemes is common practice. Sukuma medicines are composed in the same way. A protective recipe for one's crops, for example, is structured around the stem 'seeds' to which *shingila*, 'entrances', are added. The entrances act like monemes permitting classificatory extensions. For instance, night and forest both enact liminality. The monemes have typical metonymic qualities: a bit of elephant trunk that stands for perpetrators, nocturnal nakedness to express stealth, domestic water to identify the seeds as of the home, a potsherd to evoke death, and two lines of roasted maize crossing at the house's threshold to summon the protection of the ancestral spirits on both paternal and maternal side. Each ingredient translated, the medicinal message sounds as follows: 'Through this magic secretly administered, any perpetrator of fields that belong to my house will incur the spell of my ancestors who joined at the threshold of my house'. The communication, inserted as a concoction in the ground or spat in a mixture at the ancestral altars, is often addressed to an indefinite set of beings: *masamva*, ancestors, or *badugu*, kin. All beings are addressed rather than any particular or limited chunk of reality because local epistemology is sufficiently empirical to admit incomplete knowledge about the invisible world, or sometimes to avoid jealousy between the spirits. To reproduce the same outcome in an atomistic (instead of holistic) universe populated by colliding particles, one would have to invent a divine being, a supernatural law or a force – anthropology's dark matter – that would permeate all individuals, gearing each of them mysteriously towards the desired outcome. I submit that, of these options, the communicative dynamic of magic in an already interconnected whole is actually the parsimonious belief. The communication of medicine always has the divinatory quality of 'subjunctivity' (Reynolds-Whyte 1997). The medicine is couched in terms that accept the uncertainty of outcome. Magic and divination are two ways of communicating with the spirit, a notoriously abstruse interlocutor.

Modes of Production, Spheres of Exchange

Magic informs the universe. It can only do so in cosmologies that do not separate modes of production. 'Your intentions will not affect the universe', the scientist retorts, isolating the production mode of human thought from the production mode of molecular interaction, and thereby undermining the foundation of magic and animism.[1] What would a cosmology be like if it had one mode of production and many spheres of exchange? Species of animals and plants, peoples, artefacts, commodities, and so on, would be the subject of separate spheres of exchange, imposing their own principles. Yet, all would participate in the same mode of production: life. On animism among Amerindians, Descola (1994) similarly contends that the belief in one consciousness of which all beings partake goes hand in hand with 'multi-naturalism': the conviction that species have their own bodily realities operating in their own circuits of communication and exchange. Viveiros de Castro (2004) quotes Lévi-Strauss's paradigmatic example of Amerindians hanging corpses of white settlers into the water of the river to check if putrefaction is the same, while across the Atlantic, Jesuit priests were debating if the primitive mind had a conscience. Although we would not simply extrapolate the animism of Amerindians to our African region of study, both areas have long entertained a special relation with the forest. And both differ equally from the only real eccentric, the modern West.

Western modernity has made technological progress by achieving the capitalist inversion: everything can be exchanged in the one sphere of exchange called the market (except humans belonging in a separate realm of affection), whereas the modes of production have to be distinguished, because other conditions of labour and profit apply in the north and the south, heaven and earth, for kings and commoners, priests and their followers. A hegemony ensues, keeping social classes in power that bring to bear on the one market the profits of their privileged mode of production.

Modes of production and spheres of exchange provide a theoretically grounded framework to compare societies. Applying the two axes of our anthropological scheme, the spheres of exchange correspond to the experiential frames advocated by actor-idealism. They are balanced by the structure-materialism of modes of production. The two diagonally opposed quadrants should bring our applied framework more towards the centre. Neo-Marxist Bohannan wrote the structure-materialist work of reference on the Tiv in Nigeria, whose spheres of exchange are applicable as well to equatorial Africa.[2] In those various instances, the minimal partitioning (contextually porous still) stipulates that the sphere of commodity transactions is a social field that should not be confused with that of prestige goods such as medicinal knowledge and titles, nor with the highest-ranked third sphere for marrying people. The actor-idealist will translate the three spheres of exchange into frames of experience so as to explicate that everybody in that society thinks differently about commodities (by which one legally incurs debt) than about sacrifice (whose success depends on collective acceptance) or about gifts (wherein building up a relationship is central). The frame is experiential and the sphere is social.

Separate spheres of exchange do not preclude the existence of one mode of production, and reproduction. On the contrary, numerous cultural histories worldwide point to a cosmology where everybody depends on the same source of good fortune, such as 'life' or 'pacha mama'. Life holds the separate circuits of exchange together. Why would the king obey another mode of production? He too is mortal and sanctioned by the spirits of the dead. His special position only stems from his special access to that source. As in the logic of hunter societies discussed in Part I, the right medicine such as a charm or augural sign enhances access to the one source. Victor Turner's distinction between healing rituals and rites of passage as different modes conceals that those practices are felt to tap from the same source of life.

The Cultural Transmission of Medicine: Open, Empirical, Collective, Relational

From the capitalist inversion follows the misunderstanding that traditional medicine refers to a primitive mode of production. Compared to the scientific conquest of 'nature' and the unchained creativity of 'culture', African communities come across as traditionalist, slow on progress and invention. The stereotypical explanation is that their tradition-oriented structure of cultural (re)production would be merely habitual, and not at all based on empirical investigation; that it would be collectivist, discouraging individual creativity; and that it would close itself off to other cultures (cf. the 'closed' predicament, Horton 1967). A different picture emerges from ethnographic research into traditional medicine (Stroeken 2008). The precariously unitary mode of production we coined 'fertility' causes strong affects about external influences. Given the mix of desire and fear, the healer's attitude to foreign goods and other medicinal epistemologies should actually be qualified as open. Add the empirical interest in plants that cure, and the slow progress of his or her knowledge admittedly becomes a conundrum. A countervailing force is at work, I argue, that propels the endogenous development of knowledge in non-linear directions. It is the search by healer and client for a collective and relational truth.

The orientation on collective truth is not directed negatively against individual creativity (as Enlightenment discourse presumes) but positively towards truths that all members of the community would endorse. In 'all', the ancestral or nature spirits are included, which restrains individual creativity of the purely cerebral kind. How to obtain a collective truth? Healers travel around. They visit colleagues. In the evenings at the compound of an influential healer where I lived I could overhear conversations. Which new diagnoses are popular? Is it true that these days one had better not make sacrifices to the ancestral spirits because once satiated the spirits are no longer reliable? Oracles let ancestors speak to reveal collective truths.

Coupled with the truth of the collective is another secret knowledge the healer searches for: the symbolic relations that dominate life and death. Plants, animal parts, ingredients – it is a kind of truth one must get initiated into. Initiation can be expensive, and sometimes may require ancestral invitation, and is never finished. Does this secret knowledge, or *gnosis* in Mudimbe's (1988) words, not account for the ubiquity of initiatory cults in the region? An empirical sense as well as openness to the other's knowledge are implied in the widespread practice of medicine. These traits in the transmission of medicinal knowledge reflect the open, empirical, collective and relational structure of cultural transmission that is essential to comprehend the history of institutions in equatorial Africa.

Healers are eager to discover more about the materiality of symbols. Through dreams inspired by the spirit they learn about the relations between the constituents of the forest. And they obtain truth of a collective value, because rather than mechanically applying an autonomous (e.g. empirical) procedure, it is a truth accountable to the entire community, including the invisible world and its demands. In *nkula* initiation, the *Mukula* tree (*Pterocarpus angolensis*, the Rhodesian teak) that will be cut *is* the spirit (*mu-kishi*), Turner (1968: 73) hears from his informants. The figurines (*an-kishi*, same stem) carved from wood pegs are medicated on the head by a mixture of Mukula bark, red clay, bits of slaughtered rooster, red feathers of the grey parrot, body-residues from a person with albinism and from each patient, and the red lourie feathers worn by the patients (ibid.: 74). The figurine represents the baby the barren woman in this cult wishes for. The figurine is placed in one half of a cut calabash before being reunited with the other half, filled with the medicine. The resulting *ilembu* charm stands for the womb (*ivumu*). Despite the resemblance with a play, the sequence of actions changes life.

The open, empirical, collective and relational traits account for the widely experienced fact about severe illness that no matter how strictly observed, the medicinal procedures do not guarantee success. In the hunter's cult of Ihamba, the tooth dodging its capture expresses this well. Success of curing largely 'depends on the moral condition of the patient and his group' (Turner 1967: 114). Public admission of held grudges can persuade the tooth to be removed (ibid.: 152). An Ihamba shrine is erected for those public confessions (ibid.: 156). Healing is a moral domain in the broad sense, intervening in mental, social and biological facets yet permeated with the patient's concern of doing the right thing. Nobody knows exactly what is right. What 'people' and 'the ancestors' expect is truth at a collective level, which no individual masters. The healer dreams and travels, visits colleagues faraway to search for things that get the relations right and harbour truth (*ng'hana*, Suk.) at the collective level. The debate at dusk never closes, because patients are known to prefer healers who innovate to outsmart the cunning witches. The healers must feel comfortable in different spheres of exchange and manage the corresponding frames of experience. They must lead their patients out of the disempowering frame of bewitchment, via divination, into the empowering space of magic to beat their witch with countermagic (Stroeken 2004). Tell them to disentangle the mode of (re)production – life – and they lose their power to heal.

Fractal + Extension: A Niger–Congo Logic?

In cases as wide apart as Komo initiation and Zande ethnic relations, the one mode of production underwent classificatory extensions and resurfaced at different levels of symbolization. Part I compared the cultural dynamic to a fractal. The flexibility precludes cultural orthodoxy. The dynamic tallies well with the hypothesis that Bantu-speaking communities, and possibly their neighbours brought up in the encompassing Niger–Congo family of languages, have predominantly been cultural and linguistic assimilators. Can we find tangible evidence for this long-term influence of a cultural structure? Language itself carries the marks. The similarities between among others Lele, Ndembu, Komo and Sukuma initiations suggest the acculturation to operate according to the dual principle of a fractal (fertility) and its classificatory extensions. Let us consider how the production modes and exchange spheres of a society may be reflected in the structure of its languages. We begin with a few paragraphs enumerating cohering data, in Turner's work among others, before we propose the argument.

Several examples from our region under study concur on the structure of fractal and classificatory extension. Medicinal recipes consist of a powerful substance – the stem – and a symbolic 'entrance' – the class. Extended families apply classificatory kinship to expand their social network. Fieldworkers seeking to integrate into a host community benefit by becoming classificatory sons or daughters. The use of cash instead of livestock for fees is in a way a 'hybridization' between old and new (Turner 1967: 130). It is also a classificatory extension apparently arousing no moral dilemma.

What happens when the researcher does not take into account the classification prowess of his or her hosts? In the popular attributions of illness to witchcraft, Turner distils a historical change whereby witchcraft has replaced ancestral curse. We seem to witness Ndembu modernity at work: 'Belief in the moral power of the ancestors weakens, as belief in the maleficent power of the living increases' (ibid.: 129; although see the central role of witchcraft already in the ancient Ihamba ritual). Yet, ancestors always were whimsical too, hence not so moral and not so predictable a curse. Are the witch and the ancestor not interchangeable, classificatory extensions of the same thing? An ancestor responsible for death is considered evil and a curse for the family because of the violent death this ancestor suffered in the past (cf. in Kisukuma: *wacha malali*, 'one who died outside the home'). The 'moral power' this angry ancestor has, differs from the legitimate authority of an elder or content ancestor. At the level of experiential frame, the moral power is akin to the frightening claim the witch lays on someone's life. The ease by which a Sukuma oracle switches between the two culprits or combines them is indicative. An actor-idealist approach to culture registers such contextual modifications.

About hunt and oracle, a similar tendency of classificatory extension imposed itself. Not all Ndembu rituals are preceded by oracles. In Turner's account the ritual treatment of bewitchment follows after 'a traditional hunting ritual' (ibid.: 128). Is that not the point at which other groups with less affinity with hunting, Sukuma for instance, consult an oracle? Mary Douglas among the Lele acknowledged the oracular meaning of testing one's luck at hunting. A good catch augurs well for the intended ritual, so motivates to go ahead with it. We may conclude that the acts of oracle and hunt experientially belong to the same symbolic class. The hunt is a classificatory extension of the oracle, just as the witch extends the class of angry ancestors.

Now, I am unwilling to ignore the strong resemblance of this cultural structure with the particular structure of nouns in the Bantu family of languages and the encompassing Niger–Congo family. In a compound, the affix (classificatory extension) added to a stem (fractal) determines a noun-class, one of a dozen that identify semantic spheres. These classes include humans (but not the gender), animals, natural and manufactured things, and their plurals, as well as abstractions, locatives, and more classes whose original meaning has become diffuse. Does this principle of linguistic classification not reflect the region's cultural system of structuring social exchange into spheres, namely circuits of communication obeying their own principle, in analogy with an affix? Moreover, do the spheres not resort under one mode of production? They all 'are'. Remember, in Bantu languages there is no 'having' next to 'being'; you can only have something by literally 'being with' it, -*wa na*. These languages, moreover, have markers to denote a 'habitual' tense, which places activities in the flow of life and being, instead of either in past, present or future.[3]

Do differences between cultural structures of groups of *homo sapiens* that split thousands of years ago manifest themselves at the formal level of grammar? Although unorthodox, the hypothesis is not far-fetched, at least not if we find its equivalent in other languages. An interesting case to contrast with the Niger–Congo family are Latin and German: those languages limit the classes of nouns to two or three, such as gender and neuter, but specialize in denoting cases in grammatical agreement with actions (ablative, accusative, dative, genitive). Does this not correspond to the diversification of modes of production in modern Western societies? At the same time, an inverse process may affect the spheres of exchange: conflation. The market, and making profit, forms the one encompassing sphere. In brief, I am not excluding that linguistic structures are suggestive of cultural structure, in this case of an endogenous logic that eventually contributed to the ideology of capitalism.

Endogeneity and Cultural Drift

The structure of stem and class allows one to study cultural drift, which is cultural change irrespective of external influence. Societies vary in the leeway their members have for endogenously generating variants on a given theme. The Bantu specialty of classificatory extension frustrates attempts at historically reconstructing external influences or conquests that account for cultural changes. A genuine contribution of meso-anthropology is to determine for particular groups the extent of cultural change possible without effort of adoption, (major) adaptation, inertia or resistance. The normal situation, without proof of external influence, is endogenous development. Going by current ritual symbolism in the region, the Neolithic transition from hunter to farmer may have been mostly endogenous, harnessing the Bantu art of classificatory extension. To the hunter's fractal of reciprocity with the wild outside we only need to add the scalar extensions of time and space to explain current ritual symbolism.

In terms of temporal scale, the hunt's outcome auguring for the group's direct future is on a (classificatory) par with the longer-term predictions of the rains for farmers. Extend the timeframe and the hunt can remain the model in agriculture: an oracle anticipates the farmer's annual harvest, or someone's treatment of illness. The contingency of a hunt expedition (as well as a geomantic toss) enables the classificatory extension. In terms of spatial scale, the successful reciprocity with the forest entailing good fortune for the band of hunters is replicated without effort at the expansive scale of the farmer's relation with the land and with the community comprising neighbours and non-kin. The right sacrifice will keep the rains coming and safeguard the fertility of both land and people.

Through such classificatory extensions proper to Bantu-speaking communities, we may understand the mysterious persistence of shamanic hunter's symbolism in the agricultural village. Hunt and divinatory association have remained part and parcel of local cosmologies since the Neolithic revolution of agriculture, despite the disparity between the cultivated steppe of the communities today and the forest-within cosmology of their initiations. Perhaps the influence of autochthonous hunting bands in Bantu acculturation has been underestimated? In any case, the ecological-economic transition from hunt to agriculture in east and central Africa has been fed by endogenous cultural logic.

The Introduction distinguished three types of endogenous rule that commonly existed in parallel, and in some areas succeeded each other: divinatory, medicinal and ceremonial. It is at this 'anthropological' level of production modes, spheres of exchange, endogenous evolutions and experiential frames that cultural comparison works. I wish to demonstrate next that once the fundamental level of cultural structure is deserted and the cosmologies are juxtaposed as sets of beliefs, the exercise may falter. Then one concrete belief, denuded of context, may be wrongly compared to another. The method of fieldwork and the theory of endogenous anthropology must ensure we focus on similarities that matter.

A Recent Case of History without Anthropology: Anti-colonial Bodies

Magic is a frame of experience. Bewitchment is another. And positivist science draws on an experiential frame too. What blander proposition does one need in the postmodern era, than one avowing the plurality of frames within culture? Yet, the consistent application of the insight is no easy task. In her critique on anthropological projections of alterity on Africa, Florence Bernault (2006: 220) digs into the imaginary of West Equatorial Africans. Her plausible point of entry is that Europeans and Gabonese have together re-enchanted the human body in the colonial era. The issue will be whether her historical analysis can bespeak the varying contexts within society that an ethnography would evince.

Bernault sets off by describing sacrifices as messengers of wishes to the dead, which tallies well with our communication paradigm of magic. She also offers an enthralling take on magic in equatorial Africa following the paradigm of embodiment that has informed anthropology since the 1990s: '[P]eople's bodies and corporeal fragments did not differ ontologically from ritually empowered charms. As multiple and fragmentable, immaterial and material, the body could not be described simply as a neutral biological entity guided by an individual mind. . . . it was entirely submerged by power' (ibid.: 214). The quest to endogenize history and raise the bar of interpretation begins right there. Bernault's suggestive generalization of body parts into a worldview of charms will ring true to scholars working on witchcraft in sub-Saharan Africa. At the same time her description of the magical frame of experience omits other frames, as in the moment when the body is not submerged by power; when it engages in ordinary or prosaic activities or disappears in the background of speech. The multiple body requires we acknowledge the multiplicity of reality, permitting contradictory frames in one and the same society, lifetime, person. Bernault enumerates the body entities in local terminologies, on which ethnographers rely too. It would be unfair to treat her analysis other than as a token of common practice among established Africanists. My criticism regards all of us writing about beliefs, often necessarily in abstraction of the contextual frames. Ethnographers, I argue, should consciously avoid structure-idealism, the inclination to assign beliefs to actors irrespective of context.

We should acclaim the historian's endeavour to single out the Equatorial African conception of the body. Maniema discriminate between visible body, invisible body and intelligence. Fang, Lingala and Kikongo terminologies do so between living body, corpse and ancestor. According to Bernault, these terms 'differed spectacularly from the univocal dimension of the same term (in French, *corps*) indiscriminately before and after death, in parallel with the perceived material continuity of the medicalized body' (ibid.: 215). I contest that the French do not distinguish a body before and after death. Perhaps her English translations fail to evoke how 'spectacularly' different the concepts are. I see similarities with 'body', 'soul' and 'mind', the usual three constituting the person in Christian beliefs. And does the English language's 'body' and 'corpse' not discriminate before and after death?

Bernault, aware of the tendency of Christianized informants to import European concepts, avoids describing ancestors as disembodied souls (ibid.: 215; 216, n30). She follows Günther Tessman (and his translator Laburthe-Tolra) who from his Cameroonian Fang informants in 1913 learned that:

> all living things, including people, possessed a force that remained in each fragment of the living entity, even if detached from it. [. . .] The integral identity and power of an individual could therefore remain in certain bone fragments, a belief crucial to the widespread cult of relics throughout the region. These notions, however, have been largely obscured by Christian inspired attempts to force local cosmologies into western categories. (Bernault 2006: 215–16)

At closer inspection, though, is the possession of force not recalling the Catholic practice of revering the relics of saints, touching the bones or shrine to acquire their protective blessing? Furthermore, the practice of communicating intentions through the charm, on which Bernault concurred earlier, does not sit well with the just quoted belief in fragments carrying and transmitting power – a process for which, by my knowledge, no Bantu words, specific or generic, exist. The Sukuma and Luguru healers I worked with were familiar with procedures to safeguard an object's medicinal efficacy (e.g. at the crossing of a river), but not with things sacred or beaming force, independently of social context.

The case of a Gabonese prisoner whose corpse was buried after execution tempts Bernault to surmise that the community was prevented from capturing the criminal's witch-substance for their magic, and that the white officers must have seemed competitors on the market of spiritual ingredients (ibid.: 219). The author does not mention whether the prisoner was accused of witchcraft (Was he not a thief resorting to mundane means?), neither whether anyone had actually expressed the need for dissecting the executed (Was the search for witchcraft-substance not reserved for witchcraft-related crimes and for unknown causes of death?), nor whether the use of a criminal's body part could cause 'collective healing' (ibid.: 218) – which is doubtful as well, because poison ordeals and bodily infused medicinal preparations were exceptional and took place at the periphery of society, literally outside the village borders. Body fragments for medicinal purposes are the subject of specialized knowledge. Also, we learn in a footnote, at Bernault's site of research it is only specialists who collect bones, and they do so in secret (ibid.: 234, n93). If the collection is no public or collective endeavour, why would its prevention due to the colonial requirement of immediate burial impede social reproduction and reconciliation in the family (ibid.: 233)?

Furthermore, why would alternative means of acquiring body remains be seen locally as a breach (ibid.: 236), given the accepted skill of classificatory extension in symbolizations? The author overestimates the Christian ploy of emphasizing the symbolic value of Biblical sacrifice in contradistinction to local sacrifice (ibid.: 228). Symbolization is communication, thus completing the magical act. In the classificatory logic of magic users, a prohibited deed can be replaced by a metaphorically similar one, like synonyms in communication. Mimesis, the since Taussig (1993) widely discussed effect expected from inserting a sample of 'white power' in medicine, has been applied since time immemorial without requiring the association with Western fetishized white bodies (Bernault 2006: 233).

Anthropologizing history is a never-ending task. The impact of colonial policy on village life will be overrated if relying on colonial archives. Across Equatorial Africa interracial contacts, mentioned in those archives, rarely reached all layers of the rural community. Instead of assuming that a criminal's imprisonment would locally appear as the white man's competitive tactic in the universal struggle over body parts – the author's laudable attempt of moving 'away from a dominant/subaltern dichotomy' (ibid.: 220) – one should ask why imprisonment of an individual never seemed an adequate measure or punishment in central and eastern Africa. Physical isolation cannot stop the communication of magic?

Ethnographic evidence should complement historical archives wherever possible. The quote of a missionary signalling the enthusiasm of villagers to sacrifice their fetishes and get rid of the objects' dangerous powers (ibid.: 222) proves little more than that people threw the fetish away to replace it by the missionary's better magic in Biblical format. To return to the earlier definition of magic as communication, did the object's power not concern the effectiveness of the object's message, for which ingredients and formula of speech were employed? Did the dangerous force exist mainly in the eye of the white beholder?

The metonymic link with hair or nail of the client has less to do with the body than with the purpose communicated. As in the rest of Bantu-speaking Africa visited by travellers in the 1500s, metaphoric objects and plants that communicated a meaning played a greater role in magic than bones and other actual remains of the body. We find confirmation of that for the Gabonese case in a footnote citing Tessman that only skulls of relatives were acceptable body parts in ancestral rites (ibid.: 234, n94). Most medicinal matter comes from the forest instead of the body. In her description of relic boxes and their fabrication Bernault indeed makes no reference to the bodily parts she placed centrally at first (ibid.: 235). Does it in fact matter? She traces the use of body fragments 'at least to the end of the nineteenth century' (ibid.: 208). I would argue that metonymic materiality has existed, with peaks of use, long before those recorded events. The pitfall this chapter warns against is to approach institutions as historical events instead of enactments of cultural structure. Positively put: anthropologize history.

Bernault proclaims to nuance Vansina's view of colonialism as a cultural rupture because 'we cannot go far enough in identifying in which qualitative ways the colonial episode informed symbolic configurations at work in modern Africa and in the world at large' (ibid.: 238). I would rather insist that, due to the absence of precolonial data, the precolonial continuities have always been minimized in African studies, and the colonial influences, elaborately reported in archives, magnified. The chapters on medicinal rule have deliberately zoomed out from the colonial episode to trace endogenous continuities with precolonial roots. A complementary approach is to zoom in to see how colonial authorities dealt with magic, like in Kishina's account. The risk when shifting attention from an institution to people, 'whites' and 'Africans', is that virtually all combinations of people understanding and misunderstanding each other are possible. The first part of Bernault's article evinces the clash of ideational systems (ibid.: 220). The second part of her article is replete with suggestions that 'colonizers and Africans shared mutually intelligible ideas and symbolic systems' (ibid.: 238). The antinomy is possible because the 'Africans' in her account are never categorized. Her personal heated discussion with a white missionary is the closest we come to receiving a 'local' point of view. By lack of ethnographic data, the historian has little recourse other than to read people's experience of colonization into events elevated to social symptoms. Yet, the reading should be culturally sound. A perplexing example is the gruesome murder of a white trader's wife that would be symptomatic: 'The killers' cruelty and greed, and their lack of clear political motive, replicated the failure of the colonial project to promote a public order based on anything other than physical violence' (ibid.: 229). The acts seemed to this reader as those of two psychopaths, *tout court*.[4] No similar practices in society were mentioned that warrant the claim of a cultural structure at play, inverted or otherwise.

Interviews on 'urban legends' (ibid.: 236, n102) do not qualify as reports on sentiments in the population. We read that '[i]n the realm of magic, ritual specialists are less than ever perceived as invariably enforcing collective prosperity' (ibid.: 236). The reason may be that the population thinks differently about magic, but it could also be that the perception changed because healers increasingly fail at their work. The actor's frame of experience matters. Most people may have turned against the age-old medicinal epistemology after the banning of village initiation. Another issue is whether ritual specialists 'invariably' enforced collective prosperity. That could be the view of urban dwellers educated and French-speaking, with a tradition of presenting villagers as gullible. Rural Africa has in the past decades boasted prevalence figures of around 80 per cent on consultations of traditional healers in case of grave illness (Stroeken 2012). Yet Bernault (2006: 237) states that 'popular opinion tends to see foreign *marabouts* or self-proclaimed *banganga* [healers] as destructive outsiders working for the sole benefit of predatory leaders'. Should we keep a positive reservation about initiated healers? Since the area no longer has a formal initiation into healing, most *banganga* are self-proclaimed, which may render the scholar's statement about as dismissive as the Pentecostalist sermon against witchcraft.

Is the derivation of cultural structure, without which I think the pitfalls surfacing in this section are inevitable, a dirty deed akin to colonial essentialism? The alternative is rather the above analysis moving from specific events to general discourse, and back, switching between the extremes of the anthropological spectrum – from historicism to, well, culturalism. If indeed belief in body fragments containing and transmitting identity and power were the matter, one would find Bantu-speakers obsessively cleaning up and burying their own and their children's nails, hair, licked items, bodily refuse and so on. And the search for power substances would not be limited to medicinal specialists. No informant who shared the discourse on 'zombified victims' (ibid.: 209) with me in the late 1990s seemed other than recounting sensational stories, which could not preoccupy anyone as much as actual situations of personal bewitchment – the stuff people went to visit healers for. A variant on sensational culturalism is the belief 'in whites as ancestors' – as spirits, that is (ibid.: 219). Such first-contact thoughts never last long. Soon after the interlocutors engaged in social, sexual and economic exchange, they came back to their senses, probably gasping out like the great-grandfather of chief Kaphipa of Bukumbi in his conversation with the first German settlers after they had been staring at each other for a few hours on the banks of Lake Victoria: *Binadamu tu*, 'Just people'. Notice the advantage of detecting the actor's experiential shifts in concrete practices. We should all be wary of the idealist lure of perpetuating historical moments into fixed beliefs and collective traits, beyond context and frame. Cultural structure – here of medicinal rule and its derivatives such as magic as communication – reminds us that the dynamics of practice are not the same everywhere.

Notes

1. Latour's (1993) critique on the 'modern constitution' of nature and culture questions the two modes of production. Their separation is destructive, keeping up the illusion that how we think would not be an integral part of the ecological disaster worldwide. The relation between self and environment, articulated in a type of materiality, conflicts with the single mode of production in which all life participates. In the 'modern constitution', nature and the body can be known because they are molecular, consisting of things that can be isolated, tested and recombined in a laboratory, whereas society and the mind will always be too complex, holistic and subjective to be objects of science.
2. We lack the space to draw a comparison between equatorial African cultural systems partitioning spheres of social exchange. A good starting point are the works of MacGaffey (1986), Vansina (1990) and Thornton (1998), especially in relation to the cultural translation work needed regarding the meanings of slave, pawn and tributary.
3. In Swahili, the marker *hu-* in a verb denotes habitual or repetitive actions. In Sukuma, a habitual aspect in the past can also be created through the marker combining affix *-ka-* with suffix *-aga*.

4. By lack of contextual data, one may feel compelled to agree that 'the assassination confirms . . . the order of the transgressive sacrifice' (ibid.: 230). The author's default context is that of postcolonial theory, *in casu* Joseph Tonda's thesis that the colonizer reversed the symbolic economy by making 'transgressive sacrifices' without returns.

Chapter 7

TIO SHRINES OF THE FOREST MASTER

The book from 1973 on the Tio Kingdom is the work that Vansina was most content about because it came out exactly as he intended. In his view the monograph (TK henceforth) had demonstrated, against purist historians, some of whom featured in his PhD jury and he had courageously defied, that an ethnography of the past is possible (Newbury 2007). The influence of Daryl Forde, to whom Vansina (1973: xvii) said to 'owe much of what I know about social anthropology', is more visible in this book than in any other of his, as Forde 'patiently annotated the draft of the text' with 'detailed and incisive criticism'. We notice the influence of annotation in his introduction, asserting that religion interlocks with the other societal structures (TK 18); his materialist claim that 'population density is a major element of any social system, so that changes in density would almost certainly have implied major changes in the social system' is somewhat contradicted further on in the paragraph by the more holistic insight that '[t]he low density must be considered as a stable factor caused by the total way of life of the Tio' (TK 16). The organization of Tio society is his object. Hence, in his book not oral literature but 'the value-system is described. The latter is essential to our understanding of society, whereas the former is less closely linked to it' (TK 17). A society can only scantily be known from its oral tradition. These are remarkable words coming from a historian whose main source of earlier studies had been oral literature.

The Ethnographic Present/Past

At the end of a paragraph signalling the lack of anthropological fieldwork data on Tio, Vansina affirms that '[w]ithout a period of fieldwork we could not have understood the general organization of Tio society on the grasslands of Mbe and Nsah' (TK 21). However, he does not explicate how his ethnography of current life could enlighten us about the Tio precolonial past. 'We tried to avoid as painstakingly as possible just carrying anything back in time without proof' (TK 23). The data collection during fieldwork unfortunately did not target Tio cultural structure. It was mostly meant to fill in the gaps of historical sources on certain events. Sometimes he used ethnography of the present to learn about the past. Then he implicitly acknowledged the distinction between structure and event, and the merits of these complementing each other to obtain a richer, indeed 'anthropologized' history.

Highlighting the specific timeframe for which the ethnography would be valid is a way of avoiding the trap of the ethnographic present. Vansina joined the historians who were astonished about ethnographic descriptions written in the present tense, seemingly taking for granted an atemporal and static condition of non-Western societies. In addition to my plea for the habitual tense (cf. Introduction), I would argue that writers can legitimately refrain from the past tense about events obviously pertaining to the past (as in reflections about another author's writings) if they want to shift attention from factual accuracy to logic and argumentation. The issue for the ethnographer is whether a well contextualized use of the present tense might befit the interpretation of culture, whose unit of analysis is structure and continuity instead of the fleeting event.

In practice, Vansina seems anthropological enough to not go as far as historically delimiting the value system under study. The accuracy of the past tense is somewhat of a ploy anyway, for it is always stretched to encompass longer periods and more specific events than possible. Is the ethnographer's actuality – or Fabian's (1983) coevalness with the informant – confined to the very moment of conversing with one's informant, to a couple of hours before and after it, to a week, a season, or a year when the text is published? Does time even matter when the moment is subjective? The people involved in the conversation about an institution or value system will each have their own experience of the interview situation. Whose actuality counts? To include everyone's perception of the event is impossible, not least because nobody can be fully aware of a lived experience, let alone of a past event. At the same time, so many other members of the community, living and dead, determine the sense made. The meaning, of an institution for instance, evolves somewhere between all those elements.

Vansina chose a validity period between 1877 and 1892 for his monograph in function of the availability of written sources about the reign of King Iloo. The reign began about a decade earlier, and a footnote clarifies that the information is scarce before 1880 as well as between 1885 and 1890 (TK 19, n40). The suggestion is that seven years of information are sufficient to cover fifteen years of history. Of course, there will always be a dearth of information, but what I am hinting at is to restrain the historicist obsession with a people at a certain epoch. In regions with much cultural exchange a (meso-)anthropological approach reconstructing cultural wholes from adjacent areas offers a no less valid picture, albeit taken from the angle of structure instead of event. The extended spatial relevance and extended timeframe of cultural structure make up for the lack of historical data.

The question thus acutely remains, about the Tio monograph in particular, how to infer 'the value system', or cultural structure. Describing beliefs and norms is one thing, but determination of their varied importance is a serious challenge. The quality depends on the representativeness of the pool of informants, the level of the fieldworker's integration in the community, language skills, avoidance of leading questions, ability to ferret out socially undesirable ideas, the depth of participation and initiation, the length of stay, and the good fortune of meeting the right people. For instance, the district head might have convinced me that Sukuma medicine is largely a thing of the past for educated Tanzanians, had I not by chance seen his daughter one day brought by his driver to a traditional healer I worked with. Medicinal knowledge and the ritual practices it implies are particularly contentious in Tanzania where the opposite ideologies of socialism and Christianity made magical superstition into a common enemy. Local leaders fear that admitting the presence and importance of medicine in the community could draw the interventionist attention of higher authorities, as did the Bulima king deposed by the British.

This chapter examines the case of one well-documented kingdom to test the validity of our change of focus from administration and government to medicine and fertility in interpreting the institution of kingship. Medicinal knowledge is what adults are initiated into and what makes them eligible for higher rank (the so-called aristocrats). The forest-masters acquiring a charm thanks to a nature spirit embodied medicinal rule. As soon as some of them obtained a box of charms, named *nkobi*, an intermediate rank arose between the charms of their colleagues and the royal charm of the king. The dynamic confirms, I will argue, that medicine constitutes an endogenous sort of power. Kingship and chieftaincy in central and eastern Africa obey cultic principles. Going by oral traditions, in some cases the royal clans were actual offshoots of an initiatory association after a male or female member emigrated with some followers.

Charms

Vansina writes about the *ibili* charm of the headman that it lent prestige, yet concludes that because the charms could be bought, 'their possession did not mean much. Much more important as an indicator of leadership and authority was the ability of the *wookuru* to protect his people against illness and death' (TK 76). Besides the difficulty of determining what a certain institution meant for people a century ago, an antinomy appears: what other way was there to protect against illness and death than to possess the right medicine? A commonsense reasoning about the materiality of medicine being secondary to religious belief seems to be hindering his insight in cultural structure. Moreover, he extends the alleged insignificance of the charm to an indefinite period, in fact to as long as common sense might apply, presumably infinitely. This section and the next exemplify how an alternative interpretation may shed new light on the African historian's data, specifically on two pivots of medicinal rule: the role of chiefs as masters of the forest, and their reliance on shrine and charm.

What do Tio charms, *kaa*, mean to the people involved if their exchange amounts to the establishment of 'blood brotherhood' (TK 263)? The charm is not just representing but 'having' the owner's life, like blood does. Since 'having' something in Bantu languages is 'being with' the thing (rather than immanence), a sort of 'partnership' materiality can be implied whereby owned thing and owner are interchangeable. This experiential frame anchoring the practice seems like a plausible entry point to equate leadership with a charm.

The cultural structure mostly applied by Jan Vansina to the Tio kingdom is that of the *homo economicus* pursuing his personal interests, or what Sahlins (1976) in his critique of Marvin Harris's cultural materialism termed 'practical reason'. Two explanatory principles surface in Vansina's descriptions of social change: people and land. Demographics and ecology are treated as material factors. Founding a village that attracts adherents makes a person a headman, *wookuru* (from *wa ukulu*, 'of the great one'), its first meaning being 'elder' (TK 75). The elder is a 'big man' and was once an ambitious young man gathering thirty to forty peers in a group (TK 76). Vansina mentions no cosmological or spiritual elements informing the ambition. After the fact of material necessity, which denuded of culture attains the value of historical objectivity, comes the headman's 'attempt to formalize his ascendancy though the acquisition of an *ibili* charm' (TK 75). The political decision to found a village at a certain spot subsequently calls for religious legitimation – namely, a diviner is sent for, who 'chase[s] the evil spirits away with a great show of contortions' (TK 76). Cosmology is presented in secularized fashion as a separate domain, reserved for the diviner, high priest or shaman occupying a religious and non-political office encountered the world over.

In light of our thesis, the data tell another story. The specific name of the charm refers to the requirement for the headman to be initiated into an *ibili* cult (known as *ne-bili* towards the east of Mongo peoples). The household head prays daily to his ancestral spirits (*ikwii*) out of his own choosing (TK 41), without the intervention of a caste of priests. People are genuinely worried about being deserted by their *ikwii* (TK 43). Vansina's speculation that most people had little or no possessions to inherit except for some kitchen utensils (TK 38) is strangely at odds with his drawing a few pages further on of an average household shrine covered with protective statues of twins, medicinal amulets and containers (TK 42). Do these medicinal objects not qualify as wealth? The author does not care to mention whether medicinal objects were among the 'number of goods' that might be buried with the deceased household-head, 'especially if he was a chief' (TK 38). I suspect many were not, given the great value of ancestral charms. Wherever I travelled in rural east and central Africa to speak with initiated elders, they possessed much medicinal knowledge and could often point out a successor they had in mind who would inherit the regalia. For the transmission of a Sukuma elder's medicinal heritage the chosen descendant has proven his knowledge in a public competition of medicine (*isambingula*).

To outline the cultural structure, the close link between seniority and medicinal knowledge cannot be sufficiently underlined. The link disproves the separation of political and religious domains, which we have therefore kept together under the category of medicine. The two classic roles of king (chief, headman) and healer (diviner) have historically grown apart, but they belong to the same semantic field, as they are different applications of the same initiatory knowledge of the elder (*wookuru*, also headman), which concerns charms and the protection against evil. Despite the author's presentation of a Tio typology opposing healers to diviners (TK 173), the reader notices that concrete cases of actual rituals compel him to use *ngàà* as the unitary category 'healer/diviner' in his descriptions (TK 45, 179). The expert making or stopping rain is also a *ngàà*.

To attain the status of seniority, one must first get initiated into the same fertility rite healers specialize in. The casual observation by Vansina on the healer is revealing: 'No settlement was left without at least a minor *ngàà*, and in Mbe in 1963 every leader was a *ngàà* in addition to several other men and women. For, there were many gradations in the craft, and many tried their hand at a bit of curing and perhaps divining' (TK 173). Did the many gradations not have a political dimension as well? Did the household heads try their hand a bit, or did they have the responsibility of protecting their compound? In line with this paternal role and together with his experts, the chief organized the ritual care for the nature spirits of his chiefdom (TK 170). Why do we have difficulty picturing a leader obtaining honour and respect from medicinal knowledge?

The secondary role imparted to the charms by Vansina conflicts with a number of his own observations. The *wookuru* asks the diviner to install the village charm, *nkiini*, an altar or 'shrine' built around a hole with medicinal plants (TK 76), like the one built by the Chwezi spirit cult (and within the confines of the euphorbia bush, as is tradition too in some areas east of the Great Lakes). The *wookuru* is a healer of its own kind for possessing the *ibili* charm and the shrine, as well as carrying 'a horn filled with magic' (TK 79). Moreover, these shrines provide the basis for power. Vansina writes that the presence of two shrines in one village forewarns nothing less than a split. He remarks in a footnote about *nkiini* that '[t]he word and shrine for villages are known from Mayombe to the Sakata and even further to the Kuba. It can be presumed to be old, especially since it is not remembered as a recent introduction anywhere' (TK 77, n28). Then why limit the significance of village shrines to the mere formalizing of political relations? 'A village headman was expected to protect the people who lived with him' (TK 75). Protection against internal and external forces endangering life is the primary concern permeating the monograph. Why would that not be a better explanation for those elaborate medicinal-ritual investments than political legitimacy? All across the region, from Mayombe in the west to Kuba in the east and deep into the past, as mentioned in the cited footnote, appear those village charms. Across the region and beyond, including the northern part of equatorial Africa and all the way to the east of the Great Lakes, the connection is made between initiation and acquisition of a medicinal recipe and charm. The *nkiini* draws its strength from an invisible animal from the forest like the leopard (TK 78). In the same area, encompassing the Bantu-speaking area, the initiation system unites the village community to control the dangerous forces the households have to deal with. Why would kingship not be a supreme version of that? Have we fully gathered yet what the medicinal model implies?

Chieftaincy as Forest-Mastery: A Linchpin Claim

The application of European political terminology to the Tio kingdom has consequences. Throughout Vansina's monograph the titles of squire, lord, chief and king are presented as constituting the Tio hierarchy, above the rank of village headman that is. More than five hundred pages of data are arranged according to this compelling fourfold stratification of one territory, the kingdom, obeying one political structure with a fifth rank formed by the elders acting as headmen, *wookuru*. Fortunately, the abundance and meticulous presentation of the data enable us to explore an alternative reading. The cultural structure of medicinal rule characterizing other groups in the region raises a number of objections against the political stratification. Tio social structure does not appear to be the product of a central authority implementing its territorial division. There were no boundaries (TK 13). There was no centralized army or police force (TK 371). The king occupied the highest rank of a hierarchy rather than being a transcendent figure. Close kinsmen of the king did not address him with the standard respectful designation of 'father' (*taara*) but with the real kinship term (TK 52). Kinship plainly trumped kingship. Most of all, Tio language has two terms only for those supposed four ranks, *okoo* and *ngaa ntsi*. A literal translation is respectively 'great one' and 'landowner'. I propose to reinterpret the Tio monograph by maintaining these two endogenous concepts.

The highest power rank in Tio terminology is *okoo*, the ruler or king. It has the same meaning in central and western Mongo languages. Derived from *nkoko*, elder of village or lineage, or head of a clan (TK 440, n5), *okoo* has the same stem as the Sukuma word *nkulu* and Swahili word *mkuu*, the great one, the responsible and head. Its proto-Bantu root is *kul*, great or mature. The 'ruler of Ngenge' was also an *okoo*, yet Vansina suspects the Tio king was the actual paramount of the Ngenge people (TK 13, 372). A small group of chiefs, or 'superior lords', with a tributary relation to the king fulfil a special role at royal installation, much like the *mani* in Loanga. These ritual-medicinal functions include sending him in seclusion, initiating him into the royal charm, building a royal enclosure, keeping the perpetual fire, and preparing ritual food (TK 372–73). Their names start with *nga*. They are *ngaa ntsi*, translatable as master or owner of the land (from proto-Bantu *si* for land) for which Vansina (TK 313) uses the term squire. (In Bantu, 'owning' has a reciprocal meaning, I should repeat.) The language has no word for lord. Both lord and squire work with councils for peacekeeping in an area encompassing the extended compounds of several elders (TK 319). How do squires differ from lords? Both have charms, but the latter also own the *nkobi*, a box of charms, protecting the realm under which the squires resort and for which they collect tribute.

Corroborating our claim about the widespread fractal of 'the forest-within', the *ngaa ntsi* described his land by listing the forests. He left the boundary with another *ngaa ntsi*'s fluid (TK 313), which indicates that actual rule over resident families was not the aim. He received a tithe of the hunt in the form of a haunch, because the animals were extensions of the *nkira* spirits. His ill will could ruin the hunter's luck because his will covers the entire hunting territory. Agriculture was none of his concern (TK 317). The king carried the responsibility of the land's fertility; his will pertained to that realm. Agriculture provided livelihood, yet was valued much less than hunting (just as it is in relation to cattle-holding among agro-pastoralists). The king took care of the agricultural rites, sometimes planting each third seed together with the women (TK 118). But the rituals approached cultivation as a sort of hunt (TK 126). All holders of power had a *nkira* shrine of charms, the medicinal foundation for ruling the forest.

The king's powers too originated from the forest. He was entitled to the hind leg of killed game. A killed leopard had to be addressed ceremonially as a chief, and brought to him. On top of all nature spirits stood the spirit Nkwe Mbali, translated by Vansina (TK 126) as The Lion's Court.[1] Both squires and lords have protective powers stemming from the *nkira* spirit of the woods. Both are actually named after the spirit (preceded by *ngaa*; TK 315). Some share a name, the overlap indicating that the *nkira* came first. Together with plants and animals, spirits form the source of medicine. In sum, the ranks beneath the king would be more adequately termed masters of the forest, than of the land. The importance of the forest brings us to a cultural innovation kept under the radar due to the Tio use of ancient terms.

A Tio synonym for *ngaa ntsi* featuring in Sims' vocabulary from the 1880s is *mpfo antsii*, with *mpfo* having the same stem as *mfumu*: 'chief, king' (TK 313). We have discussed *fum/kum* as signifying either chief or healer in Bantu languages, but the Tio case again points to the earlier meaning we hinted at: a 'coming-outer' (see *nkumu* ideology in Introduction). A bit of a conundrum is *ngaa*, 'master of...', in *ngaa ntsi*. With changed tone, *ngàà* means 'healer, diviner' (TK 585).[2] In current Sukuma, *-ganga* and *-fumu* are synonyms for healer, two words probably having made their separate ways in the distant past to bump into each other again. We cover the whole range of Tio titles with a salient pair, namely two types of leadership applicable in various Bantu languages: *fum* and *gang* refer to the discontinuous vocation of the initiated who came out of the forest, to which belong chief, squire and lord, whereas *kul* refers to the grown up, matured head of a family, from which originated both *okoo*, king, and *wokuru*, headman. Matured knowledge and a connection with the spirits, *kul* and *k/fum*, together constitute medicine.

Centralization might have developed endogenously as an alternation between these two interrelated semantic tracks. Those initiated into medicinal knowledge and obtaining a charm (as a token of their autonomy as free men) can mature into headmanship (*kul*). Some of these men are picked out by a spirit and charm to transcend kindred and village community to rule a wider territory beyond kin. They become chief (*fum*). Once the spirit's call is answered and the territory expands with more such *fum* the association of them may be headed by a *kul* among them, the most mature or highest initiated. The Bantu-speaking groups originating from the area north-west of the Tio mastered the craft of sociality, living together, whereby not conquest but in our example the alternation with spirit and medicine increased centralization. The fact that their old concept of land referred in the new situation, in practice at least, to a bunch of forests is an indication of their cosmology being influenced by the local forest-based cultures. The forest had changed the migrants from the grassfields. From the interaction with autochthones and environment originated the endogenous model of medicinal rule.

Chief and earth-priest are complementary functions in West-Africa, some 2000 km to the west of Tio villages. The political relation may have been applicable for a long time in the Cameroon Grassfields, the so-called Bantu cradle, which lies between the two areas. The Tio king and land-masters are not really complementary, the preeminence of king over the other indicating that the two are ranks within the same organization. The medicinal role of land-masters suggests it to be a cult. In the classic studies of Meyer Fortes on the Tallensi of Ghana, power is shared between three counterpoised figures: the permanent inherited office of earth-chief, who manages the shrine of the land, the temporary elective office of chief, who rules a territorially bounded people, and the occasional role of the subchief electing the chief (Fortes and Evans-Pritchard 1940). Although comparisons can be made with the examples of our region, as in the council of nobles electing the chief, and the chief managing a shrine for the land, we find no one-to-one correspondence anywhere with the Tallensi triad. In fact, we should not have expected otherwise because migration from the grassfields meant leaving behind the land, and probably the shrine and office connected to it. Travelling without their autochthonous earth-chief, the migrants from the grassfields probably sought its equivalent in the autochthonous populations. Many Bantu-speaking groups have enthronement rituals that grant a key role to a member of the putatively autochtonous people.[3]

The idea of symbiosis between two cultural systems, uniting hunters and farmers, would give coherence to our scattered data and the transition we seek to unravel. The hunters' shaman who lives in the forest and with nature spirits, differs from the spirit-possessed villager for whom the forest represents the shock of the outside. What could have resulted from their union was a new cultural structure emphasizing the 'forest-within' and generating the institutions of mediumistic divination and medicine, the most coherent symbolisms of which we saw in Lele divinatory societies and Ndembu hunters' cults. The symbiosis explains the ubiquity of medicine in Bantu-speaking Africa and the local fascination with the forest from which recipe and oracle tap. A root of the transition we find in the secondary use of hunting as divination, illustrated in Part I. It recurs in the Tio institution of a successful hunt confirming the oracular identification of a witch (TK 175). The hunt is experienced as an act of contingency, and serves as a message from the forest, where the spirits reside.

The forest-masters wore painted circles around the eyes 'to see in the other world', a brass collar in case they were chiefs of the king, and they had the right to wear a cap (which female mediums also had) representing power (TK 332). Recalling the spirit's entrance during divination, they had on top of their head a bun of hair (the alleged 'state dress', TK 334) with feathers of among others the *nkenkene* bird that sees the future, and held a flywhisk in the left hand and a *mvuba* or *ndzuunu* adze in the right hand resembling an anvil (TK 334; the adze was perhaps to control the rains, which would link the symbolics of forest-mastery to rainmaking medicine). For Vansina the fact that this series of 'wonderful objects . . . rather than regular emblems, translated the lord's office' confirmed 'that the real foundation of any lord was the power he himself had been able to muster, just like his collection of curiosities' (TK 333). To adopt an emic perspective was not Vansina's intention.

At one critical point, the author mocks his Tio informants in the 1960s for still believing in the mystical bond between the squire and the *nkira* of a domain while he thought it was clear that the squire's religious practices always were legitimations of his political authority, and that he was a weaker copy of the king, who regulated government in his kingdom down to the lower ranks (TK 323; his sneer of a 'mystical bond' reiterated on top, middle and bottom of the page). Might we hear the polity prism talk? We have at least two elements to refute this predominantly Western concept of kingship. First, the *ngaa ntsi* was no proxy of the king. Vansina admits that councillors of the main settlement discussed and chose the man (TK 323). This autonomy goes further than his mentioning of the limited centralized influence because of military weakness of Tio kings. Whatever the king could expect from his subordinates was largely a bottom-up reality. And given the high autonomy of the settlers, one may wonder if their selection criteria were at all political. To substantiate his thesis that 'this was a political office', Vansina recites an anecdote illustrating that 'politics overruled ideology' (TK 323; ideology turns out again to refer to religion). A king had fooled a man named Ondzaala by giving him an 'empty' forest that actually had belonged to another squire before. The king thus appears not to believe in the unique relation of a squire with a nature spirit. Vansina's account continues with a seemingly trivial sentence: 'Ondzaala found a *nkira* in the forest and organized its cult'. For Vansina the new squire's finding a spirit without discovering that another squire came first, refutes the mystical bond. (Even less mystically, Ondzaala counted on a political alliance by giving every second haunch of the hunt to the neighbouring squire, Vansina remarks triumphantly with an exclamation mark.)

For this anthropologist, on the contrary, the story underlines the primacy granted by the 'squire' to the spirit cult. Organizing a cult means spirit possession. The ritual was more important than any particular belief or pragmatic use of beliefs. That a cult was organized by the squire confirms our thesis of leadership being based on finding a spirit, like in the Loango archetypal coming-out scene. Rule is predicated on establishing the medicinal cult dedicated to the spirit (which in Loango started as a personal obligation divulged by the spirit).

People's point of reference is not the person, whose perspective Vansina as actor-materialist adopts. The *nkira* comes first. Tio describe their group of kindred (*ibuuru*) by listing the forests (*idzwa*) of origin (TK 35). Nature spirits exist out there. Their identity is uncertain and their influence is plural, dispersed among the hunters in the woods and spread through charms, which call for medicinal circumscriptions to protect the ritual domain. The medicinal message travels with the objects. They can be sold, transferred and retrieved without losing their purpose, so that instead of some inborn quality it is the fate or luck of discovering a *nkira* that leads to being with the power. The spirit also appears to be a dynamic reality, with new *nkira* coming up, just as forest-masters do, gradually cutting up the realm and competing with already established title-holders. How else could there have been such a vast number of titles by the 1900s? Surely, if the king did not act as head of state (re)appointing them top-down, as can be derived from the data, the author has to think about how bottom-up processes happened. The new domains would typically arise at the periphery of established domains, as in the case of Ondzoola's forest, which lay on the outskirts of the former owner's set of woods and could thus give rise to a new *nkira* within a cut-up domain. I see no other way to interpret in local terms the aforementioned phrase: 'Ondzaala found a *nkira* in the forest and organized its cult'. The medicinal field further complexified with 'political' consequences. Vansina unwittingly left the reader astonished to hear about a cult in Tio society and wondering what it could be like. He had not theoretically matched cult and kingship.

As in all cults, the spirit rewards the initiated forest-master with strong protective magic. Who or what the protection aims at cannot be disputed: the Tio forest-master chases the witch. He does so by appealing to his *nkira*. A rare quote[4] in the book stages a forest-master at a village meeting in 1963 unequivocal about his main task:

> There is an epidemic among the small children, so they have to stay at home. It is not due to the witches, but just an illness. However, I am *ngaa ntsii*, I must protect the village against the witch from outside the domain, who could well come to gain from this situation (he meant the quarrels as well as the epidemic). So there should be no more quarrelling, for that opens the road for witchcraft (TK 320).

The master of the woods, like a diviner, can tell the difference between what is mere illness and what is witchcraft. His skills are wanted in case of the latter. The interpretation Vansina put between brackets does not evoke the symbolic complex. His analysis should from the start have specified the medicinal, a mixed religious-political type of peacekeeping. The domain is a protective shell, yet easily broken, thus needing ritual protection. The community enjoys peace in a precarious balance. People with strong emotions may overreact to illness, hence lose the spirit's blessing and become vulnerable to external attacks that ruin the small community – a danger averted by a person for whom leadership and healership are the same. At the level of the king's realm a complaint regularly resounds in the 1960s: 'Witchcraft now surpasses all. The witch must stop. Never was this seen under the old kings' (TK 319). 'The old kings' evoke the precolonial epoch. In eastern Bantu languages, in which the word *mfumu* means healer, the complaint sounds explicitly like a longing for a return to a time before the disintegration of medicinal rule.

Nkobi Shrines and Initiation

Succeeding a master of the woods meant learning the secrets of the *nkira* (TK 322). Vansina is probably correct in intuiting, by lack of data on the subject, that when a squire died without appointing a successor the newcomer had to learn about the nature spirit by dreaming (TK 322, n10). Is his dream not the spirit call of healers? Stronger healership was expected of the holders of an *nkobi*, the box of charms. Vansina subsumes under his dubious label of 'the body of folklore' the nine-day ritual whereby the new incumbent of the shrine goes into isolation with the opener of the *nkobi* and gets initiated into the secrets, with the witchcraft possibly killing him (TK 327). Surely, in this installation rite we recognize the healer's training into medicinal secrets, especially concerning magical protection, as well as the limits imposed on the training: the father cannot initiate the son for the ordeal is intimate and exacting. The openers of the *nkobi* form a separate group. I suspect them to be the hereditary branch of the healer or cult founder's original first assistants who train the chosen successor. Any healer of high repute will share his knowledge with a number of initiated, without privileging blood ties. This split of duties between kin and non-kin ensures the cult's perpetuity. One has the maturity and expertise, the other has the call – the semantic tracks of respectively k/*fum* and *kul* we derived earlier. The contents of the box is forbidden knowledge for the hereditary holder. The same applies to the king, surrounded by experts with more knowledge than he has on certain topics. The ritual for the *nkobi* holder is called *lisee*, exactly like the installation ritual of the king (TK 327).

The *nkobi* were allegedly given by the *nkira*, and according to some myths given by the creator Nza himself. Each *nkobi* had its own history and ranked in a hierarchy. 'All the narrators agreed that whoever had the *nkobi*, held its power' (TK 330). Such ritual idiom bracketing the game of politics, evidently did not satisfy Vansina, so he was happy to announce that his respondents contradicted each other when ranking the boxes of charms, save for the king's supreme one, Nkwe Mbali, and for some obviously lower ones depending as tributaries (*nkani*) on higher *nkobi*. He concluded that in reality things are the other way around: the variable prestige of the lords fought out in strategic games determined the rank of the *nkobi* (TK 328). Should he not be consistent then and infer from the declining careers and corresponding fluctuations of influence (TK 330) that the forest-masters are not holders of an office, let alone fulfilling a function in a fixed political hierarchy? Does it not confirm that they resemble healer-diviners with equal initiatory ranks, whose actual renown depends on competition in the medicinal field? The local cosmology personifies shrines as being less or more powerful, and some being tributaries of bigger ones. For Vansina, these are myths 'to preserve the political credo', 'very much as *baraka* did in northern Africa'. The defender of oral tradition to reconstruct African history is willing to pay a price on the same page when professing with overview: 'The ideology was always adapted to the political reality, and the myths, even about individual *nkobi*, were adapted as the need arose' (TK 328; the 'ideology' of charms which the village leader lacked would be the only thing that distinguished him from lords and squires, TK 338). For us seeking the experiential frame to decide on meaning, the strategic manipulation of beliefs by leaders is, if not always speculative, a truism. Boxes of charms with lives of their own reveal a little more about the lifeworld of these hunter-farmers. 'To live without chiefs was to live like a flock of sheep' (TK 336) does not exactly dovetail with the cultural structure we expect from the autonomous hunter or initiated farmer. The comparison of a forest-master 'ruling a country' to 'emitting sparks' reminds one more of the healer than of a state official. The king through his envoy handed a brass collar to the forest-master in confirmation of their relation, of his investiture and 'title' – but over his *nkobi*, the king had no say (TK 337), which corroborates the primacy of medicinal rule over political governance and stratification. The administrative penetration of the kingdoms in central Africa has been a bone of contention among historians. 'Congo Free State officials believed the king had no authority', Vansina adds (TK 337, n32). They were probably right if meaning the kind of authority colonials expected. Although tucked away in a footnote, the observation is a welcome balance to his portrayal of the collar-handing ceremony wherein 'the lord' accepted to kneel to greet 'the king' (yet sometimes not; TK 335, n25).

The classic trope of subjugation to the king conceals three important nuances. For all its autocratic symbolism, the *nkani* tributary system was an alliance between lower and higher ranks of medicinal knowledge. A later study by Dupré and Pinçon (1997) tends towards the thesis that forest-masters and *nkobi*-holders were joined together in an initiatory brotherhood, whose power was based on the leopard. The system permitted the chiefs not only to police their lands better but also to entwine their trade with allies far beyond the Tio kingdom (cf. Vansina 1990: 148). Secondly, the *nkani* system of pawn relations implied symbolic rules of conduct such as greeting the higher ranked as a 'wife' does (indeed by kneeling), which only superficially resembles the subjugation of the knight to his king. Thirdly, as part of an encompassing trend to be discussed at the end of this chapter, a process of social change must have been going on whereby some chiefs sought sovereignty and dreaded the dependency on medicine as well as the competition with newcomers that is intrinsic to medicinal initiation. Naming and geographically defining the shrines may have been the strategy of an upcoming class of rulers.

Vansina bases himself on oral literature to situate the origin of the *nkobi* box in the 1700s (TK 456). He explains 'the introduction of the *nkobi* ideology' from the legitimacy it gave to forest-masters seeking independence from the king after becoming wealthy from trade with the Loango. Hence the shrines would be a later invention. Although secondary to our thesis on charms, again some objections can be made. Firstly, the twelve *nkobi* represented by the twelve points on the brass collar worn by the king and by the forest-masters rather consolidate the kingdom as the sum of those twelve boxes. By lack of data on actual inventions of the shrines by the king, we may presume that the *nkobi* shrines either made the centralization into a kingdom possible, or were a medicinal extension by the court to keep the autonomy of the forest-masters in check. Without the brass collar delimiting the number of shrines, each forest-master with the right spirit would have been a potential secessor, and none indebted to the king. Our hypothesis accepts the strategic angle but inverts the benefactor, from forest-master to court. Secondly, no data are offered that political centralization existed before the shrines, or that it was ever necessary, so that the forest-masters would have to react. Thirdly, the conflict between kings and forest-masters might be overdrawn, for they all wore the brass collar (TK 417). They had all completed the highest initiation *lisee*, which included a cannibalistic transgression (TK 469). Rather than the erosion of royal authority, we see in the *nkobi* shrine the insertion of a territorial subdivision of power. The cult of charms transcending the village communities had grown in prominence and expanded its territory, which meant more governance and differentiation of ranks, one of which was the most successful, as in the case of the Loango chief being more 'chief' than his fellow chiefs.

Perhaps to anticipate the puzzling fact of *nkobi*'s linguistic antiquity, Vansina adds that 'Familial *nkobi* may have always been known as boxes to keep charms in. The political *nkobi* was invented in the Abala area by a group linked with the Ngia [ruler]' (TK 456).[5] Segregating the familial from the political domain, as in modern Europe, is not obvious. Furthermore, what was there to invent if familial *nkobi* already existed? The same nature spirits inhabit the box. The medicinal rule they fostered was just extended to a larger terrain than that of the family. We should think here of classificatory extensions creating territorial authorities to interconnect scattered populations belonging to the same cultural group. Top-down extensions of medicinal rule could come from the leader's Nkwe Mbali shrine, of which the *nkobi* was a micro-version. Bottom-up extensions could come from the family headman's altars, from which the *nkobi* was a macroversion. Both suggest *nkobi* to have established a layer of intermediate leadership.

Before the *nkobi* shrine, medicinal rule had taken root through the charms, ritual knowledge and *nkira* spirit, which implied cult and possibly rank. Like every addition of medicinal knowledge, the *nkobi* announced a new rank to get initiated into. The 'lord' was not a dignitary sent by the king (or overlord) to extend his rule to further terrain. He was a tributary (*nkani*) partner with initiative. He paid the overlord Nza Mba in return for the *nkobi* (TK 456), like one does for each initiatory promotion within a cult. The extremely expensive box of super-charms could serve to create additional ranks in an expanding system. Before the box, it was possession of a charm in analogy with the founder's medicine that created autonomy for lower ranks. During the rise of kingship until colonization in the late nineteenth century, actual wars were fought over the possession and theft of *nkobi* (TK 457), because medicinal ranks were superseded by their more dynamic differentiation through specific charms and corresponding territory.[6]

Vansina had the lucidity in 1973 to note that beliefs depend on context (TK 171, 221) and that the meaning of symbols is in part subjectively determined; but when he claimed that symbols do not form a system because they are substitutable (TK 235), he failed to consider the underlying cultural structure that allows to substitute, that reproduces a logic and does so because of root meanings experienced by the actors. Without a cultural structure, interpretations run wild (as in his suggestion that liking games of chance is a sign of status mobility and contradicts the rigid causality of witchcraft; TK 240) and theoretical inconsistencies appear, whereby materialism switches into idealism: religion is 'a *primum mobile*' of institutions and on the same page an 'ideological superstructure', hence less cause than effect after all (TK 221). The shift over the last century from nature spirits (*nkira*) to ancestral spirits in the dedication of shrines would be a new filling in of a 'slot of belief' (TK 468). Are beliefs occupying a pre-given slot (structure-idealism)? Or are they invented by an actor for personal gain (actor-materialism)? We shall discover that Tio society participated in regional developments wherein village and clan dynamics had innovated the densely populated settlements with new ideas of witchcraft, and ancestral wrath to match.

Political Healership

Have our reinterpretations of Vansina's data yielded enough elements to reconstruct the cultural structure of Tio society at the end of the nineteenth century? In that structure, the *nga ntsii* could not be a lower rank in imitation of the king. The king had more likely grown out of the success of a divinatory-medicinal cult developed by the masters of the woods.

The Tio monograph has ammunition for opposing our hypothesis of medicinal rule. 'Squires could come from only certain kinship groups which were collectively known as *baamukaana lilimpu*: "those of the kindred of authority"' (TK 321). The designation of these in the book as a class of 'aristocrats' reminds of British gentry whose landed estates generating income through a manorial system under the king formed the prime motivation for inventing their rank. In defence of our thesis, Tio squires and lords were members of a special group thanks to their *lisee* initiation, but there are no indications that their kinship groups were aristocratic, famous or related across the kingdom, or that they had occasions to meet so that some type of caste or class identification or cohesion was possible. The powerful elders, *wookuru*, heading the kindred did not belong to that group, at least in principle. But we read that sometimes 'altered conditions' (TK 319, n8) made such an elder the forest-master. The latter's special capacity, in the form of *nkira* mediumship, is something else than aristocracy. The term itself for those special clans literally reads as 'those of the category of having hats', *mpu* meaning both hat and power. Headwear as a metaphor refers to a spirit bond as well as to having power (TK 584; cf. Tio glossary). Pierre Bonnafé (1978: 16) equals *mpu* with the magical power that the *ngaa* has. Its ultimate source would be the leopard in the forest. Novices are invested with *kibyala*, 'governance'. In Kisukuma the verb's stem *byala* means 'to generate, to give life'. Just like parents, masters of initiation are said to generate, and so are healers: to invest the novices with life. Vansina (1990: 224) in his later works describes Me Lo Kima as the source of spiritual power, thus inadvertently revisiting his translation of *mpu*. In brief, the category of hat-wearers has all the features of 'cephalized' members organized across equatorial Africa, who entered the forest to be initiated, forming a pool of candidates for medicinal offices.

Our argument is of course not that the medicinal cult was without political or judicial elements. Such far-reaching specialization would actually presuppose a secularized culture. The daily enactments of governance were part and parcel of the 'luck' (good or bad, depending on one's personal view) one had in having the forest charm. The larger the cultic network, the more variation of leaderships was possible. Peaks of population density, commercialization, globalization and colonization affected the history of medicinal rule so that the white archivists during those peaks in the late nineteenth century encountered another system than the one the culture had until then been reproducing. The example today is the Chwezi spirit cult, which in the 1990s already consisted of ranks of 'chiefs' (*batemi*) and 'kings' (*bakingi*, from the English) underneath the highest authority, all of whom impose taxes on their members and return verdicts on conflicts between the members. The tribute (*ingkura*) the forest-master collected from the households is not evidence of a manorial system, which could have refuted the thesis of medicinal rule. As with the British landed gentry, taxes would in principle move up the political pyramid from squires and lords to the king. Yet, the tributes were erratic and small (TK 320–21) like the fees the Chwezi elders collect at ceremonial occasions. The squires ruled court cases but they kept the fines. With the *nkobi* holders, who could rule in appeal, they negotiated what could trickle down to the capital far away, since the exchange of gifts cemented their relations (TK 328).

One should be clear about what court ruling meant. In a later chapter Vansina nuances his earlier claim about judicial appeal: 'no clear judiciary structure with set levels of appeals existed at all' (TK 342). The head of the (matri)lineage, *mpfo andzo*, took the initiative to contact a forest-master, not necessarily one of his own domain. That is the right of families within the polycentric complex. The accused could appeal to another forest-master, whose verdict in his favour he could try to enforce by claiming this master's prestige to be higher (TK

341–42). We read this to mean that his shrine was more powerful. Forest-masters were not actively seeking to sanction violations. They mediated between families (TK 345). Their verdict 'cut the palaver' (TK 346; cf. etymology of *ntemi*, chief, in Chapter 3). The clients paid them for the costs of a verdict. They complemented the work of professional diviners (*vaa*) who organized oracles as a private business. The *nkobi*-holder, despite his mastery, could not rule a poison ordeal (*nkei*) for men unless recommended by the oracle of a *vaa mbulu*, a jackal diviner (TK 351) – an animal situated below the king's leopard and lion but belonging to the same hierarchy.

Before delving into the processes of change, a range of recurring symbols in the Bantu-speaking region should be mentioned that equate leadership with healership, and vice versa. About the women in Itsuua, the female cult of spirit possession, Vansina writes that they 'were considered to be of chiefly status. They wore the royal red and drank behind a blanket like chiefs or kings' (TK 186). Illness is a sign of something bigger to which people are called. During the ritual, the spirit *nkira* with whom they become one is incited to 'rule!' (*Nie!*; TK 185). In Itsuua and in the Nkita cult from neighbouring areas (and probably also in the similar cults of Mbulu, Uma and Ndembo) barren women could join the initiation (TK 187). They could benefit from the fertility radiating from the ritual. Women in Itsuua were chiefs because of the cult's 'powerful nature spirit such as great chiefs and kings control' (TK 186).

Vansina writes: 'It was the privilege and the duty of the chief to be the master of the *nkira*, i.e. to ask of it blessings and fertility on behalf of the community' (TK 224). Maintaining the conventional division (perhaps by lack of participatory observation in divination), the author sees the chief's two assistants as the religious experts, and divination as a 'counterweight to political leadership' (TK 198). The gap between politics and religion, or family and spirits, seems artificial because in reality the professional practice perfects what any initiated family head is expected to know. Family heads ritually address the 'shades' or ancestral spirits (*ikwii*). Kings and chiefs deal with *nkira*, which besides a nature spirit is a multi-layered concept expressing the fertility of unusual births, the animal double of mothers, and objects such as the twins' pots and the chief's shrine (TK 225). Within Tio beliefs, nature spirits pertain to the fertility of land and of women (Vansina equates *nkira* with *ngolo*, the good life, TK 226; cf. proto-Bantu *pol*, coolness). The shrine named *nkira* stood in front of the chief's house and was itself modelled after a house. What kind of entity *nkira* is – a spirit or a house? – seemed of no concern. In Sukuma villages the spirit is similarly a shrine standing outside in an extended family's compound.

Cult Dynamics

The book on the Tio kingdom takes a snapshot at the end of the nineteenth century. Inevitably the proposed political system comes across as reified by lack of information on its emergence and previous development. The twelve *nkobi* did not emerge out of the blue. Long-range histories of the Tio and Teke have been offered later on, among others by Vansina (1990) and Dupré and Pinçon (1997). Anthropologist Dupré and archaeologist Pinçon argue that since AD 1000 the Teke plateaux have been marked by a dichotomy between the masters of the people and the masters of the land, between whom the polity oscillated, which indeed reminds us of the Tallensi in West Africa.[7] Organized wealth production via trade and iron smelting centralized power. A kingdom arose whose rule was based on nature spirits and which was less centralized than Kongo and Loango, whose kings prayed to ancestors. A counterpoint can be read in Vansina's (1990) classic where his linguistic research must have convinced him that the Bantu term *ngaa*, for medicine man and for mediator with spirits, goes back too far in time to be ignored in the description of social structure. From the seventeenth century onwards, just as the slave trade produces a middle class of merchants, Vansina (1990: 224) sees spirit cults with charms emerging as a force opposing central authority. He reasons that the origin of the *nkobi* shrines must have been the Lemba cult of the Loango, operating along the Likouala trade route (cf. Janzen 1982).

Why would we need to surmise an external cult as the driving force, given that Tio, Teke, Loango and their neighbours have *ngaa*, and given the ubiquity of the generic term? Spirit mediumship and shamanistic animism in general are not inventions of the seventeenth century. Medicines, either or not institutionalized in spirit cults, never ceased to travel across the rainforest. The alleged tension between central authority and spirit cult artificially reproduces the division between politics and religion. There is permanence to the way people perceive the king, and this permanence relates to the local model of power. It is worthwhile to cite the tasks expected from village headman, chief, lord and squire alike:

> Their role was to protect, to make the good life possible. They should ward off witches, they should shield their people. The meaning of the feathers worn as emblems at the Pool shows what a good chief

should be: to be a good orator and a good judge, to foresee the future, to be a persevering worker, to have the magic to flee danger with people around him, all in addition to fighting witches and human enemies. At each level the role of being a protector is only made bigger. (TK 338)

A protector in the local cosmology is not a king in European style. These leaders, institutionalized unlike family heads, are not administrators. The list makes no mention of governance, policy making or conquest. Nor does the role include being a deputy or executive of the king.

According to the observations of the French explorer Léon Guiral, the king had no authority beyond the 'capital' where he lived, and where some did not obey him either (TK 378, n5). Guiral called him the great *féticheur*, the pope of the Bateke. Vansina (1990: 225) turned this qualification into a symptom of collapse: 'by 1880 . . . , as in Loango and Kongo, kingship survived because kings had become "but popes", as Guiral was to put it'. The chiefs still played their ritual roles at the royal installation. They operated like members of one cult, making one person the master of the encompassing *nkira*, Nkwe Mbali, inhabiting Lefini Falls. The training was oriented on magic. The lord Nganshibi (master of the *nshibi*) wore the *ikara* armring (like the Loango initiator) and had the right to open the king's shrine at his installation ritual. He was the only one together with the king who could use the *nshibi* whistle with which he announced his visit (TK 376). In case of epidemic or failed rains the king gave kola nuts (with which he too painted a circle around his eyes to see evil) to the forest-masters to offer at the shrines for their *nkira* (TK 374). The forest-master entitled Lipie wore the more common *ntsa* horn on his forearm to whistle to Nkwe Mbali to stop the rains (*ntsa* meaning antelope). The connection between the spirit cult and control over the rains, entirely absent in the monograph, is thus established. Not kingship per se but the membership into the cult permits to manage territorial fertility. The king was, however, the founder's successor, so his bare feet should not touch the ground lest they scorch the earth (TK 377). He could not cross the Congo River or travel in a boat except with his face covered in a red blanket, nor could he drink without hiding his face (cf. Loango, Kongo, Rwanda, and so on) otherwise he might affect the land's fertility. The taboo does not come out of the blue. The cultural structure of preserving luck existed in the prohibitions before a hunt. On every fourth day, named after the supreme *nkira* Nkwe Mbali, people honoured the spirit by leaving the 'land' alone, that is by not hunting in the forest or tilling the fields (TK 374). Fertility is associated with feral being, especially the lion (skin), the king's symbol and alleged guardian that gave tremendous power: 'kingship is the epitome of witchcraft' (TK 378). After his *lisee* initiation, which allowed him to wear the brass collar (*olua*) with twelve points, he was thought to no longer beget children despite coitus, for the land must consume his fertility (TK 377). During the *lisee* each of the twelve lords and their ritual duties were presented. These titles are ranks (TK 382), perhaps leftovers of an ancient cult, since the now important territories were not the defining criterion of the ranks but the shrine and duty were.

Cultic traces of rule abound. Most revealing is the Lipie forest-master, who stayed near the falls to check the condition of the six anvils stuck in a rock. The anvils represented the life force (*mpiini*) of the king, his own and that of other major forest-masters (TK 374; the Ngia ruler owned the royal *mpiini*, TK 378). He made the *ibili* charms, medicinal packages of objects cast from the falls onto the shore, which he could sell to village leaders like medicine men do (TK 374). The spirits of the past kings joined Nkwe Mbali in the Lefini to approve the new candidate. Vansina must conclude that 'the cult of Nkwe Mbali included the cult of the royal ancestors' (TK 375). There is no incompatibility between nature spirits and ancestral spirits. The royal clan might have been the first to shift its devotion from the forest to the ancestral domain, precisely because a royal dynasty can only stem from the healer's original group of novices if a certain invention is made and approved: that of descent-based inheritance of the highest title. The spirit of a forebear will likely support a hereditary title.

After the spirit's approval, the king was enthroned during a 'coming out' ceremony like a novice. Only, his rank was supreme. A new perpetual fire was lit for his reign and the shrine-holders would gather and touch their leopard skins to honour him. All present, despite their being masters, were obliged to crawl instead of walk, like in the Sukuma reunion before a *ihane*, where participants walk in duck-step to keep their head below the waste of the master of ceremonies. During seclusion the king's body was strengthened by being fumigated daily and sprinkled with iron tools dipped in water (TK 381). The similarities with the Chwezi spirit cult are striking despite the geographical distance.[8] Which then was first: kingship or spirit healing? The spirit obliquely surfaces in the description of the king's entry in 1884 on the occasion of the treaty with the French: 'The king drank, then danced, and then the palaver began' (TK 390, n31). Dance can be the spirit's manifestation. Moreover, if he was a sovereign, an uncontested ruler like we imagine Montezuma to be among the Aztecs, then why did he need to display the gifts of the French to his people in the 1880s (TK

390, cf. also 416)? Gifts made by the powerful visitors would locally resemble fees for entering the king's circle.

After using the word 'king' for four hundred pages, Vansina finally asks the key question in implicit reference to Guiral: 'He might be the "Pope" of the Tio, but was he a ruling sovereign?' (TK 390). The tribute (*ingkura*) sent by forest-masters, whose profits the king shared with the Ngeilino chief, would be the main reason to believe so. But as we argued before, in support of our thesis on basically seeing a cultic figure at work, there was no way in which the same cult could organize its activities and last over a wide territory without dividing the members in ranks, with territorial implications for the collection of gifts. The king combined his role with the function of headman of Mbe village (TK 393). Was kingship not a parallel title then? Nobody kept track of the names of previous kings (TK 408; Iloo was a 'povero vecchio' in 1884). A dynasty without genealogy: the ceremonial state was not yet within reach. What separated him from other forest-masters was that his daughters were married without bridewealth, for they belonged to 'all the Tio' (TK 393). His offspring and land seemed to stem from the same source of fertility. Moreover, he could marry any women from his realm but not the daughters of his forest-masters, 'for they were his children'. All descending long ago from the same cultic founder?

Finally, Tio kingship was not a hereditary title in the late nineteenth century. The king's successor did not need to be kin. He had to have an ancestor from one of the six villages of former kings. He was chosen by two chiefs, Ngeilino and Ngandzio, 'the foremost child of the king' (TK 394). Acting very much like the two wise elders of a cult, they drew on their dreams (cf. also Teke, TK 395 n45). They consulted other forest-masters, and organized the divination of the former ruler's wishes. The person they chose obeyed like a cult leader the obligations imposed by his spirit, the most conspicuous being food taboos. Sometimes a candidate fled upon hearing his election, but was then caught and beaten like in the initiatory ordeal of a cult (cf. TK 395).

Social Change: The King Opposing His Initiation

Global historical events affected the cultural structure. By the end of the nineteenth century the Congo commercial network reached deep into the interior and impacted on Tio society, which provided middlemen in the ivory trade. The rift widened between rich and poor, men and women, the social classes replacing the reciprocity between king and commoner, between a senior in service of the land's spirits and those benefiting from the fertility and his protection. Commercialization led to the subsistence farmer's loss of self-sufficiency. By that time, a gradual process had come to a head as farmers were losing their knowledge of smelting iron, of building canoes and of hunting with bows and arrows (TK 310). The only sort of traditional knowledge left was that of the healers.

An important test for a cultural structure is to verify how the institution reacts under radically changed circumstances. Are the factors we deemed essential indeed affected? The institution of forest-masters declined in the mid twentieth century when they no longer received haunches of the hunt (TK 493) and people no longer believed in the *nkira* nature spirits (TK 490). The experiential relation with the forest appears crucial. Vansina presents no convincing argument to conclude that kingship is the cornerstone of the whole system (TK 396). Despite his vitality, the king could not maintain the system by himself. Its driving force lay at the bottom, not at the top. Instead of the binding element, he had always been merely a forest-master at the highest level.

The cultural structure of medicinal rule impeded kingship in European style; however, some kings did not let the opportunity pass by that colonial government gave them of mirroring European autocracy. A critical moment was in the twentieth century when kings wanted to postpone their *lisee* initiation. Most significantly, forest-masters insisted on the king undergoing the ritual (TK 395). They insisted that 'kingship' is an initiation. They would lose too much if going along with the attempt at Europeanizing the institution. What prevented the historian from noticing the outright clash between medicinal rule and governance is misgivings about cultural structure.

The most prominent mark of kingship worldwide is probably tribute. How can one explain that the Tio system of tribute did not end at the realm? For example, the Tio king paid tribute to the Ngia ruler of the Ngungulu, while the Kukuya rulers paid tribute to the Tio (TK 396; and the Laadi and Tege from the Tio realm did not pay tribute or recognize the Tio king). Why would Tio, this embryonic version of Kongo and Loango, be a kingdom? The tributary groups were connected one by one and united by a common origin, expressed in the spirit-based initiation. Economic interests later on transformed the institution. Antecedents may go back to the 1600s when the centre of the realm moved to the south on the way from Mbe to the markets at the Pool (TK 397, n47). Trade created unbalance that the polycentric structure was not prepared for. The king was soon overshadowed by wealthier trading chiefs, who all enjoyed autonomy (TK 397). The wealthiest leader was the runaway 'slave' and ivory trader Ngaliema.

Not only did the local chiefs profit from the kingship trope Europeans had invented and sustained. The French administrators of Congo-Brazzaville benefited too from representing this cultic structure as a monarchy (cf. TK 396, n46: 'the French tried to represent [the king's] authority as stretching as far as possible'; they spoke even of cantons and provinces, which Vansina admits to being incorrect even if tribute was collected, TK 403). It raised the value of their treaty and staved off competing empires in the scramble for Africa. The ploy also satisfied intellectuals seeking in simulacra of European institutions the proof against 'primitivism'.

The Tio king signed a treaty with the words: 'King Makoko, who is sovereign over the lands lying between the mouth of the Lefini and Ncouna (Pool), having ratified the cession of territory made by Ngampey for the establishment of a French station and moreover ceded his hereditary rights of supremacy. . .' (TK 410). How could he cede territory against the explicit advice of his forest-masters and without the treaty stipulating any compensation for the Tio (TK 410, n8)? The reason may be the two wrong implications in the treaty he could only benefit from after its institutionalization: that the French thought his rule was that of a sovereign and was hereditary. These two aspects are glossed over by Vansina, who sees the alliance with Europeans and the promise of a commercial station as the desired compensation for his people (TK 411). In a footnote, though, we learn from Guiral that the king was not unhappy with the conflict between forest-masters as it could raise the king's power in relation to theirs (TK 413, n19). We have noted the trend of Tio kings postponing their initiation that reminded of their cultic rather than governmental role. Due to the interventions of the warring Europeans, the local tensions and occasional violent outbursts became persistent rifts between factions needing armies (TK 417–22). No real warfare broke out because the Tio kept to their tradition of power display and sporadic ambush, as opposed to the French armies burning down villages (TK 424). Cursory remarks in the monograph, for instance about King Iloo fearing the arrival of the Ngeiliino lord named Opontaba at Mbe palace because of his specialization in the 'perfect poison' (TK 417), suggest that a lot of history happened out of sight and was medicinal.

The historian Coquery wrongly attributed the lack of central power in Tio society to European intervention, Vansina contends, cogently arguing that decentralization always was a Tio feature (TK 430). Ethnographic study could have prevented Coquery's rash assumption.

Although Vansina had all the elements to conclude otherwise, he remained faithful to his denial of cultural structure, making no mention at all of the medicinal dimension in Tio politics (TK 431–35). What better way to end this exegesis of his meticulous chronicle than to prove that almost all reinterpretations I offered in this chapter to illustrate the contribution of anthropology to history were latently present in his monograph? I identify three moments when the author had the clues to lead the analysis onto new paths.

The translation of *okoo*, great one, as 'king' was only correct after the European political-economic system influenced the institution. The fact that there was a *mukoko* in 1507 when Pacheco Pereira first set foot on the coast does not prove that there was a king or that 'the Tio have been organized as a kingdom from remote times', as Vansina writes (TK 439). In fact, Pereira's (1892: 84) phrase about the Tio, or 'Anzica' as they were known in his time around 1500, is the following: '[A]head of this land Conguo, to the northeastern part, is known another province they call Anzica and whose Lord is named nowadays Cuqua Anzico'. Pereira translates *mukoko* as Senhor, 'lord' of the Anziku. In his youth he had been the Portuguese king's personal squire, so he was probably sensitive enough to the nomenclature to choose his words carefully. He must have done so based on what he knew about the Kongo, where the term 'king' was applied and the 'province' had undergone rapid transformation following the exchange of nobles during Diego Cam's first visit in 1483.

Vansina's hypothesis is that the king came from elsewhere to bestow titles upon the autochthonous local heads, and that it never was a local development (TK 442). The 'forests of origin', which I consider key in the rise of kingship, he puts between brackets for being a political invention by gatekeepers in the competition over offices. He offers disparate data that in my view could to the contrary illustrate an endogenous cultural evolution occurring independently at several spots, and further developing some regionally shared meanings. The anvils, sacred fire and royal smith relate smithing to kingship, as in Kongo and Loango, but Tio were the earliest smiths with better techniques of smelting ores. Their Teke neighbours sold anvils. Vansina does not go deeper into the connection. There may be a slip of the tongue though. 'One hardly assumes the first king brought the art of iron smelting into the country' (TK 442). Does he begin to realize the limitations of his top-down view on culture, focusing on a supreme actor driven by material motives and influencing lesser actors? In a footnote he contemplates an alternative, a bottom-up view which is undoubtedly the parsimonious hypothesis. The association between royal rule and smithing technology was 'inherited from previous lords and squires', and dates back to the introduction of smelting techniques (TK 443, n11). The implication is that kingship grew out of the link established by those petty forest-masters and lords of iron. We can speculate further. The common root of smithing and rule seems rainmaking medicine: the fire of lightning announces the rains for the land? In non-Cartesian materiality, he who can manipulate fire to make matter is a life-giver, a ruler of the sky. Were the first forest-masters members of such ancient initiatory society?

Tio were remarkably unaffected by Christianity until deep into the twentieth century. After the Second World War the colonial administration forbade traditional medicine and ritual, sending these practices underground (TK 490). According to Vansina, Christianity was to the Tio just 'a set of charms', this time administered by the missionaries. It is a pity that this local medicinal perspective on such a game changer as Christianity did not set him thinking about where the Tio priorities originally lay, or how they should have informed his version of their history. Had he not separated political and religious systems from the onset, whose joint changes he admitted only in the recent period when he could observe them (TK 493), the study of kingship in central Africa would have explored another course.

Notes

1. In the 1920s, Queen Ngalifourou made hay of her leadership in the cult of Nkwe Mbali to succeed her husband as *chef de canton* (TK 477, n17; 'Ngalifourou and her Cult').
2. However, *ngaa yuulu* is a kind of healer, a female initiated one. Vansina writes this compound with the same tone as *ngaa ntsi*, master of the land (TK 585). A Bantu-linguistic history of kingship should probably start from these words for master/healing, namely *ngaa* or *nganga* and *mfumu*, and trace the semantic bifurcations back to proto-Bantu. The links will crisscross though. For example, the Sukuma verb *-fuma* (to come out) is a reflex of the proto-Bantu **pum*, while the related *mfumu* might be a loanword (Koen Bostoen, personal communication). The similar stem cloaks the complex etymology. In MacGaffey's (1986) etymology, the Kongo term *mkumu* (from *kum/fum*) for king derives from 'free clan-member', in opposition to slave, but he took the translation of *mfumu* as 'free person' from Sims, who may not have meant it as a translation since he referred to a historical outcome of the spectacular demographic imbalance at the Pool where many more slaves lived than free men (cf. Vansina's observation that 'so few free men were left that Sims could say that *mfumu* meant both chief and free person', TK 370).

3. Systematic research into regional patterns of enthronements, which I could never complete on my own, might not just falsify or corroborate the West African cultural scenario, but also unveil migration histories, contrasting conquest and assimilation.
4. Somewhat jeopardizing the experiential depth of the ethnography, Vansina uses no quotes of respondents because he rarely did recording (TK 22).
5. Vansina mentions on the same page that Abala was a prosperous exploitation area of iron ore. If the link between iron and rain can be established, we may very well suspect the rainmaking cult to be responsible for the invention of the box.
6. Further investigation may be fruitful. Vansina (1990: 225) appears to change his identification of *nkobi*'s origins: 'from *lemba nkobe*' (and also earlier so in his book) but later on 'from Mbushi' (ibid. 457). A short paper by Wainwright (1942) gives a hint: ore was collected from the riverbed. It is one of many possible early associations (cf. de Maret 1985).
7. The co-authors describe the village headmen as people-masters keen to conserve the status quo. The land-masters are the chiefs, including forest-masters and king. I earlier proposed an alternation (*kum* and *kul*) to distinguish the forest-master and the king in figures of continuous and discontinuous power.
8. The funerary sacrifice of a slave whose arms and legs are broken also reminds of the burial of Chwezi leaders, which are preceded by the sacrifice of a sheep whose limbs are broken. After his death, the king's frontal bone and little finger were inserted in the Nkwe Mbali charm. The catafalque contained an effigy of the king, on top of which stood a little house, *ndzo ancweli* (TK 386, n20). C(h)wezi can be a derivation of *c(h)weli* (e.g. like Nyamwezi is from nya-mweli, 'people of the west').

PART III

The Ceremonial State

Chapter 8

KUBA, KONGO AND BUGANDA 'MIRACLES'
REVERSIONS IN TRANSITION

A comparative study of eight African kingdoms tempted Lemarchand (1977: 304) to zoom out beyond the historical evidence and conclude that African kings have basically always been confronted by the dilemma to retain power and be destroyed by their people, or relinquish power to endure in a largely symbolic office. A microscopic take on politics, picturing an individual king experiencing a dilemma, is often illuminating. In our view, the dilemma describes the oscillation of the pendulum between autocrat and nominal head after medicinal rule was undermined from within and political centralization peaked. A disequilibrium apt to cause general unrest arose after losing the democratizing balance of spirit call, acquisition of magic, and initiation in return for gifts, through which commoners could climb ranks and in which those excelling (or their ascendants) occupied the highest rank. The autocratic king's aversion concerned exactly these three core traits of medicinal rule: medicine, initiation and spirit mediumship, to whose opposite he attempted to revert the tasks of his office. The final chapter on the history of the Rwandan state illustrates the point with a long-term process.

The outcome of terminating medicinal rule was a state, as defined in the Oxford English Dictionary: 'a nation or territory considered as an organized political community under one government'. I venture to qualify it as a 'ceremonial' state because without elections, parties or policies the political community was only nominally organized. The government boiled down to king and court being despotically in charge, their influence centrifugally fading out to the edges of the usually ill-defined territory. The state presented itself to their commoners mainly through ceremony and the solemn execution of strict procedure. (Sacred state would be an evocative synonym if it were not for the connotation of the adjective with the opposite of secular.) In other words, these central African states did not really tally with the European political system of the *ancien régime* that was displaced by the French Revolution. The ceremonial state, consisting of an autocrat and his governing officers, was not the pinnacle of a gradual process but an exceptional occurrence, an offshoot from the time-worn model of medicinal rule, widespread because rooted in a cultural structure. Much like parliamentary democracy in the West, medicinal rule had, over the thousand years of its development, reached a certain equilibrium, in different ways across the region, to which the ceremonial state was a reaction. The final chapter explores a processual methodology to elicit a historical evolution in Rwanda from divinatory society to medicinal rule and, eventually, ceremonial state. Let us begin with some principles of medicinal rule that carried within themselves the seeds for the ceremonial state.

The Kabaka of Buganda: From Taboo to Ceremonial Procedure

Across equatorial Africa, kings have to obey rules of conduct, in a limited number of variants. Betraying the cultural structure of medicinal rule, they all refer to taboos that a spirit medium, possibly the later founder of a dynastic clan, could have obtained from his or her flight in the forest. Benjamin Ray (1991: 49) sums up the rules for the Kabaka paramount of Buganda: '[H]e never walked on the ground, he could never be looked upon in a royal procession, and he had to take his meals in seclusion'. A variant is that the king was not to leave the court unless carried. The Sukuma-Nyamwezi chiefs observed the taboo of not having a drop of their blood fall on the ground lest the chiefdom suffer drought. The first prohibition, on treading ground, recalls a contemporary initiation at the Great Lakes. At the moment of possession by the Chwezi spirit the novice's feet should not touch the ground. The feet should rest on a log to establish contact with the dead. Also, the bundle of grass held in the novice's hands has this purpose, like the elephant grass held by the Alur chief during his installation. The rule maintains the king's initiatory state and receptivity to the ancestral spirit, which the Chwezi novice only observes during initiation. Since the king's body contains the spirit's fertility, his transmission of bodily fluids should be prevented. In some cultural groups this means a strict regulation of his sexual intercourse. In the mentioned Sukuma-Nyamwezi case it means that his inner fluids, the blood, should stay inside and not come into contact with the soil.

The classificatory extensions of the cultural structure steering people's associative creativity can always be plumbed further. Might the contact between land and royal body be the union of two kindred, like incest, which is said to cause famine in the community? Or will the earth be fatally scorched by contact with the excess of fertility of him who is glorified in about every Bantu-speaking court as the 'Father of Twins' (cf. Ray 1991: 49)?

The norm prohibiting fluid transmission suits our picture of the king as a potent initiatory-medicinal condition. It brings us to the second rule on saving his bodily integrity. No pomp will suffice to prevent onlookers from perceiving in the royal procession a man on the throne and not the medicine. The same goes for the third rule, on seeing him eat or drink. All Kongo nobles closed their eyes whenever the king took a sip. A mortal body with its orifices and earthly needs demystifies. The court's challenge is less one of legitimacy, incarnating the body politic, than of the institution remaining efficacious by conserving the permanently initiated, ritualized condition that is the king. He should not be spilt. The king never dies; it is just the beans that are literally said to be spilt. He is the power of the kingdom; 'eats the kingdom' (*kulya obuganda*; ibid.: 43). He need not act as a warrior or wise elder. What counts is his lasting state of fertility.

How to prove that he is not, like Frazer argued, an incarnate god who magically controls life and whose vitality, bound up with the kingdom, shall be strengthened through human sacrifice and at the sign of weakness shall be met with regicide, followed by soul transference to a vigorous successor (Ray 1991: 41)? Ray is convinced that by pointing to the ambiguous, in certain aspects inferior status of kings he can destroy Frazer's thesis of divine kingship; that by reserving the deeper ritual knowledge for a caste of ritual masters (Ray calls priests) he can purge the king of his sacredness and reinstall him as the somewhat immaterial 'symbol' of order and power (ibid.: 44, 48). It is fighting fire with fire. Before inferring the king's 'subordinate status' from the fact that the ritual masters call the king their 'son-in-law' and 'slave', one should contextualize the meaning of these words. Socialization is the context in this case. The ritual masters have initiated the king before the ceremony of confirmation, the final stage of royal installation. They gave new life to him, as in the Bantu metaphor for being initiated, *kubyalwa*, literally 'being born'. A Sukuma bridegroom asking a man for the hand of his daughter uses the same expression to underline that the son-in-law will turn into a man thanks to the bridegiver, who himself can never be compensated, for no bridewealth of cattle can replace a human being. Ritual master and king are incomparable positions. Eternally indebted to the master giving or teaching him the medicine, the king is a slave. At the same time, the slave is the medium between the master and the people, without whom neither of them can do, like the bride is the vehicle of social exchange between clans. Subordination is too bland a term for this structural mediumship. Unlike the king, who approximates the unattached position of the spirit medium, the ritual masters act in the royal court as worldly extensions of the clan they represent (ibid.: 45). The sophisticated Buganda court has its own medium, yet contrasted with diviners possessed by Lubaale spirits, this royal medium is a 'bearer' of the king's spirit (ibid.: 43).[1]

Frazer's academic impact cannot be ignored. Well into the mid twentieth century a European rural religiosity was projected on Africa, mistaking African rulers such as the Kabaka for high priests of a church (ibid.: 214–15, n21–22). However, the way to counter Frazer's sweeping claim, in equatorial Africa at least, is not to switch to a political analysis nor to cut down on what sets a current king such as the Kabaka apart, but as always to retrace the local view on the institution, and to consider the logic behind the evolution of the subsequent guises of this institution. What does it mean when in all instances kingship is said to 'fall on' the successor as a destiny? That makes the king less a 'magician' and less an expert in control of fertility, and more a vehicle, without however functioning as a high priest either. What sets him apart from the healer is that his rain medicine and protective charm are collective. For the ceremonial state, we may follow de Heusch (1997) and contend that the king himself is the medicine.

Chapter 7 ended with the refusal by the last Tio king to undergo the ritual initiation. The forest-masters insisted that he would respect the medicinal tradition. I can think of no better way to characterize the event than as a breach of medicinal rule. The forest-masters must have sensed their cosmology to be at stake by the king's refusal. The initiation during which the spirit imposes obligations ties the chief or king to the fate of the people, to the rain that must fall. A head of state who would not want to depend on the outcome of the rituals will have priests to organize the ceremonial steps wherein he plays the scripted part. As long as the solemn procedure is observed, any autocratic decisions of his will be backed by the rituals and the clergy. Therefore

I propose to call this type of rule the ceremonial state, rather than a sacred or sacral state, which projects a gullible populace.

The centralizations in coastal Congo, Kuba and the Great Lakes displayed parallel features because of the polarity pivotal to medicinal rule. The separation between ritual specialist and chief grew in the ceremonial state, and with it the resemblance to European kingship. In Rwanda, the court of the *mwami*, king, had its own historians to learn every step in the ceremonies by heart. The double check made sure the priests did everything correctly. In the large kingdom of Buganda, the Kabaka paramount had his chiefs (*mwami, mukungu*) perform ritual duties together with his spirit mediums, without whom no ceremony could take place (Ray 1991: 144, 149).² In the middle of the royal shrine, separating the worlds of the living and the dead, stood the Twin (*mulongo*) charm, representing the king's double. Behind it in the temple area of 'the forest' (*kibira*; the Bantu stem *bir* recalls *i-bil-i* charms) stood a jawbone relic of the preceding Kabaka. The charm, shrine, mediumship and forest together form the symbolic core of chieftaincy in medicinal rule. Kingship rearranges those elements.

In the 1980s, the Kabaka and his family in the palace (*lubiri*, cf. again *bir* possibly referring to the *ibili* charm) distanced themselves from their people's worship of Lubaale spirits. They even minimized the efficacy of their own royal ancestors in their shrine ritual (ibid.: 151–52). Whether or not this royal aloofness was due to Christian influence, the anti-mediumistic and anti-initiatory sentiment is well in line with the process of reducing royal dependence on the counterparts of clans and diviners, which we also noticed in the Tio case. We will later conclude on recurring aversions to medicine's de facto democratization, and identify an endogenous tension quite different from the polity prism's tension with religion. The process began in the early nineteenth century, when Ssuuna II at his accession discontinued the ritual of 'maturation' (*kukula*, again from proto-Bantu *kul*) whereby the Kabaka would have to be submitted to initiation (ibid.: 77).³ The initiation made the Buganda king dependent. It was traditionally organized by the chiefs of other clans, just as it was by the forest-masters in Tio kingship on the other side of the continent. The divergence from medicinal rule continued when Mutesa I reduced the significance of the Lubaale spirits in kingship, and of the priesthood serving them (ibid.: 152).

Crucial to our thesis is the decline, or suppression, of ancestral worship announcing the rise of the ceremonial state. In medicinal rule, reciprocity and interdependence with the spirits are normal.

The paramount shares power with the elders of clans or lineages in a division of tasks. He behaves as the healer of the collective, making hay of his outsidership (he comes from elsewhere, cf. de Heusch 1972) to ensure the population's fertility, symbolically reproducing the exogamy principle and fractal of life at the level of his realm. He is the 'womb' offered to the autochthonous group, which latter retains territorially linked functions such as possessing the national charm or initiating the king. In this view, the ceremonial state evolved and derived from key features of medicinal rule, maintaining the king's reputation of life-giver while emptying out the conditions for his being a forest-within, reducing these to a merely ceremonial function. Cases in Part III to verify the process of transition include Rwanda through its oral tradition, Buganda through its recorded recent history, and Kuba through an anthropological reading of the historian's reconstruction. The models of medicinal rule and ceremonial state, and their transition, lend coherence to disparate data.

Kuba and the Problem of a Baseline

In lush riverine central Congo, where rainmaking is no issue, a different political system emerged than in the Congolese savanna, the Atlantic coast, the Great Lakes or in East Africa. Hidden amidst Mongo-speaking segmentary lineage groups and west of the Luba kingdom, the European traveller Leo Frobenius was shocked to discover the Kuba empire, to him a miracle of civilization for its sophisticated material culture and social structure. In *The Children of Woot* (henceforth CW) from 1978 Vansina has no qualms about making the analogy with the miracle of the classic Greek polity: how could the southern Congolese equatorial forest harbour a sophisticated civilization with kings, legal procedures and artistic traditions in striking contrast with surrounding cultures? From the late nineteenth century onwards, the Kuba kingdom fascinated Europeans for being the 'lone witness to the stately courts that had once flourished in equatorial Africa' (CW 3). Calling themselves 'the people of the king', the Kuba promise to be an excellent counterpoint to our thesis of medicinal rule.

Some doubt may be raised in advance. Why would a kingdom in 1887 be witness to how other polities were two centuries before? We should not assume a linear progress that African political systems undergo once their authorities centralize. Yet the society that Kuba kingship grew from was not unique. Much of the process must have been endogenous to the Kuba. Historically, this group originating from the southern Mongo (CW 44; and called BaKongo by their northern neighbours, CW 42) migrated south-east to escape the turmoil of trade with Europeans that was affecting communities at the Pool, the coast, and along the Congo River. The boys' initiation celebrates travel by canoe upstream on the river, replaying their people's migration (CW 34-36). At some point, when kingship became institutionalized, they compulsively conserved their traditions by fixating them in a temporal framework wherein each practice is explained from its origin, namely from the culture hero Woot, who instituted it (CW 16). The question of the Kuba kingdom's origins remains.

Shyaam and the Duplicate Court

Once again, the question of origin brings us back to the medicine man. Shyaam, born from a slave woman, figures in myths as the founder of the Matoon dynasty and inventor of Kuba civilization, including male initiation, crop-growing techniques, palm-wine making and the royal charm *ncaam mashok* (CW 60). Before claiming kingship, he travelled to be initiated into powerful charms. The teacher of medicine was his father-in-law. Shyaam's proof of skill was the hunt and the barehanded skinning he performed on an antelope coming out of the forest of its own will, upon which the old medicine man had said: 'Truly, now I see that you are able to be a famous medicine man' (CW 61). Vansina cannot ignore the role of medicine man in which Shyaam is cast, but explains it as trickery in an intermediate phase that was necessary to snatch kingship away and 'be himself the greatest king in Bushoong memory' (CW 63). The author reads medicine as the sign of myth.

Oral tradition, however, does not present Shyaam's healership as an intermediate phase. What we observe is the initiation of a healer commencing his own cult. He administers the right medicine to a woman giving birth to twins: she suffers from the archetypical excess of fertility, which only he as a fertility healer can treat. He also cures snakebites, another affliction typically handled by medicinal cults. The only non-medicinal part of his accession is the spit he manages to obtain by ruse from his predecessor passing by a rubbish heap near the palace, although even then reference is made to saliva as metonymic ingredient in potions or blessings. Vansina notices in a footnote the similarity with south-western Mongo chiefs, who are chosen by spirits through miracle (CW 329, n38). He does not make the connection with another archetypical theme: the hunter king founding dynasties among the Luba and Lunda – although he had earlier on recognized the theme in one of the Kuba myths (CW 329, n32), and noted that de Heusch in *Le Roi Ivre* did not make the connection. The hunter who comes from the wild outside and has no manners, must be civilized, but is cherished for the feral fertility he brings along and is therefore told to no longer look at blood (CW 59), that is: he should conserve his fertility so as to be their king. The kingdom is predicated not on material necessity but on fate, on the contingency of divination and classificatory extensions such as spirit mediumship and a blessed hunt in the forest. The forest activities and use of plants for magic remind the agricultural community of its hunter roots. The first true king is, according to Vansina's informants, the one who could never be deposed (CW 62). Does the novel phase refer to the spirit-based calling of King Shyaam, or rather to the end of the leader's reciprocity with spirits and people, hence the downfall of medicinal rule?

'[T]wo emblems of kingship' are said to be kaolin and an iron staff (CW 54). Whence their significance and origin? Kaolin (white porcelain clay) models kingship on the work of the healer (CW 197). Iron repeats the rainmaking trope. The prohibition on twins in the royal line of descent underlines the collective impact of the king's healing, and fertility. Vansina explains the prohibition from the norm of seniority that would be contradicted by such births (CW 55). Structure-idealism shudders at normative contradiction (which an actor's palette of frames however implies). Our comparative exercise rather starts from the observation that the symbolic association of twins with excess fertility is common across equatorial Africa. The king purifies the twins' excess ritually, or domesticates them by having them in his palace, but he could not be purified himself. Twinship on top of kingship (which in some cultures are equated symbolically) would have dire consequences for the land, as would the spilling of blood on the soil. In Kuba mythology, the risk of losing menstrual blood would be the main obstacle for having women on the throne (CW 56).

Chiefs, like the king, reigned on the condition that their magic was blessed by the spirits (CW 122). For this they underwent the same ritual of nine-days seclusion in the forest, followed by transgression (here ritual intercourse) as mentioned earlier among others in the Tio *lisee*. Kuba call the initiation *mbyeemy* (CW 121). Two names for the same institution point to a cultural structure shared in different places. 'Ritual . . . was almost always connected with a charm' (CW 7). The eldest son of the king (*mwaaddy*) was the keeper of tradition, the history and the rites. He collaborated closely with the king's ritualist, *muyum*, who lived in an exact copy of the king's court (CW 25) and guarded the charm of the realm in a forest near Kosh (CW 55). What caused the patrilineal inheritance of tradition despite matrilineal succession is unknown. And why would the royal charm lie outside the court? The duplication of the royal court at the medicinal level looks like the remainder of a transitional situation, since there is no reason to assume that the charm was an innovation. We get the same impression of a transition from the patrilineal control over ritual tradition by the king's son.

The chapter on Rwanda will make the transition explicit, which is that from medicinal rule to ceremonial state. We argue that the king's sovereignty grew as he severed his authority from the workings of the charm. Medicine and divination keep autocracy in check. The charm eventually got detached in a duplicate court, so segregated that the king, chiefs and all their clan members were prohibited from entering the settlements of the *muyum*'s clan. Was the latter clan historically the original owner of medicine? To understand the primacy of the senior prince as ritualist, we must return to our thesis. A healer with revered medicine founds a cult. To whom will the knowledge be transmitted? A split between two lines of descent may follow. On the one hand, through matrilineal succession a clan establishes the royal dynasty. The office transcends the individual member enthroned. On the other hand, patrilineal transmission consolidates succession of the ritual traditions. This knowledge will not go to the son of the senior prince, so patrilineal transmission ends with him. The medicine, a charm, is considered separate from the rituals. It does not get lost, thanks to an expert, *muyum*, maintaining the medicine in his clan and collaborating with every new king's son. The pair of *mwaaddy* and *muyum* is what remains after the traces of that history have disappeared.

The arrangement of court duties seems coherent if seen through the prism of a medicinal cult becoming a dynastic clan. From the viewpoint of the founding leader of a cult, his work is carried on by transmitting his medicinal knowledge to one of the children living in the compound. Since the group follows rules of virilocal residence, and the typical healer's compound is polygynous with him as patriarch, the male children will be his sons. The healer is necessarily the patriarch in his domain. He will respectfully greet visiting senior kin and maternal uncles, but they will have no say in his healership. A nephew from the matrilineal descent group is not a natural candidate in the first generations after foundation of the cult. The nephew could inherit a title during a brief ceremony, but not medicinal or ritual knowledge, which are learned by long-term practice and observation on a day-to-day basis in the compound. The eldest son is thus a more obvious candidate for succeeding the healer after training with the help of the main assistant (who, as said before, substitutes the father in the intimate stages of initiation into spirit mediumship). The nephew in our conjecture looks like the *mwaaddy*, and the son looks like the *muyum*. The pieces of the puzzle fall into place. A third figure specialized in narrating oral traditions is the *bulaam* – not coincidentally a dance instructor – dance performances being the main rite in mediumistic healing.

The thesis of medicinal rule tallies with the historical shift Vansina presumes from patrilineal to matrilineal descent in the Kuba kingdom (CW 51–52). The initial cultic model revolving around ritual expertise and the contingency of spirit possession was gradually replaced by a kin group protecting its interests. Such kin group fulfils the criteria of a dynastic clan. They protect themselves through rules of succession, military means and the imposition of norms. A metaphorical enactment of the transformation from mediumistic to ceremonial and normative rule seems to me the Kuba myth on the king's reign substantially growing once the clan notables had murdered a ritual expert in public for breaking a rule. The ritualist was someone the king had earlier on not dared to kill, despite the man's violation of new norms which, ironically, he himself had devised in honour of the king (CW 54).

Strict rules serve the king. The basis of the court's formalism are the royal taboos to sustain fertility. These in turn originated from the (not formalist) experience of spirit possession yielding a personal obligation, compliance of which works like a medicine.

Kete Matrilineages and the Kuba Switch (Let Youth Rule?)

North of the wide Sankuru River lies a naturally rich environment of canopy, savanna and rivers, inhabited by southern Mongo-speakers. Vansina rhetorically leaves his question unanswered why anyone would leave such a fertile area (CW 91, 104). The Lele and Wongo moved away first, possibly as far back as a millennium ago, and then the Kuba did, or at least their forebears who would later give rise to the kingdom. The Lele crossed the Sankuru River and the region of the Kete to eventually settle in their current place to the south-west, remaining the hunters that featured centrally in Part I. The Kuba trickled across the river in smaller groups to live next to Kete villages. The Kuba were used to chiefs (*kum*) with authority over a village or a set of villages, ruled together with the elders of patrilineages (CW 97). The lineages resided in (virilocal) sections of the village. They had their ancestral spirits and rituals with prohibitions, mainly food taboos. The chief's authority was based on an old Mongo complex backed by myth regarding his mystical appointment by nature spirits, which are territorially linked. He received the gift of the (leopard) hide (*ekopo*) and possessed the ball of white kaolin for ritual smearing, and a double bell. His insignia were the royal drum, the eagle's feather, a royal palisade and residence at the head of the village, probably downstream. Every chief and possibly village had a collective charm and an *ilweemy*, a medicine man for protection and war charms. Together a complex takes shape that we have systematically encountered elsewhere and named medicinal rule. However, Mongo societies were strictly speaking stateless, Vansina remarks, specifying in a footnote that the earliest chiefs must have been patriarchs of the kin group since the Bushoong term for chiefdom is *bubil*, whose root *bil* means kin in Mongo (CW 98, n18). Could the stem *bil*, mentioned earlier on in charms (*ibili*) and initiatory cult (*nibeli*), refer to the initially kin-based foundation of cults?

Before the Kete hosts embarked on their 'centuries-long symbiosis' with the Kuba they had a council (*kibanza*, a common Bantu term in the southern savanna) at the village, but no leadership beyond that level. They placated nature spirits and granted the dead a more active role in life than did the southern Mongo and presumably the Kuba forebears. The Kete hunted, and they farmed better than the Kuba. Most of all, their artisans carved pillars, spirit statues and a type of mask all of which influenced the later famous 'Kuba style'. 'But their political organization was much less coherent', Vansina finely remarks (CW 102). The Kete traced descent in the matrilineage (*bulungu*), which made them 'the most distant extension of the central African matrilineal belt' (CW 101).

Based on changes in the kinship terminology such as adoption of the Kete term 'mother' for grandparents and ancestors, Vansina draws a baffling conclusion. After they crossed the Sankuru, the Kuba switched from a patrilineal to a matrilineal kinship system. What had happened? In order to marry women of the Kete lineages, the Kuba accepted that the children would belong to their mother's family. The cost of bridewealth was lowered through bride-service by the groom, who cultivated at his in-laws during the years before marriage (CW 108).[4] In return for an expensive fee, patrilineal descent of children could be maintained, namely with 'pawn' women. For them, indeed, the original Mongo term of 'wife' was still used.

Did the Kete strike the best deal by carrying on their matrilineal system? The recompense for the Kuba was conservation of virilocal residence. They valued corporate residence more highly than descent. In a fascinating dense argumentation, Vansina demonstrates that the new system resulted in the kinship groups dispersing and losing their corporate function, making way for stronger political organization in the residential unit, the village (CW 111). The transition to matrilineal descent and virilocal residence increased the mobility of the families because husbands could demand residence in any village of a grandparent or wife. Cousins of the matrilineage lost their unity because they were dispersed among their mothers' virilocal residences. In Kuba as well as Lele groups, which both made the lineal shift, the village council (*malaang*) became pre-eminent at the expense of the kin-based authority of Kete villagers. The clan sections (localized lineages in the village) were represented in the council by their elders (*kolm*). The power broker was the young messenger-spokesperson, *itembangu* in Lele (CW 112; Douglas 1963: 71–72; cf. *nsumba ntale* in Kisukuma).[5] Gradually, in an estimated period between 1500 and 1650, the Kete found themselves in a position of social inequality, especially in the Bushoong chiefdom.

Presented in this way, the Kete come across as naive and the Kuba as strategic. But is territorialized government over other peoples something the Kete would have to naturally strive for or intuitively know the implications and consequences of? Or did the centralization arbitrarily evolve to reward some and victimize others? To avoid misinterpretation and anachronism, we should think the past not from the outcome or the present but from the earlier past. That means we should figure out the cultural structure that was relevant before the change. The Kete did not have chiefship as a cultural model. As far as we can determine, they did not know or care about territorial rule beyond the village level. The normal situation was 'decentred' government in the hands of the families. On the side of the proto-Kuba too, rulers were conceived of as healers of the collective. Their view and motives, situated somewhere on the continuum between the decentred government of segmentary lineages and the medicinal rule of the segmentary state, should not be extrapolated to explain the ceremonial legitimacy of the unitary state.

A second and third reflection concerns the author's exposition. From the onset, as the forebears of the Lele and Kuba are recounted to migrate from the lush north, the discourse is set in the key of push rather than pull factors. We saw that the matrilineal transition increased mobility. Clearly, life was vibrant across the Sankuru River.

Was it a famous place among the young people at the time, perhaps introduced to them during their rite of passage, which for the liminal phase and ordeal requires a 'wild outside' such as a forest or an opposite riverbank? What if the greater mobility, or opportunities of mobility, in the south pulled adolescents across the river? Such a mobile and perhaps liberal society could have resulted in a matrilineal system with fathers as inseminators instead of patriarchs. Vansina's direction of causality (matrilineal transition increased mobility) is thus inverted, without stretching the facts. Socio-sexual mobility created matrilinearity. A number of elements corroborate the inversion. First of all, in support of our pull factor, there are no reasons whatsoever to assume that the proto-Kuba were chased from the more fertile north. Secondly, there may have been a push factor at the intergenerational level. Since the early 'chiefs', who we should picture as charismatic healer-chiefs, operated only in one village or a few villages, they had direct contact with the entire population. Those chiefs monopolized, together with the elders, not only the village charm but the sexual network. Prospects for trade, sexual rights and self-sufficiency should have attracted adolescents fed up with a polygynous system benefiting older men. The invention of bride-service compensated for a youngster's limited capacity to deliver bridewealth on his own. The practice of working to get a wife at that new place was crucial in raising an adolescent's self-sufficiency. Matrilineal descent, in which the husband does not lay claim on the offspring of his marriage, could lower expectations of bridewealth and lighten the burden as well. The young generation extraordinarily participating in the power structure through their spokesperson confirms the hypothesis of an intergenerational dynamic. However, to assess its probability we should know how soon these customs arose after the traversal, particularly bride-service and adolescent spokesmanship.

Healership and 'Rule'

The matriliny-after-mobility argument inverting Vansina's does not aspire to an alternative history. I wanted to illustrate that, without anthropological analysis, the historical data can be interpreted in virtually opposite ways, and it should therefore be scientifically rewarding to consider the interpretation itself, that is to discern the various 'cultural structures' at hand. Within the modern constitution one may switch between political, economic and religious angles (cf. Introduction). But the modern constitution itself and its corollary (the polity prism) requires an alternative, which I propose with the medicinal perspective. This brings us to my third remark. The above study takes the political perspective on society for granted. Might the numerous applications of the verb 'to rule' and 'to govern' to depict the actions and titles in the Kuba chiefdoms prior to the rise of the kingdom (e.g. CW 116) not be replaced by 'to heal'? 'To rule', 'chiefdom' and 'subject villages' mean little if '[t]he chiefdoms were small, the duties and privileges of titleholders not quite clear, and power probably remained fairly diffuse. Control over subject villages was perhaps limited to one collection of tribute a year. In judicial matters, only cases involving murder or bloodshed may have come to the chief's court' (CW 122).

I have lived in the 'court' of cult leaders and healers. There were ranks and dignitaries with certain functions, collection of fees, as I described. The idea of each chief having a diviner (*ilumbi*) like a king has a priest (cf. CW 12) should remind us of the nagging dissatisfaction about royal bias mentioned earlier by the author. The 'founding clans' of the chiefdoms are called *mbaangt*, the Lele term for the clan of first settlers who because of their autochthony can count on ritual rights (CW 115). The ritual role did not make them politically less significant. The *mbaangt* no less than chose, advised and deposed the chief, *kum* (CW 116). They would know who, among the sons of the dynastic clan, the spirit of Woot had chosen to become equated with the deified sun (CW 122). The *ibaam* council of the *mbaangt* was headed by the *kikaam*. He initiated the chief through a ritual of seclusion during a sacred nine days, of course. One apparently becomes a chief as one becomes a healer. Hence, the case we presented for medicinal rule. The initiation ritual displayed the charms from the territorial shrine tended by the *mbaangt* (*Inam* in the case of Bushoong chiefdom). The chief foreswore all kinship ties (possibly through incest, CW 122). The endorsement by the autochthonous Cwa hunters was followed by the chief's ritual intercourse with his recently designated first wife, 'who washes with kaolin'. The ritual of installation uses kaolin from north of the Sankuru, which renders the ritual ancient, to predate the migration and ensuing rise of Kuba chiefdoms (CW 121). The ritual significance of kaolin itself is so widespread over all equatorial Africa (CW 197) that our connection between medicine and rule may be grounded in it.

Ritual and medicinal charm were not invented to 'legitimate' the chieftaincy, because historical evidence suggests they came before government. Anthropologically too, the same cultural structure subtends the chief's enthronement and that of the initiation rites of

Bantu healing cults. The Chwezi novices are convoked by the spirit to go into seclusion and get initiated by the ranked officials in a hut containing the cultic charms. They have to give up all kinship ties through a ritual act of incest with an assigned (grand)mother/ father. After a week of training in the forest and the *lutaka* nocturnal dance at the centre of the court, they solemnly receive from their teacher like chiefs the diadem of cowrie shells and bushbuck tail from the bottom of a pond, reminiscent of the Bushoong's sacred lake (But aPoong) where the *muyum* guards the national charm, or further away, of the Nkwe Mbali waterfall spilling its charms for the Tio chief and the cults in western Congo.

Just as the chief of the Chwezi cult is chosen by the spirit but has also paid the fees before reaching the highest rank, the elected successor of the Kuba chief must already have grown up to be a wealthy man with a family. He is required to pay huge gifts to the *mbaangt* clans. Each return him the favour with a wife to marry. At installation he must pay, just as the Chwezi novices do immediately before entering the final phase of their consecration as bearers of their spirit. The consecration is for men and women, and normally for more than one person at once. The chieftaincy was a variant on the spirit cult with special conditions, some of which the singers at the homage ceremony reminded the audience of: 'What is forbidden is a female king' (CW 121). Spirit cults and ritual initiation formed the people's frame of reference for comprehending and co-creating the institution of kingship that developed from chief-healership.

Shyaam is credited by oral traditions as the first king. He fashioned the titles of chiefs and dignitaries into an overarching bureaucracy located in a capital and headed by the Bushoong chief, de facto 'the king', *nyim* (CW 128). The two main categories of office to complement the king were the *kolm,* grouped in totemic sets eventually amounting to over a hundred titles which any free man could acquire (marked by a type of feather; CW 131), and the eighteen 'medicine men of the basket' (*ngwoom incyaam*) forming the crown council (*ibaam*). The basket referred to the new royal charm. Termed in Kikongo, it presumably had substances appended to the old charm *Inam*.[6] Essentially, these two categories at the upper layer of society did not form a bureaucracy organized according to a functional division of administrative tasks. They were a cult hierarchy reproducing in each layer the fractal logic of Shyaam's kingship and extending it during generations in the creative arts and ornaments for which the Kuba are celebrated today: 'Each title had its praise name, emblems and symbols, and the most important ones even boasted their own funeral and installation rituals' (CW 132). New titles are meant to attract additional supporters for the crown (CW 136), just as novices make a cult grow.

While Shyaam had managed to organize and perpetuate the institution, his original demeanour shows in his identification with a nature spirit (*ngesh*) and his 'madness' (CW 129), which could only signify spirit possession. The spirit taught him to create medicine and ritual. The year-long rituals of installation, which probably began with his successors and thus were devised for the future of the institution (CW 146), initiated the king (for eighteen days). Most of all, they implicated all segments of the population like members of a cult.

'The introduction of terms, originating in the area west of the Loange river, for "medicine man" and "royal basket of charms" makes it plausible that this aspect of kingship goes back to the beginning of the kingdom. Shyaam was, after all, remembered as "the magic king"', we get to read (CW 130). Can we speak of the medicinal as a mere 'aspect' of kingship when the heart of the palace contains drums (CW 138, 206), the king is supposed to control the most powerful charms of the region (CW 130) and he is associated with the forest to whose shot game he has rights (CW 143)? His capacities and prohibitions fit within the universal symbolic structure. Twins lived at his court. Their birth boasted fertility like an animal's litter, and their leader, *muyesh*, acted as the king's spokesperson, indeed as his twin (CW 147). Better than the Kete rainmakers, the king controlled fertility (CW 208, n50).

> [The king] could send storms or tornadoes and could ward off attacks by witches against his capital, as is shown by his mastery over lightning, thought to be an animal. He protected the fertility of villages by throwing white porcelain clay in the air and reciting a formula, but he could also withdraw his protection. A whole set of avoidances – negative ritual – was linked to his powers. These were acts to preserve the fertility of the land. A king could not walk for long, sit on the bare ground, cross a field, eat in front of his wives, cross the Kasai river, or look at tombs, corpses or wounds. A transgression of any of these, and of certain other prohibitions, made the people think that 'the ground would be burned'. (CW 208–9)[7]

True, the Kuba chiefs had a counterpart, a lord of the land who would survive Shyaam's innovations. A mysterious figure, as mentioned, the *muyum* guarded the national charm in a forest near the lake. Still in the 1950s he was living in a replica court to which king and nobles had no access (CW 206). We can only think of the right of autochthony, and perhaps a sour deal, that granted the honour to his clan, which indeed had ruled over the area before the arrival of the

Bushoong. Chieftainship remained a family business, with the eldest son (*mwaaddy*) keeping the dynastic tradition, as a healer's son does.

Transitions: Towards the Ceremonial State of Mass Killing

Inheriting a title is easy. Possessing unique qualities is another thing. Descendants of the medicine man typically fear not to pass muster. It seems no coincidence that to keep up with the healer Shyaam his successors needed a royal medicine man (*pok ibaan*, 'their [charm] pot'). As a new influential titleholder, he stripped the powerful executer of royal rituals (*mbyeemy*) of authority (CW 135, 138). His most remarkable feat was to have a charm that was released of spirit (CW 206) and thus could do without diviners who communicate whimsical wishes the client should comply with. Only village shrines were still linked to a nature spirit – *ngesh* from the western Bantu *nkisi* – which controlled fertility (CW 200).

Medicinal rule had faded for the ceremonial state to commence, with the multiplication of protocol, identity markers and offices, and the delegation of medicine to an officer who had things under control and could put a lid on oracles with democratizing tendencies the king might have to obey (see Chapter 9). A gradual social change reinforced the process. The cult of ancestors disappeared together with the declining lineages after the lineal shift (CW 198). The ancestral cult perhaps never took root in a society of men waiting until adulthood to shift residence to the matrilineage. Where would they as children have witnessed the care for their lineage ascendants? The court had been arranging for its own publicity through songs on nature spirits praising the kingdom (CW 23). The equation of the king with a nature spirit contributed to legitimacy of the state (CW 238), yet whether the people fell for it we cannot tell from a song. Later the village nature spirits were supplanted by a deity, *Ncyeem*. In the eighteenth century the ninth king Mbop Pelyeeng aNce dissolved all spirit cults in the region (CW 200).

Like Ndori in Rwanda featuring in the next chapter, Shyaam was a pivotal figure, an embodiment of a process that was ongoing. Whereas Ndori broke away from medicinal rule, whose spirit reciprocity and sense of contingency were transferred to a fleeing Ryangombe, we see that Shyaam in Kuba radiated medicinal rule, yet only to usher in a new era for his successors, establishing precise rules of succession (CW 238), protocol, tribute (if rarely mentioned in the traditions; CW

143), corvée labor (for an impressive palace, however unable to mobilize the realm for a large army; CW 144) and an army. The 'magic king' was succeeded by the 'warrior king' Mboong aLeeng (CW 127), responsible for annexation of the last province. On his instigation, the boys' initiation was organized at the capital under the leadership of one of the princes, who kept records of youth demographics (CW 180). There was room for leverage by an intermediary like the young village spokesperson. Or was it the latter's influence that the king had countered by monopolizing initiation? The age-grades and rite of passage were abolished by Kot aPe in 1908 (CW 230).

Kings were *ncyeem kwoonc*, translated as 'God on earth' (CW 135, 207). As my earlier reference to a 'second god' (cf. *mungu wa pili* in Part II) suggests, one should not take titles of publicity as proof of popular belief. In the century that followed, the kings would need more tribute to maintain their massive 100 square kilometres of fenced capital with fenced compounds. The inhabitants lived like aristocrats, paying no taxes and prohibited from farming. To feed the treasury the court created and taxed 'unfree' villages (*matoon*; CW 140) of former war prisoners, slaves and convicts. Arbitrary killings to both entertain and intimidate the masses became an alternative to winning acclaim. By the second half of the nineteenth century, ceremonial sacrifices of thousands of human lives in one go were no exception.

As a form of 'conspicuous consumption' at funerals, the killing of slaves was also supposed to furnish the deceased noble with servants in the afterlife (CW 181). What were once speculative beliefs of oracular value on the invisible world, distilled from one divination to the next, were now religious propositions taken literally and executed faithfully. We gather from fieldwork in rural communities in the Great Lakes that during medicinal rule a sense of contingency meant a practical view on belief in the supernatural: one knew the difference between fact and oracle. Would a charlatan diviner want to have mass killings on his conscience? The ceremonial state, however, segregated politics and religion, yielding a caste of priests and an orthodoxy stipulating correct procedures and concomitant interventions. In those years, many miles away in the Buganda kingdom, the same funerary human sacrifices for royals were customary (Ray 1991: 167). Apparently, the creation and segregation of politics and religion is not a Western invention. It may be structural to a highly centralized state.

That social change occurred in the African kingdoms, with centralization of the violence as well, nobody will deny. Explanations have been materialistic or particularistic at the expense of cultural, endogenous driving forces with regional roots. I argue that divination and the role of the spirit, whom Shyaam had experienced, form the link missing in Vansina's account to comprehend the transition of what he calls the Age of Chiefs to the Age of Kings, with Shyaam as the linchpin. We cannot know why during the Age of Kings the Kuba no longer addressed the diviner and healer as *kaang* (from the proto-Bantu *gang*, cf. previous chapter). Nor do we have historical data to explain why since that period the Kuba contracted the meaning of *ilweemy* (cf. *ilumbi*, official diviner in Lele) to merely refer to war magicians at the court, and why they instead spoke of all diviners as *ngwoom*, a term supposedly adopted from the Kwilu area (CW 201). We do have a cultural structure to guide our search though. It directs our suspicions to the autocratic wish of kings and the obstacle that diviners pose. The diviners with power at the court were the crown council: *ngwoom incyaam*, which Vansina translates as 'the medicine men of the basket'. Notice that above he translated the same term as 'diviner'. The crown council hence consisted of 'diviners of the basket'.

Having regularly witnessed groups of adults peering together at the entrails of a chicken before taking final decisions, I have seen oracles blend in with daily affairs, rational schemes and pragmatic issues. The council foretold the court by wisdom and, I assume, by reading signs in the charmed objects hopping in their baskets. 'Basket divination' is a common practice in southern Bantu groups (see Turner 1975). Representing the autochthonous *mbaangt* clans, the council could admonish the king, but their influence dwindled during the seventeenth century in the Age of Kings (CW 146). What could have been a strategy to marginalize them? The king might have colluded with an unattached medicinal man, the war magician, to raise the latter's stake in court, while discrediting or forbidding the commoner oracles of *bukaang*, and instead permitting *ngwoom* divination outside the council so as to let the practice inflate and break the council's monopoly. It might even be that the council members, caught in a competition with spirit mediums of the villages, did the forbidding and so eventually undermined themselves. These are the endogenous processes a historical anthropology could further unravel.

Divination, like magic and mediumship, lies at the heart of medicinal rule. It is a practice of uncertain communication with the spirit world, reproducing a cosmology of contingency. Vansina does not see divination bearing a relation with the social changes on a larger scale (CW 237). Religion is supposed to be ideology, thus he overstates the distinction between witchcraft, for which the poison ordeal was meant, and sorcery, for which the healer provided amulets of countersorcery (CW 202). In practice, oracles have the intrinsic spirit-led freedom to identify witches as well as sorcerers. The autonomy of the spirit's message on good and evil, innocence and guilt, danger and well-being, which truly mediumistic oracles would bring out, meant a medicinal rule that unitary states headed by kings were unable to cope with unless they destroyed it. This is why Shyaam wanted to be 'a diviner who won the kingdom by clever use of magic', without depending on a nature spirit, Kop aNgaan, to designate him as ruler of the area (CW 207). It is that kernel of contingency that bugged him.

Like in Rwanda, we will see, the power shift away from the oracular did not mean less ritual or less magic in the royal court or at home. The private charm, *nnyeeng*, was a common sight in Kuba in 1892. In Lele the word means both medicine and rite (CW 202, n22; Douglas 1963: 205). As among the Mongo, Yaka (Devisch 1993) and Sakata (Bekaert 1998), each Kuba village had a collective charm consisting of a small ritual forest, *nkiin*. It was dedicated to the supreme being Ncyeem, who was mentioned during communal rites.

Vansina intuits the ideological transformation. But the modern division between politics and religion lingers. He knows that chieftainship as well as kingship are 'tied' to charms (CW 206), yet because only 'scraps' of religious data exist, he sighs 'I am convinced that a much fuller history of change in religion may never be written' (CW 198). Our reinterpretations of his data hopefully contradict the statement. The pessimism might hold, though, for research into Kuba household medicine, in which a social history transcending court tribulations should be grounded. A series of entities such as *bokali* spirits and *nkady* charms, from surrounding Mongo and Lele groups, crop up in the monograph that suggest much cultural exchange of medicines at the village level as anywhere else in equatorial Africa. Kuba must have shared an etiology of illnesses and their treatments. The lack of sources on popular history cannot be remedied. But the author's choice to segregate the religious from the political can. It is a matter of cultural structure, which is better made explicit from the onset.

Shyaam's return from the forest to found kingship epitomizes the regional commonality. Institutions and idioms correspond, sometimes even the very words for charm, witchcraft, poison ordeal and spirit possession. Both historians and anthropologists should ask themselves if a holistic analysis of society does not depart from there, the overarching structure, to draw the contours of the cultural whole accordingly, instead of limiting their scope to one group or location and then being surprised when unintentionally coming across similarities a thousand miles away. It seems pointless to speak of the 'invention' of a practice with a certain name in one group and date the invention, for example spirit possession announcing 'priestly' vocation in Kuba (CW 200), if it is ubiquitous enough in the neighbouring groups to infer that their common ancestors had practised it too.

Court History

No Africanist will want to be accused of reducing a people's past to court histories. Yet, can the reduction be prevented for societies whose oral historians were paid by the court? Oral tradition is about the only source to rely on. But would the court, forming a cult of its own kind wherein descent plays a role, promote the history of cults of a rivalling kind such as the conventional medicinal associations and famous healer-diviners working in the chiefdom? Court lore will not shed much light on the community's history of medicinal, divinatory and cultic activities. For all the king cares, any medicinal cult popping up is a first.

Court history means perceiving the court as the essence and centre from which a people's activities emanate. Vansina's downplaying of Shyaam's initiation sets the tone of an analysis wherein medicine does not determine the kind of supremacy the royal court musters. African kings and their courts should basically be no different from European ones. Thinking through medicine might conjure up discussions of superstition, possibly feeding into stereotypes on Africa by non-Africanist historians. For many scholars, the slightest hint at magic in relation to Africa is exoticizing. The risk preoccupied postcolonial Africanists and probably Vansina too, despite the many classic themes that bring chieftaincy and medicine together, such as the ritual purifying twins and their hold on a chiefdom's fertility. This book has chosen to avert the risk by redefining magic within the wider frame of medicine and rule.

One implication of medicinal rule – a rule not by an individual but a thing – is that kings and chiefs figure in history in so far as they are medicinal heroes. At the fireplace outside (*ha shikome*) where Sukuma elders talk, I obtained much oral tradition on cult leaders, but little or nothing on Sukuma chiefs. Sukuma legends and songs primarily deal with magical traditions, the origin and successes of medicinal cults specializing in healing, lucky charms, snakebites, dance competitions, and so on (see Gunderson 2010). I had to visit the courts themselves to obtain any royal history. The dominance of court history in Vansina's monographs befits the ceremonial state. Igokelo palace was not so welcoming to young fieldworkers like me living with unchristian healers, who symbolized the medicinal rule the chiefs were traditionally expected to excel in, but since colonization mostly had refrained from. The chief's direct family felt closer to educated administrators. I cannot exclude that Vansina as a compatriot of the colonial administrators had privileged access to royal circles and inevitably wallowed in the richness of their lore before he could find time to learn about the average compound's narratives in the Kuba of his day. The courtly bias may be due to his high-ranked informants and their familiarity with the aristocratic oral tradition. One furtive remark of Vansina is unintentionally telling (CW 80). His ethnographic data on terminologies made linguists shift the classification of Kuba languages (Bushoong) from Guthrie's zone C to zone B, which lies in the west (a region inhabited by the Mbuun and more to the west by the Kongo, whose centuries-old exchange with Kuba shows in the similar ornamentation patterns of raffia textiles; CW 84). The historian beating the linguists at their game – quite a feat? Later the linguists reverted. They had ascertained on a closer look that Vansina's corpus contained too much vocabulary from the court. Its vocabulary was dominated by the western dialects from where the founder of the last dynasty had migrated.

Lived Meanings in the Kongo Cult of Kingship

According to popular lore, the three kingdoms of Kongo, Loango and Tio are 'all children of Nguunu'. Vansina (1966: 109) conceded that Kongo and Loango may have grown from the same origin as the Tio kingdom. Who then is that founder? Nguunu is a female diviner-healer, we learn in a footnote (ibid.: 109, n9). The gender is no trivial thing in our discussion. Her femininity countermands the centrality of the big man in founding the cult that gives way to kingship. It highlights the political importance of the queen mother in ceremonial states. Her background furthermore supports the thesis on the divinatory and medicinal origins of rule in equatorial Africa. Of the three kingdoms mentioned by Vansina as potentially forming one model, that of Kongo is the most researched, because of its contact with European missionaries since the 1500s. Kongo underwent more globalization, and sooner, in comparison with the less-changed kingdom of Loango and the smallest kingdom of Tio, which featured in previous chapters.

MacGaffey's (1986) *Religion and Society in Central Africa* summarizes the cultural traits of Kongo society in the complementary positions of priest and king. He does not consider divinatory practices, probably because the ceremonial state is his angle. There divination is regulated by 'priests'. The initiatory dimension of power, mentioned in his introduction, does not inform his analysis either. A spiritual hierarchy is schematized in terms of the oppositions benevolent and destructive, private and public (ibid.: 7, 75). The priests and chiefs are public figures, respectively benevolent and destructive, the former addressing the ancestors to serve the lineages, the latter placating the local spirits on behalf of the communities. Their counterparts in the foursome are the figures of witch and 'magician' (by which he means healer), respectively killing through ghosts and healing through charms, both operating away from the public eye in the private world. MacGaffey has the lucidity of qualifying his scheme as normative, but should not actual practice be the determinant for the anthropologist structuring culture? In practice, charms are employed by all figures. Chiefs are not just destructive, but ambiguous and a-moral. The witch does not fit in the comparison, for he or she has no commission or office. The witch exists as an imaginary figure and can be anybody using whatever means, not just ghosts, to corrupt the victim's defences. Oracles can be private or public. In practice, the oracle has the last word, hesitating in a seance between laying the blame on a witch or – leaping to the other side of MacGaffey's scheme – on an ancestor. It is the client's frame of experience and the diviner's moment of mediumship that in practice determine the classification. More even than Victor Turner's watershed division between rite of passage and healing, MacGaffey's scheme is a construct requiring no ethnographic fieldwork.

In fact, the scheme contradicts the lack of orthodoxy in Kongo religious beliefs admitted by MacGaffey (1986: 8; citing Vansina's remark on the Tio). Ambivalence, mixing benevolence and destruction, characterizes both chief and healer. The Christian undertone of the Manichaeist scheme prompts one to harbour reservations about the evidence cited by MacGaffey and documented in the cahiers written by the Congolese collaborators of Laman, a Swedish missionary.[8] Are these lived meanings, that is interconnecting social institutions, ritual symbolism, everyday activities and people's livelihood?

Basing himself on the limited historical archives of Van Wing, MacGaffey proposes a classification of three cults of the ancestors in precolonial Kongo: the clan head placating the ancestors at grave or altar, secondly the *mfumu mpu* (in the same paragraph ironically translated as both chief and priest) placating a matrilineal ancestor with a basket of ancestral relics (*lukobi lwa bakulu*) after the oracle of a *nganga ngombo,* and thirdly the rituals initiating the smiths so that they could consecrate chiefs (ibid.: 65). MacGaffey remarks that the smiths normally address nature spirits (*bisimbi*) and not ancestral spirits (*bakulu*). He notices himself that the cults address the ancestors as well as chiefs and clan heads without differentiating the categories. Is this not enough reason to seek the endogenous logic of lived, practised meanings? An ethnographically based comparison embedded in the wider region could go beyond normative scheme and discourse.

Private versus public may be a preoccupation of the court, but is rather secondary, I should stress, in rural communities with collective orientations on clan or group and without individualist responsibilities. The difference between healer (*nganga*) and priest (*kitomi*) should be a matter of degree, whereby the so-called priest does a healer's job of ritual in public with a large non-kin group participating. Indicative is that Dapper in the 1600s did not mention the priest. The ceremonial consecration of chiefs was done by smiths (ibid.: 65), the priest possibly being the consecrated later version of a smith (ibid.: 196). Research on what kind of healer a smith originally was would be handy. In general, the thesis of medicinal rule has been nuancing the opposition between healer and chief, relating them as original model and classificatory extension respectively, whereby the sharpness of distinction may characterize the level of political centralization.

Citing John Thornton's (1983) work on the Kongo kingdom to underline the concurrence in scholarship, MacGaffey specifies the structure of Kongo religion, allegedly unchanged since the sixteenth century:

> 'The complementarity of chief and priest in public functions; the contrast between public and private functions, specifically, between *kitomi* and *nganga*; the opinion that those who resorted to magic were greedy for personal gain; and the likelihood that a magician would be suspected of witchcraft'. (MacGaffey 1986: 196–97)

Opinions of respondents, often couched in socially desirable terms, cannot overrule the fieldworker's observation of practices, nor the underlying cultural structure he or she derives from those observations. The popular Christian opinion on the greed of the user of magic conflicts with the general attraction and sometimes high status of potions for protection, love and business, and with the diviner's daily dealings with clients' greed and jealousy. Many respondents will confide that a strong healer has lethal magic, but that will not prevent them from consulting him or her. The occult and evil ways imputed to the diviner-healer recede in the background when clients suspect someone of witchcraft, often a neighbour or close kin member, and want to consult an oracle.

Nevertheless, MacGaffey's study of Kongo religion offered the necessary counterpoint to the political focus of Vansina. The previous chapters have inferred an evolution from initiation to chiefship in the rural areas, and towards kingship in the commercial hub, where the *nganga* (healer) branches off as a profession with limited public function. The kernel of our diachronic account can be found in MacGaffey's synchronic opposition between commission and office (or hereditary title), more exactly in this geographical contrast: 'The great tutelary spirits, *min'kisi mya nsi*, are not known in the east because this is an area characterized by very small political sovereignties, in which chiefship was a collective affliction cult and a commission rather than a perpetual office' (ibid.: 139). Applying a diachronic logic to his opposition, a shift could have taken place from the commission acquired through the initiatory fee towards the hereditary office of the proto-king, a clan-based entitlement. In sum, kingship could have arisen out of the collapse of the original cultic model of rule. At an early stage, 'chief' was a title and charm obtained through healing ritual, commissioning him to perform certain duties within the cult.

The commercial hubs occasioned an inflation of charms and ranks, culminating in the hierarchy of the Kongo royal palace (ibid.: 35). The gifts with which wealthy Kongo men could buy titles had replaced the sacrifice of an individual submitting him- or herself to spirit possession (cf. ibid.: 35, 139). This social transformation should not be mistaken for a linear cultural evolution. As far as we can tell, the first kings such as Shyaam initially *reverted* to the model of diviner-healer to end the accumulation of titles, and then centralized these titles into a hierarchy with a hereditary office at the top. The Rwandese ceremonial state in the next chapter illustrates the evolution of kingship after an anti-divinatory phase. Before that, I wish to reflect on a few seminal studies approaching kingship as a worldwide historical institution. How does medicinal rule relate to these? And can our hypothesis remedy the European obsession with divine kingship in Africa?

The Body Politic: Medicinal versus Sacral

'The king is dead. Long live the king.' The medieval formula proclaimed in a European country by a peer of the king instantiates the transfer of sovereignty as the heir ascends the throne. The transfer was immediate to prevent war over succession. A throne occupied meant peace in the realm. In most of equatorial Africa, rules were observed by ruler and ruled to ensure uninterrupted continuity of the land's fertility. One of these was the prohibition on words, with their magical capacity, that declare the king dead. The set formula in Sukuma chiefdoms declared the drum to be broken. Two similar practices of eternalizing kingship in Europe and Africa appear to have different intentions at origin.

In Europe, what had to be transferred was the right to rule, which was seen as divine. According to Ernst Kantorowicz in his classic *The King's Two Bodies* (1957), the medieval citizens developed a political theology that sought to imagine how the king as a mortal person with a body natural could perish without affecting the realm. They invented a spiritual counterpart, namely the king stood for the body politic, the organized group of citizens. At stake in European cities as well as in the feudal system was the organizing of unity. In the chiefdoms of central and east Africa, and also in the kingdoms it seems, no separation was made between natural and spiritual body. In kingship, fertility was transferred, conferred on the body of the king, whose double was a tangible object of medicine, a charm or a drum, that guaranteed the flow of life. Luc de Heusch (1972) went a step further in that direction by squarely equating the king with the medicine.

To obtain a similar perpetuity for the king embodying the community, we may argue, the West had split natural and spiritual ('supernatural') worlds. The dual mode established the political and the religious as distinct realms. The split, on which the very idea of 'religion' hinges, has not ceased to bedevil Western scholarship on Africa. The haunting image is that of a realm created for arational, affect-based and transgressive acts of sacrifice, which may serve the purposes of the worldly realm. The spectre is a separate mode of production eluding the commoner.

The duality, replicated in that of church and state, had many precursors, possibly dating back to the druids making and unmaking the king, and performing human sacrifice, as recounted by Julius Caesar in 'the Gallic wars': 'because they think that unless the life of a man be offered for the life of a man, the mind of the immortal gods cannot be rendered propitious, and they have sacrifices of that kind ordained for national purposes'.[9] The uninterrupted flow of killings to regenerate life reminds of the mass sacrifices in Inca society, and those in the ceremonial states of Kuba and Buganda. The model of medicinal rule, exemplified by the chief's charm permanently containing the desired fertility, seems like a sustainable alternative. Every medicine of the initiatory associations celebrates the hunter's bond with the forest. The druidic cosmology of the agricultural cycle contrasts with the hunter cosmology of discontinuous sacrifice in return for a good catch. In a theory of reversible evolutions, the original model can determine the meaning of an institution long after that model has become historically obsolete.

Hocart (1970: 165, 192) illustrated the dual political organization of staff (priest) and sword (king) in India, of terrestrial (hereditary) king and his subordinate celestial (elective and law-making) king among the Yoruba in Nigeria, of King of Kings and Great (law-making) King in Nepal, and of left-hand chief (war maker) and right-hand chief (peacemaker) in Papua New Guinea. Dumézil had, in an ambitious attempt at cross-cultural history, acknowledged the two roles of this-worldly (sacerdotal) law making and other-worldly (sovereign) power within the Indo-European political function under the Roman god Jupiter. Wolfram (1997:15) cites the work of Tacitus from AD 98 on the German polity to distinguish two types of kingship, those of ruler (*rex*) and commander (*dux*), the first chosen for nobility, the second for audacity. Asymptotic cases for both would be the prevailing types of state leadership in Europe, respectively the monarch who has a largely ceremonial title and the president who is elected after public debate. In the background lurks the dichotomy of secular and sacral. The Middle East has seen an alternation between two similar types, the theocratic ruler exemplified by the ayatollah, and the nationalist leader heading the army. Across the Polynesian islands of the Pacific we recognize the tension between the statuses of *toa* (warriors) and *ariki* (chiefs). The politico-anthropological literature contrasts Melanesia's big-man societies with Polynesia's chiefdoms. Hawaii is a special case, it having transformed the chiefdom into a system of possibly indeed 'divine' kingship wherein the ruler's exchange with the gods is direct, including the give and take of human sacrifice.

Another intriguing parallel is that of the cultural concept of god reflecting the local social structure. As the latter centralizes so does the pantheon (Hocart 1970: 167). The wellspring of all human action being life, Hocart reasons, the cult of saving and giving life precedes the institution of kingship. Our ethnographic museums delving into human origins are replete with fertility charms. Ethnographies describe ritual after ritual because that practice is the primary technique of lifesaving (ibid.: 33). Communities can fulfil all social functions without requiring central government, but once rituals involve more people, concentrated around a centre, their organization develops into a government (ibid.: 30, 38).

The parallels leave the reader somewhat perplexed, and without tools or ways to improve the research. The trouble with the 'structural history' by Hocart and colleagues is that it eclipses specific antecedents and cultural histories that would normally refract the meaning of fertility. This kind of comparative approach does not provide any cultural ground for the established parallels. A regional comparison with a historically based cultural rationale does, as we have attempted to show.[10] Therefore we searched in our central and east African cases for the reasons of commonality. We proposed a model or logic that links royal initiation, hereditary charms, ritual experts, and the forest.

After Frazer

Divine kingship has been a contentious issue for good reason. If we follow Gordon's (2016) historical critique, divine kingship used to be an anthropological stereotype about Africa that needed to be remedied with information on the pragmatics of local government. The controversy concentrated on the now century-old thesis of Frazer, succinctly recapitulated by Graeber (2011: 3) that 'all religion was to some degree derived from fertility cults centered on the figure of a dying god, and that the first kings, who embodied that god, were ritually sacrificed'. In a more prosaic moment, Frazer contended that the king incarnated the apogee of a magician terrifying his community. In contrast, Luc de Heusch (1972, 1987: 22) explored the more loosely defined stance of 'sacred' (instead of divine) kingship: in order to control nature and in particular the rains, a king must transcend the order of the lineage, namely commit incest and become like a living fetish, destroyed if ineffective, which would explain (the historically rare) regicide.

My response throughout this book has been to drop the sacred and think the medicine. Both divine and sacred kingship play on the European trope of secular versus profane figures. Both theses do engage with cross-cultural data on early kingship, so cannot be discarded without empirical footing. Because of our ethnographic focus on ritual medicine, we relocated the data on which the theses are based, in a society without administration and without worship. The dying god enacted by the king is a mythological translation of a known practice, the healer's spirit possession. In the Chwezi spirit cult, an act of ritual incest completes the initiation and announces the onset of healing and subsequently the power to heal others (Stroeken 2006). The qualification of 'divine' or 'sacred' kingship ignores the experience and meaning of spirit, on which royal power draws. An incumbent who does not experience it must be good at feigning it, during his entire public life. That is what I imagine to detect in the unsure look of some kings surrounded by courtiers on pictures in the colonial collections of the African Museum in Tervuren. The reader must keep in mind a society where the link or reciprocity with spirit, which struck the commentators of kingship as transcendental, is but a token of the initiatory sacrifice that awaits every adult in the medicinal cult, and at which some adults are more adept irrespective of pedigree. In precolonial sub-Saharan Africa, god was an impersonal being, often a creator at the beginning of time yet in the everyday barely a force. God did not arouse feelings like ancestral or nature spirits do. A 'divine' king then means little more than someone granted a privilege in mythological times, which is not what anthropologists like Frazer hoped to prove. The king brings actual powers into play, which refers us back to the role of medicine and spirit. Frazer desperately sought to generalize the Biblical and Christian theme of messianic sacrifice. A personal sacrifice makes no sense in rural equatorial Africa unless as a symbolic part of the ordeal during the liminal phase of initiatory ritual. The near equivalence of kingship and life-giving appeared in every succession to the throne and instalment of the shrine, such as the ancient Sukuma custom of replacing the embalmed head of the previous king.

Historians Vansina, Mauny and Thomas (1964: 86) denounced 'the obsession of divine kingship' in Frazer and Murdock. They did not acknowledge its European bias or basis. The majority of African states would be founded on the belief in the divine origin of kings, which presumed a quite familiar, almost Christian concept of belief in supernatural power. Only some state systems had secular authorities without divine kingship. The Shilluk in their view were the odd one out, having divine kingship without a state system. Finally, the authors went on, there are kings that rule by divine right, having a power delegated by the creator (ibid.: 87). Economy further specified the type of polity, with trade creating the 'secular' groups that led to political centralization.

The sacred stood for primitive origin preceding the separation of church and state. Yet, from the perspective of medicine, of things believed to give power, the distinction between sacred and secular makes no sense. The most obvious barrier for Western scholarship is to imagine god in a society without worship, without personal relation with the creator, and without churches or priests, hence with much medicine but no religion in the strict sense. The spirit is an entirely different figure from the (demi-)god. The spirit is capricious, corruptible and liable to strike a deal with, but is most of all personally related through kinship, clan or spatial proximity. Divinatory rule more adequately than divine rule expresses the contingency of such a basis for power.

The outcome of medicine, like sacrifice, is a fate. The king controlling the main charm and shrine of the realm safeguards fertility, but it cannot be expected to do miracles. Stories of his control over weather phenomena are hyperboles and not essential, against what divine nature would suggest. He himself depends on unison with the royal spirits.

The Euro-Christian theme of kingship by divine right, spawned from the pious insight that only God ought to be the divine king, hence that the king rules by *dei gratia* as in the days of Charlemagne, misses the point of medicinal purchase and magical communication expected from the chief. The next chapter makes a last call to African studies to rethink kingship in terms appropriate to the continent's unique history.

Notes

1. The compound verb *kukongoja*, 'to bear', is a possibly later term than *kulagula*, 'to possess' ('to treat' though in KiSukuma), which would suggest it was adapted to the new kingship.
2. New Sukuma cults habitually adopt another cult's paramount title as a lower rank, for example the common highest rank of *ntemi* ('the cutter', chief) of chiefdoms winds up ranking under *kingi* (from the English) in Chwezi. For the highest title they invent their own name, like the Chwezi *malamala* ('the completer'). The logic is their rivalry with other cults, to overshadow them, and the relentless competition over new customers. In Buganda the Rwandan paramount, *mwami*, is subjugated nominally by becoming a rank under the *kabaka*. Is chief- or kingship basically a cult, like Kishina implied, and thus manipulating to attract customers?
3. A separate cross-cultural study into the transgressive moment during enthronement rituals could reveal strong patterns. One should start in Buganda with the Butaka place of ritual where the *kukuza* is a stepping over the ritual sister, which signifies as much as sexual intercourse, like in the Chwezi cult's ritual incest (ibid.: 87).
4. Bride-service is a common practice among the patrilineal Sukuma. So is the gift of one head of cattle by the mother's brother as part of the bridewealth paid by the groom's father. Vansina considers these practices among the Kuba as traces of matrilineal descent. I join my Sukuma informants defending these as strategies to balance the exacting patrilineal costs of marriage.
5. The *nsumba ntale*, 'big adolescent', fulfils an important role in the village. He is the direct contact the people have with the village council, in which the heads of each extended family gather. Much of the day-to-day decision making is in his hands. Almost every evening after sunset he

walks on the narrow paths between compounds to whistle his horn and shout the message of the day, which may be an invitation for a gathering, a communal cultivation on an elder's field or a public work such as digging a well. The *nsumba ntale* looks after security in the village. He convokes his peers for search parties, and has become a key figure in the Sungusungu vigilante structure since the 1980s. It is unfortunate that Vansina gives no details on the initiatory background of the Kuba power broker. Traditionally, among Sukuma the *nsumba ntale* had to be initiated. He was in fact a member of the *busumba* age-grade group, who after going through the basic initiation like his peers, climbed to the highest rank via gifts of beer bouts.

6. They sang songs to a small drum at new moon, which was an innovation by Shyaam (CW 146), suggestive of cultic developments.
7. The relation of twins to kings in the entire region would deserve a separate chapter. Sukuma cosmology denotes twins as *nsebu*, 'hot' and endangering fertility, possibly scorching the land, causing drought, if not ritually purified. Part II made piecemeal mention of the link with kings, in that the courts adopt twins from commoner parents, and twins symbolize the king. The first Kuba who was a *cikl*, a substitute Kuba king during interregna, was the twin brother of the first chief; he followed a Luba custom (ibid.: 120).
8. The collaborators' contact with modernity was gauged not only through Christian orthodoxy but also in terms of the 'grand dichotomy' between private and public (see Weintraub and Kumar 1997), where certain folk practices have to be kept from the scrutiny of the public eye, where individual progress is emphasized, and where the state's bureaucratic system impinging on life has to be curbed.
9. Chapter 16 in http://classics.mit.edu/Caesar/gallic.mb.txt.
10. Another possibility is the sociostructural explanation we have been obliquely integrating in our accounts of historical change. For example, Feeley-Harnik (1985: 279) cites Meyer Fortes criticizing Hocart's surmise that a common historical origin should account for the similarity of installation rites in different regions. Fortes reckons sociostructural constraints.

Chapter 9

FROM DIVINATORY TO CEREMONIAL STATE
NARRATIVE PROOF FROM RWANDA

The region of the Great Lakes in Africa, also known as Interlacustrine Africa, stretches from the western shores of lakes Tanganyika, Kivu, Edward, George and Albert in central Africa, to the eastern shores of Lake Victoria and Lake Kyoga, totalling a surface of almost one million square kilometres. The hills in the west roll into dramatic mountainous scenery in the north around the Virunga and Ruwenzori range, which together with the lakes form natural borders for Burundi, Rwanda, Uganda and Tanzania. The fertile, densely populated hills of Burundi and Rwanda descend into the semi-arid plateau of cultivated steppe in south-west Uganda and north-west Tanzania. The Great Lakes exhibit wide climatic diversity between those two ecological zones, the mountainous and the lacustrine, but on the whole the zones each developed a proper livelihood that facilitated demographic growth and political centralization. Each combined mobility and a major source of energy: along the lake, the canoe and banana ensured spare time. On the hills, cattle were the source of wealth, prestige, and in fact manure to fertilize the farmer's fields (Chrétien 2003: 350). A reciprocal agro-pastoral system emerged whereby the donors of cattle were associated with an ethnic group: the Tutsi in Rwanda and Burundi, the Hima in western Uganda. The white colonizers interpreted the ethnic relations in terms of political rule and cultural superiority, and institutionalized the latter as a right of governance.

East of the communities of Tutsi and their Hutu partners, and south of the communities of Hima and their Iru partners, begins the plateau inhabited by agro-pastoral Nyamwezi and Sukuma, who live at the edge of the Great Lakes region, bordering it like Zande in the north-west. Except for a brief spell of conquest rule by King Mirambo, the Nyamwezi-Sukuma exemplified medicinal rule. They did not have centralized government, nor did they install ethnic cleavage.

At the time of first colonial contacts, in the second half of the nineteenth century, the societies of the Great Lakes displayed about the same political system. In the hilly zone the monarchies of Rwanda and Burundi dominated, ruled respectively by the Nyiginya dynasty and the Ganwa dynasty. They were surrounded, from Lake Kivu in the north to Lake Tanganyika in the south, by the tiny kingdoms of Buhavu, Bushi, Bufuriru, Bushubi, Buyungu, Muhambwe, Ruguru, Bujiji, Bushingo and Heru. *Mwami* was the title of their kings. In the plateau west and north of Lake Victoria the *Kabaka* of Buganda ruled supreme. North-west of him lay the kingdom of Bunyoro governed by the Bito clan, as well as Toro, Buhweju, Igara and Busoga in the northeast. They named their king *Mukama* as did the dynasty of Karagwe in the south and its neighbours along the south-western shores of Lake Victoria: Kiziba (also ruled by the Bito clan), Bugabo, Kyamutwara (ruled by the Nkango clan), Kyanja, Ihangiro and Bukerebe. Finally, Nkore between Rwanda and Buganda name the king *Mugabe*, as do the polities of Buzinza, Kimwani and Rusubi south of Lake Victoria. The Hinda dynasty delivered the kings for Nkore (a Mugabe), Karagwe (a Mukama), Buzinza, Ihangiro, Kyanja and Kimutwara (ibid.: 483, 474). All these communities speak Bantu languages of Guthrie's zone J. They call the healer *mpfumu* (from *kum*), which elsewhere means chief or king. In that respect Sukuma traditions fit in the zone of the Great Lakes.

The names of the clans refer to an ancestral figure honoured to this day for clearing bush and founding a residential group. We may assume that this person was a cultivator and that he was worthy of being commemorated for bringing novelty, such as introducing the sedentary agricultural lifestyle to the bands of hunters, which entailed expansion of descendants and dependents. Or he had given proof of medicinal knowledge that justified cultic membership, yielding group formation and expansion; or both. The originator of a dynastic clan, such as R/LuHinda, was deemed a master of fertility for possessing the medicine for good harvests and health. The shift from hunting to farming meant investing the land, the rains and the annual seasonal cycles with the animism of the forest to which they had been used as hunters. Domesticated fertility grounded medicinal rule. Healing and kingship could become independent developments as the originator's power became hereditary – a mediumistic call anybody may claim to have. A charm containing the power of a nature spirit located deep in the forest or a shrine dedicated to an influential ancestor could be transmitted from generation to generation. The materiality of the charm permitted the commencement of kinship-based inheritance of a title.

Our hypothesis of domestic fertility as the endogenous logic of political evolutions in forest-fringe cultures offers an alternative to the classic duality, of which Jean-Pierre Chrétien (2003: 135) noted the contradictions in his study *The Great Lakes of Africa: 2000 Years of History* (henceforth referred to as GL). Scholarly interpretations of the relation between initiation systems and dynastic clans 'vary between two extreme positions: religion as instrumentalization by the powers that be, or religion as the ultimate site of contestation, reflecting the oppressed's aspirations and the former elites' nostalgia' (GL 134). Vansina's work, we have seen, often exemplified the first position; Vidal and Berger, we will see, the second. Chrétien's solution is to emphasize the continuum and variability between positions over time. In Rwanda and Burundi, the cults of Ryangombe and Kiranga respectively and their initiatory practices of *kubandwa* are controlled by the monarchies, which for about two centuries have ordained the cult's initiators like priests of a church. Known as Chwezi elsewhere, the cult has also inspired revolt against the state, as in the Nyabingi movement a century ago at the border with Uganda (Feierman 1995). Kingship competes with the religious cult, Chrétien argues, because both revolve around a mediumistic actor, albeit the first with a terrestrial vocation, the second with a celestial one (GL 136). Agreeing with David Newbury, Chrétien sees in the mysticism of the cult the abstracted essence of kingship. He also remarks that the Nkore have the same term for royal grave and Chwezi shrine; that in Burundi the sound of kings, drums and Chwezi initiates are likened; that in Buha the Mwami has a Chwezi name – for him ever so many indications of the convenient assimilation of royal and priestly authority in history (GL 134). Earlier on, he had discovered that the Haya term *kutendekwa* means both to enthrone and to initiate.

For us, the terminological associations point to a common origin of cult and kingship, not their assimilation. The equation of enthronement and initiation belongs to a time preceding the reification of medicinal rule into kingship. A king assimilating the cult is to anachronistically presume a previous split of politics and religion. Kingship is a cult in its own right. The fractal of domesticated fertility lives on in everyday medicine, thus it can be revived where the other cults are forbidden. In the communication attempted by magic (via symbolic 'entrances') an actor relives the cultural structure of spirit and contingency. From this experience he or she can muster the courage to harness mediumship, like in Nyabingi, to oppose the court. The solidarity the cults offer beyond the lineages is a well-known Africanist trope (GL 136), but the complementarity should not be a functionalist structure in history denying the agency of mediums. The latter continue the traditions, which chiefs and kings gave up on because of the colonial and postcolonial imposition of a governance model of rule.

The history of Rwanda and Burundi is one of particularly effective modernization and Christianization, which by the 1990s resulted, among others, in less than 0.1 per cent of Rwandan respondents reporting the use of traditional healing.[1] Moreover, the colonial secularizing of worldly power happened to coincide with an ongoing internal process (analysed further on), accelerating and intensifying the royal attack on spirit reciprocity and on the sacrificial logic of domesticated fertility. The annual *muganuro* festival organized by the king of Burundi has, since the 1920s, been purified of its pagan elements, and Christianized; the original cult objects were forbidden, and the sacred woods of the royal shrine became the favoured spot for building a mission (GL 270). Similarly, the functions of the Rwandese king's diviner and the *mwiru* master of the *muganuro* ritual were abolished (GL 274). The missionaries convinced the baptized king Rudahihgwa to bury the Imandwa cult (GL 275). Simultaneously, cultural practices that benefited the colonial administration's obsession with stability and control were restored and to be sanctioned in native courts (GL 272). Institutionalization caused feudalization. The *buhake* contract of cattle-lease inflated, for it was tolerated as part of the vassalage (*bugaragu*) that the colonizer considered the foundation and 'main cement of native society'. Religion and culture were taken together and seen as separate from and, most of all, peripheral to *primum vivere*, the market and the economy where cultural traditions were obstacles. Inklings shine through of an African 'modernity' in part emerging endogenously rather than just awaiting the advent of colonialism.

However, the rituals and initiatory cults regenerating the fabric of fertility in society were pragmatic in their medicinal orientation, rather than religious or worship-oriented. Colonial administrators and their researchers such as the aforementioned Edouard De Jonghe reported on initiatory societies as movements of revolt. From religion would spring the riposte against political hegemony, as echoed by Chrétien: 'In Rwanda, as in Burundi, these reforms and the general hardening of social relations aroused prophetic-style revolts between 1927 and 1930 against Tutsi chiefs deemed responsible for these new constraints' (GL 272). Why, we should ask, were they directed against the chiefs instead of the colonizer? These initiatory associations looking after the community's protection and well-being had long permeated the Bantu-speaking world. The chiefs had always been in their playing field, the medicinal one, same for all. May I go so far as to submit that their radical reaction was against the changed tenor of rule? The court had adopted the profound political impact of the colonizer to affect everyday life in new ways. The first half of the twentieth century saw protests across equatorial Africa against the attack on medicine that was being waged by the elites and the church. The cultural war revived the attempt by monarchs to distance themselves from the cultic domain their dynasty had sprung from.

Converted aristocrats were instrumental in the prohibition of rituals and charms. In Bukoba the Mukama's son burned the main shrine of the Chwezi cult in the name of Christianity (GL 264). Modern aspirations erupted in certain layers of the population, which took the colonial administration by surprise and frightened them, conjuring the spectre of 'Bolshevist' nationalism (GL 266, 353). For the administrator, a safe bet seemed to be the neo-traditional option of sustaining ethnic clichés and creating tribes, mostly confederating them, each preferably identified with a king, a recognizable office acting as spokesperson. Some salaried anthropologists at the time were naive enough to treat the ensuing artefact as preserved culture, and convinced others of this, including historians at first, who on the rebound were disappointed, and logically by independence in the 1960s lost interest in the concept of culture and in the possibility of a cultural structure they might have to reckon with. The social engineering of the administration consisted in selective interventions that wiped out grassroots authorities. In Buha the king's princes (*batware*) were given the final say at the expense of the *batiks*, the autochthonous custodians of the land and territorial shrine (GL 265). In Burundi, the initiatory society of *abashingantahe*, elders climbing grades in function of their organization of beer ceremonies (cf. *bunamhala* among Sukuma), ensured frequent gathering and facilitated alliance between the kraals scattered along the villageless hills. As a council for the *mwami*'s chiefs we may assume that they counterweighed centralized power, yet with diminished purchase since colonization. Also, the term for chiefs, *batware*, lost salience in favour of *baganwa*, princes, after the colonizer systematically appointed the princes to chieftaincy. The colonizer inadvertently reinforced a long-term process of state formation. A key period locally had been around 1800 with the conquests of King Ntare II Rugamba doubling the state's territory and naming as territorial chiefs his sons, the *baganwa* (GL 268, 177). Kings appealed to individual loyalties (GL 169), which points to a cultic rather than administrative structure. Exclusive reliance on blood ties does suggest dwindling cultic alliance.

In the colonies, royal rituals were reinvented in the image of Catholic liturgy. The colony and the postcolony, the administrator and researcher, have been surprisingly alike in assuming that interventions in culture are peripheral, sparing the fabric of society. Was cultural disintegration not a factor in the genocide in Rwanda and Burundi? The colonial intervention coincided with the accelerated decline of medicinal rule, the banning of shrines and charms, the removal of magical elements from annual ceremonies, the undermining of local councils and chiefs, and the support of courts and their history of a king divine.

Summed up, the colonial pitfalls are functionalism (a cultural slot would exist in society, once filled up by pagan superstitions, but now by modern religion), materialism (economy and politics are at the centre of society and come before culture and religion, which only in extreme cases such as inequality inciting revolt can influence the former two big operators), idealism (cult objects and sacred woods are substitutable by Christian items because the material and medicinal dimensions are secondary to the actual internalized beliefs), institutionalism (not experiential frames or dynamic cultural systems/ fractals but institutions such as native courts and customs are the 'foundation' of society; restoring them is safeguarding culture), and universalism (in the end, all humans will want the same: modern education and wealth; cultural structures can be obstacles to that social equality). Each pitfall boils down to overlooking the possibility of a cultural fractal structuring the whole of society. The possibility of radical difference is denied. The epistemological challenge pertains to academia too.[2]

Chrétien suggests a joint process of ethnic differentiation and declined reciprocity under the reign of Kigeri Rwabugiri in the late nineteenth century (GL 188). The new chiefs being mostly Tutsi, recognized for owning many cattle and letting others do the agricultural work, endowed the ethnic category with a hierarchical connotation, substituting the ranking between clan memberships (GL 189). The *bugabire* pastoral contract underwent

> a shift from a logic of reciprocity, one of gifts and counter-gifts (according to the spirit Marcel Mauss defined), to a logic that, at least in principle, was redistributive and increasingly hierarchical to the point of perverting the personal ties that were central in this pyramid of power.

In countries less touched than Rwanda by this logic of discrimination – Burundi and Buha, for example – the logics of exchange remained more visible in the nineteenth century. The *bugabire* combined simple Bahutu and Batutsi in various configurations. Exchanges of beer, sorghum, and bananas were central to social life. (GL 188)

According to our macro-analysis of Rwandan oral history, coming up next, the shift was a gradual process that had begun a century earlier. The medicinal rule requiring reciprocity with spirit and outsider transformed into the ceremonial state characterized by national ritual, procedure, taxation and hierarchy (but no actual policy or administration of services). The analysis also indicates that the formation of the Rwandan state coincided with ethnic differentiation. The latter is not imaginable without erosion of clan authority and, most of all, without erosion of the initiatory and marital alliances cross-cutting the clans. Although the state probably never had a grip on people's everyday lives like in the colony, it must have implemented a number of centralizing interventions over time that concerned land and cattle. Chrétien mentions the army system under Cyrima Rujugira in the mid eighteenth century (GL 186). The allotment of cattle herds led to 'bovine armies' under the control of 'bow chiefs'. It cannot be a coincidence that the centralized states of the Great Lakes took root in the most popular well-watered places, which groups might want to claim for themselves and defend. In a time of competition over land between herders and farmers, Gahindiro instituted in the early nineteenth century the *gikingi*, grazing land assigned to cattle raisers befriended to the court. The discrimination of Hutu by Tutsi appeared more and more, in the evolution of the *buhake* contract that became less equal, and in the agricultural corvée *buletwa* (a Swahili word of the porters), probably introduced by King Rwabugiri as late as 1850 (GL 181, 186).

King Mutaga of Burundi, who fought his Rwandese neighbour Cyirima Rujugira in the eighteenth century (and had acquired the same seminal reputation as Ndori for Rwanda a century earlier), left traces of his success in the form of 'many sacred woods and descendants' (GL 163). Besides this noteworthy medicinal measure of success, there was the collective summoning capacity of the drum. How can we link Turner's and Janzen's cults of affliction with kingship? Membership of the royal dynasty, hence descent from the first king, was traditionally expressed through the healing idiom. 'To come from the drum's belly' means royal descent in KiRundi (GL 172); in BuNyoro those with a royal blood tie are BaBito, 'of the drum' (*b'ebingoma*, cf. also Banang'oma in KiSukuma). Because of its importance for the social structure and for motivating individual claims, we may assume the terminology to be stable, possibly harking back to the original model of rule. Of course, the drum would become the sign of royalty, backed by mythical tales that attribute agency to the drum, carrying a name and a personality on which the kingdom depends: among others Kalinga in Rwanda, Rusama in Bunyoro, Timba in Buganda, Nyabatama in Karagwe, Bagyendanwa in Nkore, Karyenda in Burundi, and Rugabo and Buhabugari in Buha (GL 127). The commonality seems to me quite mysterious unless these are all names of a *ngoma* healing drum that evolved into a kingdom. The polity prism has no room for drum and dance.

Historically the medicinal reference of the drum came first, so must somehow have determined political evolution. The agency of the drum pursues a medicinal logic. The parts of the drum, a mortar on which animal skin is stretched, evoke fecundity. The name, *ingoma*, signifies kingdom, according to Chrétien (GL 125). The drum as kingdom should rid us of the polity prism. Chrétien concedes that the enthronement is a ritual of initiation and that the king is 'a kind of medium' being imbued with the predecessor's force and becoming the father of the nation, bringing the nation back to normalcy after the predecessor's death. After removing his headgear for divination, he becomes the diviner's leader. In this last phase he is an impartial ruler who has broken with his family. All the elements are there to infer from the last phase a process of innovation that drew on cultic initiation. The sacred diadem (*ishungwe*) of cowries and beads worn by the king (see Illustrations 4 and 5), the river crossing and planting of the Erythrina tree, the hunt in the forest, and the ritual at the termite mound are, among others (cf. GL124), enacted in the initiation of the Chwezi cult (Stroeken 2006).

Finding examples of kings who were famous diviners (GL 159) or were assigned by diviners (GL 151) is no evidence of the institutions' common origin. However, the further back one goes in history the more chance that kings are portrayed as diviners. Might this tendency not be a trace of the original model? The Western connotation of the oracular with the mythical dismisses the magical background of kingship as fable. We have mentioned the *abashingantahe* elders in Burundi, climbing ranks on the basis of beer treats like 'chiefs' of the Chwezi cult. In a footnote (GL 176, n69) we learn that the term for appointing them is *kwatirwa*, the same as mediumistic initiation into the Chwezi cult. Again we note the absence of a religious versus political differentiation.

In Buganda, King Tebandeke's mediumship turned madness led around 1700 to the court's intervention to separate the offices of king and priest (GL 157). In this way a stage in the creation of the ceremonial state became thematized. For Rwanda, Chrétien situates a similar transition to what he calls the monarchical state in the mid eighteenth century, as political centralization and military expansion reinforced each other (GL 186). Standardization of rituals was possible in the same period after the court controlled the Chwezi cult or 'cult of Ryangombe' (GL 161). Does this contradict our hypothesis of the kingdom having arisen much earlier from such cult? Not at all. The surrounding kinglets spawned by Rwanda were headed by ritualists (GL 160). They led the provinces of a cult.

In other parts of the Great Lakes such as Buzinza and Buha, centralization was never achieved to the same extent as in Rwanda and Buganda (GL 153). The latter two are extreme cases, excelling in the mentioned anti-medicinal or anti-divinatory modifications. For our thesis on a transition, the smaller labile kingdoms better elucidate the process of origination. Consider the following statement: Ndorwa (Mpororo) was 'the kingdom of the Murorwa drum inherited from the mysterious queen Kitami' (GL 149). The female healer-diviner Kitami set up a drum of affliction. Its dynasty lasted two generations. That was short enough to safeguard the truth in oral tradition, namely that the actual source of kingship is the mediumistic cult. How many established courts have not manipulated their oral history to cover up this medicinal origin and meaning of the drum? Another example is the short-lived Sibula dynasty of the Buhavu kingdom, whose founder's grandfather Lubambo is the spirit for the diviners' cult in Burundi (GL 118, 119). The polity prism, accepting only a political-governmental focus or its religious-divine counterpart, seems like the myth embraced by courts and advocated after witnessing the colonial's technology of governance. Two centuries later the chiefs of Ndorwa (Mpororo), who clandestinely rebelled against the colonial administration, had become mediums of Queen Nyabingi '[a]ccording to the logic of initiation', illustrating 'kingship's possible avatars' (GL 149). Our reinterpretation warrants the exact opposite for the entire region spanning central and east Africa: kingship is an avatar of the medium – the founder of a cult with initiatory hierarchy. The hypothesis is historically sound for the Great Lakes, where the birth of ceremonial states was presumably preceded by Kitara society with a culture named C(h)wezi, whose 'collapse' is dated to the sixteenth century (147, 95). A culture, or cultural structure, does not collapse, but survives and reshapes itself, transforming drums into kingdoms.

When criticizing Western scholars for presupposing Nilotic, 'Hamitic', and ultimately Egyptian origins of kingship in central Africa,

Chrétien only needs a light pat on the back to fully embrace the oral traditions, such as in Bushi, that situate the birth of the institution 'in the bush, the result of exploits, magic' and that picture a hunter with leopard skin on his way to collect initiatory material, crowned by outsiders to be their king (GL 118). The putative 'amalgamation' of chronicles by nineteenth-century Rwandan court historians into one narrative understandably inspires caution (GL 115). As we will demonstrate next, the *bitekerezo* tales maintain a reflective dimension though, escaping the narrator's intentionality. Contrary to Chrétien's claim, the ethnic dimension of Rwandan conflicts does gradually come to the fore in the oral traditions on precolonial history. The main challenge for understanding the history of kingship from the perspective of the (various) cultural systems in which it was conceived at the time is to devise a method free from anachronistic and ethnocentric terms of incipience. At the microlevel of analysis, ethnographies and situational analysis avoiding the outsider's objectivism allow for insider's observations. At the macrolevel, anthropologists have developed structuralist analyses which pimped for our purpose can bring out the cultural terms of oral histories. The second half of this last chapter focuses on the latter method and applies it to Rwandan history.

From Oracular to Ceremonial Rule: A Cultural Process in Rwanda

What is the historical value of Gakaniisha's collection of twenty tales covering four centuries of dynastic wars in Rwanda? A method is proposed here so as to lay bare in the narration of successive epochs a cultural structure. A political model sui generis comes to the fore detailing the components of early Rwandan kingship, comprising changes in spirit reciprocity, divination, medicine, ritual, autocracy, ethnicity, and nation building. By integrating diachrony in the structuralist method, the institution of kingship can appear as a cultural process instead of an invented or imported practice.

Historians such as Clifford (1988) had serious impact on anthropology, so much as inaugurating the postcolonial era of studying culture. After half a century of anthropological emphasis on structure, they brought the event, and with it agency, back into the picture. The historicizing of anthropology confronted authors with their making of culture and entailed a 'reflexive turn' that benefited two generations of postcolonial ethnography. This book has envisaged the other direction of influence, seeking to 'anthropologize' history, as it were, so that historians consider the frame or structure – the relations between cultural elements – through which they interpret events. Materialist or idealist frames, micro- or macro-oriented interpretations yield very different histories. In this chapter, we verify whether Western concepts can be replaced by locally conceived 'variables' of practice (e.g. ritual, divination, ethnicity) and belief (e.g. providence, nation, spirits). Evolutions in these determine the history of the institution at hand, kingship. We attempt to link up the tenor of the previous chapters with a new structure-oriented method.

Anthropologists have no methodological tool to derive structure from ethnographic data, not at least in ways that outsiders could verify. Despite efforts such as Grounded Theory to systematize qualitative data analysis, ethnography has remained an art, granting the privilege of interpretation to the insiders, the authors and their informants. Is there no external source to validate the cultural logics that the ethnography lays bare? Oral tradition is a likely candidate to be harbouring such collective structure. To verify the claim, we systematically analyse the collection of twenty historical narratives, known as *bitekerezo*, learned by rote and transmitted by Rwandan elders, in this case by Gakaniisha (Coupez and Kamanzi 1962).[3]

The collection recounts four centuries of dynastic wars and royal tribulations. Indirectly, though, each tale characterizes the ethos of the epoch during a certain reign: people's way of life, norms and cultural logic. Jan Vansina (1985), who pioneered the discipline of African history by remedying the lack of written sources with oral tradition, sought to extract fact from tale after purifying the latter of its fabricated and added elements. This chapter treats tales not as eroded history but as evocations of epochs. The remoteness from the recounted events and the lesser orientation on facts are an advantage rather than a handicap, because of the greater freedom of the narratives to foreground the cultural elements pointing to historical process. The ideologies and interests of elites informing the stories should be seen as data instead of biases of the truth.

Pierre Smith (1970: 9), an expert on Rwandan mythology, similarly defended his structuralist quest against Vansina's positivism. Rwandans' scrupulous iteration of the *bitekerezo* tales, whose literal meaning is 'reflections', must be attributed to their esteem for a different sort of history, one that reflects on the past as a whole, thus recounting the life and transformation of collective institutions.[4] Our methodology to elicit these reflections will permit kingship to appear as an institution that came into being, rather than as a given, an event or an imported idea. This diachronic methodology will be complemented with the author's ethnography as an observer and participant of the Chwezi cult in western Tanzania.[5] The Chwezi are the last vibrant remainder of the spirit cult founded by Ryangombe and formerly known as Kubandwa, which will appear to lie at the heart of the politico-religious transformation during the reign of Ndori. King Ndori is a pivotal figure in the process. That much our diachronic narrative analysis and the chronicle of Vansina agree on.

After questioning the dominant approaches to Rwandan history, we propose a method to closely trail the 'reflections' within the successive tales about kings, diviners and ethnicities so that what suffuses them can surface: an anti-oracular process, separating magical and initiatory dimensions, while undermining the encompassing role of medicine. The gradual, multilayered nature of the process suggests that the narrative evolution is not fabricated history. We claim to obtain data no other method as yet could produce.

Applying the Two Anthropological Dimensions to History

The Introduction touched on anthropologizing moments in the discipline of history bolstered by the Annales school and the later 'cultural turn'. In the meanwhile, neo-Marxist scholarship had fostered world-systems theory, which recognized the explanatory power of structures in history – not ideational but material structures this time, primarily socio-economic. The differences between the two schools are captured by our two axes, the one opposing agency to structure, the other opposing materialism to idealism. What interests us in these four extremes is the corresponding biases in presenting Rwandan kingship (Figure 9.1). The four quadrants correspond to distinct methodologies. Can we devise a method representing the approach in the middle?

As explained in the Introduction, the first combination, actor-materialism, basically claims that culture and change result from humans acting according to their self-interest. We have illustrated how the presumably universal cultural structure of *homo economicus* oriented on material needs surfaced in Vansina's reconstructions of history. His reconstruction should be counterbalanced with the opposite, structure-idealism, which is exactly the approach his compatriot Luc de Heusch (1966) adopted in his work on Interlacustrine Africa. How could the reconciliation be done without repeating old mistakes? In its pure form, structure-idealism claims that culture follows an internal logic steering people's minds (e.g. functionalism and structuralism). Vansina (1983) notoriously reproached de Heusch for

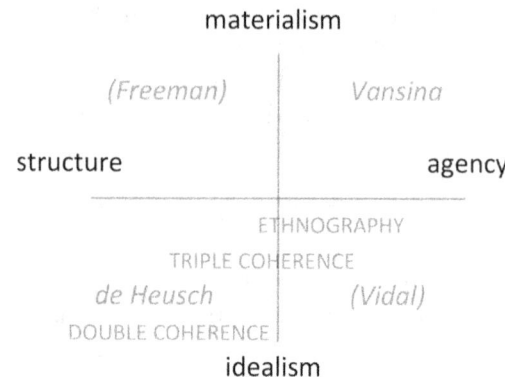

Figure 9.1 Methods on two anthropological dimensions of culture. Figure by the author.

aiming to convince the reader of such structures through analytical elegance instead of evidence. Structuralism lacked the criterion of falsification necessary to be scientific – a criticism we will nuance in the method section. A more cogent critique on structuralism came since the decolonizing 1970s, after interpretive anthropologists improved the participatory techniques of ethnography to grant more agency to the subjects and thus give way to actor-idealism, the third approach in Figure 9.1. From this perspective, Claudine Vidal (1985) faulted Luc de Heusch for presenting cognitive structures as so deeply entrenched that people would live according to them; that there would be historical truth, for example, in the Rwandan mythological structure of an eternal quaternary cycle whereby cattle-king is succeeded by two warrior-kings and a fire-king. For Vidal (ibid.: 578) ethnography was an antidote as well to the fourth combination, 'structure-materialism' (e.g. neo-Marxism), typically overstretching the purchase of material structures on culture, of which Jim Freedman's (1974) representation of pastoralists 'worshipping' the god Nyabingi seemed a case in point.

During a century of debate on culture, anthropologists have navigated to spiral towards the middle of the four theoretical poles. Reflexive, interactive ethnographies have dominated the postcolonial era. But the risk of their denying cultures an endogenous dynamic has always lurked. Figure 9.1 is telling in that sense. If interpretive ethnography is the actor-idealist method par excellence, and survey is that of structure-materialism (for example, applying correspondence analysis, cf. Bourdieu 1979), then which technique can make the ideational structures of a culture appear, compensating for the current bias among both historians and anthropologists towards actor-idealism? The next section introduces a method to derive historical process in such inductive manner that is reproducible by external researchers.

Method: Triple Coherence

Contrary to Vansina's claim, structuralist analysis does have a criterion to falsify its interpretations. The criterion is not empirical evidence, as in finding facts to reject hypotheses, but the coherence of the interpretation in relation to the data. This approach recognizes the holistic and hermeneutical character of meaning in all analysis. Following Lévi-Strauss's (1972) application of Saussurian linguistics to culture, we can speak of internal and external coherence, referring respectively to syntagmatic and paradigmatic relations with the data.

The syntagm, also known as the constitutive relation, stands for the sequence of units (i.e. words such as 'Marc' and 'reads') *constituting* structures (i.e. phrases such as 'Marc reads') that are well formed according to syntax. Transposed to the cultural domain, the syntagm is the relationship between ideas (or *relata*, terms related to the referent) together forming a meaningful story, description or other message. To comprehend the myth of Ryangombe, Luc de Heusch (1972) proposes a syntagm of four relata: relations of kinship and alliance, relations between the sexes, socio-economic relations, and relations with royalty. These are schematized in Table 9.1 as horizontal arrows expressing the interrelation between the columns. The syntagmatic claim would be falsified if someone found a fifth unit whose addition would better capture the essence of the tale (then the relata would not be exhaustive) or if one unit could be subsumed under the others (then the relata would not be mutually exclusive). Together the relata form a cultural syntax, or cultural structure.

The second type of relations is the paradigm, also known as the associative relation, which concerns the choice of unit among a set of possibilities *associated* with a particular syntactic role, such as 'John' for the word 'Marc' in the example above. Transposed to the cultural domain the paradigm is the relationship between a set of relata and their alternatives. These are schematized in Table 9.1 as vertical arrows relating the text fragments of a tale to the theme heading the column. In Ryangombe's myth, the equality of father and son concerns their relation of kinship. That paradigmatic claim would be falsified if the equality of father and son was absent in the data (here in the myth), or if their equality was contested to be about kinship.

Befitting the hermeneutics of the humanities, which views 'facts' – like kinship in the above example – as constructed, the objective is not a one-to-one correspondence with empirical reality but a structural correspondence of the cultural syntax, simultaneously at the levels of syntagm and paradigm. With ethnographically informed analysis (for example in our case, showing matrilineal descent to assign symbolic fatherhood to the maternal uncle) the proposed cultural syntax can be refuted. The refutation is not absolute like in testable hypotheses (or in the factual verification Vansina had in mind) but relative because the set of cohering relata will be adapted.

The double coherence can be recognized in Luc de Heusch's ideational structure subtending the spirit possession cult of Ryangombe. In the myth, Ryangombe defies the norms in all four domains of relationship (Table 9.1). Ryangombe is an equal to his father and does not obey his mother, who blocks the door to prevent him from going to hunt in the forest. He leaves his wife, does not care about cattle breeding, rejects feudality, and rebels against the king. His sense of freedom is testified also by his self-praise. His subversive position, de Heusch (1972) goes on showing, is supported by ethnographic data on the cult. Membership is open to all social classes and negates the caste system based on cattle ownership (although in Rwanda separating Hutu and Tutsi sections). The cult optimistically celebrates the prosperous time inaugurated by the tragic death of Ryangombe, and thus counteracts the angry, capricious ancestors who dominate daily life and putatively motivate pessimism about life's outcome. The structuralist method allows for disclosing the meaning of Ryangombe, whose role in people's collective memory has been underestimated, according to de Heusch.

However, the moral message the structuralist connects to the death of Ryangombe as the price paid for his excessive freedom reveals a limitation of the method in terms of historical consciousness. Firstly, it is not abnormal for heroes to die in myths, certainly not if biography is intended. Ryangombe's death may have been given undue significance by de Heusch. Secondly, the self-praise is an oratory style featuring in most Rwandese tales from a certain era onwards, so with the benefit of historical oversight we know that little weight should be given to that conduct of the hero. Thirdly, the transgression Luc de Heusch finds in this one story, of the hero defying the will of the gods, could in a body of narratives spanning a longer period be seen in the light of a historical evolution that reached its momentum in the epoch of Ryangombe and Ndori, as we will argue. To bring cultural process to light, in the indirect manner we envisage here, it is advisable to

Table 9.1 Three levels of coherence between the symbolic relations of Ryangombe's myth

DATA	Kinship/ alliance	Relations between sexes	Socio-economic relations	Kingship
TALE 1	Ryangombe equals father and disobeys mother	R ignores marital contract	R depreciates pastoralism	R rebels against Tutsi king and feudality
TALE 2				

study a body of narratives that cover consecutive periods, referring as parts to a whole – 'history'.

Consequently, our remedy to improve the validity of double coherence is to extend the syntagmatic and paradigmatic relations with a third, diachronic dimension. It verifies relations across tales from successive episodes (see arrow across the rows in first column of Table 9.1). The cultural syntax we derive should cohere with no less than three types of relations, and this *simultaneously*: between themes (relata or units), between those themes and the data, and between the tales.

From Text to Cultural Structure

To practically go about obtaining triple coherence, we began the analysis by reading all tales chronologically and identifying themes that recur. The chronological ordering of the twenty stories had already been done by Coupez and Kamanzi based on internal references to ruling kings, the succession of which is known from the Rwandan court's genealogical list. The first columns in Figure 9.2 cover the tale's chronological rank and, if applicable, its name, the period and name of the ruler, and a brief summary of the plot. From the fourth column onwards events are arranged under the themes we clearly established as recurring, yet we must consider as provisional because defined by our etic perspective. The columns were provisionally entitled: 'war or battle', 'oracle' (prophetic/ secular), 'ritual' (fixed/magic), 'royal power' (absolute/ controlled), 'ethnic talk', 'nation reference', 'custom invented', 'plan or ruse', and 'self-praise'.

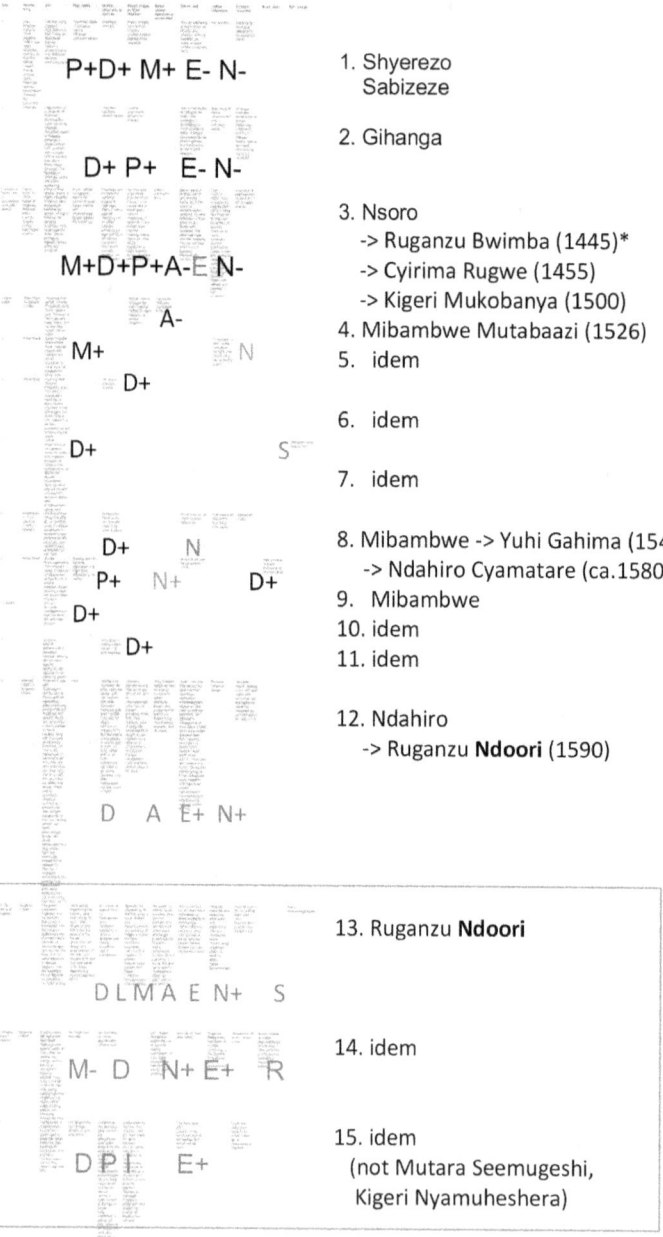

P+D+ M+ E- N-   1. Shyerezo
                   Sabizeze

                2. Gihanga

D+ P+   E- N-

                3. Nsoro
                   -> Ruganzu Bwimba (1445)*
                   -> Cyirima Rugwe (1455)
M+D+P+A-E N-   -> Kigeri Mukobanya (1500)
     A-   4. Mibambwe Mutabaazi (1526)
M+   N   5. idem
   D+
                6. idem
D+   S
                7. idem

    D+   N   8. Mibambwe -> Yuhi Gahima (1543)
  P+ N+   D+   -> Ndahiro Cyamatare (ca.1580)
  D+   9. Mibambwe
       D+   10. idem
                11. idem

                12. Ndahiro
                   -> Ruganzu **Ndoori** (1590)

   D A E+ N+

                13. Ruganzu **Ndoori**
   D L M A E N+ S

                14. idem
  M- D N+ E+ R

                15. idem
   D P I   E+   (not Mutara Seemugeshi,
                   Kigeri Nyamuheshera)

                16. Ruganzu -> Mibambwe
                   Seekarongoro **Gisanura** (1671)
  F D- N+ E+   R   (not Yuhi **Mazimpaka**, **Rwaka**)

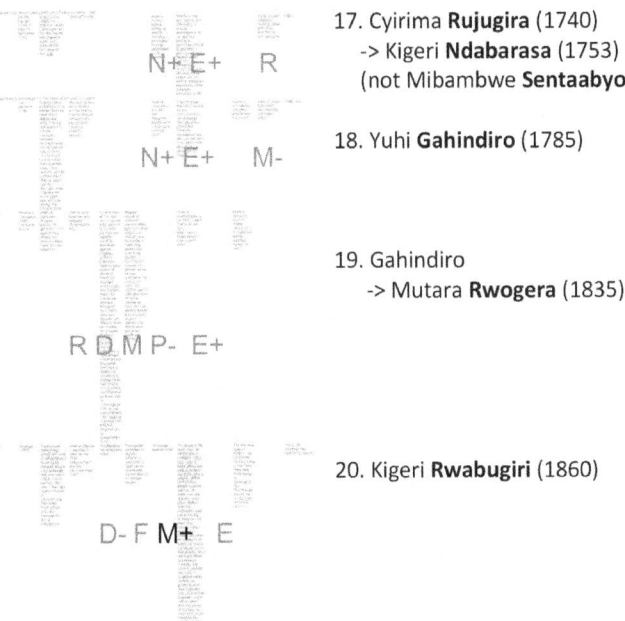

Figure 9.2 Gakaniisha's 20 tales in terms of chronology, variables and reigns. Figure by the author.

What makes a set of themes fit together as a cultural syntax is their joint presence in a story as well as their variation across the whole collection, like variables on which stories can score positive or negative values. The columns of provisional themes act as a canvas on which to mark the definite themes. These are the variables, which structuralists call relata. We formulate the variables in the way they appear together in the first story: belief in providence (P), consulting diviner before important decision (D), applying magic (M), absence of ethnic labelling (E), and absence of discourse on Rwanda as a nation (N). Like all variables, the relata are tentatively named. Their co-occurrence and variation form the basis for deriving cultural process, but the choice of relata by the author remains a subjective moment in the analytical chain, a textual hermeneutics drawing on ethnographic experience and knowledge of the relevant literature. Nevertheless, our historical correction of the structuralist method introduces a third, diachronic dimension that ups the ante. Text fragments are compared in all tales instead of just one, hence raising the requirement for deciding on the syntagm (i.e. on the relata that are mutually exclusive and exhaustive).

In order not to overlook any relata of the cultural process, we decided to err on the side of exhaustiveness, at the expense of mutual exclusiveness, so we also included less recurrent themes whose meanings may overlap with the former variables: autonomy in relation to tradition (A), self-praise (S), using ruse as main strategy (R), and formalism in execution of rites (F). Two variables only appear once in the collection, but the moment of their appearance seems crucial for our discussion: the figure of a cult leader as main character (L), and the question of who invented initiation rites (I).

The analysis in Figure 9.2 consists in determining for each tale which variables it articulates. The variable's first letter is written in large font onto the cell corresponding to the story's row and the theme's column. In an explicitly positive or explicitly negative articulation, a plus or minus is added to the letter. To express this information in Table 9.2 we recast the values of the variables: blank for absence of variable, '0' for negative presence, '1' for presence and '2' for positive presence. For instance, on the variable Divination a high score of '2' (or D+) will be attributed to a story in which a king counts

Table 9.2 Gakaniisha's 20 tales in terms of their values on all eleven variables

	P	D	E	N	A	S	L	I	F	R	M	
1	2	2	2	2							2	10/10
2	2	2	2	2								8/8
3	2	2	1	2	2						2	11/12
4					2							2/2
5				1							2	3/4
6		2										2/2
7		2					1					3/4
8		2		1								3/4
9	2	2		0								4/6
10		2										2/2
11		2										2/2
12		1	0	0	1							2/8
13		1	1	0	1	1	0			1		5/14
14		1	0	0					0	0		1/10
15	1	1	0				0					2/8
16		0	0	0				0	0			0/10
17			0	0					0			0/6
18			0	0						0		0/6
19	0	1	0						0	1		2/10
20		0	1						0	2		3/8

on divination to make a decision. The score will be only '1' (or D) if divination is performed but the king's subsequent decision deviates. A score of '0' (or D–) expresses a negative attitude to this relatum, as in a king rejecting the institution of divination.[6]

Figure 9.3 based on this table will visualize the changing values of co-occurring variables in the tales during successive epochs. A quick glance at Table 9.2 already betrays the striking pattern, linking our themes to an evolution in the institution of kingship.

Deriving Cultural Process: The Rise of the Rwandan Kingdom

The first story of Gakaniisha recounts the era prior to the establishment of the Rwandan kingdom. This is the time when the Nyiginya clan led by Shyerezo migrated to the area and was assigned land by the local clan named Zigaaba, headed by Kabeeja (pronounced Kabeza in southern Sukuma, cf. the ancestor of Kishina). The story familiarizes the reader with the perspective of Shyerezo's wife Gasani, who at menopausal age hopes to give birth to a son. The miracle happens, as the child is born out of milk by the intercession of Imaana, which Rwandan historians traditionally translate as Providence, an impersonal omniscient force (see Bantu verb *ku-ma(a)na*, 'to know'). Figure 9.2 thus begins the analysis by marking P+ for tale number one. The miraculous milk refers to the use of magic, hence M+. The child called Sabizeze will later father Gihanga, the renowned inventor. There is no indication of nation building, nor of ethnic labels (hence N– and E– in Figure 9.2). The suggestion is of roaming clans looking to settle down, but still with hunting as the main activity. The clans intermarry following the rule of reciprocity. In anthropological terms we may contrast this political model of alliance between (segmentary) lineages with the model of a state and nation socially (including ethnically) categorizing. The diviners are prophetic, as testified by their exact predictions regarding the death of host and original settler Kabeeja. The tale thus additionally scores D+ and P+.

In the second story we obtain a first justification of the suzerainty of the Nyiginya clan over other groups in Rwanda. A cataclysm took place after which Gihanga, the clan-head, managed to save the few remaining cattle. Not only did he allow cattle to multiply again and clans to expand across the country down to BuHa around today's Kigoma in Tanzania, to Indorwa and to Ubunyabungo in East Congo, which would become new kingdoms (Burundi is not part of Gihanga's descent, it is underlined). He perfected the skill of hunting and invented techniques of pottery, metallurgy and woodwork. The verb *ku-hanga* in Kinyarwanda indeed literally means 'to invent', which as many commentators have argued, points to the fictitiousness of the name. Gihanga's heritage is enormous, yet none of his achievements are possible without Imaana, Providence, creating the phenomena (P+ in Figure 9.2). To know Providence is to make things well. Diviners come in two kinds: prophetic (*bahunuuzi*) and diagnostic (*bapfumu*). The former are needed in court, while the latter serve both the king and the common people. Divination (D+) is not so much registering the situation as it is changing it by looking for good omens. The prophetic oracle is presented as a performance in itself redressing the situation. All ensuing events will be as predicted. The best diviners are thought to come from afar. The Ubukara consult spirits for prophetic purposes. Another source of life is the forest, from where the first milk is brought by a girl as a remedy for a Gihanga in distress. The nomadic Twa (Pygmy) are mentioned by the narrator as hired killers, which implies a professional category, not an ethnic label (E–). Conflict is limited to quarrels with wayward hunters. The nation of Rwanda only exists, in the narrator's words, as an anticipated reality (N–).

The 'history of Nsoro, son of Saamembe', totalling over two hundred verses, covers the subsequent period of three generations, from Nsoro (prior to 1445), father of Ruganzu Bwimba, to Cyirima Rugwe (1455) and finally Kigeri (1500).[7] As small battles unfold, involving vengeance and the search for influence through magical means and intermarriage, the nation of Rwanda gradually takes shape. At the same time, ethnic labels appear. In the second half of the recounted seventy years or so, the term 'Hutu' begins to emerge in the narrative. Going by the derogatory connotation in the story, illustrated among others by explicit ruminations on the blander style of clothing among Hutu women, more is meant than the professional category of servant. Social and ethnic features are intertwined in the category, whilst Tutsi means nobility. Reciprocity is suggested though: kings and Tutsi nobles need Hutu witnesses because of the latter's authenticity and distance from the Tutsi court's intrigues, hence the E in Figure 9.2 (meaning that the issue comes up, yet not in a one-sided manner meriting the maximum value of 2). During this era, the royal dynasty becomes the most powerful corporate and military group in the region, which irritates neighbouring peoples complaining about 'those Tutsi', one of the non-Rwandans exclaiming 'if you meet Tutsi, slash them with knives (*imihoro*)' (Coupez and Kamanzi 1962: 115). The main enemies of the royal clan appear to be the Shi, living in Igisaka, west of Rwanda. They are spoken of as rebels, suggesting that Rwanda occupies the centre while the Shi belong to a recalcitrant periphery. That does not prevent the Shi from harbouring the most sought-after diviners. Illustrative of the way the royal clan begins to identify itself with the people in its country, the daughter of Nsoro is willing to make a sacrifice for peace in the region by marrying Kimenyi, chief of the Shi. All of this has been predicted by foreign diviners (D+) looked for in the forest, living afar, yet knowing about the court's preferred sacrificial materials. Medicinal procedures, stipulated by oracles, abound (M+). Some customs are suggestive of a different lifeworld than that of the narrator's mostly Christian audience. For instance, Nsoro helps Cyirima to become respected by the people by having him marry the girl who is admired by the court's women for having slept with two kings. The nation of Rwanda is not yet formed (N–). Before Cyirima commands the chiefs of the hills and can seek to establish sovereign rule over all neighbouring peoples, he has to go through some ordeals such as accepting a blood pact with a Hutu (who followed the advice of his elders to refrain from killing him). It is a half-hearted attempt from Cyirima at alliance though. In the eyes of the Rwandan kings, the narrator interjects, all who refuse their rule should be expelled. In practice, we notice something else. As in the conflict with the Shi, the elders and diviners counterbalance and boldly contradict the Rwandan king (hence A– in Figure 9.2: the king's rule is not absolute or autocratic). They warn King Cyirima against imposing his will on other peoples. He should wait until he obtains good omens. Providence always has the last word (P+). Kigeri, his successor, indulges the Hutu groups who distrusted him and wanted to test his intentions after giving portions of their land. He proves his benevolence by donating the best cattle and women. But when the Hutu host dares to ask for the gift of the royal drum Karinga, it is the sign for Kigeri to kill him.

The following six short stories concern King Mibambwe Mutabaazi, purportedly ruling in the mid sixteenth century. After dealing with his servants' critique (A–), Mibambwe challenges King Kimenyi of rivalling Igisaka. Who is the most refined and noble, and has the best horned cattle? Who possesses the magical hidden stone of Bagenga (probably for rainmaking, the fertility of the land being a king's responsibility)? In the next story Nyoro threatens to annihilate Rwanda. The concept of a state and people is taking root, albeit in calamity (N as a rising issue): 'Rwanda is going awry' (*Rwanda va mal*). Magical means are needed (M+) and divination to know the correct procedures. All predictions materialize (D+).

Oracles play the main role as well in the sixth story on the drought inflicted by Mashira on the Rwandan outer chiefdom of Ubugesera. The king's throne and life are in danger when the steps prescribed by the oracle are not completed. The steps are not customarily prescribed, but reflect the (whimsical) wish of royal ancestors expressed in an oracle. In the seventh chronicle, Chief Karemeera of Ubugesera consults the spirits because of a curse on his possessions, leaving everything sterile. The girl Imparakazi, diviner and witch (*umulozi*), lifts the curse by finding a better place for him to build and live in Ubugusera. In the next tale, the reader learns again about the danger of ignoring the diviner's advice (D+). The elderly Mibambwe eventually applies protective medicine using papyrus before enthroning Yuhi Gahima after whom King Ndahiro will follow. Meanwhile the kingdom of Rwanda seeks a wider spatial reference and expands its influence through an alliance with the king of BuHa in the south (N). During dialogues the custom emerges of self-praise in rhetorical poem, which allows individuals to take centre stage amidst the collective. Figure 9.2 grants this textual element an S, which means a score of 1. We interpret self-praise as an innovation deviating (if moderately) from the traditional belief in Providence as the benefactor in life.

The ninth story details the work of the diviner Runuukamishyo from Indorwa, who serves Mibambwe in consulting the oracles of chicken and bull organs to detect an excellent omen (*ishirya*) for the kingdom. That omen will not work should the king touch those organs afterwards. For the first time we hear the expression that sets Rwanda apart: '*Imaana* (Providence) spends the daytime elsewhere but the night here', meaning that Rwanda is the divinity's home. Mibambwe's reign would represent the epoch when Providence and nation began to be equated, an important moment in the process we are describing (P+ and N+). It is added that Burundi will never be an enemy. The next two stories emphasize the importance of divination for the well-being of the country and its king, because an oracle can end a tragedy by finding the cause of that tragedy (D+). The Ubugesera region that turned its back on a diviner named Runyota paid the price of drought and famine. Divination helped to exonerate the Hima accused of causing a bovine epidemic.

By now it should be clear that oracles partake of Rwandan history, sometimes skewing the relation between past and future, since an able diviner can influence fate. Strikingly, divination is key in the political-religious equation of nation and providence during Mibambwe's reign, while it no longer is during those of his successors Ndahiro and Ndori.

Ryangombe and Ndori: Narrative Evidence of an Anti-divinatory Revolution

The twelfth chronicle is pivotal. The nation of Rwanda and the ethnicity of Hutu, Tutsi and Twa within the state become established issues (N+ and E+). The king has provincial chiefs (*abatwale*). The main characters up the ante of ethnic stereotypes ('Hutu is always in a hurry', 'Twa is easily impressed') with the statement 'Hutu and we (Tutsi) have always hated each other' (Coupez and Kamanzi 1962: 217). At the same time, a second track of changes begins, one whose significance is clear because of the role of oracles in the past. Disagreements between king, advisors and diviners occurred before, but now comes the first sign of the king's criticism of oracles (D instead of D+). King Ndahiro is convinced that the Rwandan nation is in danger because of the neighbouring Abakongoro Hutu. They never accepted his rule, so he decides to provoke them into war. The Ubukara, who perform divination for the king and keep his saliva, disagree with him and try to prevent war (A). Their oracles project the danger away from the Hutu neighbours and onto an individual suspected of witchcraft, the girl Nyira-Kimuuzanye. After mocking the diviners, Ndahiro agrees not to go further into battle. Nevertheless, he is caught by Abakongoro soldiers. He is killed by strangling, as his wish conveyed to the captors was not to be cut by the machete. In the cosmology of Bantu-speaking peoples, a king is not supposed to have his blood spilled on the soil lest the land lose fertility. His son Ruganzu Ndori can escape thanks to Twa hunters, who as a cultural group since that day are entitled to insult nobles. Ndori retrieves the royal drums from the forest that his father had lost.

While the old king Ndahiro struggled to free himself of diviners and their unpredictable oracles intervening with his royal strategies, his successor will be able to replace the dyad of ruler and diviner by another political model. In the person of Ndori we observe the completed shift from a symbolic king incarnating the land's fertility and enjoying carnal delights to a strategic king ensuring autocratic rule. The outcome is absolute power via military force, ruse, strict regulation and administration. A break is made with royal dependency on whimsical oracles and ancestors, which only legitimized the king's rule on the condition of reciprocity with those diviners, neighbouring peoples, Twa and other social categories. If we consider this break as a new beginning, we may understand why Jan Vansina (2004) named Ndori the first king. However, he assumed Ndori to be an immigrant from the north, importing this model of kingship with slight innovations.

In the north, he admits though, there were no large chiefdoms. In Gakaniisha's collection we rather obtain the picture of a gradual and endogenous process, which started with the predecessor, supposedly 'father'. The tales do not explicitly contrast old and new customs, nor do they even articulate a cultural change. The contrast and change can be indirectly derived, as we did above, by comparing the various stories in terms of the dialogues, the actors' motives, the outcomes of events and the narrator's priorities, all articulating the themes illustrated in Figure 9.2.

Corroborating our thesis of a long-term process, the initiated transition intensifies in the thirteenth tale. The elders and court diviners have no power anymore (D). Led by Ndori, the army conquers the neighbouring lands and massacres the autochthonous inhabitants of the hills, burning their houses and systematically looting – each man on average killing '50 Hutu' (Coupez and Kamanzi 1962: 245; E in our Figure). Ndori places himself above customs (A), among others by cursing his rivals, the Shi people and their leader Nzira. The wars seem necessary antecedents to Ndori's organization of the country, including the land of Bunyabungo. Across the territory he emplaces chiefs and a tributary system, for himself as *mwami*, supreme king (N+).

Just as Rwandan kingship reaches its pinnacle, a formidable counterpart and contrasting figure emerges, the legendary Ryangombe, supposed founder of the Imandwa spirit cult, known today across the Great Lakes as the Chwezi cult. A spiritual leader, he is everything the new king is not. It may be why the king seeks to establish an alliance with him. Would they really have been contemporaries? The point of Ryangombe's entry seems more symbolic than historical. It is clear that Ryangombe belongs to another world (L). Unlike the rhetorically refined and belligerent king, he stammers and is weak at fighting and playing strategic games. His attempt at self-praise is a travesty compared to the '*autopanégyriques*' the king and his soldiers abundantly engage in (S). But he proves to be powerful in magic. He can command the sun, regulate warm and cold (mimicked today in the *lutaka* mud massage by Chwezi novices to restrain their spirit possession) and deal with witchcraft (cf. the Chwezi magic *lushilo* reputed to end all bewitchment). His promiscuity is notorious, and perhaps not so different from the mores of the early kings, but again a contrast with the bodily self-restraint of the new king. The forest, where initiation takes place, is Ryangombe's home, as it was for the Hutu hunters of old and still is for the Twa. In many ways he represents the model of medicinal rule, which continues in the cult and lost grip at the court. The divinations he performs at the Eurythrine tree are of a special kind, aiming to predict and thus empower the client's diurnal acts, turning them into magical acts (M). He decides to assist Ndori in his war with the Shi by enchanting his acts, such as the tapping of the soil and the making of firewood from rival Nzira's tutelary tree. In return Ndori wants to donate to Ryangombe half of his land. He refuses the gift, telling the king that he does not own all that land anyway (which indicates that state building was ongoing rather than completed). He settles for the right to incessant polygamy. By refusing land, Ryangombe sticks to his nomadic life. He is, like the spirits in his Chwezi cult, roaming over the world and keeps his autonomy instead of filling in the vacant position after the divinatory-medicinal model of rule collapsed. The new kings from now on manage to keep the invisible world of ancestors at bay, but at the same time they have to cope with this realm, separate and thus a source of uncertainty. They still need its magic. They conspicuously pretend to have the certainty of executing ritual procedures, claiming to follow prescriptions orally transmitted from a divine past.

The second tale of Ruganzu Ndori makes no mention even of oracles in the unfolding of events (D). Ruse, such as false accusations, replaces magic (R and M–). The king reigns despotically and cannot accept or even imagine the existence of another ruler in the region (N+). He makes sure the last Hutu rebels are exterminated (E+). The following story recounts the death of Ryangombe. It is not Providence communicated through oracle that kills the cult founder, but the attraction of the forest (P). At his own peril he ignores his mother's intuitive warning about not hunting that night. He crawls under the belt she tied at the door, which according to Smith (1970: 17) symbolizes the second cut of the umbilical tie. The combination of forest, nocturnal hunt and maternal resistance evokes male initiation rites. Indeed, the narrator then exceptionally elaborates to explain that initiation rites are human inventions. It is unclear whether his intention is to address his listeners, possibly Christian members of the colonial administration who might regularly have participated in Church services, hence in similarly man-made ceremonies. But the choice of making the origins of initiation an issue in this story seems not coincidental (I). It matches the cultural crisis in Rwandan society in that epoch when divine and secular interventions are differentiated. By this time it was children who were performing divination, and not elders benefiting from life experience and secular wisdom (D). The children are supposed to be real mediums, like Ryangombe possessing the right talent and purified of all worldly secular influences. Ethnic labelling is present (E+).

Under Mibambwe Gisanura (the narrator skips the reigns of Mutara and Kigeri) the various elements of the nascent process fully come to the fore. The court members do not indulge in divination but in discussion about the correct rites. Rather than just disappearing, oracles are replaced (D–), moreover paired with ritualism. Interlocutors seek to show their better knowledge of the customs and rules, which suggests that the court has in the meanwhile formalized ceremonial procedures (F). Following drought across the land – 'Rwandan affaires go bad' – an internal discussion has arisen over the correct rites of enthronement during the last succession. Rituals are secularized, pragmatic procedures. Members of the Rwandan court are requested to identify with the nation, and sacrifice themselves if necessary (N+). There is no magic but ruse (R). The ethnic labels are part of the social structure. Only the king has no ethnicity (E+).

King Cyirima Rujugira (1740) has a well-trained army, coping with the country's *frontière permeable*' (N+), especially due to cattle-raiding and other infiltrations from Igisaka. The army goes to battle with sophisticated tactics, fortifications and traps (R). The trouble with Igisaka continues under King Gahindiro. In the next tale he suffers from an internal dispute with General Biyenge of his Abakemba army, which enjoys much autonomy at a great distance from the court. The king feels that 'foreigners always want to subjugate Rwanda' (Coupez and Kamanzi 1962: 309). He fears poison (*ubumara*) from Igisaka, not magic (M–). We learn about ethnic stereotypes in those days (E+): 'Don't hit a Hutu first because then you curse your spear', and 'however courageous you are, you will always be but a Hutu' (ibid.: 307). The royals seem self-conscious about their natural drives: eating in public destroys the honour of a man.

Situated in the last days of Gahindiro and the succession of King Rwogera (1835), the nineteenth story describes a period of internal conflict and intrigues, accompanied by explicit stereotyping: the 'Hutu' is superstitious and a liar, 'the habit of Hutu' (E+). Again it seems that instability in nation-forming go together with ethnification. At the heart of a massive internal dispute (R) stands general Rugaaju. He does resort to witchcraft, sacrificing a black goat before taking the old king along to hunt. When the king notices bad omens, like his stumble in the morning and a sneeze, the general mocks him for 'Hutu superstitions' he should not have – a reaction that was unthinkable in the first stories. It appears we have reached the peak of a gradual process whereby Providence does not exist (P–) and a secular approach to magic is taken as established (M), while the ethnic category of Hutu represents an anti-person (E+). By lack of alternatives to properly mourn the king's untimely death, secret forms of divination momentarily return on the scene (D). Two groups from the court look for retaliation against Rugaaju, albeit discreetly and without success. Neither prophets nor diviners of spirits find an omen favourable to attack. The recommendation is to 'follow the poets'. Dynastic poets from the court specialize in a secular art. Their oracular predictions turn out to be correct, but only in part.

The last chronicle about King Rwabugiri's reign, starting around 1860, narrates the internal disputes that led to war with the Shi in Ubunyabungo, ruled by Kabego. These external enemies are eventually 'exterminated'. The battle is not preceded by divination (D–), but a young bull is ritually sacrificed to the Itariro spirits before the fight. That sacrifice is the procedure by then (F). The reader may notice another change, as the enemies and absolute 'others' are again Shi, while Hutu are vassals part of society. Through the traditional contract of cattle in return for vassalage (*buhake*) they climb the social ladder. Although not equals, the Hutu farmers are relative outsiders for the dynastic members to establish relations with (E). Like in the days of Nsoro, Cyrima and Kigeri two hundred years earlier, ethnicity is a social category, whereby 'Tutsi' nobility is something the rich in cattle achieve. The Shi are treated as opponents, yet are acknowledged to have their own rules of honour, such as the prohibition to kill a captive king on their own soil.

The Cultural History of Instituting Kingship

Were Ndori and Ryangombe contemporaries? Was it common in King Rujugira's epoch to speak depreciatingly of 'Hutu'? Did Mibambwe scrupulously obey the oracles? The data above do not permit to make such factual statements about events. What our comparison can reveal is cultural process, namely historical patterns hardly attributable to chance. While the double coherence of structuralism is incommensurable with historiography, the triple coherence we introduced does contain a diachronic dimension to demonstrate cultural process.

From just reading the chronicles a cultural process cannot readily be established. Nor does such process ever seem part of the narrator's awareness or intention. Nevertheless, a pattern clearly emerges in Table 9.2. In a time span of four centuries, the dominant cultural themes shift from scoring positively in the beginning (underlined by the bold font of the 2s) to neutrally halfway (the standard font of the 1s) to negatively at the end (light grey 0s). The transition reaches its peak in the twelfth story when Ndori becomes king. By then the royals no longer seem to be believers in Providence (P) and do not consult diviners (D) before important decisions. They have rid themselves of this reciprocity with, and dependence on, the whimsical spirit world. The liberation goes together with their governing a kingdom with provincial chiefs and their talking of Rwanda as a nation (N). The same kings moreover engage in discourse ethnically labelling social groups within their country (E). In this transitional phase the autocratic tendency in ruling and the autonomy in relation to traditional expectations increase (A). Oratory self-praise becomes common among nobles (S). Since Ndori, nobility is a quality that shows in disciplined food-intake. The Rwandan nation-state has sought to inscribe itself on the body, in the way suggested by Chris Taylor (1999). Nothing should come in between King Ndori channelling for the nation the flow of fertility, equated with Imaana. Taylor did not hesitate to describe the cultural structure of flow and blockage as the cosmology behind the genocide in 1994.

Contrasted with Ndori, the figure of cult leader Ryangombe comes to the fore in the thirteenth chronicle. Ryangombe and his cult stand for a leader and institution that cannot be subsumed under the king, which points to radical change. The cult leader is a healer and expert in magic, at ease with hunting and life in the forest amidst animist forces, while the king is not, or at least not anymore. The contingent, spirit-led rule of divination and medicine that generally overshadowed the person of the king has left the court. The diviner-healer is presented as belonging to another world, a clearly new concept that assumes the invisible world of spirits to be separate from the diurnal realm. The separation conflicts with the cosmological reciprocity that allowed commoners to do divinations themselves and to perform rituals for the ancestral spirits at home, a ritual freedom many Sukuma-speaking farmers still cherish today.

Soon after, in the fifteenth account regarding the death of Ryangombe, the secularist issue emerges of the invention of ritual and initiation (I). Strategies in war and conflict have been secularized as well, for the events revolve increasingly around planning and ruse (R) instead of heeding oracular advice. In the more recent period of the kingdom, since Gisanura's reign, the last word at the royal court is given to formalist execution of prescribed rites (F), with emphasis put on knowledge of the court's procedures. That, next to criticism of the diviners' capacity, is another way of marginalizing oracles, mediumistic communication and spirit-led medicinal powers, for which the cult of Ryangombe is better suited. In other words, the double function of mystical and military rule, which according to Smith (1970: 19) pervades the whole of Rwandan mythology and society, appears in our narrative evidence as a division that emerged over time and historically contrasts with the previous union of both. In the union, no distinction is made between sacred and profane. The *bitekerezo* tales 'reflect' on the historical split of this union. The process can be named secularization for constraining the influence of spirits on the world, hence limiting their social significance (cf. Bruce 2011: 2). At the same time the court's procedures are sacralized, imbued with a quality deserving obedience and veneration by commoners, for the integer body of King Ndori, and his successors, channels Imaana. The combination of these two tendencies makes the rise of Rwandan kingship into a particular religious process, whereby kings, nobles and spirits become predictable and disciplined, no longer at the mercy of spiritual or mystical grace. The divine kingship recognized by Africanist historians in the 1960s in fact referred to the sacralization characteristic of an exceptional evolution in a very limited number of states, such as Buganda, Kuba, Kongo and Rwanda. That transition was still endogenous, for it hinged on the collapse of the very pivot of the earlier model.

The last column of Table 9.2 marks each story through a fraction whose numerator totals the obtained scores on the themes and whose denominator is the number of themes present in the respective story, multiplied by the maximum score of 2. Those fractions can be expressed as decimals (note that absence of a theme does not affect the fraction). Figure 9.3 expresses the decimals (in the form of a bold x) on the y-axis of a two-dimensional system of coordinates, whose x-axis represents the chronology of stories. The same figure shows vertical lines for each story, whose direction, upward or downward, depends on the respectively positive or negative scores in Table 9.2, and whose length depends on the number of 2s or 0s scored (with a maximum of five lengths positively or negatively, see +5 and −5 in Figure 9.3). Horizontal lines show the number of 1s for each story (with variable thickness) which is more informative than adding the 1s to the vertical lines as if the values ranging from 0 over 1 to 2 represented a continuous variable.

Figure 9.3 schematizes the process of instituting Rwandan kingship, underlining its gradual nature. The scores pertaining to the epochs of the first 'kings' are high, with several reaching up to five maximums. In the middle a transitional phase appears. The lateral lines of 1s announce the politico-religious transformation: the thickest lateral line in column 13 indicates five 1s. In the second half of the figure, dealing with epochs since AD 1600, the scores drop dramatically, the vertical lines reaching down to five negative scores. The

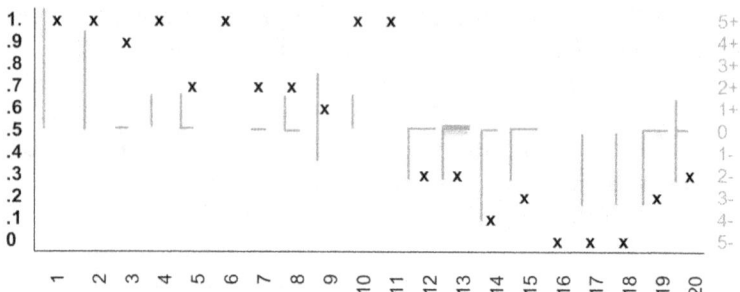

Figure 9.3 Decimals (x) and positive/negative/neutral scores of variables in Gakaniisha's tales. Figure by the author.

cluster of scores in the first half describes a divinatory and medicinal model of rule with a reciprocal attitude to the spirit world. This model evolves in Gakaniisha's tales to take a politico-religious turn. Each tale evokes an ethos of a certain era. Implicit is a shift from one ethos to another. If at both ends of the timeline we must speak of 'kingdoms', these mean two very different things. From our analysis we may conclude that Vansina was right to focus on Ndori, for his reign meant the beginning of the Rwandan kingdom that developed from the 1600s. But Vansina (2004: 46, 220) also claimed that Ndori was an immigrant from the north who imported or created ex nihilo a 'new kingdom'. The least we can infer is that Rwandan oral tradition has for generations reproduced a cultural structure and process that contradict this. In the narratives, Ndori's kingdom meant the end of a previous model of rule while evolving from it. The firmness with which Vansina (ibid.: 10) drew his conclusion is not only unwarranted, given the imperfection he admitted about the sources of Rwandan history. The factualism that led Vansina (ibid.: 217) to dismiss all stories dating before Ndori as 'predynastic fairy tales', and to mercilessly denounce the Rwandan historian Alexis Kagame (1952) for taking these seriously, excluded an important cultural source for reflection on Rwanda's history. Surely, one cannot attribute the gradual, subtle, multilayered and consistent evolution we established in the recounted epochs to fabrications by Rwandan narrators or courts? The invaluable 'reflection' (-*tekerezo*) on history we obtain after the above painstaking analysis is firmly lodged in the *bitekerezo*.

The institution of kingship evolved from reciprocity to autocracy, implying cultural reorganizations of what could be differentiated as religious, political and ethnic relations. The reorganizations were not written down, but since they informed people's priorities and ethos at the time, we may expect oral tradition about the epoch to retain some of their ethos – not unlike the suggestive clichés transmitted across generations about Celts, Romans, Vikings, cowboys or swashbucklers, trickling through in European popular culture and film genres. The collective intangible is the level of cultural process our method registers. The tales disclose the transformation of ethnic relations, at least in the era's ethos, from being reciprocal to becoming hierarchically fixed, even if there were apparent interludes of lesser 'ethnification'. One cannot ignore their relevance for the post-genocidal debate on how culturally entrenched the ethnic dualism of Tutsi and Hutu was and on the role of the Belgian colonizer in rigidifying the categories. The reign of Rwabugiri around 1860, which still represents the pre-colonial period, is recounted as recovering some of the early ethnic reciprocity. The historical fluctuation of ethnic categorizing concurs with Danielle de Lame's (2005: 223) informant reminiscing about pre-genocidal times when a Hutu rich in cattle could become a Tutsi noble. The opposite thesis, on the colonizer arriving after the ethnic damage had already been done, presumes a certain type of society. Its unverified claims can be put to the test with the methodology we proposed here. The method provided us with a 'structure-idealist' corrective to actor-materialism.

The pivotal shift was the king's search for control over spiritual relations. The control over Providence (hence 'death' of its contingency) and the rise of legal formalism imposed by the court ensured predictable outcomes for participants in the ritual sphere. The temptation might be to deduce a process of secularization, in an African version predating Europe's Enlightenment by a century or two. The importance of nation building and ethnification indicates a more subtle internal change, cross-cutting religion, economy and politics, and operating at the pre-conscious level of the actor's decisions, irrespective of social domain. That we are not just dealing with a process of secularization can be observed too in the role of magic (M). The relevance of magical practices in society at large seems unaffected by the Rwandan politico-religious transition, as magic returns with a vengeance in Gakaniisha's final account. Yet, medicinal knowledge becomes a specialization, an art of the occult. At this stage the advantage of ethnography becomes apparent for raising one's sensitivity to local distinctions. The use of magic such as amulets for protection requires a certain level of belief in spirit reciprocity, but not in the consequential way that consulting an oracle does.

Belief operates at another level than the pragmatic motives of the *homo economicus*. For Vansina (2004: 12), local knowledge on ritual and divination belongs to the category of 'esoteric data, [which] are precisely those that are most easily manipulated'. Our study demonstrates the value of such data for historians willing to integrate ideational structure in their interpretations of events. Why did the early kings consult foreign diviners? Vansina (ibid.: 219) opted for the rational motive of them obtaining 'a more stable form of alliance [that] resulted from the more powerful lord delegating the ritual powers to his weaker associate'. He did not consider the subject's cultural necessity to address outsiders to receive the pure, unmediated truth from the spirits. In north-west Tanzania, where the decline of 'traditional religion' has been much slower than in the rest of central and eastern Africa, clients search for diviners living afar to make sure that the oracle will be mediumistic and not fabricated from rumours. Unravelling one's secret path and obtaining correct predictions from the oracle means receiving help from the ancestral spirits, or from Providence, for history to take a propitious turn.

Vansina (2004: 297n8, 218) categorizes oracles under 'the literary genre of cryptic prophecies, related to riddles, [which] seems to have been as much liked by the common people as detective stories are today'. In Gakaniisha's tales, however, the attitude to divination constitutes the crux of Rwandan royal history. Oracles contain structure internalized by members of society. They are inadvertently illustrative of the ethos of a distant past. For anthropologists such data lead to more significant history than information about singular events whose occurrence only the actual witnesses can attest to. Actor-materialism and sociostructural factors cloak cultural structure in history. Out of the blue the reader is thus confronted with a sweeping statement that does not emanate from Vansina's analysis: '[A]t the Nyiginya court, to govern meant, above all, to ensure the performance of the appropriate rituals' (ibid.: 58). This is what we understand by the ceremonial state. However, what is the value of such a statement by an author neglecting 'esoteric' data? Without the data to distinguish ritual formalism from spirit reciprocity, how could he fathom the cultural change that took place during Ndori's reign?

Notes

1. See 'International Religious Freedom Report 2007: Rwanda', by United States Bureau of Democracy, Human Rights and Labour (14 September 2007); cf. http://www.state.gov/ g/drl/rls/irf/2007/90115.htm.

2. Hearing of culture, images come to Chrétien's mind of customs that colonial powers sought to modernize or abolish if their pagan alterity was irremediable. 'It is no longer possible to entertain a caricaturized ethnographic notion of tribal atavisms' (GL 347). The author mentions in the same breath the tribal illusion and the one tool for researching culture. Is he not reifying culture as a static given instead of a holistic dynamic? Reiterating the colonizer's educative mission, 'to march towards progress' (GL 267), a culture's accumulated trial and error, wisdom and maturity, is replaced by a vacuum, to be filled by education, new institutions, 'real democratic practice': 'Europe was not made in a day' (GL 356). The envisaged ideal of global citizenship contrasts with the fieldworker's hard-won insight in the far from inferior life of farmer or herder, away from the artificial happiness and fake liberties of consumer society. Cannot both be African? If only the former is considered realistic, one may conclude like Jean-Pierre Chrétien by wishing for everyone the historian's skill, which 'is in reflecting on long-term processes and past ruptures and challenging fixed memories. Africa also needs this pedagogical shift'. Rwanda and Burundi, profoundly Christianized, are hardly representative of Africa – if such a community existed. Furthermore, is it fair to demand a shift where annihilation took place? The history of the invisible cultural fabric has never been written. The ongoing damage to its cohesion and reproduction remains unacknowledged. That is why Chrétien can, without further due, attribute the success of Islam and Christianity to people's perception of the lesser potency of their *lubale* cosmology (GL 209). More obvious for an ethnographer working in Tanzania is the rapprochement between the local cosmology's take on Christian redemption and the active efforts of White Fathers adapting ('enculturating') the gospel to local beliefs. Christianities arose in the plural.
3. The little we know about Clément Gakaniisha is what Coupez and Kamanzi (1962: 6–7) disclosed: born in 1895, nominally Catholic after 1933, an illiterate narrator and vassal of chief Gashugi. The recordings totalling 585 minutes began in 1952.
4. The main distinction in Rwandan lore is threefold: *imigani*, translatable as moral legends and proverbs, *amakuru*, referring to informative short stories, and *bitekerezo* (also *ibitéekerezo*), chronicles, which due to their reflective nature – their 'philosophy of history' (Smith 1975: 16) – are held in higher regard (I thank Koen Peeters for telling me about the unexcelled Pierre Smith). Vansina (1985: 53) categorizes Gakaniisha's *bitekerezo* as historical narratives, whose versions alter less across time than those of popular tales and epics.
5. After two years of ethnographic fieldwork in a Sukuma-speaking village, I participated in Chwezi initiation ceremonies in 1997 and 2000. Ng'wana Hande, the master of ceremonies, recently confirmed in a personal communication to me that BuChwezi, BuChweeji, BuChwengele, Kubandwa (which he named BuBandwa) and Ryangombe (pronounced

Lya Ng'ombe) refer to the same cult (Nyang'holongo, 11 September 2015).
6. For the sake of presentation in Table 9.2 and Figure 9.3, the first variables (P, D, E, N, M) form the reference, so that the additional variables negatively correlating with these receive an inverted score. For instance, a high level of royal autonomy (A+) will yield a score of 0. An alternative would be to name the variable 'absence' of royal autonomy, as we did with variables Ethnicity and Nation Formation. It would of course not change the pattern established.
7. All date estimations in this section are based on Vansina's genealogical list of Rwandan kings published in Coupez and Kamanzi (1962: 58–59). Vansina (2004: 208ff) later improved the dates and erased some names as fictitious, yet without consequences for our chronology.

Conclusion

REVERSIBLE TRANSITIONS

Kalinga in Rwanda, Rusama in Bunyoro, Timba in Buganda, and so on. Why is each kingdom in the Great Lakes represented by a drum? Because the origin of the kingdom is a drum of affliction. That, in a nutshell, is the gist of our book. It makes the many gathered pieces of the puzzle fall into place, from the call of spirits and the hunt for life in the forest to the king's embodied obligation. Merge the two classic studies of the region by two authors mature enough to look beyond the ethnographer's locality – Vansina on the polity and Janzen on healing – and what does one get? Medicine that rules.

A controversial thesis? Not if one looks at the evidence and gives endogeneity a chance. How to uncover the endogenous logic? The logic is socialized. Initiation conveys its main thrust. Ritual initiation turns out, invariably and in defiance of Victor Turner's watershed division, to revolve around the application and acquisition of medicine. The Sukuma bundle of magical plants entitled 'forest within the home' epitomizes the core act of power in the region (see left sphere in Figure 0.3 in the Introduction). It is a power that heals, not one that subjugates. It is only logical that the most revered member of the community should excel in it. A model of rule has a cultural basis: what is new?

Why then did medicinal rule remain unacknowledged in African studies? Why could initiatory power not inspire research about political, economic and other systems? It is not that the 'value system' was never considered. On the contrary, numerous applications of local terminologies and schemes of African cosmologies in analogy with Western belief systems have been published. The challenge has been more fundamental, for the author's very premises are at stake. In European (endogenous) history, power is impact is government – an evolution leading to the monarch's hegemony, against which the alternative emerged of parliamentary democracy. The polity prism: that is how I hazarded to coin this model of European civilization rooted in the Greek and Roman 'miracle'. A polity conflates society and political organization into so-called citizenship. That is not how society works in our region under study. The polity type of kingship, governing a geographically demarcated population through a state, has been exceptional, a freak phenomenon, as discussed in Part III. True enough, this type of state resembled European monarchies, but its roots were entirely different. We encountered a major sociostructural similarity with European rule in how politics and religion split – the latter justifying the former – because that is what the formidable Buganda state did around 1700: it separated the offices of king and priest, which oral tradition recounts in terms of King Tebandeke's mediumship turned madness. This book has concentrated on the endogenous factors determining the evolution to kingship. Before specifying these, a quick intermezzo is in order on the Western perception of magic.

How come the obvious difference between cultural backgrounds of kingship gets so easily overshadowed by the sociostructural similarities of such rule across the world? An unspoken premise says that all societies have in origin been magical, so their salient cultural differences will not be found in that premodern past. This is the dominant way of thinking about magic, as a universal practice, supposedly natural (e.g. due to a cognitive module) and overcome through modern civilization. The other way, embraced in this book, is that magic partakes of the broader set of practices oriented on well-being, (mis)fortune and healing, which we call medicine. Medicine has a regional history from which various principles and experiential frames developed.

The kingship proper to the ceremonial state had its own regional roots. It evolved out of medicinal rule by magnifying certain elements: taboo and ceremony. We remember the 'come-out' (namely consecrated) recipient of medicine in seventeenth century Loango, as described by Dapper. I argue that the personal obligation he or she obtained in the forest carried the seeds for the later ceremonial, instituted obsession with prohibition: 'Follow the rule, or things will go wrong'. More importantly, at the same time this kingship attacked the pivots that had made centralized power possible in central and east Africa: divination and mediumship, initiation, association and medicine (see middle sphere in Figure 0.3). Together they specify the fertility fractal of the forest-within. They allow for the divinatory, contingent experience that is life. Aversion to contingency motivates the more autocratic type of reign. The reversions presented in Parts I, II and III, and summarized below, bespeak the transition.

Vansina saw an Age of Kings succeed the Age of Chiefs. This book's main contribution has been to demonstrate that the transition has been from medicinal rule to ceremonial state. There is no reason to assume that it was other than an endogenous evolution, ultimately rooted in the divinatory societies of hunters. What the ceremonial state actually did was to undermine something that European Christians would never associate with spirit possession: the democratizing effect of depending on spirit guidance. To that, autocrats were aversive. Indeed, we should ask ourselves who the 'coming-outer' was, from which developed the *kum*, meaning both chief (in the equatorial west) and healer (in the equatorial east). The answer is: the same chosen and receptive individual as in divinatory societies. So long as spirits roam in the forest, to be discovered and inhabiting a charm, virtually anybody can claim a forest and attract customers for a cult, which one day or in the next generation might mature into an association with titled ranks, to eventually geographically outline a chiefdom. To extend this endogenous logic to the fringes of Bantu-speaking Africa, I have subsumed mediumship as well as magic under the medicinal. They are all forms of communication with the spirit world. The dramatic type of trance, such as dissociation or speaking in tongues, is not how spirit mediumship commonly showed. Dancing or dreaming medicine articulates the forest within. Most communities privilege plant knowledge above the old shamanic-like experience. In all directions of the compass, save in the humid rainforests, an agricultural concern appears. So long as fertility, and by extension rain medicine, could be inherited by descendants of the cult founder, there were communities requesting to be given the medicine. We encountered intermediate situations. Southall observed Mambisa leaders collaborating without paramount chief. None of them was confirmed yet in a 'coming out of the forest' ritual like the Alur rulers. They were trying to translate medicinal capacity into rule in order to win over the local community for what must have been a nascent kind of chieftaincy. The equation of power and medicine – how to adequately bring it home?

Time stood still during a day of fieldwork in the mid-1990s. A medical anthropologist, after visiting me in the field, confided in the evening that the people I was working with in the healer's compound were marginal figures because they were patients, and several of them moreover were possessed by a spirit. I was a bit speechless, for the renowned healers teaching me about medicine had not made a secret of their own former illness or their flight for months in the forest long ago: a kind of madness, certainly, that had started off their career. It is the sacrifice that men and women are willing to make before they morally guide the community. Nobody can heal unless having been there too. Every patient is a potential healer after recovery. The experiential frame enacted by sacrificial medicine or spirit possession is the beginning of all rule, which no worthy head of a group, cult or chiefdom will want to escape. The preconscious cultural structure shines through. In a society where the sole mode of production is life, interconnecting all beings and things, someone's health cannot be separated from other social events (cf. left sphere in Figure 0.3). Nobody feels untouchable except in a game of make-belief, because basically 'What goes around comes around' as we would say, so also positively the invisible other may be hoped for to act upon one's sacrifice. Why would the idea of plural modes of production, which would carve up our life into the workings of nature, society, rationality, affect, and so on, be empirically more sound?

The cult founder, whose descendants transformed the spirit-mediated medicine into a hereditary rule, sometimes was a woman. We had enough reason to conclude, among others, that the female healer-diviner Kitami set up a drum of affliction from which sprang the Ndorwa kingdom with the same name. Its dynasty was sufficiently short lived to prevent the court historians from covering up its cultic basis. Such basis intrinsically jeopardizes the hereditary claim on the throne by descendants without mediumistic call. Indicatively for our thesis, the spirit call is across the region the condition for initiation into chiefship, underlined by the rites of enthronement and transgression. Several specific histories could be reconstructed in support of the cultic basis of chieftaincy. For example, after the invasion of the Kitara empire by a Luo clan around 1700, the survivors of the dynasty moved south, according to oral tradition in the form of a cult to which the kingship had reverted, headed by the spirit medium Ryangombe. Not much later the first chiefdoms emerged in the Sukuma-Nyamwezi plains. Every time, however, we historically situated an event, doubts arose on how unique the phenomenon was, and on whether reversions would not be a better way of presenting the evolution.

A certain medicine for 'rain-trying' was the bare meaning to which Kishina's chieftaincy was reduced. Although the sociostructural reduction was characteristic of the colonial period, the meaning of medicine was not a new reality after (post)colonial interventions. From his historical account we learned that medicine had always been central in his Sukuma chiefdom. Remarkably, it was also a transmittable trade of title and fee, as was the chief's ritual purification of twins. The trade of chiefly expertise as if it was cultic knowledge did not undermine the meaning of his rule because cult and chieftaincy are cognate. Kishina himself had made the suggestion in our interview. In the chief we might as well see a cult founder operating in the same field as healers do, all excelling in the one mode of production. Hence, well into the postcolonial period, the few Sukuma chiefs who pretended to continue their rule and were succeeded, could do so while being treated respectfully by elders, as if doing their duty as they always had, and without being conspicuous to the government or district heads, since the purely political-governmental implications were typically limited, and not of the kind alarming a state virtually absent in rural areas.

An important addition is that the chief's healing was meant for the collective. This level of influence was dramatically reduced by the colonizer. Moreover, medicine pertained to the entirety of life and society, so could not be a separate mode of production. Therein the colonizer had created a new situation, which Fortes and Evans-Pritchard did not fathom, as they placidly commented on the 'ritual functions' (which they admittedly put between quotation marks) that African kings spontaneously retain under European rule. As I have argued, the medicinal charm refers to the one mode of production on which also chiefship draws, and which the concepts of ritual and religion artificially split.

Historical accounts may detail for a certain group which institution came first: cult or chieftaincy. The risk is to overlook, by lack of information, evolutions in the past. It is impossible to record all the times the institutions reverted to the other pole. Is to discern the polarity not the advance an anthropologized history should content itself with? The ease with which the one transforms into the other should draw our attention. Why is the main medicinal plant of initiation called *ntemi*, 'the chief'? Why are the holders of high ranks, responsible for collecting the fees of initiates in the districts, denoted literally as 'chiefs' under the head of the cult? The two institutions of cult and chieftaincy have a cultural model in common so that the one readily evolves into the other. They directly influence each other. Their rivalry should not be seen as proof of cultural distance, or structural opposition as literature on the Great Lakes has suggested: the cult's resistance to hegemony, of chief or colonizer, was possible due to the mentioned democratizing force of spirits, a shamanic practice known by hunters, but the political resistance did not culturally inhere the institution. Initiatory societies were persecuted by colonial governments, and have been dealt a bad hand in anthropology too. Evans-Pritchard was convinced that the Zande triad of magic, witchcraft and oracles could do without the fourth of cults (which comprises initiation and association). Our cultural comparison of magic and our analytical map divulging the cultural diversity and influences in the Zande complex both pointed to the contrary. A perplexing consensus reigned the discipline in the mid twentieth century that the institution interchangeably denoted as cult, closed or initiatory association and sometimes religious movement, was a fairly recent reaction to centralized rule. Some presumed that cults came after such institution, despite important archaeological findings such as those by Pierre de Maret on shells dating from around AD 800, which suggests no commercial value other than social payment for an initiatory association. Not only politics but the economy itself might have to be subsumed under medicine in this part of the world.

Positivism is a veil disguising influences that cannot be seen. Replete with what it positively exposes, it rarely divulges what cannot be proven. An unpleasant reminder of the positivistic veil were the historical estimations, among others by Vansina and Ranger, of the age-old practice of spirit possession in certain locales. Absence of a specific verb or noun for spirit possession, except for metaphors like 'climbing' (the spirit), led them to assign a date for the practice that corresponded with the first observations and written reports, typically the decades of sociopolitical upheaval at the end of the nineteenth century when colonization peaked. The advent of our civilization and exploitation were supposed to be the cause, rather than just stimuli of new cults. Past shamanic traditions that interconnect Bantu-speaking groups were conveniently forgotten. Little corrective could be expected since cultural comparison died out, and the ethnographers culturally particularized groups, as if isolated from the surrounding region and humanity. It had become the accepted antidote to wretched universalism. A meso-anthropology of regional history has been our alternative.

The case that set us thinking fundamentally about 'anthropologizing' the historical method was the lexico-positivism of Vansina's reliance on words and/as things. In large parts of eastern Africa, not least in those areas where these medicinal associations were most influential, cults have been denied their vibrant ongoing past, quite simply by lack of a local generic name for the institution. The sour deal has persisted up to now.

Further nuances must be made, first of all, about the drum of affliction or healing cult. Its meaning should be broadened to include what Europeans understand by the political. The ritual initiation in the forest exudes the power on which the community as a whole relies, and from which the ill incidentally tap. It is healing in René Devisch's

(1993) sense of life-giving, an affect not to be reduced to the medical field of illness and treatment. The rites of passage on the one hand and the cults treating a certain type of affliction on the other are different specializations of the same power. The affliction resorts under the many situations that lack 'coolness', from the proto-Bantu stem *pol*. The ritual of life-giving restores it. Therefore, we treat the drum, a container resounding thanks to animal skin, as a charm communicating with spirits. To broaden the meaning of medicine to comprise leadership and rule, we should ask how kings represent themselves, for they tell us, quite directly, about their origin, and about the ongoing significance of that origin, through the emblems of drum, leopard skin, birth of twins, and rain. What these share is the contact with the forest, the wild outside, which can be domesticated for the good of the land and the people. The incited dance, chant or possession: all frame an experience, an affect, that matters and that transcends the medical aspect of medicine.

As a second nuance regarding the regional history of chiefs and kings, the 'come-out' consecrated healer with word stem *kum* (and *gang*) is joined in an alternation by the matured 'great one', with word stem *kul* (and *tem/ten* among others). The two, translatable as chief and headman, complement each other, their polarity occasioning further divisions of rank. Their complementarity should not tempt one to recognize in it the polarity of politics and religion, or secular and sacred rule, for both base their power on the initiatory ritual. The Tio case illustrated the dynamic in its complexity, after we reinterpreted Vansina's data, having to meticulously disentangle these from the polity prism.

Thirdly – and the most critical readers may exclaim their relief at this stage – I am aware that this book offered mainly a rationale for how three types of rule relate to each other, while the differentiation of each, which would have interested many, has not been done. One reason is that my focus on endogenous 'cultural' factors scantily exposed sociostructural factors. I doubt that any would have been of significance to our argument though. I hinted at a few alternative paths. For instance, the centralization of states in south-eastern Africa differed from the growth of ceremonial states in central Africa and the Great Lakes. In the chiefdoms out of which grew the Zulu and Swazi kingdoms, general meetings beyond the village level took place: the *pitso* assembly among the Sotho, and the *libandla* among the Nguni.

Another reason for little subcategorization is the obvious limitation of cases. Much more ethnographic material on the precolonial situation could have been involved. Archives could have been consulted to verify the authors' works we exegetically reinterpreted. So much has not been done yet that Africanist anthropology might do one day. Right now, I am content to have a rationale close at hand to help colleagues in their debates, for instance on whether 'the African polity is government' or 'the African polity is religious', where I might make them agree that both are true but applicable to different times and types of rule in east and central Africa.

Finally, we must distinguish the reversions that surfaced at key moments in the book's three parts. Let me emphasize that I do not reject the word 'evolution' in relation to history and society, nor its sister 'transition', as long as the evolution is seen as reversible. Reversions at the social level, which show in aversions at the personal level of affects, have been pivotal to our approach. Reversions offer another take on history, allowing for an ongoing past, beyond the events. Instead of phases in a linear evolution, or the tree-like multilinear construct we began our search with in the Introduction, we obtain a culturally logical scheme of poles of endogenous transitions. In the background (hence the dashed lines in Figure 0.3) lingers the cultural fractal of domesticated fertility, the forest-within, symbolizing life as the one mode of production. Chiefs and kings are placed between quotation marks, for they are our Western transplanted terms, labels tagged to moments in the process. The process itself stands out as the central issue. The double arrow points out the sociocultural tensions pivotal to it. The aversions and reversions are identified as endogenous factors of change.

Can our scheme be falsified? An important test for a cultural structure is to verify how the institution it supposedly spawned reacts under radically changed circumstances, and quite plainly if that institution is changed. We cannot do without historical data to establish the key matter: whether the factors we deemed essential are affected in practice during the transitions. The next paragraphs illustrate some of the pivots discussed in the chapters.

Suppression of the role of divination and medicine announced the rise of the ceremonial state. The colonial factor cannot be denied. The annual *muganuro* festival organized by the king of Burundi was, from the 1920s, purified of its pagan elements and Christianized. The original cult objects were forbidden. The mission was haughtily erected in the sacred woods of the royal shrine. Similarly, the functions of the Rwandese king's diviner and the *mwiru* master of the *muganuro* ritual were abolished. The missionaries convinced the baptized king to abolish the Imandwa cult, the local version of the Chwezi cult. In Bukoba the Mukama's son burned the main shrine of the Chwezi cult in the name of Christianity.

However, Christianity exerted an effect that roughly repeated what had happened centuries earlier in those societies whose chieftaincy transformed into ceremonial state. In the 1980s the Kabaka and his family in the palace distanced themselves from their people's worship of Lubaale spirits; they minimized the efficacy of their own royal ancestors. But the Christian influences had merely emboldened the existing anti-mediumistic and anti-initiatory sentiments in the court during the long royal search for independence from clans and diviners. In the early nineteenth century, Ssuuna II at his accession had discontinued the Kabaka's ritual of initiation, or 'maturation' (from proto-Bantu *kul*), organized by the chiefs of other clans. The divergence from medicinal rule continued when Mutesa I reduced the significance of the Lubaale spirits in kingship, and of the priesthood serving them.

Before Christian impact, states had been forming where local cosmologies underwent an anti-shamanic phase. The personal obligation or inherited charm transformed into a veneration sanctioned by priests collaborating with the court. The Rozvi empire in the southeast personified the Mwari spirit into a deity at a shrine championing traditional law and custom. Further south, Shaka expelled all rainmakers from his Zulu kingdom to become an autocratic ruler. The anti-medicinal move permitted the emergence of his conquest state.

Shyaam initially epitomized medicinal rule. He founded the Kuba kingdom, though, by ensuring that his successors were left with precise rules of succession, protocol, tribute, corvée labour and an army. His first successor cunningly organized the initiations of young men at the capital under the leadership of a prince. In the eighteenth century the ninth king of Kuba dissolved all spirit cults in the region. Earlier on, the court had arranged for its own publicity in songs on nature spirits praising the kingdom; later it introduced a deity. The age-grades were abolished in 1908. The kingdom knew an anti-associational moment.

The critical moment in the Tio kingdom came as late as the twentieth century, when kings wanted to postpone their *lisee* initiation against the forest-masters insisting. Soon the anti-medicinal and anti-initiatory process sped up but its outcome was not a new phase or stronger centralization. The Tio institution of forest-masters withered away in the mid twentieth century when they no longer received haunches of the hunt and people no longer believed in the *nkira* nature spirits. The king could not maintain the system by himself. Without the cultural structure initiated, the house of cards collapsed with him on top. For the rest, it seems that, across the region, the kings who colluded with the colonial government and did not let the opportunity pass by of mirroring European autocracy also disappeared with decolonization.

Evidence of the above processes, albeit in the long-term and in one fairly linear direction, we found in Rwandan oral tradition on kingship. Ndori's reign was the linchpin of a transition that took place during successive dynastic reigns. The reciprocal model of rule, hinged on divinatory logic and initiatory membership transcending social classes and categories, evolved into a model of autocratic rule, allowing the king to keep spirit matters at bay as well as safely formalized in rigid court-controlled rituals while an ethnically hierarchical nation could be built. The string of twenty narratives covering several centuries lays bare the generationally transmitted and collectively shared, if largely implicit, ideas about epochs. In this and all the reinterpreted cases, more historical investigation is needed to falsify or corroborate, but the Rwandan narrated ideas exhibited with impressive homogeneity a structure and a change in time that confirmed our ethnography as well as our comparative analysis for the wider region of central and east Africa. Narration, in the Rwandan tradition of evoking historical trends, articulates the evolution of institutions indirectly yet distinctly. We learned to understand 'institution' as a noun derived from the verb 'instituting' – that is, not as a given but as a practice and a process that is contextually and historically situated.

At the microlevel we were thrilled to discover that the offshoot known as kingship resided, endogenously, in the most diverse societies of the region. Lele communities of hunters in the rainforest had been replacing about every ten years the fortune magic of their divinatory societies by the rule of the witch-finding cult. The cult superseded people's reciprocity with the spirits. The witch-finding transcended village communities, like a kingdom does, for it also silenced the diviners traditionally convening at district level in a nascent form of chieftaincy. Sooner or later the orthodox witch-finding cult collapsed under its own contradictions. The point of gravity in society could revert to the cross-cutting divinatory societies. The alternation succinctly captures the medicinal, including divinatory reversions that have marked the history of the region.

The unwritten past of precolonial Africa confronts the scholar with an intriguing puzzle. The old solution has been a well-argued surmise about sequences of historical events on the basis of what has been collected and encountered in pits, lexicons and stories. The ethnographically based cultural structure through which we have systematically compared societies seems no less feasible an approach to comprehending 'kingship'. The correct tense, past or present or habitual, for speaking about our scheme of transition may remain a moot question, but the anthropological perspective lending coherence to the data, and more fundamentally the obtained insight into alternative perspectives, should not be ignored by the Africanist historian. The dialogue has just begun.

REFERENCES

Abraham, D. 1964. 'Ethno-history of the Empire of Mutapa', in J. Vansina, R. Mauny and L.V. Thomas (eds), *The Historian in Tropical Africa: Studies Presented and Discussed at the Fourth International African Seminar at the University of Dakar, Senegal 1961*. London: Oxford University Press (IAI), pp. 104–126.

Appadurai, A. 1996. *Modernity at Large*. Minneapolis, MN: University of Minnesota Press.

Bateson, G. (1972) 1990. *Steps to an Ecology of Mind*. New York: Ballantine.

Bekaert, S. 1998. 'Multiple Levels of Meaning and the Tension of Consciousness: How to Interpret Iron Technology in Bantu Africa', *Archaeological Dialogues* 5(1): 6–29.

Bernault, F. 2006. 'Body, Power and Sacrifice in Equatorial Africa', *The Journal of African History* 47(2): 207–39.

Biebuyck, D., and K. Mateene (eds). 1969. *The Mwindo Epic from the Banyanga (Zaire)*. Berkeley, CA: University of California Press.

Binsbergen, W. van. 1977. 'Regional and Non-Regional Cults of Affliction in Western Zambia', in R. Werbner (ed.), *Regional Cults*. London: Academic Press.

Bonnafé, P. 1978. *Nzo lipfu, le lignage de la mort: la sorcellerie, idéologie de la lutte sociale sur le plateau kukuya*. Nanterre: Labethno.

Bourdieu, P. 1979. *La Distinction: Critique Sociale du Jugement*. Paris: Minuit.

———. 1980. *Le Sens Pratique*. Paris: Minuit.

Bradbury, R. 1964. 'The Historical Uses of Comparative Ethnography with Special Reference to Benin and the Yoruba', in J. Vansina, R. Mauny and L.V. Thomas (eds), *The Historian in Tropical Africa: Studies Presented and Discussed at the Fourth International African Seminar at the University of Dakar, Senegal 1961*. Oxford: Oxford University Press, pp. 145–164.

Broushaki, F., et al. 2016. 'Early Neolithic Genomes from the Eastern Fertile Crescent', *Science* 353(6298): 499–503.

Bruce, S. 2011. *Secularization: In Defence of an Unfashionable Theory*. Oxford: Oxford University Press.

Bruman, C. 1999. 'Writing for Culture: Why a Successful Concept Should Not be Discarded', *Current Anthropology* 40: S1–25.

Burke, P. 2015. *The French Historical Revolution: The Annales School 1929–2014*. Cambridge: Polity.

Chabal, P., and J.-P. Daloz. 1999. *Africa Works: Disorder as Political Instrument.* Bloomington, IN: Indiana University Press.

Chrétien, J.-P. 2003. *The Great Lakes of Africa: 2000 Years of History.* New York: Zone.

Claessen, H. 2011. 'On Chiefs and Chiefdoms', *Social Evolution & History* 10(1): 5–26.

Clifford, J. 1988. *The Predicament of Culture: Twentieth-Century Ethnography, Literature, and Art.* Cambridge, MA: Harvard University Press.

Comaroff, J., and J.L. Comaroff. 1993. 'Introduction', in J. Comaroff (ed.), *Modernity and its Malcontents: Ritual and Power in Postcolonial Africa.* Chicago, IL: University of Chicago Press, pp. xi–xxxvii.

Cory, H. 1951. *The Ntemi: Traditional Rites of a Sukuma Chief in Tanganyika.* London: Macmillan.

Coupez, A., and Th. Kamanzi. 1962. *Récits historiques Rwanda: Dans la version de C. Gakanisha. Texte et traduction.* Tervuren: MRAC, coll. Annales, Sciences humaines, linguistique, Vol. 43.

Dapper, O. 1668. *Naukeurige beschrijvinge der Afrikaensche geweste.* Amsterdam: Jacob Van Meurs.

De Craemer, W., J. Vansina and R. Fox. 1976. 'Religious Movements in Central Africa', *Comparative Studies of Society and History* 18: 458–75.

Descola P. 1994. *In the Society of Nature: A Native Ecology in Amazonia.* Cambridge: Cambridge University Press.

Devisch, R. 1993. *Weaving the Threads of Life: The Khita Gyn-Eco-Logical Healing Cult among the Yaka.* Chicago, IL: Chicago University Press.

Douglas, M. 1963. *The Lele of the Kasai.* London: International African Institute (IAI).

Doyle, S. 2007. 'The Cwezi-Kubandwa Debate: Gender, Hegemony and Precolonial Religion in Bunyoro, Western Uganda', *Africa* 77(4): 559–81.

Dupré, M.-C., and B. Pinçon. 1997. *Métallurgie et politique en Afrique centrale: Deux mille ans de vestiges sur les plateaux batéké Gabon, Congo, Zaïre.* Paris: Karthala.

Eglash, R. 1999. *African Fractals: Modern Computing and Indigenous Design.* New Brunswick, NJ: Rutgers University Press.

Evans-Pritchard, E.E. 1937. *Witchcraft, Oracle and Magic among the Azande.* Oxford: Oxford University Press.

———. 1958. 'The Ethnic Composition of the Azande of Central Africa', *Anthropological Quarterly* 31(4): 95–118.

———. 1960. 'A Contribution to the Study of Zande Culture', *Africa* 30(4): 309–24.

———. 1963. 'A Further Contribution to the Study of Zande Culture', *Africa* 33(3): 183–97.

———. 1965a. 'A Final Contribution to the Study of Zande Culture', *Africa* 35(1): 1–7.

———. 1965b. *Theories of Primitive Religion.* London: Clarendon.

Fabian, J. 1983. *Time and the Other: How Anthropology Makes its Objects.* New York: Columbia University Press.

Feeley-Harnik, G. 1985. 'Issues in Divine Kingship', *Annual Review of Anthropology* 14(1): 273–313.
Feenberg, A. 1998. *Questioning Technology*. New York: Routledge.
Feierman, S. 1972. 'Concepts of Sovereignty among the Shambaa and their Relation to Political Action'. Unpublished doctoral dissertation, Oxford University.
———. 1995. 'Healing as Social Criticism in the Time of Colonial Conquest', *African Studies* 54(1): 73–88.
Fortes, M., and E. Evans-Pritchard. 1940. 'Introduction', in M. Fortes and E. Evans-Pritchard (eds), *African Political Systems*. Oxford: Oxford University Press, pp. 1–23.
Freedman, J. 1974. 'Ritual and History: The Case of Nyabingi', *Cahiers d'études africaines* 14(53): 170–80.
Geertz, C. (1973) 1993. *The Interpretation of Cultures*. London: Fontana Press.
Geschiere, P. 1997. *The Modernity of Witchcraft: Politics and the Occult in Postcolonial Africa*. Charlottesville, VA: University of Virginia Press.
Gluckman, M. (1956) 1970. *Custom and Conflict in Africa*. Oxford: Blackwell.
———. 1940. 'The Kingdom of the Zulu of South Africa', in M. Fortes and E. Evans-Pritchard (eds), *African Political Systems*. Oxford: Oxford University Press, pp. 25–55.
Goffman, E. 1974. *Frame Analysis: An Essay on the Organisation of Experience*. Harmondsworth: Penguin.
Gordon, D. 2016. '(Dis)Embodying Sovereignty: Divine Kingship in Central African Historiography', *The Journal of African History* 57(1): 47–67.
Graeber, D. 2011. 'The Divine Kingship of the Shilluk: On Violence, Utopia, and the Human Condition, or, Elements for an Archaeology of Sovereignty', *HAU* 1(1): 1–62.
Gunderson, F. 2010. *Sukuma Labor Songs from Western Tanzania: 'We Never Sleep, We Dream of Farming'*. Leiden: Brill.
Gwassa, C. 1972. 'Kinjikitile and the Ideology of Maji Maji', in T. Ranger and I. Kimambo (eds), *The Historical Study of African Religion*. London: Heinemann, pp. 202–217.
Heusch, L. de. 1966. *Le Rwanda et la Civilisation Interlacustre*. Brussels: Université Libre de Bruxelles.
———. 1972. *Mythes et rites bantous: Le Roi ivre ou l'Origine de l'État*. Paris: Gallimard.
———. 1985. *Sacrifice in Africa: A Structuralist Approach*. Manchester: Manchester University Press.
———. 1987. 'Power, Process and Transformation: Essays in Memory of Max Gluckman', *Social Analysis: The International Journal of Social and Cultural Practice* 22: 22–29.
———. 1997. 'The Symbolic Mechanisms of Sacred Kingship: Rediscovering Frazer', *The Journal of the Royal Anthropological Institute* 3(2): 213–32.
Hocart, A. 1970. *Kings and Councillors: An Essay in the Comparative Anatomy of Human Society*. Chicago, IL: University of Chicago Press.

Hodder, I., and S. Hutson. 2003. *Reading the Past: Current Approaches to Interpretation in Archaeology*. Cambridge: Cambridge University Press.

Holbraad, M. 2007. 'The Power of Powder: Multiplicity and Motion in the Divinatory Cosmology of Cuban Ifá (or Mana, Again)', in A. Henare, M. Holbraad and S. Wastell (eds), *Thinking through Things: Theorising Artefacts Ethnographically*. London: Routledge, pp. 189–225.

Holmes, C., and A. Austen. 1972. 'The Pre-colonial Sukuma', *Cahiers d'Histoire Mondiale* 14(1): 377–405.

Horton, R. 1967. 'African Traditional Thought and Western Science', *Africa* 37: 50–71, 155–87.

Janzen, J.M. 1982. *Lemba (1650–1930): A Drum of Affliction in Africa and the New World*. New York: Garland.

———. 1992. *Ngoma: Discourses of Healing in Central and Southern Africa*. Berkeley, CA: University of California Press.

Jerardino, A., et al. 2014. 'Cultural Diffusion Was the Main Driving Mechanism of the Neolithic Transition in Southern Africa', *PLOS ONE* 9(12): e113672.

Kagame, A. 1952. *Le code des institutions politiques du Rwanda précolonial*. Brussels: Institut royal colonial belge.

Kalb, D., and H. Tak. 2005. *Critical Junctions: Anthropology and History beyond the Cultural Turn*. Oxford: Berghahn Books.

Kantorowicz, E. 1957. *The King's Two Bodies: A Study in Medieval Political Theology*. Princeton, NJ: Princeton University Press.

Kisangani, E. 2016. *Historical Dictionary of the Democratic Republic of the Congo*. New York: Rowman & Littlefield.

Kishina, S. n.d. *Historia ya Bulima*. S.l.

Kodesh, N. 2007. 'History from the Healer's Shrine: Genre, Historical Imagination, and Early Ganda History', *Comparative Studies in Society and History* 49(3): 527–52.

———. 2010. *Beyond the Royal Gaze: Clanship and Public Healing in Buganda*. Charlottesville, VA: University of Virginia Press.

Kopytoff, I. 1999. 'Permutations in Patrimonialism and Populism: The Aghem Chiefdoms of Western Cameroon', in S. McIntosh (ed.), *Beyond Chiefdoms: Pathways to Complexity in Africa*. Cambridge: Cambridge University Press, pp. 88–96.

Lagae, C.R. 1926. *Les Azande ou Niam-Niam: L'organisation Zande, croyances réligieuses et magiques, coutûmes familiales*. Bibliothèque Congo Vol. 18. Brussels: Vromant.

Lame, D. de. 2005. *A Hill among a Thousand: Transformations and Ruptures in Rural Rwanda*. Madison, WI: University of Wisconsin Press.

Latour, B. 1993. *We Have Never Been Modern*. London: Prentice Hall.

Leach, E. 1960. 'The Frontiers of "Burma"', *Comparative Studies in Society and History* 3(1): 49–68.

Lemarchand, R. 1977. *African Kingships in Perspective: Political Change and Modernization in Monarchical Settings*. London: Cass.

Lévi-Strauss, C. 1949. *Les Structures Elémentaires de la Parenté*. Paris: PUF.
———. 1972. *Structural Anthropology I*. London: Penguin Books.
Luhmann, N. 1995. *Social Systems*. Stanford, CA: Stanford University Press.
Luongo, K. 2006. 'If You Can't Beat Them, Join Them: Government Cleansings of Witches and Mau Mau in 1950s Kenya', *History in Africa* 33: 451–71.
MacGaffey, W. 1986. *Religion and Society in Central Africa: The BaKongo of Lower Zaire*. Chicago, IL: University of Chicago.
Mahieu, W. de. 1985. *Qui a Obstrué la Cascade?: Analyse Sémantique du Rituel de la Circoncision Chez les Komo du Zaire*. Cambridge: Cambridge University Press; Paris: Editions de la Maison des Sciences de l'Homme.
Malinowski, B. 1922. *Argonauts of the Western Pacific*. London: Routledge and Kegan Paul.
Maret, P. de. 1985. *Fouilles archéologiques dans la vallée du Haut-Lualaba, Zaire*. Vol. 120. Tervuren: MRAC/RMCA.
Millroth, B. 1965. *Lyuba, Traditional Religion of the Sukuma*. Uppsala: Almqvist and Wiksell.
Mudimbe, V. 1988. *The Invention of Africa: Gnosis, Philosophy, and the Order of Knowledge*. Bloomington, IN: Indiana University Press.
Newbury, D. 2007. 'Contradictions at the Heart of the Canon: Jan Vansina and the Debate over Oral Historiography in Africa, 1960–1985', *History in Africa* 34: 213–54.
Ogot, B. 1964. 'Kingship and Statelessnes among the Nilotes', in J. Vansina, R. Mauny and L.V. Thomas (eds), *The Historian in Tropical Africa: Studies Presented and Discussed at the Fourth International African Seminar at the University of Dakar, Senegal 1961*. Oxford: Oxford University Press, pp. 284–304.
Oliver, R. 1966. 'The Problem of the Bantu Expansion', *The Journal of African History* 7(3): 361–76.
Ortner, S. 2006. *Anthropology and Social Theory: Culture, Power, and the Acting Subject*. Durham, NC: Duke University Press.
Packard, R. 1981. *Chiefship and Cosmology: An Historical Study of Political Competition*. Bloomington, IN: Indiana University Press.
Parkin, D. 1966. 'Voluntary Associations as Institutions of Adaptation', *Man* l: 90–94.
———. 2007. 'Introduction: Emergence and Convergence', in D. Parkin and S. Ulijascek (eds), *Holistic Anthropology: Emergence and Convergence*. Oxford: Berghahn Books, pp. 1–20.
Pereira, D.P. 1892. *Esmeraldo de Situ Orbis*. Lisbon: Imprensa Nacional. Retrieved 30 April 2018 from https://archive.org/details/esmeraldodesitu00peregoog.
Radcliffe-Brown, A. 1940. 'Preface', in M. Fortes and E. Evans-Pritchard (eds), *African Political Systems*. Oxford: Oxford University Press, pp. xi–xxiii.
Ranger, T. 1973. 'Territorial Cults in the History of Central Africa', *The Journal of African History* 14(4): 581–97.

Ranger, T., and I. Kimambo. 1972. 'Introduction', in T. Ranger and I. Kimambo (eds), *The Historical Study of African Religion*. London: Heinemann, pp. 1–26.

Ray, B. 1991. *Myth, Ritual, and Kingship in Buganda*. New York: Oxford University Press.

Reefe, T. 1981. *The Rainbow and the Kings: A History of the Luba Empire to 1891*. Berkeley, CA: University of California Press.

Reynolds-Whyte, S. 1997. *Questioning Misfortune: The Pragmatics of Uncertainty in Eastern Uganda*. Cambridge: Cambridge University Press.

Richards, A. 1940. 'The Political System of the Bemba Tribe, North-Eastern Rhodesia', in M. Fortes and E. Evans-Pritchard (eds), *African Political Systems*. Oxford: Oxford University Press (IAI), pp. 83–120.

Robertshaw, P. 2012. 'African Archaeology, Multidisciplinary Reconstructions of Africa's Recent Past, and Archaeology's Role in Future Collaborative Research', *African Archaeological Review* 29: 95–108.

Rose-Hunt, N. 1999. *A Colonial Lexicon: Of Birth Ritual, Medicalization, and Mobility in the Congo*. Durham, NC: Duke University Press.

———. 2016. *A Nervous State: Violence, Remedies, and Reverie in Colonial Congo*. Durham, NC: Duke University Press.

Sahlins, M. 1968. 'Notes on the Original Affluent Society', in R.B. Lee and I. DeVore (eds), *Man the Hunter*. New York: Aldine.

———. 1976. *Culture and Practical Reason*. Chicago, IL: Chicago University Press.

Schoenbrun, D. 1997. *The Historical Reconstruction of Great Lakes Bantu Cultural Vocabulary: Etymologies and Distributions*. Cologne: Rüdiger Köppe.

———. 2006. 'Conjuring the Modern in Africa: Durability and Rupture in Histories of Public Healing between the Great Lakes of East Africa', *The American Historical Review* 111: 1403–39.

———. 2012. 'Mixing, Moving, Making, Meaning: Possible Futures for the Distant Past', *African Archaeological Review* 29(2): 293–317.

———. 2013. 'A Mask of Calm: Emotion and Founding the Kingdom of Bunyoro in the Sixteenth Century', *Comparative Studies in Society and History* 55(3): 634–64.

Smith, P. 1970. 'La Forge De L'intelligence', *L'homme* 10(2): 5–21.

——— (ed.). 1975. *Le récit populaire au Rwanda*. Classiques africains, Vol. 17. Paris: Association des Classiques Africains.

Soper, R., and B. Golden. 1969. 'An Archaeological Survey of Mwanza Region, Tanzania', *Azania* 4: 15–80.

Southall, A. 1956. *Alur Society: A Study in Processes and Types of Domination*. Cambridge: Heffer.

Strathern, M. 1988. *The Gender of the Gift*. Berkeley: University of California Press.

Stroeken, K. 2004. 'In Search of the Real: The Healing Contingency of Sukuma Divination', in M. Winkelman and Ph. Peek (eds), *Divination and Healing*. Tucson, AZ: University of Arizona Press, pp. 29–54.

———. 2005. 'Immunising Strategies: Hip Hop and Critique in Tanzania', *Africa* 75(4): 488–509.

———. 2006. '"Stalking the Stalker": A Chwezi Initiation into Spirit Possession and Experiential Structure', *Journal of the Royal Anthropological Institute* 12(4): 785–802.

———. 2008. 'Sensory Shifts and Synaesthetics in Sukuma Healing', *Ethnos* 73(4): 466–84.

———. 2010. *Moral Power: The Magic of Witchcraft.* Series Epistemologies of Healing, Vol. 9. Oxford: Berghahn Books.

———. 2012. 'Health Care Decisions by Sukuma "Peasant Intellectuals": A Case of Radical Empiricism?', *Anthropology & Medicine* 19(1): 119–28.

———. 2017. 'The Individualization of Illness: Bewitchment and the Mental in Postcolonial Tanzania', in W. Olsen and C. Sargent (eds), *African Medical Pluralism.* Bloomington, IN: Indiana University Press, pp. 151–169.

Taussig, M. 1993. *Mimesis and Alterity: A Particular History of the Senses.* London: Routledge.

Taylor, C. 1999. *Sacrifice as Terror: The Rwandan Genocide of 1994.* Oxford: Berg.

Tcherkézoff, S. 1983. *Le Roi nyamwezi, la droite et la gauche: révision comparative des classifications dualistes.* Cambridge: Cambridge University Press.

Thornton, J. 1998. *Africa and Africans in the Making of the Atlantic World, 1400–1800.* Cambridge: Cambridge University Press.

Turner, V. 1967. *The Forest of Symbols.* Ithaca, NY: Cornell University Press.

———. 1968. *The Drums of Affliction: A Study of Religious Process among the Ndembu of Zambia.* Oxford: Clarendon Press (IAI).

———. 1975. *Revelation and Divination in Ndembu Ritual.* Ithaca, NY: Cornell University Press.

Van Bockhaven, V. 2013. 'The Leopard Men of the Eastern Congo (ca. 1890–1940): History and Colonial Representation'. Unpublished doctoral dissertation, University of East Anglia.

Vansina, J. 1966. *Kingdoms of the Savanna.* Madison: University of Wisconsin Press.

———. 1973. *The Tio Kingdom of the Middle Congo, 1880–1892.* London: Oxford University Press (IAI).

———. 1978. *The Children of Woot: A History of the Kuba Peoples.* Madison, WI: University of Wisconsin Press.

———. 1983. 'Is Elegance Proof? Structuralism and African History', *History in Africa* 10: 307–48.

———. 1985. *Oral Tradition as History.* Madison, WI: University of Wisconsin Press.

———. 1990. *Paths in the Rainforests.* Madison, WI: University of Wisconsin Press.

———. 1995. 'New Linguistic Evidence and "the Bantu Expansion"'. *The Journal of African History,* 36(2): 173–195.

———. 2004. *Antecedents to Modern Rwanda: The Nyiginya Kingdom.* Madison, WI: University of Wisconsin Press.

Vansina, J., R. Mauny and L.V. Thomas. 1964. 'Introductory Summary', in J. Vansina, R. Mauny and L.V. Thomas (eds), *The Historian in Tropical Africa: Studies Presented and Discussed at the Fourth International African Seminar at the University of Dakar, Senegal 1961*. London: Oxford University Press (IAI), pp. 59–103.

Varkevisser, C. 1973. *Socialisation in a Changing Society: Sukuma Childhood in Rural and Urban Mwanza, Tanzania*. The Hague: CESO.

Vidal, C. 1985. 'Rêve et réalité en ethnohistoire: Note sceptique sur J. Freedman et L. de Heusch', *Cahiers d'études africaines* 25(100): 573–85.

Viveiros de Castro, E. 2004. 'Exchanging Perspectives: The Transformation of Objects into Subjects in Amerindian Ontologies', *Common Knowledge* 10(3): 463–84.

Wainwright, G. 1942. 'The Coming of Iron to Some African Peoples', *Man* 42: 103–8.

Wolfram, H. 1997. *The Roman Empire and Its Germanic Peoples*. Berkeley, CA: University of California Press.

INDEX

academic specialization,
  anthropology and, 21
acculturation
  Bantu migration and, 109–10
  Loango and, 51
  state formation and, 32
actor-idealism
  anthropology and, 15–18,
    264–65
  history and, 23–24
actor-materialism, 284
  anthropology and, 15–18
  Vansina and, 20–23, 263–64
adoption, 130n8
adulthood. See bunamhala
affliction, drums of. See drums
affliction rituals, life-crisis rituals
  versus, 65–68, 73–74
Africanist anthropology, 12–15,
  25–31, 40n6
African Political Systems (Fortes and
  Evans-Pritchard), 25–27, 135
African political systems, four-
  faceted structure of, 142–43
agency, anthropology and, 14–18
alliance, state formation and, 31–34
alterity
  Africanist anthropology and, 13
  Zande openness to, 154–65
Alur, 32, 143–51
Alur Society (Southall), 143–50
Amadi, 158–61
Amerindians, 177
ancestral spirits
  Kuba and, 116
  nkira spirits and, 212
ancestral tradition, Vansina on,
  114–17
ancestral worship
  ceremonial states and, 225–26,
    237
  Kongo and, 243–44

animal hides, initiation and, 11–12
animism, Sukuma and, 10
anthropology, 39–40nn3–4
  academic specialization and, 21
  actor-idealism in, 15–18,
    264–65
  actor-materialism in, 15–18
  Africanist, 12–15, 25–31, 40n6
  agency in, 14–18
  archaeology and, 23–25
  culture concept in, 3–4
  endogeneity and, 18–21
  ethnographic present and, 30,
    116, 192–94
  history and, 21–25, 29–30,
    117, 184–89, 192–94,
    263–65, 285n2
  meso-, 18, 64
  ontological turn in, 14–15,
    17–18
  praxeology in, 18
  structure-idealism in, 15–18
  structure-materialism in,
    15–18
anti-sorcery cults. See witch-finding
  cults
Appadurai, A., 3
archaeology, anthropology and,
  23–25
aristocracy, forest-mastery, Tio,
  versus, 207
army system, in Rwanda, 258
associational model, of
  centralization, 124–29
associations
  brotherhoods versus, 128–29
  Zande and, 151–63
Austen, A., 96–100, 106

Bali, *mambela* cult and, 127
banang'oma, chieftaincy, Sukuma,
  and, 84–85, 90, 92, 99, 105

Bantu migration, 129n1
    acculturation and, 109–10
    language and, 111–14
Bantu rule, Nilotic rule interacting with, 133–34
baotale. See seniority, Lele and
Barth, Frederik, 16
Bashu, 126
Bateson, G., 175
Bekaert, S., 20, 240
Bemba, 140–43
Benin, 132–33
Bernault, Florence, 184–89
Biebuyck, D., 62–63
bitekerezo tales, 262, 267–84, 285n4, 296
body fragments, as charms, 185–89
body politic, medicinal versus sacral conception of, 245–50
Bonnafé, Pierre, 207–8
Bourdieu, Pierre, 18, 154–55
Bradbury, R., 30, 132
bride-service, 250n4
bridewealth, 130n3
    Crow kinship and, 117–18
    Kete and, 231
brotherhoods, associations versus, 128–29
Broushaki, F., 20
Buganda, 222–26, 238, 250nn2–3, 259–60, 288, 295
buganga. See divination
bugemi wa mbula. See rain medicine
Buha, 256
bunamhala (adulthood), Sukuma and, 9, 11, 106, 130n9
Bunyoro-Kitara empire, 28–29, 148–49
bureaucracy, of Kuba, 235–36
Burundi, 255–58, 274, 285n2, 294
busunzula ceremony, chieftaincy, Sukuma, and, 92–94
bu ya mu kaya. See forest-within

Caesar, Julius, 246
Cartesian dualism, magic challenging, 174–75
centralization, 25, 27–31, 294. *See also* ceremonial states; state formation
    associational model of, 124–29
    cultural heterogeneity and, 26
    forest-mastery, Tio, and, 199
    initiation and, 36
    Mongo and, 117–18
    Vansina on, 117–29
ceremonial states
    ancestral worship, decline of, and, 225–26, 237
    Buganda and, 222–26, 259–60, 288
    Kongo as, 242–45
    Kuba as, 229–42
    religion as separate in, 238
    Rwanda and, 258, 260–63, 284
    spirit possession and, 289
charms
    body fragments as, 185–89
    Buganda and, 225
    forest-mastery, Tio, and, 193–97
    hereditary title and, 254
    hunters' societies and, 77
    initiation and, 11–12
    Kuba and, 240
    nkobi and, 193, 203–7, 210, 218n6
    nkula cult and, 179–80
chieftaincy. *See also mani*
    Alur and, 143–50
    Bashu and, 126
    Bemba and, 140–43
    forest-mastery, Tio, as, 197–203
    kingship versus, 27–28
    language for, 112, 122–23
    Mwindo epic and, 60–61
    Ndembu and, 69–71
    nkumu as, 119–24
chieftaincy, Sukuma, 80, 107n2, 167
    banang'oma and, 84–85, 90, 92, 99, 105
    busunzula ceremony and, 92–94
    colonialism and, 84–88, 106–7, 290–91
    cultic knowledge and, 90–94, 290–91
    death of chief in, 101–2
    drums and, 105–6
    end of, 106–7
    festival-based, 94–96

history, emic, of, 83–89
history of, 95–106, 241–42
igunguli and, 100
language for, 113
as medicinal cult, 91–94
mfumu and, 95, 102–5
ng'oma ya mabasa twin ceremony and, 105–6
as non-hegemonic, 99–100
ntemi ng'hoja and, 103
polity prism limited salience for, 102–6
rain medicine and, 81–82, 84, 89–91, 99–101, 172
succession struggles and, 35, 84–90, 100–102
The Children of Woot (Vansina), 115, 226–42
Chrétien, Jean-Pierre, 254–61, 285n2
Christianity
embodiment and, 185
forest-mastery, Tio, and, 217
Christianization, 257
Burundi and, 255, 285n2, 294
Rwanda and, 255, 285n2, 294–95
Chwezi cult, 24–25, 208, 222–23, 254–55, 285n5
bitekerezo tales and, 276–77
colonialism and, 256, 294–95
initiation and, 11–12, 57–58, 94, 121, 168, 170, 235, 248
Ndori and, 263
sacrifice and, 218n8
titles and, 250n2
circumcision. *See also gandja*
Maniema and, 127–28
Mbole and, 127
Ndembu and, 67, 71–73
Claessen, H., 28
classificatory extensions
cultural drift and, 182–83
of fertility, 180–82
of forest-within, 75–76
hunters' societies and, 75–76
collective healing, 291
ilumbi and, 50
witch-finding cults and, 50
collective truth, cultural transmission, of medicine, and, 179–80

colonialism, 4–5, 27, 35, 187–89, 190n4
Alur and, 145
Burundi and, 255–58
chieftaincy, Sukuma, and, 84–88, 106–7, 290–91
Chwezi cult and, 256, 294–95
forest-mastery, Tio, impacted by, 214–17
Great Lakes region and, 255–57
polity prism and, 260
radical difference denied by, 257
Rwanda and, 255–58
Zande and, 151–52, 161–62
colonization
Africanist anthropology and, 13–14
witch-finding cults and, 46
communication, magic as, 173–76, 185–89
conquest, state formation and, 31–34
cooling, 74–75
initiation as practice of, 37
ntemi ng'hoja and, 103
poja as, 7
Cory, Hans, 85–86, 102–6
Coupez, A., 285n3, 286n7
court duties, in Kuba, 229–30
court history, 241–42
Crow kinship, 117–18
cultic knowledge, chieftaincy, Sukuma, and, 90–94, 290–91
cultural drift
classificatory extensions and, 182–83
endogeneity and, 182–84
cultural heterogeneity, centralization and, 26
cultural transmission, of medicine, 178–80
culture concept, in anthropology, 3–4

dancing, magic and, 174
Dapper, Olifert, 43–44, 50–55, 123, 244
de Heusch, Luc, 224, 228, 246, 248, 263–67
de Lame, Danielle, 283
de Mahieu, Wauthier, 56–59

de Maret, Pierre, 292
democracy
    medicinal rule versus, 141
    spirit possession and, 289
Descola, P., 177
Devisch, René, 19, 292–93
diffusion from centre, of language, 111–12
divination. *See also* ilumbi; oracles
    bitekerezo tales and, 271–80
    Great Lakes region and, 259
    Komo and, 57, 59
    Kuba and, 239–41
    Lele and, 44–49, 296
    Mwindo epic and, 61
    power differentiation and, 45
    subjunctivity in, 176
    Sukuma and, 61, 66, 98
    Vansina on, 239, 283–84
Doko, 118
Douglas, Mary, 13, 44–50, 181
drums, 287, 292–93
    chieftaincy, Sukuma, and, 105–6
    as kingdom, 258–59
Drums of Affliction (Turner), 65–78
Dupré, M.-C., 210
dynastic clans, initiation and, 254–61

Edo, 132–33
Eglash, Ron, 58–59
embodiment
    Christianity and, 185
    magic and, 184–89
endogeneity, 34–35
    anthropology and, 18–21
    cultural drift and, 182–84
    history and, 20, 124
    transition and, 19–21
    witch-finding cults and, 46–47
enthronement, initiation and, 254, 259
ethnic differentiation, Rwanda and, 257–58
ethnicity, *bitekerezo* tales and, 272, 275, 277–80, 283
ethnographic present, 30, 116, 192–94
Evans-Pritchard, E.E., 12–13, 40n7, 48, 151, 154–55, 166n8, 291–92
    African Political Systems by, 25–27, 135
    magic and, 152–53, 161–63, 173–74
evolution, 294

fame. *See lu-kumo*
Feeley-Harnik, Gillian, 1, 251n10
Feenberg, Andrew, 40n5
Feierman, Steven, 6–7, 50, 162, 254
fertility, 5, 20, 247–48. *See also* forest-within
    classificatory extensions of, 180–82
    Komo and, 58–59
    Kuba and, 236
    nkira spirits and, 211–14
    Sukuma and, 10, 58
    Zande and, 153–63
festivals, chieftaincy, Sukuma, and, 94–96
fluid transmission prohibition, 222–23
Forde, Daryl, 191
forest-mastery, 9–11, 37
forest-mastery, Tio, 37, 119, 191–92, 210, 295–96
    aristocracy versus, 207
    centralization and, 199
    charms and, 193–97
    chieftaincy as, 197–203
    Christianity impact on, 217
    colonialism impacting, 214–17
    hereditary title and, 213, 215
    ibili cult and, 195
    initiation and, 195, 203–7, 212–17, 224
    judicial appeal and, 208–9
    mpu and, 207–8
    ngàà and, 196
    ngaa ntsi and, 198–203
    nkira spirits and, 198, 201–3, 206–7, 209, 211–14
    okoo and, 197–98, 216
    sacrifice and, 218n8
    shrines, *nkiini*, and, 196–97
    shrines, *nkobi*, and, 203–7, 218n6
    social change impacting, 213–17
    tribute and, 212–15

witchcraft, protecting against, 202–3
wookuru and, 194–97, 207
forest-within *(bu ya mu kaya)*, 9–12, 287
    classificatory extensions of, 75–76
    Zande and, 153
Fortes, Meyer, 25–27, 135, 199–200, 251n10, 291
founding clans, Kuba. *See mbaangt*
fractal of life, Komo, 58–59
Frazer, James George, 223–24, 248–50
Freedman, Jim, 264
Frobenius, Leo, 226
funerals, denial of, witch-finding cults and, 47

gandja circumcision ceremonies, Komo and, 56–58
Geertz, Clifford, 17
gender equality, Zande and, 153–54
Gluckman, Max, 13–14, 32
Goffman, E., 175
Golden, B., 96
Gordon, D., 248
governance, kingship interpreted as, 1–2, 25–31
Graeber, D., 248
The Great Lakes of Africa: 2000 Years of History (Chrétien), 254–61
Great Lakes region
    colonialism in, 255–57
    divination in, 259
    overview of, 252–54
Guiral, Léon, 211, 215

habitual tense, 182, 189n3
Harris, Marvin, 16
hat-wearers, Tio. *See mpu*
headman, Tio. *See wookuru*
healer/diviner, Tio. *See ngàà*
healing. *See* collective healing; *specific topics*
hereditary title
    charms and, 254
    forest-mastery, Tio, and, 213, 215
The Historical Study of African Religion (Ranger and Kimambo), 134–40

history
    actor-idealism and, 23–24
    anthropology and, 21–25, 29–30, 117, 184–89, 192–94, 263–65, 285n2
    chiefs, Sukuma, invoking, 95
    court, 241–42
    endogeneity and, 20, 124
    oracles and, 284
    of Sukuma chieftaincy, 83–89, 95–106, 241–42
    Vansina and, 21–23
Hocart, A., 247
Hodder, I., 23–24
Holmes, C., 96–100, 106
hunters' societies, 37
    charms and, 77
    classificatory extensions and, 75–76
    ihamba gun-hunters' ritual and, 75–78
    Ndembu and, 75–78
hunting
    ngaa ntsi and, 198
    oracles and, 181–83, 200
Hutson, S., 23–24

ibili cult, forest-mastery, Tio, and, 195
igunguli (sub-chiefdom), chieftaincy, Sukuma, and, 100
Ihamba cult, 180
ihamba gun-hunters' ritual, 75–78
ihane initiation, Sukuma and, 8–11, 56–57, 66, 75, 106
ilumbi (diviner, Lele), 49–50
Imandwa cult. *See* Chwezi cult
initiation, 43, 287. *See also busunzula* ceremony; *ihane*
initiation, Sukuma and
    animal hides and, 11–12
    bitekerezo tales and, 276–77, 280
    Buganda and, 225, 250n3
    centralization and, 36
    charms and, 11–12
    Chwezi cult and, 11–12, 57–58, 94, 121, 168, 170, 235, 248
    cooling, as practices of, 37
    dynastic clans relation between, 254–61

Index

enthronement and, 254, 259
forest-mastery, Tio, and, 195, 203–7, 212–17, 224
Komo and, 56–59
Kongo and, 120–21
Kuba and, 227–29, 234–36, 295
Lele and, 44
Loango and, 53–55
Ndembu and, 67–73
nkula cult and, 179–80
nkumu and, 119–24
Sukuma and, 223–24
symbolic relations and, 179
women and, 209
International African Seminar, 1961, 29–30
Itsuua, 209

Janzen, J.M., 5–7, 120, 130n4
Jerardino, A., 20
judicial appeal, forest-mastery, Tio, and, 208–9

kaa. *See* charms, forest-mastery, Tio, and
Kabaka, of Buganda, 222–26, 295
Kagame, Alexis, 282
Kamanzi, Th., 285n3, 286n7
Kantorowicz, Ernst, 246
Kete, 230–33, 250n5
Khoi-San, 19
Kimambo, I., 134–40
Kingdoms of the Savanna (Vansina), 30–31
kingship. *See specific topics*
kingship, Euro-Christian conception of, 245–50
The King's Two Bodies (Kantorowicz), 246
Kishina, Stanislaus, 83–95, 136
Kodesh, N., 6, 50
Komo, 56–59
Kongo, 120–21, 129, 242–45
Kopytoff, I., 29
Kuba, 115, 226
ancestral spirits and, 116
bureaucracy of, 235–36
ceremonial state in, 229–42
charms and, 240
court duties in, 229–30
divination and, 239–41

fertility and, 236
initiation and, 227–29, 234–36, 295
Kete and, 230–33
mass killing and, 238
mbaangt clans and, 234–35, 239
Mongo and, 227
Shyaam and, 227, 235–37, 239–41, 245, 295
spirit possession and, 236
taboo and, 236
twins and, 227–28, 236, 251n7
virilocal residence and, 229, 231–32
ku-wa (na), being with, 142, 182, 194

Lagae, C.R., 162–63
language
Alur and, 147–51
Bantu migration and, 111–14
for chieftaincy, 112, 122–23
for chieftaincy, Sukuma, 113
diffusion from centre of, 111–12
lexicological positivism as approach to, 113
modes of production and, 180–82
spheres of exchange and, 180–82
Vansina and, 111–14, 116, 130n6, 292
Zande and, 157, 166n8
Latour, Bruno, 189n1
Leach, Edmund, 65
Lele, 39, 44–50, 181, 230, 296
The Lele of the Kasai (Douglas), 44–50
Lemarchand, R., 40n8, 221
Lemba cult, 120, 130n4
Loango and, 52–55
nkobi shrines and, 210
Lendu, 146, 151
Lévi-Strauss, Claude, 62, 125, 265
lexicological positivism, language approached via, 113
life-crisis rituals, affliction rituals versus, 65–68, 73–74
linear time, 30–31

Loango, 43–44, 50–56, 123
local terms, for kingship, 2–3
Luba empire, 9
lubanga, Alur and, 148–49
Luhmann, Niklas, 175–76
lu-kumo (fame), Sukuma and, 123–24

MacGaffey, W., 120–21, 217n2, 242–45
magic, 288. *See also specific topics*
  bitekerezo tales and, 271, 273, 278
  Cartesian dualism challenged by, 174–75
  as communication, 173–76, 185–89
  dancing and, 174
  embodiment and, 184–89
  Evans-Pritchard on, 152–53, 161–63, 173–74
  modes of production and, 176–78
  multi-naturalism and, 177
  spheres of exchange and, 177–78
  temporal element of, 175–76
  Zande and, 152–53, 161–63, 173–74, 291–92
Magufuli, Paulo, 175
Malundi, Ng'wana, 107
mambela cult, Bali and, 127
Mambisa, 149–50
Mangbetu, 127, 158–61
mani (chief)
  Lele and, 44
  Loango and, 52–53
Maniema, 126, 127–28, 129
marriage
  Ndembu and, 73
  Sukuma and, 73
mass killing, 238, 246
Mateene, K., 62–63
matrilineage, Kete and, 230–33
Mauny, R., 249
mbaangt clans (founding clans, Kuba), 234–35, 239
Mbole, circumcision and, 127
Mbomu, 158–61
Mbudye, Luba empire and, 9
mediation, stateless societies and, 26
medicinal rule. *See specific topics*

mfumu, 95, 102–5, 123, 217n2
Miangba, 158
migration
  Bantu, 109–14, 129n1
  Vansina on, 32–33
missionaries, 4–5
mobility, Kete and, 232–33
modern constitution, 189n1, 233–34
modernity
  African, 255
  Africanist anthropology and, 14
modernity, Western
  modes of production in, 177
  spheres of exchange in, 177
modes of production. *See also* fertility
  language and, 180–82
  magic and, 176–78
  modernity, Western, and, 177
  Niger-Congo, 180–82
Mongo, 117–18, 227, 231
Mpororo. *See* Ndorwa
mpu (hat-wearers, Tio), 207–8
Mudimbe, V., 3, 179
Müller, Ernst Wilhelm, 119–20
multi-naturalism, 177
Mwantiyanvwa, tribute for, 68–71
Mwindo epic, 59–63
mwine, Bemba and, 142
myth
  Mwindo epic as, 59–63
  Sukuma and, 62–63

nation building, in *bitekerezo* tales, 275, 278, 280
Ndembu, 67–78, 181
Ndori, 237
  bitekerezo tales and, 275–77, 280–82, 296
  Chwezi cult and, 263
  Vansina on, 282
Ndorwa (Mpororo), 260
Neolithic transition, 19–20, 22
Newbury, David, 23
ngàà (healer/diviner, Tio), 196
ngaa ntsi (landowner, Tio), 198–203
ngaa yuulu, 217n2
Nge, 125
ngoma, 5–7
ng'oma. *See* drums

ng'oma ya mabasa twin ceremony, 105–6
Nguunu, Kongo and, 242
Niger-Congo, modes of production in, 180–82
Nilotic rule, 28, 133–34
nkang'a puberty rites, Ndembu and, 72–73
nkani, 125–26
nkani tribute system, Tio, 204–6
nkiini shrines, forest-mastery, Tio, and, 196–97
nkira spirits, 198, 201–3, 206–7, 209, 211–14, 212
nkisi
    Loango and, 50–56
    spirit possession and, 54–55
    witchcraft and, 53
nkobi, 193
nkobi shrines, 203–7, 210, 218n6
nkula cult, 68–69, 74, 179–80
nkumu (chieftain), 119–24
nsumba ntale, 250n5
ntemi. See chieftaincy, Sukuma
ntemi ng'hoja (cool cutter), 103
Nyabingi movement, 254–55
Nyanga, Mwindo epic and, 59–63
Nyerere, Julius, 106

obligation, Loango and, 51–52, 55
Ogot, Bethlem, 28–29, 134
okoo (ruler, Tio), 197–98, 216
Oliver, Roland, 109–10, 129n1
ontological turn
    Africanist anthropology and, 40n6
    anthropology and, 14–15, 17–18
oracles. *See also* divination
    history and, 284
    hunting and, 181–83, 200
Ortner, S., 17

Packard, R., 126
paradigmatic relations, 265–66
Pasha, Emin, 7
Paths in the Rainforests (Vansina), 18–19, 109–29
patrilineage, 99–100
    Mongo and, 118
    Sukuma and, 87
Pereira, Pacheco, 216

Pinçon, B., 210
poison ordeal, Loango and, 52–54
poja, 7
political stratification, Tio lacking, 197
polity prism, 1, 287–88
    Africanist anthropology and, 25–31
    chieftaincy, Sukuma, limited salience for, 102–6
    colonialism and, 260
    Vansina and, 114, 129, 226, 233–34
polycentrism, Sukuma and, 11, 31
power differentiation, Lele divination and, 45
praxeology, anthropology and, 18
private/public dichotomy, 243–44, 251n8
Providence, *bitekerezo* tales and, 271, 273–74, 277, 280, 283

Qui a obstrué la cascade? (de Mahieu), 56–59

Radcliffe-Brown, Alfred, 12–13, 16–17, 40n7
Ragem, Alur and, 147–48
rain medicine
    Alur and, 143–50
    chieftaincy, Sukuma, and, 81–82, 84, 89–91, 99–101, 172
    smithing and, 217, 218n5
Ranger, T., 134–40
Ray, Benjamin, 222–25
religion
    ceremonial states and, 238
    Western conception of, 246–47
Religion and Society in Central Africa (MacGaffey), 242–45
reversions, transitions and, 294
Richards, Audrey, 140–43
ritual masters, Buganda and, 223–24
Robertshaw, P., 24
Rose-Hunt, N., 35, 154, 162
Rozvi empire, 295
ruler, Tio. *See okoo*
ruse, *bitekerezo* tales and, 277–78, 280

Rwanda, 21–23, 39, 96, 255–63, 267–84, 285n2, 294–96. *See also* *bitekerezo* tales
Ryangombe, 265–67, 276–80

sacrifice, 184, 186, 190n4, 218n8, 249, 289–90
    mass killing as, 238, 246
Sahlins, Marshall, 19, 194
Sakata, 20
Schoenbrun, David, 6, 114, 122, 124
Schoffeleers, Matthew, 135, 137
schooling, Sukuma and, 15–16
secularization, *bitekerezo* tales and, 281, 283
segmentary states, Alur and, 143–50
self-praise, *bitekerezo* tales and, 274, 276, 280
seniority, Lele and, 45
sexual relations, *ilumbi* and, 49
Shaka, 27, 32, 295
Shambaa kingdom, 7
Shilluk kingship, 28–29, 249
shrines
    Alur and, 146–48
    Bemba and, 142–43
    Buganda and, 225
    forest-mastery, Tio, and, 196–97, 203–7, 218n6
    nkiini, 196–97
    nkobi, 203–7, 210, 218n6
    Sukuma and, 171
    Zande and, 171
Shyaam, Kuba and, 227, 235–37, 239–41, 245, 295
slaves, kings as, 223–24
Smith, Pierre, 262, 280–81
smithing
    rain medicine and, 217, 218n5
    Tio and, 216–17
social structure, Vansina on, 114–17
Soper, R., 96
Southall, Aidan, 29, 32, 143–50, 289
spheres of exchange
    language and, 180–82
    magic and, 177–78
    modernity, Western, and, 177

spirit mediums, kingship origin in, 131–32
spirit possession, 121, 123
    ceremonial state and, 289
    as democratic, 289
    Kuba and, 236
    nkisi and, 54–55
    origin of, 138–39
state formation. *See also* centralization; ceremonial states
    acculturation and, 32
    alliance and, 31–34
    conquest and, 31–34
    medicinal rule, originating in, 6, 34–35, 221–22
    processual typification of, 29
    territorial cults, South-East African, and, 138
    witch-finding cults and, 48
stateless societies
    mediation and, 26
    Mongo as, 231
structure-idealism
    anthropology and, 15–18
    de Heusch and, 263–64
structure-materialism, anthropology and, 15–18
sub-chiefdom. *See igunguli*
subjunctivity, divination and, 176
succession, equatorial African versus European, 245–46
succession struggles, chieftaincy, Sukuma, and, 35, 84–90, 100–102
Sukuma, 130n2, 193. *See also* chieftaincy, Sukuma; Chwezi cult; *ihane* initiation, Sukuma and
    animism and, 10
    bride-service and, 250n4
    bunamhala and, 9, 11, 106, 130n9
    divination and, 61, 66, 98
    fertility and, 10, 58
    forest-mastery and, 9–11
    initiation and, 223–24
    lu-kumo and, 123–24
    marriage and, 73
    myth and, 62–63
    nsumba ntale and, 250n5
    patrilineage and, 87
    polycentrism and, 11, 31

schooling and, 15–16
shrines and, 171
territoriality and, 97
titles and, 250n2
twins and, 251n7
war and, 99–101, 103–4
symbolic relations
    cultural transmission, of medicine, and, 179–80
    initiation and, 179
syntagmatic relations, 265–66

taboo, 288
    Buganda and, 222–24
    fluid transmission prohibition as, 222–23
    Kuba and, 236
Tallensi, 199–200
Taussig, Michael, 174
Taylor, Chris, 280
Tempels, Placide, 3
territorial cults, South-East African, 134–35, 139–40
    as ritualist, 136
    subjugation of, 137–38
territoriality
    Kete and, 232
    Sukuma and, 97
Tessman, Günther, 185, 187
Thomas, L.V., 249
Thornton, John, 244
Tio. *See also* forest-mastery, Tio
    ngaa yuulu and, 217n2
    nkani tribute system and, 204–6
    political stratification absent from, 197
    smithing and, 216–17
The Tio Kingdom of the Middle Congo (Vansina), 191–217, 218nn4–6
title associations
    Edo and, 132–33
    Yoruba and, 132–33
titles, cult, 250n2
Tiv, 177–78
Tonda, Joseph, 190n4
transition, 8, 35–39, 294
    endogeneity and, 19–21
    Neolithic, 19–20
tribute
    forest-mastery, Tio, and, 212–15

for Mwantiyanvwa, 68–71
nkani as, 204–6
triple coherence method, 265–71
Turner, Victor, 13
    Ndembu and, 65–78, 181
    watershed division and, 7, 64–68, 178
twins, 105, 107n2, 148–49
    Kuba and, 227–28, 236, 251n7
    Sukuma and, 251n7

Urewe, 24

van Binsbergen, Wim, 137, 139
Vansina, Jan, 5, 7, 107n1, 129n1, 250n4, 285n4, 286n7
    actor-materialism in, 20–23, 263–64
    ancestral tradition in, 114–17
    centralization and, 117–29
    The Children of Woot by, 115, 226–42
    court history in, 241–42
    divination and, 239, 283–84
    historical interpretation in, 21–23
    Kingdoms of the Savanna by, 30–31
    language in, 111–14, 116, 130n6, 292
    migration and, 32–33
    Ndori and, 282
    Paths in the Rainforests by, 18–19, 109–29
    polity prism and, 114, 129, 226, 233–34
    Rwandan kingship and, 21–23
    social structure in, 114–17
    The Tio Kingdom of the Middle Congo by, 191–217, 218nn4–6
Vidal, Claudine, 264
virilocal residence, Kuba and, 229, 231–32
Viveiros de Castro, E., 177

Wanga, 163
war, Sukuma and, 99–101, 103–4
watershed division, Turner on, 7, 64–68, 178

Weaving the Threads of Life (Devisch), 19
witchcraft, 3, 14
    Alur and, 144
    forest-mastery, Tio, protecting against, 202–3
    Ndembu and, 181
    nkisi and, 53
witch-finding cults, 46–50, 296

Wolfram, H., 247
wookuru (headman, Tio), 194–97, 207

Yoruba, 132–33

Zande, 151–63, 166n8, 171, 173–74, 291–92

www.ingramcontent.com/pod-product-compliance
Lightning Source LLC
Chambersburg PA
CBHW072144100526
44589CB00015B/2084